Also by Marjorie Garber

Vice Versa: Bisexuality and the Eroticism of Everyday Life

Vested Interests: Cross-Dressing and Cultural Anxiety

Shakespeare's Ghost Writers: Literature as Uncanny Causality

Coming of Age in Shakespeare

Dream in Shakespeare: From Metaphor to Metamorphosis

DOG LOVE

Marjorie Garber

Simon & Schuster

 SIMON & SCHUSTER
Rockefeller Center
1230 Avenue of the Americas
New York, NY 10020

Designed by Francesca Belanger
Dog tails illustration on page 283 by Laura Hartman Maestro

Manufactured in the United States of America

1   3   5   7   9   10   8   6   4   2

Library of Congress Cataloging-in-Publication Data
Garber, Marjorie B.
Dog love / Marjorie Garber.
p.   cm.
Includes index.
1. Dogs—Behavior.   2. Dogs—Psychology.   3. Human-animal
relationships.   I. Title.
SF433.G37   1996
636.7'001'9—dc20   96–27109
CIP
ISBN 0-684-81871-X

Permissions to reprint previously published
material begin on page 343.

To Wagner and Yofi

ACKNOWLEDGMENTS

It is a pleasure to acknowledge the generous assistance of many friends and colleagues: Jonathan Aaron, Ann Balas, Charles Balas, Mary-Claire Barton, Bruce Cratsley, Dan Danielsen, Carolyn Dever, Rebecca Folkman, William Germano, Pat Johnson, David Kennedy, Thomas Laqueur, David Perkins, Katherine Rowe, Kathryn Schwarz, and Carol Thompson were among those who shared dog stories and dog lore. Jeffrey Reiser, Barbara Akiba, Francesca Delbanco, Paul B. Franklin, Theodore Gideonse, Toby Kasper, Denise Roy, Rachel Tiven, and Rebecca L. Walkowitz assisted in obtaining images and permissions and in numerous other ways. Andrew Parker suggested to me, in a phrase I found immensely helpful, that in a way all my books are about love.

My editor Rebecca Saletan and my agent Beth Vesel were, once again, invaluable in their advice and support. Barbara Johnson, my most demanding and most forgiving critic, tried valiantly, as always, to keep me out of the doghouse while keeping an eye on the dogs. Nietzschie (1980–1992) trained me patiently in the art of being a dog owner. Wagner and Yofi, to whom this book is dedicated, taught me that dog love is love.

CONTENTS

Introduction   13

A Dog's Life   43

Talking Dogs   81

Unconditional Lovers   119

Sex and the Single Dog   141

Breeding   159

Dog Law   203

Dog Loss   241

Coda   283

NOTES   287

INDEX   329

DOG
LOVE

Introduction

Drawing by Shanahan; © 1992 The New Yorker Magazine, Inc.

I love a dog. He does nothing for political reasons.

—Will Rogers

All knowledge, the totality of all questions and answers, is contained in the dog.

—Franz Kafka, "Investigations of a Dog"

When a three-week-old puppy was found discarded in a city Dumpster and her picture shown on television and in the newspapers, the Animal Rescue League of Boston received more than five hundred phone calls offering to adopt her—from as far away as Arkansas and Wisconsin. Several calls were from lactating human mothers who were willing to nurse the motherless pup.

A British Airways captain diverted his jumbo jet a thousand miles to save Louise, a Shih Tzu flying in the plane's hold. A heater stuck on full blast had threatened Louise's life, and when Captain Rex Gravely consulted the two hundred passengers over the plane's public address system they overwhelmingly voted for him to change his route, landing in Boston rather than continuing on to Houston. Louise had emerged from six months of British rabies quarantine and was en route to join her American owner, who said with relief, "They saved her life. . . . I wanted to kiss every single passenger and the crew." The cost to British Airways was $31,000. Captain Gravely was awarded a plaque by the Royal Society for the Prevention of Cruelty to Animals.

Human lives, of course, are unspectacularly saved every day by alert captains, flight crews, and engineers. The passengers wouldn't be polled, however; nor, except in the most dramatic cases, do the personnel get medals. When the threat is to a dog, curiously, the stakes go up, not down, and the resultant publicity is amazing. Why should this be so?

Why is it sometimes easier to say "I love my dog" than "I love my spouse"? Dogs, we often say, offer unconditional love, where human lovers and human beloveds are often, well . . . all too human in their inconsistencies, frailties, and willfulness. But what is "unconditional love," and what are the conditions that produce and nurture it? Dogs provide "human interest" on the evening news and in the morning paper. The plight of an abandoned puppy or a mistreated older dog can sometimes provoke spontaneous generosity or public outcry in a way we *wish* were the case for the subjects of individual human tragedy. Homeless persons, abused children, refugees of war are so commonly reported that we have become dulled to their particular tragedies. The vividness of our feelings comes back when the story is about dogs. It's not that people feel less, or less strongly, about other people than about their dogs—at least for the most part. It's rather that the overwhelming dimension of human need sometimes makes the task of reparation seem hopeless. Dog love is local love, passionate, often unmediated, virtually always reciprocated, fulfilling, manageable. Love for humans is harder. Human beauty and grace are fitfully encountered: a child grows up and grows away; a lover becomes familiar, known, imperfect, taken for granted. But dog love is not an evasion or a substitution. It calls upon the same range and depth of feelings that humans have for

humans. Historically as well as in modern times it has often brought
out the best in us.

Dog stories find a place in our ongoing folklore as the real embodiment of what we would like to think were "family values" among human
beings. Sheba, a Rottweiler mix in Oakland Park, Florida, was chained
up by her owner after giving birth to nine puppies. The owner, who
didn't want the pups, buried them alive, but Sheba broke from her
chains and dug them out. The puppies—and the heroic mother—were
rescued; the owner faced charges of animal abuse that could land him
in prison for up to five years. In another very similar incident, the
mother dog rescued her puppies from a trash compactor into which her
owner had tossed them. In default of any consensus about social policy,
family planning, even what constitutes "the family," in a populace increasingly weary of economic struggle and social divisiveness, "family
values," like other values, are—it is fascinating to note—now often
passed on in popular culture not through human stories, but through
stories of, and love for, dogs.

The dog becomes the repository of those model human properties
that we have cynically ceased to find among humans. Where today can
we find the full panoply of William Bennett's *Book of Virtues*—from
Courage and Responsibility to Loyalty and Family Values—but in
Lassie and Beethoven and Millie and Checkers and Spot?

"Humane societies," after all, evoke in their very titles the good
qualities of *human beings:* kindness, mercy, compassion. How we treat
animals becomes a litmus test for "humanness." Consider the case of
Fred and the police commissioner.

Fred was a stray beagle, old, fat, and out of shape. He hung around
the First Police Precinct in New York City, where officers fed and cared
for him. But when Fred made a mess on the precinct's gym floor, one of
the officers took him to the ASPCA, which at the time ran the city's animal shelters. The officer told the shelter that Fred was a homeless
stray; he didn't identify him by name, or identify himself as a police officer, nor did he mention that the precinct's officers had clubbed together to pay Fred's veterinary bills in the past. Predictably, Fred was
kept in the shelter's kennel for three days, failed to attract a new owner,
and was put to sleep.

When Fred's absence was noticed at the station, there was an investigation. The police sergeant who had taken Fred to the ASPCA was

fired, as was another officer who reportedly struck the dog after he soiled the gym floor. Police Commissioner William J. Bratton, an animal lover who keeps five cats and a dog in his city apartment, explained why he had taken the maximum possible action against the two officers: "I just saw a conscious pattern of deceit, a calculated deceit. If they're this callous in the treatment of an animal, then it's indicative of how they might in fact deal with members of the public." The Sergeants Benevolent Association protested Bratton's action, calling the firing "a classic example of the punishment not fitting the crime," but the commissioner stood firm, calling the men's actions deliberate, not a "mistake of the heart" but "a mistake of the mind."

The story of Fred the beagle made headline news for days in the New York press—and also in Boston, where Commissioner Bratton had formerly been head of police. Bratton was known as the man who had once snubbed President Clinton in order to take his dog, Charlie, for a regular walk. But the point he was making by firing the officers who had maltreated the ill and elderly Fred was unmistakable. It was a point that could not, perhaps, have been made so dramatically about any human-on-human crime. And yet its "message" was all about how people treat other people. The homeless Fred, incontinent and dependent, was a reminder of mortality, human as well as canine. The officers' actions spoke eloquently, and unforgivably, of man's inhumanity to man's best friend.

Dogs in need can also bring out the best in people. When nearly eighty cocker spaniel and Irish setter puppies were discovered ailing in an overcrowded kennel in New Hampshire, Roland Wetherbee and his wife, who own a kennel on the other side of the state, took them in and nursed them to health. Shortly they were overwhelmed with scores of adoption offers. Volunteers answering the phone at the Wetherbees' Beau Meadow Farm hardly had time to hang up on one call when the next came through, and the local police station was kept busy directing traffic toward the farm. So many people asked directions from a nearby road-paving crew that members of the crew sent for specific driving instructions so as to be able to pass them on. Said one woman who stopped by, "I think we love animals better than we do people sometimes."

Tetley, a Chihuahua, was snatched from her owner, Glenn Edwards, as he stood on a New York City subway platform with his wife and son. Tetley (a dog the size of a teabag?) had been tucked away in a shoulder bag grabbed by the thief, who was dangling between two cars on the moving train. When Edwards's wife, Cindy Powers, went into a local copy shop to make "lost dog" posters, the shopkeeper suggested she try a media blitz, notifying local television stations and newspapers of Tetley's plight. Within days Tetley was back home, returned by a woman who had bought her for twenty dollars from a man near a subway station a few stops from the scene of the crime. Tetley, said the woman, had seemed "sad all the time," even when she fed her. And when Cindy Powers shouted her name over the telephone, Tetley, according to her rescuer, wagged her tail. "People ask me why I love living in New York," said a delighted Powers. "It's because there are great people in this city." And, apparently, great dogs.

Sometimes it's the dogs who rescue the people. Lyric, an Irish setter who is a trained medical dog, became an instantaneous national heroine when her human companion stopped breathing and Lyric dialed 911. Actually what she did—what she was trained to do—was knock the receiver off the hook and press a button that dialed 911, barking into the handset as she did so. The enhanced 911 system alerted medics to the situation, and within minutes an ambulance had brought oxygen to the stricken patient. Lyric's exploits brought her national media exposure: appearances on network television and at Disneyland, an audition for a part in NBC's situation comedy *Mad About You*, and guest stints with Jay Leno and Maury Povich.

A study conducted by the State University of New York at Buffalo Medical School suggested that in times of stress a dog is likely to be more help in calming you down than a spouse or partner. One hundred twenty men and women, assigned stressful activities of various kinds like making a speech, solving math problems, and dipping a hand in icy water, were monitored for heart rate and blood pressure. Spouses upped the tension level most; dogs, apparently, were the most steadying company. Most dog owners can guess the reason why: dogs never judge us and never compete with us. (Besides, we know we're better than they are at speechmaking and algebra. As for plunging into cold water, however . . .)

The more stressful the profession, the more necessary the dog. Take the case of Bailey and the governor of Tennessee. Don Sundquist adopted Bailey, a golden-haired dog he thought was a stray. Bailey had been hanging around a local restaurant, where a kindly waitress had fed him scraps. But it turned out that Bailey was only a block from home—a fact his family learned when a neighbor saw him on television in a story on Tennessee's "first dog." Governor Sundquist, who had "bonded," he said, with Bailey, was reluctant to give him up, but when the dog and his ten-year-old owner were reunited it was clear whose dog Bailey was. Returning Bailey was "a very emotional thing," said the governor. He plans to get another dog.

Relationships between politicians and dogs, in fact, have a long history in the United States. Indeed, it seems to be a maxim in politics: if you want to make a man appear more human, show him with a dog—a lesson learned by presidents from Roosevelt to Nixon to Bush.

The stiff and stolid Herbert Hoover was sold to voters in 1928 in part through a photograph of an uncharacteristically smiling Hoover with his dog King Tut. Hoover's arms rest on the shoulders of the also smiling Tut, whose paws he holds in both of his. The voters responded, whether to this or to other blandishments, and elected Hoover president. Hoover, it turns out, owned numerous dogs besides Tut, including an Irish wolfhound, an elkhound, a collie, an "Eskimo dog" and a "police dog," a setter, a Scotch collie, and two fox terriers. It was Tut, however, who drew attention to himself in the White House, by assiduously—some thought obsessively—patrolling its gates and fences. He became known as "the dog that worried himself to death," and, when Hoover sent him away from 1600 Pennsylvania Avenue to be on guard, actually pined away and died.

Political dog stories are bipartisan. Franklin Delano Roosevelt's Scottie, Fala, traveled virtually everywhere with the President. When Roosevelt met Winston Churchill in Newfoundland's Placentia Bay on the U.S.S. *Augusta* to sign the Atlantic Charter in 1941, Fala sat at their feet. On another ship, the cruiser *Baltimore* en route to Hawaii, tufts of Fala's hair were plucked by sailors to send home as a souvenir of the presidential voyage. In the 1944 reelection campaign a rumor circulated that Fala had been left behind on the Aleutian Islands, and that a destroyer had been sent to pick him up at taxpayer expense. Roosevelt addressed these accusations in one of his most famous "fireside chats," turning the rumors into political gold.

"These Republican leaders," he observed with (mock?) indignation, "have not been content with attacks on me, my wife, or on my sons. No, not content with that, they now include my little dog, Fala. Well, of course I don't resent such attacks," Roosevelt drawled in his inimitable voice, "and my family doesn't resent these attacks, but Fala does. You know Fala is Scotch and being a Scottie, as soon as he learned that the Republican fiction writers in Congress and out had concocted a story that I had left him behind on the Aleutian Islands and had sent a destroyer back to find him at a cost to the taxpayers of two or three, or eight or twenty million dollars—his Scotch soul was furious. He has not been the same dog since."

That consummate political animal, Richard Nixon, heard Roosevelt's speech and remembered it. When his initial vice-presidential campaign was in trouble, then-Senator Nixon performed a reprise of the Fala maneuver, this time using the new medium of television. In effect Nixon "became" Checkers, the beloved family cocker spaniel. Accused of being on the take from campaign contributors, about to be booted off the Eisenhower-Nixon ticket, Nixon went on television in 1952—long before it was common for politicians to do so—and turned on the pathos: "You know, the kids love that dog and I just want to say this right now, that regardless of what they say about it, we're going to keep it." Mamie Eisenhower, we are told, wept sentimental tears as she watched, and "several of the men [in the Eisenhower group] clutched handkerchiefs and dabbed their eyes." (Remember, this was 1952, before men were allowed to cry.) Darryl Zanuck called to say it was "the most tremendous performance I've ever seen."

"We're going to keep it" became the political message, rhetorically sublimated through the Checkers speech. Nixon stayed on the ticket. It would be years before he reverted to bad-dog status and told the country, quite falsely as it turned out, "You won't have Dick Nixon to kick around any more." In Oliver Stone's film *Nixon*, the Checkers speech is uncannily recreated by Anthony Hopkins, complete with trademark hunched posture and combative-defensive delivery. The indifference bordering on dislike shown by King Timahoe, a later (and more aristocratic or "presidential" family dog), serves as shorthand in the film for Nixon's loneliness and sense of isolation.

Since the time of Checkers, it has become virtually de rigueur to keep a dog or dogs in the White House. Millie, George Bush's springer spaniel, went so far as to write her own autobiography. Lyndon Johnson, notoriously, had beagles, whom he picked up by the ears before photographers, producing howls of protest across the country. The beagles were called Him and Her; Him's dog license tag proclaimed him #1, while Her was #2, another political faux-paw. (Johnson also had a beloved random-bred called Yuki, whom he picked up in a Texas gas station and permitted to attend Cabinet meetings. Yuki once showed up, uninvited but appropriately, at the signing of a new law called the Wholesome Meat Act.) President Gerald Ford's golden retriever, Liberty, was so popular that she sent out paw-printed photographs to her fans. The Clinton family cat, Socks, developed her own ailurophile following, but the absence of a dog was felt, and at one point Bill Clinton bid $3,500 on a golden retriever being sold to benefit daughter Chelsea's private school. The dog sold for $3,700. When Clinton failed to win the gold, other dogs were offered to the first family. To be truly American, exemplarily American, was apparently to have a dog. (The Clintons had had a dog in Arkansas, but it was hit and killed by a car.) Even the sometimes ironical Senator Bob Dole, in his quest for the presidency, brandished his photos of the family and its dog. Dole, a longtime Republican stalwart, had watched the success of Checkers and Millie and their owners. Now he proffered a snap of his own dog, optimistically named Leader: "He's the one on the right." (As so often with Republican candidates, though, it wasn't clear whether this Leader was far *enough* to the right.)

The public consciousness of the "family dog" assumes a whole new dimension when the Family is Royal and the "dog" plural, as in the case of England's Queen Elizabeth II. One knowledgeable commentator on the Buckingham Palace scene observed, "The Queen's corgis and 'dawgies' [which he described as "an unplanned cross" between corgies and dachshunds] are the only almost constant companions of the Queen who are unaware that their mistress is also the sovereign. They form as integral a part of her life as her children." What effect has this canine court had upon Elizabeth II's *other* family? "To this day it is not unknown for one or other of the royal children to complain about how difficult it is to get to see Mummy on her own, *and without the dogs.*"

Dog Days

When *Vanity Fair* asked clothing designer Bill Blass, "Who or what is the greatest love of your life?" he answered, succinctly, "My dogs." In literature and popular culture, in psychology, animal behavior, and fashion, the last years of the twentieth century could be called the Decade of the Dog, and our canine passion shows no sign of abating. The success of books like as Elizabeth Marshall Thomas's *The Hidden*

Life of Dogs (1993), Stanley Coren's *The Intelligence of Dogs* (1994), Vicki Hearne's *Animal Happiness* (1994), Peter Mayle's *A Dog's Life* (1995), and Willie Morris's *My Dog Skip* (1995) has coincided with the renewed interest in dog movie stars and TV stars, and with a general fascination with putting on the dog.

A remake of *Lassie* by Paramount Pictures and a celebrity biography of the eight (male) collies from Pal to Howard who have starred in the (female) title role has provoked a series of new "Lassie" articles and clothing tie-ins (like the beguiling "win a trip to meet Lassie in 'person' at Bloomingdale's"). In Britain a long-running series of popular advertisements made the "Dulux dog" (known to friends and family as Fernville Lord Digby) a star. Detective stories featuring dog-owning sleuths and grouped under headings like "Canine Capers" and "Dog Lovers' Mysteries" represent a new kind of niche marketing in the murder-mystery trade.

Dogs have also wriggled their way into cyberspace, which might almost be dubbed the Interpet. On-line dog groups discuss everything from what breed to buy to fleas, ticks, and how to deal with a family dog that misbehaves. In one telling instance a mother posted a message on a kids newsgroup about her household dog, who was stalking her three-year-old son, Henry. Misc.kids users overwhelmingly suggested putting the dog to sleep. But when a dog lover copied the same message into the *dog* newsgroup the range of suggestions was quite different, ranging from training tips, to hints for separating the child and dog, and even to a joking proposal: "The choice should be obvious: get rid of Henry." Computer search programs called "Fetch" and "Golden Retriever" ("faithfully helps students do senior project research") hit the market, a screen saver called "Bad Dog" allowed a cutely misbehaving pup to amble across an idle screen, and a CD-ROM called "Dogz: Your Computer Pet," invites users to "click on a doghouse and choose a pup; she'll wiggle, overeat, and frisk among your icons. (A similar CD-ROM, P.A.W.S., for "Personal Automated Wagging System," is distributed in the U.K.) For those who prefer time-honored low-tech wireless connections, there is still a thriving business in dog telepathy: in 1994 a British biologist set up experiments that seemed to prove (via split-screen videotape) that the family dog can be so in touch with household members that she senses when they *leave* their place of work and stations herself at the window to await their return.

On the Internet and in personals ads from the Web to the weeklies, romance between humans can be facilitated by dogs: "Dog lovers a plus," concluded an ad in the *New York Press* after cataloguing the advertiser's charms, preferences, and desires. And Americans are not the only dog-love entrepreneurs. In Japan, suitors in search of romance rent dogs by the day ($50 for a poodle, $80 for a golden retriever). "Young men rent an animal in order to grab their dates' hearts," said one pet shop owner, and another observed that "having a dog generates a lot to talk about." Even collective dog watching can be a social activity with romantic promise: just ask the crowd that hangs around the dog run in New York's Washington Square. "What a nice [Rottweiler; Shih Tzu; Labrador; or, when in doubt, just plain "dog"]—what's his [or "her"; never "its"] name?" is a good, low-key conversation opener virtually guaranteed to be nonthreatening. Followed up two days later by "Hello, Rover" [Rex; Chablis; Beauregard—you get the idea], it establishes you as an FOD (Friend of Dogs) rather than a crass social opportunist. If you don't believe me, watch how many conversations, increasingly intimate, take place in the presence of, and are ostensibly directed at, dogs. ("Does Chelsea like running in the park? She does? So do I. . . ."). Dog walkers who gather in the playground near my house often know the dogs' names but not those of the owners. A tall man with a moustache is "Brandy's owner," an older woman in a green parka belongs to Zeus. On a summer evening the dog owners break out the zinfandel (or mineral water; this is Cambridge, after all) and indulgently look on as their charges sniff and mingle. Dogs are good matchmakers. The old maxim "Love me, love my dog," is, it seems, often more effective the other way around.

A front-page article on Max, the Jack Russell terrier in the Jim Carrey movie *The Mask,* appeared in the Arts and Leisure section of *The New York Times.* Another telegenic Jack Russell, "Frasier's Pal Eddie," made the cover of *Entertainment Weekly* as "TV's Top Dog—He's Hot. He's Sexy. He's Purebred." *EW* also featured, in another issue, a page of dog-celebrity look-alikes, or "dogs that do celebrity impersonations": A shar-pei as John Goodman, a Chinese crested hairless as Joan Rivers, and so on. If your dog is not yet a celebrity, but aspires to become one, *How to Get Your Pet into Show Business,* by Captain Arthur J. Haggerty, who "trained Sandy for Broadway's *Annie,*" can teach him or her all the tricks of the trade. (Sandy, a multitalented mongrel, was an author as well as an actor, producing his own rags-to-riches life story, *The Autobiography of a Star.*)

Around the turn of the last century anthologies like *Praise of the Dog, The Dog's Book of Verse,* and *The Dog in British Poetry* (dedicated "To the Cynics"—the word "cynic" comes from a Greek word meaning "dog") were assured a welcome by what one editor appropriately called "the great dog-loving public," and dog fiction was as popular as dog verse. The same public today annually snaps up dog calendars, dog coffee-table books, collections like *The Literary Dog,* and dozens of self-help and how-to books that could be titled, generically, something like *The Courage to Heel.*

Books by William Wegman and Thierry Poncelet feature dogs dressed in human clothes, embodying human foibles and illustrating the classics of "human" childhood. Poncelet buys family portraits from the eighteenth and nineteenth centuries, paints out the human faces, and replaces them with dogs. Photographer Wegman's weimaraner Battina stars as Cinderella and Little Red Riding Hood; as the latter, in a dramatic and reflexive encounter, she meets the wolf. (Fay Ray, Battina's mother, plays the Fairy Godmother and the Evil Stepmother in *Cinderella,* and the Grandmother and the Mother in "Little Red Riding Hood." "Fay is very versatile," comments her spokesperson at the Wegman Studios.) The title of an earlier Wegman volume, *Man's Best Friend,* draws attention to the exchange of properties: the "Man" of the title is in fact the dog (Wegman's first weimaraner, Man Ray, named after the surrealist), while the "best friend," by process of elimination, must be photographer Wegman, the man. Man (the dog) himself was originally to be named "Bauhaus"—a *great* dog name—but his new owner decided the puppy "didn't look like a Bauhaus"; a Bauhaus, he thought, should be black, white, and square. Fay Ray, Man Ray's successor, was, of course, named after the movie actress Fay Wray, whose classic encounter with King Kong raised its own questions about pathos, the human/animal boundary, and the ineluctable mysteries of desire.

Meantime, in another man-bites-dog reversal, a Samoyed named Samson became his own man's "best man," standing up for his master in a wedding ceremony that made the evening news. The reporter—obviously not a dog person—wondered how he had managed to carry the ring. The social integration of dog into human culture—and human into dog culture—is, we might say, at an all-time high.

Putting on the Dog

A *New York Times* editorial recounting the unexpected pleasures of summer in the city noted that "the local dogs are lapping up refreshment at yet another new amenity—the water bowls for canine passersby that have suddenly appeared in many a shop entrance," and mused, rhetorically, "Is it the heat or some kind of collective unconscious bent on making New York a kinder, gentler place that accounts for the mini-cafés, the benches, and the doggie water bowls?" A company called Frosty Paws has begun marketing an "ice cream" made especially for dogs. Its chief ingredients are water, whey, soy flour, and fat; apparently dogs love it.

Chicago's Comiskey Park, home of the White Sox, planned a Dog Day of Summer to woo canine fans and their masters to low-attendance weeknight games. Featuring a pregame costume parade (with dogs dressed as players), Rin Tin Tin reruns on the Jumbotron, and free admission, treats, and water for the guests of honor (owners buy their own hot dogs), the event was calculated to make the lucky dogs rr-root-rrroot-rrroot for the home team, whether from dugout or bull(dog) pen.

All over New York, pampered pets and bandanna-wearing free spirits are stepping out in dogwear that apes human fashion. "Dog owners like to dress up their dogs," said an expert at Dog-O-Rama on Seventh Avenue South. "They have a sense that they're a person and should dress up like a person." "You feel stupid buying dog clothes when people are homeless," admitted the owner of two well-dressed poodles, "but I do other things for charity." But canine fashion shows can be charitable draws. At a high-powered fund-raiser for POWARS, the Pet Owners with AIDS Resource Service, a Jack Russell terrier and his master wore fuschia shirts and ties by Gene Meyer, and the model Tomiko posed with two Maltese, Happy and FouFou, all wearing Fernando Sanchez's pink-and-aqua ostrich-feather jacket. (POWARS provides food, dog walking, and other services, enabling people with AIDS to keep their pets.) Even in cyberspace there is a site for "fashion dog" (http://www.carpi1.shinyit/fashiond/fashiond.htm).

Sometimes the dogs don't *wear* the fashion items, they *are* the fashion items. "Dogs make the perfect accessory," declared *The New York Times Magazine.* "At least one English sheepdog . . . has been mistaken for a pillow on a chintz couch. Dalmatians are always at home on a black-and-white checkered kitchen floor."

Or—for a touch of hair of the dog—consider the book *Knitting with Dog Hair.* "Stop vacuuming and start knitting," urge the authors. The projects they recommend include a golden retriever scarf, a cardigan sweater made of Samoyed hair, and perhaps the ultimate in self-referential recycling, a dog sweater for a pet pug made of yarn spun from a Newfoundland. (This is not a new thought, though it may sound surprising: in World War I in England the hair of the chow was used for weaving sweaters and cloth, and a Kentucky woman in the thirties made bed-sized coverlets out of dog fleece with the aid of a spinning wheel. One dispassionate account from the same period reported that "some dog owners have tanned the skins of dogs that have passed away and have made useful floor pieces from them. If a color match could be had, we believe that the coat and skin of certain breeds of dogs would make excellent fur coats for human wear.")

Scores of catalogues peddling dog-related items are mailed out to be pawed through by potential purchasers, from companies like Pedigrees, the Pet Catalog; Drs. Foster & Smith, the Company Owned and Operated by Practicing Veterinarians; and The Company of Dogs, Gifts and Gear for Dogs & the People Who Share Their Lives. They include helpful guidelines like "how to measure your dog for collars and clothing" (for the latter, "hold tape measure at collar and measure to base of tail"), as well as products that range from dog life preservers ("a must for boating dogs"), a doggie bathrobe ("after a bath or strenuous workout, your dog will love relaxing in his own kimono with double layers of terry"), a doggie backpack, and a pair of (human) socks with a pocket for carrying keys on the daily walk.

Some catalogues skip the dogs entirely and go straight for the masters, like the popular Black Dog catalogue circulated by a bakery and tavern in Martha's Vineyard, Massachusetts. Black Dog T-shirts have been worn by dog fans from Minneapolis to Moscow; actress Brooke Shields was wearing one when she was photographed for a cover story in the *National Enquirer,* and a Martha's Vineyard newspaper editor calls the Black Dog logo Ts and sweatshirts "the ultimate nonfashion statement of hipness . . . the antialligator." The logo depicts a black Lab, though the original black dog was a brindle boxer-and-Lab mix. (An authorized biography of the eponymous black dog is now in its third printing.) Why a Lab? The catalogue describes the Classic

Dog T as "the shirt that prompts the response 'It looks just like my dog.'"

In Britain the same "dogged devotion" is clearly on display, from the Bones Dog and Catalogue to the neoclassic kennel in grey and gold with domed top and foliate bal finial on auction at Christie's. (Expected to fetch about £5,000.) A miniature green and gold Harrods bus, selling for only £1,500, has a sleeping section and compartments for grooming aids and fashion accessories, and there are shops catering to the sophisticated urban dog as well as the hearty country canine. In October 1995, a Labrador named Oscar toured the U.K. as a hypnotist. Celebrated (human) specialist Roger Mugford of the Animal Behavioural Clinic ("the Anthony Clare of the canine world") cares for "dotty dogs" suffering from maladjustment and separation anxiety (vet referral required). *Dogs Today* magazine and *Our Dogs* newspaper circulate to the U.K.'s estimated 6.5 million dog owners, and in 1996 painter David Hockney exhibited 45 oils of his beloved dachshunds Stanley and Boodgie.

Dog collectibles (I mean here art and tchotchkes, not scoopables) have long been favored by fanciers, from the wealthy turn-of-the-century patroness Geraldine Rockefeller Dodge, who owned more than six thousand items of dog-themed art from paintings to bronzes, all the way to designer Betsy Speert of Boston, whose kitchen includes a wooden pipe rack with two carved dogs (used for wooden spoons), ceramic dog-shaped planters (now holding spatulas), a terrier lamp, and a sculpted dog head attached to a kitchen cabinet that clenches a dishtowel in its teeth. A New York City art gallery advertised "antique dog and animal art and accessories" as "ideal gifts for the holidays," and George Rodrigue, painter and author of *The Blue Dog Book*, was available to sign copies at a SoHo Gallery, The Time Is Always Now, that featured recent "Blue Dog" paintings under the fetching headline "Who can bear the burden of unconditional love?" Dog cookbooks are also a hot market item, featuring tempting and healthful treats like Pogo's Light Biscuits for Belly Draggers, Ruthie's Breakfast Bagels, and Tess's Nice Breath Biscuits (key ingredients: mint and parsley). In response to consumer demand, a popular Southern California restaurant offers two separate menus—one for humans and the other for canines. Staff and owner at the Park Bench Cafe in Huntington Beach, about an hour south of Los Angeles, sport T-shirts emblazoned with the motto "Bone Appetit."

Pet superstores have become big business, backed by venture capitalists and experienced superstore retailers, who scent money in the fifty-three million households that own pets nationwide. *Barron's,* the financial weekly, advised investors that "a new breed of pet businesses" was "cashing in on [the] love fest" between humans and pets, merchandizing products from car safety seats to press-on toenails, from premium pet food to pharmaceuticals. "Who's to say," *Barron's* concluded optimistically, "America isn't going to the dogs?" Three pet chains went public in thirteen months: Petsmart, Petstuff, and Petco Animal Supplies. (Pet Nosh, a New Jersey superstore, wins my personal blue ribbon for best store name.) "Everybody spoils their pet," said a marketing specialist at Coopers & Lybrand (convincingly if ungrammatically), adding: "They are treated as family and nothing is too good for them." Customers are encouraged to shop with their pets. New products like poultry-flavored toothpaste and "Crispy Beef"–flavored sparkling water are creating their own demand. And a series of dog boutiques, like My Dog in Harvard Square ("Unique supplies, gifts, and natural food for dogs and the people who love them," telephone 617-87MYDOG) cater to upscale customers for whom the suburban superstores are inaccessible or de trop, selling everything from car seatbelts for dogs to inflatable dog bowls (just toss in the back of the Range Rover for your portable pet) to leashes that attach to a belt around the owner's waist (easier to jog with JoJo), to pad-protecting dog "feet" that fasten with Velcro and protect the dog's feet from salt and snow ("flying out of here," reported the store owner in the first days of winter). An article in the *New York Times* business section, commending the boom in pet superstores, reported that the "bare-bones" costs of owning a dog was $11,580, assuming a dog life span of ten years.

Health insurance for dogs is now available from several companies, including Veterinary Pet Insurance and Fireman's Fund Insurance Company (both in California), with coverage for the treatment of diseases like cancer and diabetes and special, more expensive policies for elder care. "Our surveys show that seven of 10 American pet owners now think of their pets as children," reported Honey Niehaus, deputy director of the American Animal Hospital Association. "We now regularly hear comments along the lines of 'I'd go bankrupt before I put him to sleep,' or 'If she gets sick, money is no object.'" The owners of Stormy, a Belgian sheepdog in Los Angeles, spent $5000 on cancer-fighting surgery and chemotherapy, and followed up the successful treatment with a $3,000 hip replacement. (After death, dogs can be interred in pet cemeteries with caskets, headstones, or crematory urns—or freeze-dried by a Florida company for a cost of from $400 to $1,800, the latter price for dogs as large as Doberman pinschers.)

In the midst of life, it seems, most dogs are happy campers—some of them literally. Camp Wingford in Avoca, Michigan, offers swimming, orchards to roam in, and 733 acres of grounds. The summer camp run by Shady Spring Kennels in Maryland features dog-paddling, Frisbee, and hiking, a Bark-and-Ride camp bus, a camp spa with hairdo and pedicure, and bunk photographs for the proud parents to take home. "People treat their dogs like their children," says camp director Charlotte Katz Shaffer. "They look for a kennel like they look for a pediatrician." At Happy Trails Pet Resort in Crownsville, Maryland, VCRs play films like *The Incredible Journey, Homeward Bound, 101 Dalmatians,* and *Lady and the Tramp* in a continuous loop from morning to night, and dog guests are encouraged to bring their own home videos. The resort owner, who has taken courses in dog psychology as well as dog grooming, says "movies are a very important factor in keeping them happy." At Camp Gone to the Dogs in Putney, Vermont, people and pets vacation together, sharing a room. The bathing-suit pageant features owners and dogs in matching swimwear. For traveling vacationers, a series of guidebooks now points out inns and resorts where dogs (and their owners) are welcome. There is even a dog club for the dogless, a New York City establishment where, for a fee, dogless dog lovers can pet a borrowed canine or take one for a walk. The main drawback? Patrons become too attached to their fantasy pets. As the proprietor notes, "It can be very, very hard to say good-bye."

Following the lead of this boom in pet care and pet products, dog day-care centers have opened all over the country, from Boston to Louisville to San Francisco, expanding the services offered by dog walkers to include play groups, sofas and chairs to snooze on, and classical music. ("One of the advantages of being a dog walker is that you don't have to like people," said one experienced New York City walker.) The tab for this comes high, $75 to $100 for a five-day week, or $6,000 to $8,000 per dog at a Somerville, Massachusetts, day-care center. "I'm sure E.P. would love to go every day," says the "father" of a springer spaniel puppy, "but once a week is all we can afford at this point."

But if dogs are sharing some of the pleasures of human society, they are also sharing some of its problems. According to the Animal Veterinary Medical Association, dogs are now taking Prozac. It seems they, too, suffer from anxiety, depression, extreme shyness, aggression, and obsessive-compulsive disorders. Dog problems from separation anxiety to "high-rise syndrome" (they fall out of unscreened windows) afflict urban pets. Many of these ailments can be found in a hefty classification of animal behavioral disorders analogous to the American Psychiatric Association's *Diagnostic and Statistical Manual.* (This was familiar canine territory for me: our old dog Nietzschie was a martyr all his life to linoleo-phobia: fear of slipping on linoleum floors. He also barked vociferously at statues, whether of persons or animals. His spirited vocal challenge to a statue of the wolf who suckled Romulus and Remus became famous in certain circles.)

Dog phobias, like their human counterparts, are often associational, provoked by a chain of events or ideas rather than by the frightening or hated object itself. Sam, a sheepdog, was afraid of thunder, and came to realize that when lightning flashed thunder would follow. So he began to fear lightning. Then, when someone took a photograph of him, he was startled by the flash and thought it was lightning—so he cowered and ran. Before long he would quake whenever he saw a camera, even though there was no flash, no lightning, no thunder. His amused owners told me this story. The "moral" of the tale, if there is one, is certainly not—or not only—a lesson about the mental life of dogs. Substitute any modern human phobia for the inadvertently frightening camera Sam imagined to be the cause of thunder and lightning and you may have a social narrative of quite a different kind.

Therapy for pets, with or without drug treatment, is a fast-growing business. A speaker on holistic healing ("Holism: What It Means"; "Nutrition: Herbs; Homeopathy; Bach Flower Remedies") spoke to an overflow crowd at a kennel club in Pennsylvania, outdrawing another presentation on a more traditional topic, "Born to Win." In the film *Down and Out in Beverly Hills* a dog psychiatrist is called in to counsel the family dog, Matisse, a picky eater, and diagnoses him as suffering from "nipple anxiety." (The part of Matisse was brilliantly played by a canine actor named Mike the Dog, who, as critic Leonard Maltin noted, easily steals the film.) The producer of *The Pet Show,* a nationally syndicated radio program, suggested that quality time was more effective than pills: "Sometimes just rotating the use of toys and spending more time on the floor with your animals is the best solution for a cranky or depressed animal friend." "How ironic," observed the president of the National Psychological Association for Psychoanalysis ruefully, "that we seem to care more about the happiness of animals than humans."

What is behind the current cultural obsession with crossover relationships between human beings and their dogs? Does the modern attachment to dogs and dog stories tell us something about the present state of *human* affairs? Are we asking dogs to act out our own stories so as to take a new look at ourselves? Or is it only ourselves we see even when we look at other species? This question may have something to do with the return of anthropomorphism in several recent studies.

The New Anthropomorphism

A lively new pack of dog writers has captured the popular imagination in a genre that might be called ethohumanism. Discussing entities like "happiness," "intelligence," and a "hidden life," these widely marketed, best-selling, and often moving and evocative books explore the once forbidden terrain of canine consciousness, with the objective of finding out not only whether dogs think, but what they think about *us.*

These are "crossover" books in the publishers' sense, books with one foot—or paw?—in a learned or scholarly field and another in the domain of the popular. Elizabeth Marshall Thomas, the author of the highly successful *The Hidden Life of Dogs,* is described on her book's jacket flap as a "novelist and anthropologist." Stanley Coren, author of *The Intelligence of Dogs,* is a "renowned psychologist and award-winning dog trainer," and Vicki Hearne is "a poet and philosopher" who has taught college English and trains dogs professionally.

The border-straddling nature of these works is underscored by the difficulty bookstores have in deciding where to display them: *The Intelligence of Dogs,* for example, is marked on the book jacket "Pets/Psychology," and turns out to define "intelligence" as a version of "obedience." It is no exaggeration to say that such books in fact constitute a respectable new form of pop psychology and self-help, the flip side of a subgenre more directly aimed at that market niche, like Clarissa Pinkola Estés's best-selling *Women Who Run with the Wolves,* or its sardonic send-up, Barbara Graham's *Women Who Run with the Poodles. Poodles* cheerfully offended Jungian feminists by including a section on "Reclaiming Your Sacred Inner Bitch." But unlike *Poodles,* which sees the inner bitch in the woman, *Hidden Life, Intelligence,* and *Happiness* all see the inner woman in the bitch—or, more usually, the inner man in the dog.

"The dread practice of anthropomorphism," as science writer Natalie Angier notes, has long been a "sin" among researchers who study the behavior of nonhuman animals. Traditionally, "to ascribe to the creature under scrutiny emotions, goals, consciousness, intelligence, desires, or any other characteristics viewed as exclusively human" has been regarded as unscientific. "The truly objective biologist will refrain from projecting personal feelings onto the animal"; "a scientist should never presume that an animal has intentions, or is aware of what it is doing, or even that it feels pain."

But lately a new wave of "neo-anthropomorphists" has arisen: animal behaviorists who believe that anthropomorphism can actually help them "do their science," as scientists like to say. "Anthropomorphism is really just another word for empathy," they claim. "For many biologists," said a Berkeley scientist who studies pit vipers, "the major reason they study animals . . . is that they really wonder what it's like to be that animal." *When Elephants Weep,* a book by former Freud archivist Jeffrey Moussaieff Masson and collaborator Susan McCarthy, set out to explore and legitimize "the emotional lives of animals," and wound up on the best-seller list.

Not everyone, not even all humanists, agree that such complete communication is desirable. "It is necessary to stop humanizing animals for fear that we start predicating animal attributes on humans," asserts Richard Klein, a professor of French, in a thoughtful piece on America's "obsession" with pets. Worrying that "animals are not only being assimilated to humans; they are being made into the destiny of humans," Klein argues that "we ought to resist the anthropomorphism of real animals." (By "real" he means not animated, non-Disney.) Klein sees anthropomorphism as dangerous: "By anthropomorphizing pets we are encouraging the tendency to blur the distinction between humans and animals." He fears that with this loss of distinction we will be encouraged to kill with the same lack of conscience as animals do, which may lead to "the worst form of biologism, racism or naturalism."

But to worry about humans becoming more bloodthirsty by seeing themselves as cats and dogs seems to me exaggerated. Humans hardly need anthropomorphism to encourage them to become natural-born killers. And the argument that we should "reserve" humanness for humans and preserve the "fundamental ethical difference between animals and humans" fails to take account of the "humanizing" effect that care, affection, and even institutions directed at animals have upon *people.*

Why, the new "critical anthropomorphists" ask, should science insist that there is a fixed boundary between human beings and the rest of the living world? Indeed, as one researcher points out, the desire to establish a firm borderline somewhere, anywhere, between humans and other beasts—a desire inherited from both Judeo-Christian religion and the philosophy of Descartes—has resulted in a kind of scientific gerrymandering, a constant redrawing of boundaries to suit the intellectual politics of the time. The "sine qua non of humanness," rather than residing in any particular property, is constantly being revised; the borderline keeps moving. The definition of humanness, said one animal psychologist, "keeps getting pushed away to preserve human exclusivity." Are human beings the only ones with the ability to feel? To think? To speak? To suffer? What are the bounds of "humanity"? This is a border region now being encroached upon by machines as well as by animals, with the advent of chess-playing computers and artificial intelligence. As an observer at a chess match between IBM's Deep Blue supercomputer and chess master Gary Kasparov noted, "We have a habit of perpetually redefining 'creativity' as that which humans do and 'brute force' as the stuff of machines. In each age, we have redrawn the borders of the inviolably human." Vacillating between "artificial intelligence" and "emotional intelligence," the "human" (as contrasted with the animal *or* the machine) is contested territory.

But if some dog writers are now embracing anthropomorphism, others, still skittish, shy away from the concept even as they deploy it. They are, we might say in Pavlov's sense, *conditioned* to do so by the scorn that traditional behavioral scientists (and some philosophers and linguists) have heaped on the idea. Notice the note of defiance with which author Elizabeth Marshall Thomas begins *The Hidden Life of Dogs:*

> This is a book about dog consciousness. To some people, the subject might seem anthropomorphic simply by definition, since in

the past even scientists have been led to believe that only human beings have thoughts or emotions. Of course, nothing could be further from the truth. . . .

After all, thoughts and emotions have evolutionary value.

Thomas's approach is, she suggests, *more* "scientific" than that of some scientists, since it takes "evolutionary value" into account.

Where Thomas, an anthropologist, uses the language of science to defend anthropomorphism, literature professor Hearne uses the vocabulary of the humanities. "Having something to say about what animals are like—about the problem of animal consciousness," Hearne says, has become a "ubiquitous . . . way of providing a rhetorical and conceptual frame for investigations of human consciousness." "The family of tropes damned as 'anthropomorphic,'" she maintains, "points us to the places where the greatest secrets of animal thinking, and thinking in general, begin to be revealed." The dog trainers she knows have the habit of "talking in highly anthropomorphic, morally loaded language," she says, a practice that offends some "academics," among them philosophers or psychologists who think that only people can "love."

In Hearne's own books about dog training, the names of poets and philosophers serve as frequent reference points, illustrating homely anecdotes about dogs and their owners. She cites poems by Milton, Sidney, Shakespeare, Wordsworth, and Byron, by John Hollander, Donald Davie, Wallace Stevens, and James Merrill. Her dogs exemplify the ideas of philosophers like Ludwig Wittgenstein and Stanley Cavell. "Many people think Airedales are the best dogs, as did the poet and critic Yvor Winters," she will say. The performance of Sam, a pointer, strikes her as "an illustration of what T. S. Eliot called 'the eternal struggle between art and education.'" She imagines her Airedale, Drummer, "by himself, meditating," and wonders whether he is "hoping that I would, in Matthew Arnold's phrase, overhear his meditation."

This connection between the canine and the canon is hardly new, of course. The impulse to compare our dogs with major—and minor—characters in literature is almost irresistible. In his wonderful essay on "The Character of Dogs," published in 1883, Robert Louis Stevenson compared a vain and spoiled dog, "with his whining jealousies and his foible for falsehood," to Sir Willoughby Patterne, the title character in George Meredith's *The Egoist*. Stevenson wrote of his Skye terrier, Woggs, unaccountably rejected by females of his kind, "Had he been

Shakespeare, he would then have written *Troilus and Cressida* to brand the offending sex; but being only a little dog, he began to bite them."

Vicki Hearne's interest in seeing the dog as meditating, speculating, and exemplifying what Arnold called "the best that has been thought and said" calls attention to the ways in which anthropomorphism today functions almost as a species of moral philosophy. Through her dogs Hearne revisits the touchstones of traditional literary and philosophical culture. Their actions and attitudes paradoxically confirm her understanding of what is human.

In fact, the fascination of many dog writers with the major poets and philosophers is a clear sign of something we might call "caninization": the recurrence, in many of these contemporary books about dogs, of scenes from Homer, Shakespeare, and other "great" authors, the use of dog stories as universal narratives of love and loss whose universality is demonstrated by the way they recall the classics. At a time in modern culture when claims about the universal and the timeless have to compete with the need for historical and cultural specificity ("Is this a story about *me* or not?") dog stories transcend the personal, permit thoughts about the general instead. Few human readers of *Lassie* will set her experiences aside because they can't identity with a collie; few audiences watching *101 Dalmatians* are likely to ask whether the film is relevant to the lives of cocker spaniels. Mutts remain in a special category, that of Cinderella or the Little Engine That Could, since rooting for the "underdog" has become second nature (second "human nature"?). But whatever the pedigree (or absence thereof) it is somehow easier for many people to "identify with" a dog than with a specific person (a "hero" or "heroine") in literature or history. Readers and writers, adults as well as children, anthropomorphize in order to regain their sense of a collective human experience. Paradoxically, the quintessence of the "human" is often found in the dog.

A review of two children's books about dogs described them, in a headline, as "Two novels in which adolescents learn from the experts how to love and trust." The experts—it was almost needless to day—were the dogs. Successors to classics like *Old Yeller,* these books, and books like them, aspired to an emotional place aptly described by reviewer Linda Gray Sexton as "so intense and durable that I can recall those stories quite precisely decades later." It is not only children's books that do this, as the enormous popular success of tales like *James Herriot's Dog Stories* makes clear. The very same school reader that instructed mid-twentieth-century Americans in the shape of the ideal family also told us that no nuclear family was complete without its Spot. As one dysfunctional character says to another in Sam Shepard's play *Buried Child*, "It's like a Norman Rockwell cover or something. Where's the milkman and the little dog? What's the little dog's name? Spot. Spot and Jane. Dick and Jane and Spot."

To Love, Honor, and Obey

Perhaps the most symptomatic development in the new cultural permission to anthropomorphize is the wide currency of the term "marriage" to describe a relationship between two canines, and the insistent description of them in recent books as "husband" and "wife."

In *The Hidden Life of Dogs*, described on the flyleaf of the book as "a sort of deeply truthful ethological poem," Elizabeth Marshall Thomas chronicles in affecting terms what she repeatedly calls the "marriage" of the huskies Misha and Maria. Misha "had married my daughter's husky, the beautiful Maria," says Thomas. Maria "would wait near the door for her husband." As historian Harriet Ritvo cogently pointed out in *The New York Review of Books*, Thomas "evidently wishes to imply that the range of canine behavior includes the highest kind of mutual devotion and fidelity," but the result is both "distracting" and "coy."

Significantly, in this account of a dog marriage Thomas once again directly addresses the question of anthropomorphism, again with the consciousness that in doing so she trespasses on conventional wisdom. And again she has recourse to the concept of "evolutionary value."

> Popular prejudice might hold that romantic love, with its resulting benefit of fidelity, sexual and otherwise, is not a concept that can be applied to dogs, and that to do so is anthropomorphic. Not true. Fully as much as any human love story, the story of Misha and Maria shows the evolutionary value of romantic love. The force that drove Romeo and Juliet is no less strong or important if harbored by a nonhuman species, because the strength of the bond helps to assure the male that he, instead of, say, Tybalt or Bingo, is the father of any children born and that both parents are in a cooperative frame of mind when the time comes to raise those children.

Notice that Shakespeare is evoked as the humanistic "evidence" of an emotional standard: "the force that drove Romeo and Juliet" appears here as a fact, not a fiction, while the beguiling fantasy of a litter of baby Montagues sired by Romeo on his Capulet "mate" serves to corroborate the "evolutionary value of romantic love." It's perhaps just as well not to take this flight of fancy literally. In canine terms the mating of Juliet with her cousin Tybalt would be an example of line breeding, a procedure "that has been the basis of producing the very best dogs," whereas Romeo is regarded by the Capulets as a dangerous enemy from a rival house. In this sense the marriage of Romeo and Juliet, even though both have "pedigrees," might seem less like Misha and Maria than like Lady and the Tramp.

As it happens, elements of Shakespeare's *Romeo and Juliet* also turn up in another love story between dogs, Ivan Reitman's film *Beethoven's Second.* This popular family movie featuring a romance between two St. Bernards has more than a little in common with *The Hidden Life of Dogs.* Missy the St. Bernard, imprisoned by her wicked step-owners on a first-floor apartment house balcony, is wooed by the love-struck Beethoven, and—in a move Juliet might have envied—she leaps over the railing to join him for an afternoon on the town. Once again the reference to Shakespeare (rather more accurate than in Thomas's account) is used as a shorthand for "romantic love."

The appearance of puppies some weeks later confirms the carnal nature of their relationship (Beethoven's introduction to his new brood is less traumatic than Misha's, and results in a longer-term parental commitment), but the affair is presented in distinctly romantic—and manifestly "anthropomorphic" terms. (The filmmakers appear to have wrestled with the problem of how to make this pair of beefy canines look heterosexual, and have solved it by giving Missy a pink hair ornament. Lesson: if the bitch looks butch, put on a bow.) Rather than sniffing one another's rear ends in doggy style the two St. Bernards go out together for a hot dog, take a ride in a bicycle buggy, and wind up necking (or should we call it petting?) at a drive-in movie.

To talk about dog "husbands" and "wives" is not, of course, a new practice among ethologists. Konrad Lorenz wrote about a similar kind of "animal husbandry" forty years ago in *King Solomon's Ring,* where he described the mixed "marriage" of his Alsatian and his wife's chow. "We discovered," Lorenz reports, "as an unexpected hindrance, a new property of Lupus dogs [dogs like malamutes, huskies, and chows, which were, Lorenz believed, descended from the wolf]: the monogamous fidelity of the bitch to a certain dog."

Now, what Lorenz called Lupus dogs may in fact be more "monogamous" than what he called Aureus dogs (like German shepherds or golden retrievers) but erotic constancy is not in general a trait we associate with the canine world. In any case, the discovery of sexual fidelity in a species not particularly known for that trait—despite the generic name "Fido"—is an interesting commentary on another species (homo sapiens) whose track record in marriage is in fact getting worse all the time. If "Fido" ("Faithful") is a stereotypical dog name, so, after all, is "Rover."

But the recurrence in these accounts of the word "fidelity" can hardly be an accident. As the name Fido suggests, "popular prejudice" does associate dogs with fidelity, but of a slightly different kind. We expect dogs to be faithful to human beings, not to each other. They are supposed to be *our* "best friends."

Home Is Where the Dog Is

Any dog owner knows that the sweetest moment after a long day comes when you put your key in the door and the dog comes running. In a moment you can leave work and the commute behind you. Today's dual-career-couple dog owners sometimes telephone during long workdays to let their dogs hear their voices on the answering machine, giving a new meaning to the concept of calling home.

In his 1918 memoir *A Man and His Dog* (*Herr und Hund*) Thomas Mann had described his weary homecoming from the city: "And then it happens that the embodiment of my own domesticity, as it were, my very retirement, comes to meet me and salutes and welcomes me not only without reproach or touchiness, but with extreme joy, and reintroduces me to my own fireside—all in the shape of Bashan [the dog] himself." For Mann the dog was the very embodiment of "my own domesticity" on "my own fireside." In modern life this image of the dog on the hearth has become such a traditional sign of welcome (even in households without a hearth) that pet catalogues and specialty shops now carry a range of indoor-outdoor floormats ("in 15 Breeds," from basset to Yorkie to three different colors of Lab) depicting a smiling dog on a hearthrug. Home is where the dog is—whether or not you actually own a dog.

It's symptomatic, too, that there have been so many dog movies with "home" in the title: not only the classic, *Lassie Come Home,* in endless versions and variations dating from the forties to the present, but also a couple of highly successful features from the nineties: *Homeward Bound: The Incredible Journey* (1993)—a remake of Disney's 1963 film titled simply, like the popular book that inspired it, *The Incredible Journey*— and *Far from Home: The Adventures of Yellow Dog* (1995). These rather ungainly double-barreled titles suggest that the studios recognize there are two important buttons to push: the one marked "dog" (or "dog story") and the one marked "home." Thus when Chance, the bumptious new dog in the household, completes his arduous journey in *Homeward Bound,* arriving (of course) just as the family is sitting down to a turkey dinner that looks a lot like Thanksgiving, his thoughts are the film's last word: "At last, for the first time in my life, I was home." As is clear from their titles, *Homeward Bound* and *Far from Home,* like *Lassie Come Home,* draw both literally and liberally on the quality of "nostalgia," a bittersweet longing for things, persons, or situations of the past, a kind of cultural homesickness, from the Greek word *nostos,* a return home. Home is where the dog is.

The *canis classicus* here of course is Argus, the faithful dog of Odysseus, who recognizes his disguised master after twenty years— and promptly dies:

> There, full of vermin, lay Argus the hound. But directly he became aware of Odysseus' presence, he wagged his tail and dropped his ears, though he lacked the strength now to come nearer his master. Odysseus turned his eyes away, and . . . brushed away a tear. . . . As for Argus, the black hand of Death descended on him the moment he caught sight of Odysseus—after twenty years.

Once again we can see that not for nothing is "Fido" the pet name of man's best friend. And that "home" is the same as "death" is a lesson we do not need to learn from Freud.

"Nostalgia, in a dog? Well, why not?" ask Jeffrey Masson and Susan McCarthy. Darwin speculates on dog memory in *The Expression of the Emotions in Man and Animals,* offering a challenge to those who doubt canine consciousness. "But can we feel sure," he wonders, "that an old dog with an excellent memory and some powers of imagination, as shewn by his dreams, never reflects on his past pleasures in the chase? and this would be a form of self-consciousness."

"The dog has an enviable mind," remarks dog trainer Barbara Woodhouse. "It remembers the nice things in life and quickly blots out the nasty." That dogs remember—remember people, remember places, remember smells, remember each other—is a proposition that hardly seems to require proof. Our dog Nietzschie had been to the Oberlin Inn once, as a puppy. When he was brought back there some three years later, it was clear from his joyful sniffing that he remembered it very well. And some years after Nietzschie died, Wagner, who was five years younger and had, we were sure, looked up to him, happened to come upon a toy with which they had both played, and which had since been forgotten. Not only was Wagner (now a relatively dignified eight-year-old) enraptured with this toy, he played with it like a puppy—like, in fact, the puppy he had been when he was given it, and when he and Nietzschie tussled about it together. Was Wagner remembering his lost friend? Or his puppyhood? This may be too much to ask, or to answer. But he was remembering *something.*

"Of the *memory* of the *dog,* and the recollection of kindness received, there are a thousand stories," remarks the author of the mid-nineteenth-century treatise *The Dog,* "from the return of Ulysses to the present day, and we have seen enough of that faithful animal to believe most of them. An officer was abroad with his regiment, during the American war. He had a fine Newfoundland dog, his constant companion, whom he left with his family. After the lapse of several years he returned. His dog met him at the door, leaped upon his neck, licked his face, and died."

Whether exemplified in classic literature (the story of Argus and Odysseus or Ulysses), in ethological description (Konrad Lorenz or Elizabeth Marshall Thomas), or in the daily lives of pet owners, it is an article of faith that Bowser remembers. Remembers good times. Remembers *us.* But if home is where the dog is, the ultimate homecoming of modern-day dog lore belongs, needless to say, to Lassie. And home in Lassie's terms has become associated with a lost vision in America, "the place where, when you have to go there, / They have to take you in"—or, in the same poet's words, "something you somehow haven't to deserve."

Rescue Me

The association of the dog with the concept of home makes the pathos of the homeless dog, the dog abandoned or given away by its owner, take on the poignancy of all our human fears of abandonment and rejection.

The photo of a "Senior Dog" waiting to be adopted stared up at me from the Yankee Golden Retriever Rescue League flyer. "I'm waiting!" said the inscription beneath the photograph. "Are you interested in a friendly, affectionate companion who enjoys quiet walks and relaxing at home?" The model looked uncannily like my own older dog, Wagner. The urge to call them up was overwhelming—but what would I do with a third big dog around the house? And, more important, how would Wagner handle it? Not well, I decided instantly. He's possessive, proprietary, bossy, and likes to be in charge. (Who says dogs resemble their owners?) And while our junior golden, Yofi, is a paragon of tractability when it's time for him to get off (or on) the couch, he's a double handful on the leash, and he weighs a good bit over a hundred pounds. The irresistible pull of the senior dog who was waiting would have to wait.

The phrase "senior dog" is clearly coined to evoke the same dignity and respect for age implied by the use of "senior citizen" for human beings. Yet despite the supposed charm of films like *Grumpy* (or *Grumpier*) *Old Men*, homeless or family-less senior *persons* without resources often wind up in shelters or nursing homes, whether or not they have medical problems. Photographs of "adoptable" elders do, occasionally, appear in human interest stories in the local newspaper, especially around Christmastime, or may be used, more calculatingly, in advertisements for HMOs or charities seeking contributions. But just as puppies are more readily adopted than mature dogs, older or younger, so older citizens may have a difficult time if they are in financial—or emotional—need.

The field of "pet therapy" has developed to partner dogs and human elders temporarily, whether in nursing homes or in their own houses or apartments. Lollipop, a Corgi described as the "founding dog" of the Pets & People Foundation in Randolph, Massachusetts, made over three hundred visits to nursing homes in the company of "co-founder" Stanley Wald. The Lollipop Memorial Award in 1995 was given to Deucie, a golden retriever, and Ann Batchelder, her human companion, who together made over a thousand daily visits to a nursing home in Wellesley. Deucie was also honored at the Bay Colony Cluster Dog Shows as a "Dog of Distinction" for her "extraordinary and distinctive service in the public interest"—a citation she shared with a dog who had saved a person's life, another who had rescued a puppy from traffic, and several search-and-rescue dogs who had been to Oklahoma City in the wake of the bombing. "Pet therapy," according to one friend whose dog participates in the program, is a somewhat problematic term, since it conjures images of dogs on couches telling their troubles to therapists. What happens is usually the opposite: the human being confides his or her troubles to the dog.

Dog love is not the special realm of childhood or of boyhood, no matter what the movies keep telling us. It is highly significant, I think, that at *both* ends of the human life span the bond between human and dog speaks with an insistent clarity—if we have ears to hear.

Pet Share is "a pet companion program that brings unconditional love and friendship to elders in nursing homes." One of several services offered by a charitable organization called the Good Age Fund, it was brought to my attention by an advertising circular that told the following story:

Rose sits alone in the TV room.
    She stares vacantly at the television set. Since entering the nursing home two years ago, Rose has spent every morning like this . . . silent and utterly alone.
    A nurse enters the room and asks Rose if she'd like visitors. There is no response. No sign of interest. She does not speak. Rose hasn't spoken to anyone in two years.
    From the hallway, the sound of a jingling collar is heard. A moment later, a small black and tan dog trots in on a leash, followed by her owner.
    Nuzzling for attention, the little dog thrusts her inquiring face into Rose's lap. Rose remains motionless. Puzzled, the dog looks up and begins to lick a tired, worn hand. Slowly, almost imperceptibly, the hand inches down to touch the soft, warm, silky fur.

The dog responds with a curly tail wagging so rapidly that her entire body wags along too. A smile grows on Rose's face. She leans forward, strokes the animal . . . and then, a small miracle takes place.

"Nice dog. Good dog."

Four simple words. Uttered by a woman who had been silent for years.

Rose pets the dog, tears in her eyes. "I used to have a dog when I was raising my family. I can't remember his name. When he died, my boys gave him a funeral in the back yard. I wish I could remember that dog's name."

A week later, when the little dog, Foxy, and his owner returned to visit Rose, she had remembered. "His name was Shep," she said.

This is a story intended to tug at the heartstrings, and it does. Where is Rose's family now? "Join Foxy. . . . Join us," invite the Fund's officers in a postscript. If they think that Pet Share is the most likely way to solicit contributions for elder services, they are, I believe, entirely right.

The concept of the "humane society" began as a way of *dogs* rescuing *people,* not the other way around. The first Humane Society was founded in England in 1774 for the purpose of saving not dogs and cats but drowning persons. One of the most famous and frequently reproduced paintings by the dog portraitist Sir Edwin Landseer is called *A Distinguished Member of the Humane Society* and pictures a black-and-white Newfoundland dog. The word "shelter" is one that I was brought up to understand as meaning a harborage for homeless dogs and cats, and carried with it the painful consciousness that not all animals brought or born there will survive to find good homes. This is a pathos we can manage—barely. The pathos of homelessness, of "shelters" for the *human* strays, the lost and the unwanted, is something we find much harder to deal with. Yet it is not substitution, or anthropomorphism, that produces the human love of dogs, and the current, often even comic, preoccupation with them in our culture. It is with dogs that, very often, we permit ourselves feelings of deepest joy and deepest sorrow. In this sense, one could almost claim, it is the dog that makes us human.

A Dog's Life

*"Speaking personally, I haven't had my day,
and I've never met any dog who has."*
Drawing by Stevenson; © 1992 The New Yorker Magazine, Inc.

Whether dogs might be a suitable subject for musical treatment, following the huge success of *Cats,* is something on which we can only speculate.

—Reinhold Bergler, *Man and Dog:*
The Psychology of a Relationship

"Yesterday I was a dog. Today I'm a dog. Tomorrow I'll probably still be a dog. There's just so little hope of advancement." The speaker is Charlie Brown's dog, Snoopy, as personified by Bill Hinnant in the 1967 musical comedy *You're A Good Man, Charlie Brown.* Despite this gloomy viewpoint, however, the life of the dog has frequently been, for at least the past hundred years, an exemplary tale for the advancement of learning—that is to say, *human* learning. Just as the pathos of human love and loss is most effectively retold, in modern stories, through the vehicle of the steadfastly loyal and loving dog, so the human hero has increasingly been displaced and replaced by the canine one.

Once the hero had a dog. Now the hero *is* a dog. Once our models of adventure and companionship were pairs like Ulysses and Argus; Tintin and Milou; Superman (or Superboy) and Krypto; Buster Brown and Tige; Actaeon and his hounds. Now fiction, films, and newspaper deadlines all proclaim the dog to be the hero, while the owner, master, or handler all too often plays the secondary role, if not the part of knave or fool. "I have known dogs, and I have known school heroes that, set aside the fur, could hardly have been told apart," Robert Louis Stevenson wrote in 1883, "and if we desire to understand the chivalry of old, we must turn to the school playfields or the dungheap where the dogs are trooping."

The phrase "a dog's life" originally meant a life of suffering and abjection: "Mrs. Ford afterward had a dog's life among them" (from the sixteenth century); "She domineers like the devil. . . . O Lord, I lead the life of a dog" (a husband's plaint, from the eighteenth century); "They've been leading him a dog's life this year and more" (nineteenth-century schoolboys: *Tom Brown at Oxford*). In late-twentieth-century culture the phase has been taken up and played upon in various more neutral or even complimentary terms: Peter Mayle's fictional account of Boy, the dog he and his wife adopted in Provence (told, irreverently, from the dog's point of view) uses *A Dog's Life* as its title, as does a nonfiction book on the history and everyday life of the dog; a celebrity biography of Lassie bears the subtitle *A Dog's Life, the First Fifty Years*.

This change in use is partly just the natural migration of proverbial language over time, from figurative image to (ironic) liberalization: the underdog of figure becomes the top dog of narrative, the abject negative becomes a droll (or coy) positive. But with or without the quotation marks, a dog's life has changed over the years—or at least, to be more accurate, some dogs' lives have. While many unwanted dogs still live and die in obscurity (maltreated, abandoned, or, as a last resort, humanely euthanized), the "life" of the dog of fiction, biography, and canine autobiography is now often to be found in the news, in the libraries, or on the best-seller lists. The dog, alone, or with his or her human companion, has become a literary lion.

In 1940 Dylan Thomas entitled a collection of his autobiographical essays *Portrait of the Artist as a Young Dog.* The title was a wry homage to (or parody of?) Irishman James Joyce's more solemn—and, Thomas may have thought, pretentious—*Portrait of the Artist as a Young Man.* The word "dog"—here meaning fast-living, fast-loving man-about-town—was emphasized by twin photographs on the book jacket, showing the poet and his insouciant canine alter ego each with a cigarette dangling from his mouth. Thomas's book is not in fact about dogs, though it includes a vignette about a paternity suit in which the magistrate, unable to decide which of the two young men is the father of which young woman's child, describes their behavior as "just like little dogs!" But the autobiographical memoir of today is likely, on current evidence at least, to reverse the paradigm, and to offer up what might be called *The Portrait of the Dog as a Young Artist.*

An Eminent Victorian

An undervalued and often delightful genre in the world of letters, the canine biography is a genre that has followed closely upon its counterpart in the chronicling of human affairs. Recent celebrity bios of Lassie, Millie Bush, and Sandy, the star of the Broadway show *Annie*, tell us as much about what we look for in theatrical and political life stories as any earnest narrative of the human subject.

But the classic of the genre is Virginia Woolf's *Flush: A Biography*, a sympathetic tongue-in-jowl reimagining of the life of Elizabeth Barrett Browning's beloved spaniel. *Flush* was a manifest send-up of Woolf's friend and rival Lytton Strachey, himself the inventor of a new and witty mode of critical biography (*Eminent Victorians, Queen Victoria, Elizabeth and Essex*). "I wanted to play a joke on Lytton—it was to parody him," wrote Woolf to Lady Ottoline Morrell. "Flush is only by way of a joke. . . . I lay in the garden and read the Browning love letters, and the figure of their dog made me laugh so I couldn't resist making him a life." But *Flush* (the name comes from a characteristic activity of hunting spaniels in the field) is a masterpiece in its own terms. Much of it written in free indirect discourse ("Flush thought . . . ," "Flush knew . . .") it explores the mind of a dog, and in the process takes a fresh and often wicked look at things that human beings take for granted, such as the "human" and the "literary."

Flush is himself an eminent Victorian, "a dog of birth and breeding," and very much aware of the fact. When Miss Barrett finds him "examin[ing] himself carefully in the looking-glass," she concludes affectionately that he is a philosopher: "On the contrary, he was an aristocrat considering his points." His predilection for mirror-gazing includes not only the looking-glass but Miss Barrett herself. The first meeting between dog and mistress, a tour de force rendering of love at first sight, is brilliantly imagined:

> For the first time she looked him in the face. For the first time Flush looked at the lady lying on the sofa.
> Each was surprised. Heavy curls hung down on each side of Miss Barrett's face; large bright eyes shone out; a large mouth smiled. Heavy ears hung down on either side of Flush's face; his eyes, too, were large and bright; his mouth was wide. There was a likeness between them. As they gazed at each other each felt: Here am I—and then each felt: But how different! Hers was the pale worn face of an invalid, cut off from air, light, freedom. His was the warm ruddy face of a young animal; instinct with health and energy. Broken asunder, yet made in the same mould, could it be that each completed what was dormant in the other? She might have been—all that; and he— But no. Between them lay the widest gulf that can separate one being from another. She spoke. He was dumb. She was woman; he was dog. Thus closely united, thus immensely divided, they gazed at each other. Then with one bound Flush sprang on to the sofa and laid himself where he was to lie for ever after—on the rug at Miss Barrett's feet.

The mirror, literal and figurative, seems in fact to have played a key role in the Barrett-Flush relationship, producing speculations both philosophical and psychoanalytic:

> She would make him stand with her in front of the looking-glass and ask him why he barked and trembled. Was not the little brown dog opposite himself? But what is "oneself"? Is it the thing people see? Or is it the thing one is? So Flush pondered that question, too, and, unable to solve the problem of reality, pressed closer to Miss Barrett and kissed her "expressively." *That* was real at any rate.

Woolf is here transposing a passage from a letter written by Barrett to her friend Hugh Stuart Boyd, a blind classical scholar. Flush, writes Barrett, "can't bear me to look into a glass, because he thinks there is a little brown dog inside every looking glass, and he is jealous of its being so close to *me*. He used to tremble and bark at it, but now he is *silently* jealous, and contents himself with squeezing close, close to me and kissing me expressively." Where Barrett's Flush sees "another" dog, and is jealous, Woolf's Flush sees "himself," and ponders the problem of reality.

Neither Woolf nor Barrett (much less Flush) had the benefit of reading that classic of modern psychoanalysis and culture, Jacques Lacan's *Le Stade du miroir comme formateur de la fonction du Je* ("The Mirror Stage as Formative of the Function of the I") with its suggestive account of the child produced as a social subject through a (mis)recognition of his own image in the mirror. Lacan describes the "jubilant assumption of his specular image by the child at the *infans* stage"—that is, before he is able to speak (Latin *infans*, "unable to speak," is the root of the English word "infant"). According to Lacan, the child looking in the mirror appears to himself (or herself) as he or she might wish to be, exchanging a "fragmented body image" for the "armour of an alienating identity," the inner world for an outer world of others, that is, for the world of social interaction. So also with Flush ("Was not the little brown dog opposite himself? But what is 'oneself'? Is it the thing people see? Or is it the thing one is?"). Unable to solve the conundrum, Flush resolves it, instead, by kissing Miss Barrett "expressively"—the word is taken by Woolf from Barrett's own account of the episode to H. S. Boyd.

But Flush's developmental narrative does not end with the mirror stage.

Before he was well out of his puppyhood, Flush was a father.

Such conduct in a man even, in the year 1842, would have called for some excuse from a biographer; in a woman no excuse could have availed; her name must have been blotted in ignominy from the page. But the moral code of dogs, whether better or worse, is certainly different from ours, and there was nothing in Flush's conduct in this respect that requires a veil now, or unfitted him for the society of the purest and the chastest in the land then.

Through this droll invocation of difference between moral codes for dogs and men (and, even more, between dogs and women) Woolf is able to hold up to ironic scrutiny the existence of such codes. No polemic would serve her as well.

Flush's story, once under way, follows a familiar narrative pattern. Born—or, in this case, adopted—into a household of high degree, he is pampered and doted upon in his childhood, then subject to a series of reversals of a kind familiar to any reader of Victorian fiction. He is several times stolen by a gang of dognappers (a common fate of Victorian pets) and ransomed by his doting owner, who had to conceal these transactions from a father who would certainly have disapproved. This Dickensian setback, which lands the unprepared Flush briefly among thieves, is followed by a crisis of a different kind, as a rival for Miss Barrett's affections appears on the scene. It is, indeed, a Rival Poet: Mr. Browning.

Flush becomes aware of a change in Miss Barrett, of her waiting for the postman, and of her preoccupation with something other than himself.

> What was horrible to Flush, as they talked, was his loneliness. Once he had felt that he and Miss Barrett were together in a fire-lit cave. Now the cave was no longer firelit; it was dark and damp; Miss Barrett was outside.
>
> Flush touched her. She recalled him with a start. She patted him lightly, joyfully on the head. And smiling, she gave him the oddest look—as if she wished that he could talk—as if she expected him too to feel what she felt. And then she laughed, pityingly; as if it were absurd—Flush, poor Flush could feel nothing of what she felt. He could know nothing of what she knew. Never had such wastes of dismal distance separated them. He lay there ignored; he might not have been there, he felt. Miss Barrett no longer remembered his existence.

On the eighth of July, we are told, he could stand it no longer, and bit Mr. Browning. But this bold action became food for further reflection on the nature of human—and canine—emotion:

> Things are not simple but complex. If he bit Mr. Browning he bit her too. Hatred is not hatred; hatred is also love. Here Flush

shook his ears in an agony of perplexity. He turned uneasily on the floor. Mr. Browning was Miss Barrett—Miss Barrett was Mr. Browning; love is hatred and hatred is love.

Love and hate, as Freud and Flush alike observe, are near allied. But the extravagance of emotion directed by Flush—once the cynosure of his mistress's eye—toward the interloper Mr. Browning pales beside his jealousy when he is confronted, after her marriage, with a new rival for her affections. Banished for a time from her side, he is at last taken up to his formerly accustomed place, her bedroom, in the arms of a maid.

They entered the bedroom. There was a faint bleating in the shadowed room—something waved on the pillow. It was a live animal. . . . Mrs. Browning had become two people. The horrid thing waved and mewed by her side. Torn with rage and jealousy and some deep disgust that he could not hide, Flush struggled himself free and rushed downstairs. . . .

". . . for a whole fortnight he fell into deep melancholy and was proof against all attentions lavished on him"—so Mrs. Browning, in the midst of all her other distractions, was forced to notice. And when we take, as we must, human minutes and hours and drop them into a dog's mind and see how the minutes swell into hours and the hours into days, we shall not exaggerate if we conclude that Flush's "deep melancholy" lasted six full months by the human clock. Many men and women have forgotten their hates and their loves in less.

But Flush "had sworn to love and not to bite," and gradually, from his vantage point beneath the sofa, he began to develop a sneaking affection for the baby. "Did they not share something in common—did not the baby somehow resemble Flush in many ways? Did they not hold the same views, the same tastes?"

Woolf's tone of mingled irony and admiration finds its source in two models: Strachey's droll new mode of biographical writing, and Barrett Browning's letters. Where Strachey is by turns arch and devastatingly cool, Browning exclaims and wonders. Yet more of her tone carries over into *Flush* than one might, perhaps, expect. Here, for example, is Elizabeth Barrett on canine consciousness, in a letter to her friend Mary Russell Mitford, who had given Flush to her.

My poor Flush. He was sitting on my sofa wagging his tail into the very ecstasies of a tail (if you understand the metaphysics and physics of *that*) while he watched Arabel lacing on her boots. She said to him, "Flush, I cant [*sic*] take you out with me. I am going to the bazaar." The tail stopped. Poor Flushie! He turned round & looked at me,—significantly, as he always does in trouble,—and then began to cry!—What do we mean by *understanding*?

Flush is "no hero," concluded Elizabeth Barrett when he fled, shrieking, from an attack by Catiline, the "savage" Cuba bloodhound. "But why was he no hero?" Woolf asks rhetorically, and answers for Miss Barrett: "Was it not partly on her account? She was too just not to realize that it was for her that he had sacrificed his courage." Comforting him with milk, cake, and just a bit of partridge, Miss Barrett sees that he has chosen her life as his own: "He had refused the air and the sun for her sake."

Ever the modernist, Flush is indeed "no hero." But this fact only underscores the expectation of canine heroism.

Hero Worship

A throbbing rhythm from the percussion, a hint of "Over There" in the melody, a dimming of the house lights, and Act Two is under way. As the curtain opens we see a familiar figure silhouetted on the top of his doghouse, seated bolt upright, his arms outstretched before him, a scarf around his neck and the goggles of his leather helmet pulled down firmly over his eyes. The music and lights help SNOOPY *throughout in telling his story of bravery and heroism.*

SNOOPY: Here's the World War One flying ace high over France in his Sopwith Camel, searching for the infamous Red Baron. I must bring him down.

Snoopy's dreams of glory may seem far-fetched (to use a dog-friendly term) if we fail to take into consideration the wartime exploits of noncartoon dog heroes. Rob, the "para dog" of World War II, a black-and-white random-bred with a black patch over one eye, made over twenty parachute landings while serving with British troops in North Africa and Italy. Judy, a purebred English pointer born in Shanghai in

1936, was captured by the Japanese and spent two years as a prisoner of war before she was liberated, with her fellow prisoners, in 1945. Beauty, a wirehaired terrier, pioneered the use of dogs in finding buried air-raid victims during the war. (The first beneficiary of his skills was a cat trapped under bomb wreckage.)

Punch and Judy, a boxer dog and bitch, saved two British officers from a terrorist attack in the territory of Israel; a dog named Rifleman Khan rescued a soldier from drowning under heavy shell fire. Brian, an Alsatian dog attached to a parachute battalion in Normandy, made so many jumps that he became a fully qualified "paratrooper," and Antis, another Alsatian, owned by a Czech airman, served with his master in the Free French Air Force and the RAF, and then, having returned with him to Czechoslovakia after the war, "substantially helped his master to escape across the frontier when . . . he had to fly from the Communists." So declares the official citation from the service medal awarded to Antis in 1949.

All these courageous canines were winners of the Dickin Medal, known in Britain as "the animals' Victoria Cross." Instituted during World War II by Mrs. Maria Dickin, founder of the People's Dispensary for Sick Animals, the medal, bearing the words "For Gallantry" and the motto "We Also Serve," commended the "conspicuous gallantry and devotion to duty" of eighteen dogs, three horses, one cat, and thirty-one pigeons.

Britain, legendary for its dog lovers, was the last Western European country to set up a war-dog school. The Germans had been subsidizing village breeding clubs since 1870 and training dogs for specialized army tasks, so that, when war broke out, some six thousand were available for service. Britain had one army dog, an Airedale who went to France with the troops and was killed in action on the Aisne. But in 1916 Lieutenant-Colonel E. H. Richardson and his wife founded a dog training school in Essex, drawing their students from "Dog Homes" (where many had been dumped because of food shortages) and patriotic civilian households. Dogs were "volunteered" by their owners ("We have let Daddy go and fight the Kaiser, now we are sending Jack to do his bit") and offered back to their owners at war's end. The number of recruits was overwhelming, catching authorities by surprise. Seven thousand dogs were offered for service within a few days in 1916. "My husband has gone, my son has gone," wrote one woman to the War Office. "Please take my dog to bring this cruel war to an end." In the messenger dog record book kept by the Imperial War Museum are chronicled the successes and the failures: Jock, Bruno, and Champion did yeoman service during an advance in the Dieppe forest; others, deemed of "no use to the service," were given away or shot.

In World War I the most popular "war dog" was the Airedale, in World War II the German shepherd, always described in official British reports as an "Alsatian." The French favored chiens de Brie, large, shaggy sheepdogs. Dogs were used to carry grenades, to lay telegraph wire across no-man's-land, and to pull machine guns or medical supplies. Until the advent of radio communications made them obsolete, messenger dogs moved through enemy lines three times as fast as human soldiers—and, comments author Jilly Cooper, "how seriously they took their duties. One Australian officer, seeing a Welsh terrier 'running, hopping, jumping, skipping over the terrible shell holes' was impressed by the 'earnest expression of the dog's face as he passed.'"

"No animal has served men more nobly in war than the dog," declares Cooper, who writes frequently about animals. "Guarding outposts, detecting mines, racing messages through an inferno of gunfire—he acted out of love, not because he was made to. He is the only animal who can be trusted to think for himself." "Earnest," acting "out of love" and "not because he was made to," trusted "to think for himself," the heroic dog of war became the ideal soldier, embodying and in effect "personifying" all the qualities for which his human counterparts also strove. Or were told to strive.

Canine war sacrifices were likewise vivid. During World War II the Russians—later to send Laika into space—used dogs as suicide troops, strapping bombs to their backs and sending the dogs to crouch under Panzer tanks until they and their enemy targets were simultaneously blown to bits. In subsequent theaters of war, from Vietnam to the Falklands, trained dogs have sniffed out mines and explosives, traced suspected terrorists, and been used, often controversially, to control riots. "The handler," explained a spokesman, "has to learn every mood, expression, and nose twitch of his dog. If he keeps indicating at a particular spot, you must undo the wall even if you know there's nothing there, just to show you've got faith in him." As always in wartime, strong bonds developed between soldiers subjected to harrowing experiences together, and when one of the warriors was canine the passions were especially strong. The relationship between handler and dog has in fact been described as a kind of marriage. "Great trouble is taken to 'marry up' the right handler to the right dog, and there is no questioning the strength of devotion that grows between them." Tales of extreme fidelity are legion and legendary: a dog who pined and refused to eat when the handler went on leave, so that the human partner hastened back early to his companion's side; a World War II dog who escaped from her kennel four times in twenty-four hours to join her handler at his hospital bedside. When the war was over, these wartime romances often led to difficult emotional human-dog triangles.

It was often hard to return dogs to their prewar owners—hard for both the handler and the dog. A Corporal A. McClellan wrote to the People's Dispensary for Sick Animals that when he had to accompany his Alsatian, Peter, to the dog's owner, Peter "told me in his own way he wanted to come with me. I had to pat him, and bid him stay. At the word 'stay' he lay down and the pathetic look in his eyes, I shall never forget. The tears ran down my cheeks as I patted him again." On the other hand, Dodo, a random-bred Alsatian cross, described by his handler and other military experts as grown too ferocious to return to civilian life (he had spent eighteen months guarding German prisoners of war) ran eagerly to his former master at the train station and, like many another old soldier, put the war years firmly behind him.

But not the glory. Although the Dickin Medal recipients were all bona fide war heroes, the public appetite for canine heroism had been whetted. In America, at least, the emphasis now fell upon the dog hero as police detective, drug sleuth, action hero, team mascot, or private citizen.

"Treat Your Dog Like a Hero and Collect These 'All-Star' Heroes," invited the makers of Milk-Bone dog biscuits in a 1992 promotional campaign.

> Introducing the real "All-Stars" in the fight against drugs: U.S. customs Drug Detecting Dog Trading Cards from Milk-Bone. Learn about dogs like "Snag," who discovered $783 million worth of drugs concealed in a gas trailer! Or "Corky," who has a total of 52 drug seizures to date and has appeared on the TV show "Top Cops." Let these heroes show your kids how we're winning the war against drugs.

The slippage in addressee from headline to text is worth noting; presumably it is the child reader who collects trading cards, but it is the watchful parents, ever in need of role models for their children, who will "show your kids how we're winning the war against drugs." From "your dog" to "your kids" is a short step but a key one. Parents in quest of heroes, the manufacturers suggest without irony, had best look to the dog.

Milk-Bone is, of course, hardly the only brand to recognize the commercial appeal of canine heroism. Since 1954 Ken-L Ration has given an annual award to dogs who have rescued their masters or other humans from catastrophes such as fire, animal attacks, traffic accidents, and drowning. The Massachusetts Society for the Prevention of Cruelty to Animals gives two awards each year: an Animal Hero Award, presented to an animal who has shown remarkable loyalty and/or bravery on behalf of humans or other animals, and a Human Hero Award, to a person who has saved the life of an animal or has significantly promoted the welfare of animals. The degree to which art influences life in conceptualizing these heroic figures may be seen in a headline advertising the MSPCA hero search: "Calling All Lassies," it declared.

To old-time Lassie fans, this was not a surprise, for in the post–World War II period the previously domestic and bucolic collie had become a war hero on screen, going to the front in both *Son of Lassie* (1945) and *Courage of Lassie* (1946) and, inevitably, saving both her master and the Allied troops. But even the first Lassie film was, allegorically at least, a war film, in which the heroic prisoner escapes from captivity in a foreign land (Scotland) and swims across the border to safety. Dedicated to *Lassie* author Major Eric Knight, who had died bravely in American uniform in the Second World War (having fought along with his native English troops in the First), the film was drenched in patriotism as well as sentiment. The link between the single dog-loving "boy" and "our boys at the front" was an easy one for Hollywood to make.

Since Lassie has become the prototype of the dog as hero, it may be worth taking a look at the Lassie story in some detail. For in it we find embedded, not only the story of love and canine heroism, but also the structure of a national epic. Lassie, as we will see, is not—or not only—the faithful Argus, waiting at home for her master, but also the quest hero Odysseus (or Ulysses), crossing a fearful and unknown terrain in search of home and love.

Lassie Come Home

The original "Lassie Come-Home," a short story published in 1938 by
Eric Knight in *The Saturday Evening Post* (and expanded two years
later into a novel), might be described, despite its deceptive brevity, as
a canine epic in miniature. It begins, like all epics, in medias res, with
the return of the collie to the boy and family that had raised her:

> The dog had met the boy by the school gate for five years. Now
> she couldn't understand that times were changed and she wasn't
> supposed to be there any more. But the boy knew.
>
> So when he opened the door of the cottage, he spoke before
> he entered.
>
> "Mother," he said, "Lassie's come home again."

Lassie, a handsome black-white-and-gold collie who is apparently the
family's only financial asset, had been sold in hard times to the Duke of
Rudling (the story takes place in the Yorkshire ridings). Her return—
or rather, the fact of her recurrent return ("Lassie's come home
again")—marks not the end of the story, as we might expect, but rather
the beginning. Her return is a problem as well as an (apparent) solution: the agonizing fact (agonizing to the reader as well as to the boy) is
that Lassie is *not supposed to return,* since she has a new "home."

The fact that "Lassie's come home again" thus provokes a crisis.
Moreover, the father, who has been laid off after seventeen years in the
mines, and who loves collies in general and Lassie in particular, is
painstakingly honest, and the father's honesty, too, will become an unexpected *problem* with which the story will have to deal. So the boy and
his father return the dog to the duke. "Bid her stay," instructs the father, and the boy does his bidding.

> "Stay here, Lassie, and don't come home no more," he said.
> "And don't come to school for me no more. Because I don't want
> to see ye no more. 'Cause tha's a bad dog, and we don't love thee
> no more, and we don't want thee. So stay there forever and leave
> us be, and don't never come home no more."

(This is a passage I defy the most sophisticated reader to read aloud
without a lump in the throat.) The boy hopes, of course, that Lassie will
continue to disobey, will hear the lie in his voice, will come home yet
again. But his father is quick to disabuse him. "Tha' might as well have

it. Tha'll never see Lassie no more. She run home once too often, so the
duke's taken her with him up to his place in Scotland, and there she'll
stay. So it's good-bye and good luck to her, and she'll never come home
no more."

But of course she does.

Here is where the element of epic invades this modest little story,
turning Lassie not into Argus, the faithful waiting hound of Homer's
tale, but into Odysseus the adventuring hero—generalized now in epic
high style as "a dog," "a collie," escaping dogcatchers, taking refuge
with kindly old couples for a time, but heading always, relentlessly,
south. "Ah, a thousand miles of tor and brae, of shire and moor, of path
and road and plowland, of river and stream and burn and brook and
beck, of snow and rain and fog and sun, is a long way, even for a human
being. But it would seem too far—much, much too far—for any dog to
travel blindly and win through."

"And yet"—for of course there is a "and yet"—there comes a day
when a dog meets a boy at a school gate once more. And this is indeed
now a dog that resembles the aged Argus: "Not a dog, this one, that
lifted glad ears above a proud, slim head with its black-and-gold mask,
but a dog that lay weakly, trying to lift a head that would no longer lift,
trying to wag a tail that was torn and blotched and matted with dirt and
burs," swept up in the arms of the boy. "Then who shall picture the ur-
gency of a boy, running, awkwardly, with a great dog in his arms running through the village . . . ? Or who shall describe the high tones of a
voice—a boy's voice, calling as he runs up a path: 'Mother! Oh, mother!
Lassie's come home! Lassie's come home!'"

Lassie's come home *again*. The narrator's text does not disappoint.
"Nor does anyone who ever owned a dog need to be told the sound a
man makes when he bends over a dog that has been his for many years;
nor how a woman moves quickly, preparing foods," even "raw egg and
brandy, bought with precious pence," until the day when "a dog lifted
itself to its feet for the first time to stand over a bowl of oatmeal."
Lassie's come home to life again, but not, it seems, to the cottage. For
the father is too honest, and the dog must be returned to its rightful
owner, the duke.

As it happens, the duke and his favorite granddaughter, Philippa,
come to seek the man in the cottage, and the boy knows it must be because of the dog. "Mother! T'duke is back and he's coming to take
Lassie away." Desperately he pleads that the father should hide her,

but his mother is sure of one thing: "Thy feyther'll not lie." And she counsels him, as mothers do, about the great schism between demand and desire: "Tha must learn never to want nothing in life like that. It don't do, lad. Tha mustn't want things bad, like tha wants Lassie." But the mother, it seems, has misunderstood: "It ain't that, mother. Ye don't understand. Don't ye see—it ain't me that wants her. It's her that wants us! Tha's wha made her come all them miles. It's her that wants us, so terrible bad!" Confronted with this revelation, about the son as well as the dog, she surrenders. She will talk to the father, though she is sure he will never lie.

Thus, when the duke arrives, he finds a boy barring his way, and a boy who says to him something defiant and heartbreakingly revealing: "Thy tyke's net here!" "Tyke," a general term for a child, especially a boy, is also a regional word in Scotland and Yorkshire for a female dog, as well as for a mongrel or cur. "Thy tyke's net here!" No direct announcement of Lassie's presence could be more definitive.

The duke is no fool. "Now, ma lad, what tyke of mine's net here?" he asks. What dog of mine isn't here? And of course the boy compounds his error: "No tyke o' thine. Us hasn't got it. . . . No tyke could have done it. No tyke can come all those miles. It isn't Lassie. It's another one that looks like her. It isn't Lassie!"

A primer in psychoanalysis could hardly put the point more clearly. "What's the boy talking about—a dog of mine being here?" demands the duke of the boy's mother, and she returns, defensively, to the literal. Nay. . . . He didn't say a tyke o' thine was here. He said it wasn't here." "Well, what dog of mine isn't here, then?"

It is the father—the relentlessly truthful father—who saves her the trouble of a lie. For "Joe Carraclough, the collie fancier," stands before them with a dog, a dog with one ear up and one ear down, with patches of black on its coat, with black paws where Lassie had white paws, and declares: "This is t'only tyke us has here. Does it look like any dog that belongs to thee?" And "having told no lie, having only asked a question," Carraclough receives a "gentleman"'s answer, as the duke (who knows dogs, and knows Lassie), wordlessly inspects the damaged paw pads of a dog who has traveled five hundred miles from Scotland. "I never owned this dog. 'Pon my soul, she's never belonged to me!"

The story has a satisfying ending, for the duke's errand with the boy's family, it turns out, has not been to find Lassie but to hire the elder Joe as his dog handler. The Carracloughs will now live on the duke's land in his cottage, but they must "get rid" of the "eyesore of a misshapen mongrel." This, the boy says happily, will be easy to do. "In a day or so we'll have her fixed up and coped up so's ye'd never, never recognize her." "I don't doubt," puffs the duke as he goes to his car, "ye could do exactly that."

To whom, and to what emotional place, has Lassie come home? The duke is teased by his granddaughter about being a sentimentalist ("And I thought you were supposed to be a hard man") and replies, roundly, that for five years he's sworn he'd have the dog by hook or crook, "and now, egad, at least I've got her." If he had to "buy the man" before he could "get his dog," that may not be the worst part of the bargain, says the shrewd Yorkshireman. But like Scrooge playing Santa, the duke has (we may imagine) a twinkle in his eye. Just as the mother thought it was the boy's desire that exceeded any hope of fulfillment, and was silenced by the boy's invocation of the primacy of the *dog's desire,* so the duke's desire to own Lassie as a portable possession has been converted into a relationship, not with the dog, but with the family (it is the wife, the true sharp "Yorkshireman," who strikes a good financial bargain for her husband's wages and cottage).

Lassie's ultimate homecoming, not as an "aristocrat" (a word twice applied to her in the story) but masquerading as a tyke or mongrel, makes possible a different kind of "homecoming" for the boy (now regarded by his mother as a "man"), the father, "Joe Carraclough, the collie fancier" (whose former occupation, that of "collier" or miner, is replaced by his natural calling as a dog handler), the mother, who secures a cottage as well as a living wage, and, arguably, even for the duke, whose fierce Yorkshire pride (and vernacular use of the Yorkshire dialect when speaking to his "people") are matched by the laborer father's resolute honesty, leading the duke to "speak as a gentleman should" in standard English, man-to-man, when he disavows ownership of Lassie: "She's never belonged to me."

To whom *has* she belonged, and does she now belong? The simple answer, the answer that provides one abiding Anglo-American cultural myth, is "the boy." This is the answer that provided much of the impetus for the Lassie industry of Hollywood and television—an answer that erased, incidentally, the Yorkshire roots of both boy and dog. "Lassie come home" became a synonym of loyalty, fidelity, perseverance, and rescue.

"Lassie," it might be argued, is in a sense "that which cannot belong to anyone." The power of the "Lassie principle" for the imagination, and the emotions, is the power of the lost-and-found, the lost-in-order-to-be-found, the found-only-to-be-lost-again, that which waits at the gate. Lassie could be counted on to come home even when home was a movable place in the heart. In fact the "home" theme in the *Lassie* story was emphasized at every possible moment, from *Courage of Lassie* (1946) (with Lassie as a war dog who rejoins her master at the front, a necessary home away from home) to *The Hills of Home* (1948), to my favorite of all the sequels, *Challenge to Lassie* (1949), which boldly appropriates the entire nineteenth-century saga of the loyal Edinburgh Skye terrier Greyfriars Bobby—"Auld Jock" dies, dog establishes his place on master John Gray's grave, town rallies to feed and honor dog, magistrate gives dog the "freedom of the city of Edinburgh" as a citizen so he won't need a license—except that the dog is a *collie* and its name is *Lassie*. Thus blithely, by what might well be called "poetic (dog) license," is revisionist history inscribed in the cultural imagination.

In the postwar fifties Lassie became an *American* hero—or rather, an American heroine. A 1993 public television special made to commemorate fifty years of Lassies in American cultural life did not hesitate to drive home the moral. "Values" and "family values" were constantly mentioned, and the audience was treated to sentiments like "There was a time when things were a little more peaceful, a little more decent—and safer for all of us" and "As long as there is that yearning in our heart for undemanding loyalty—for a love that asks nothing in return—Lassie will live forever."

Here's an example of how much a part of the cultural mainstream *Lassie* has become. In the 1994 comedy film *Speechless* Michael Keaton, an experienced political speechwriter, explains to his girlfriend, Geena Davis, a speechwriter for the opposing candidate, that the Democratic candidate needs what he calls a "Yaseetimmee." What's that? she asks. At the end of every *Lassie* episode, he tells her, Timmy's mother sits him down and says, "You see, Timmy . . ." A "Yaseetimmee" is a moral lesson, a social truth or truism, a maxim about humanity drawn from the exploits of America's favorite dog.

Fifty years after the release of the first Lassie movie, *Lassie Come Home*, in 1943, PBS assured the nation that "Lassie's message is still being seen and heard." And what is that message? "A boy and a dog—

it's always there, like Mom's apple pie." And again, "The companionship, the helping one another—that you can't really get from, say, a boy
and a cat." What about a *girl* and a dog? Shirley Temple told the *New
York Post* in 1956, "I class myself with Rin Tin Tin. At the end of the
Depression, people were looking for something to cheer them up. They
fell in love with a dog—and with a little girl." Audiences for *The Wizard of Oz* (1939) got both at once in the irresistible pairing of Dorothy
and Toto. The musical *Annie*, based on Harold Gray's Depression-era
cartoon strip Little Orphan Annie, reviewed the same winning combination of upbeat girl and dog. And Elizabeth Taylor professed herself
"thrilled to be working with Lassie." But "a boy and a dog" has been
the primary message of film after film, television program after television program, from *Rin Tin Tin* to *White Fang* to *Far from Home* to
Fluke. (It's worth noting that the two boys in *Homeward Bound* both
have dogs as pets, while the girl has a cat.)

There are always exceptions to any rule, and the idyllic relation of
boy and dog has made it an occasional target for satire or critique. In
the 1975 cult film *A Boy and His Dog*, Don Johnson's early foray into
black comedy, the adolescent boy and his telepathic (and far more intelligent) sheepdog, foraging for life and love in a future-world reduced
to rubble by World War IV, meet (and later eat) an attractive but calcu-
lating young woman. Her mistake is to try and separate boy and dog;
given a choice, as his canine companion and mentor lies dying of star-
vation, Johnson's character does not hesitate. In fact there is a distinct
gleam in his eye as he realizes the solution to both of his problems: how
to save the dog, and get rid of the girl. But even this ironic saga can't
help being curiously sentimental about the primacy of the boy-and-dog
bond; it would be a hardhearted viewer who failed to snicker, if not to
cheer, when Blood, the talking dog, resumes his instructional narrative
at the close while licking his chops.

"What are little boys made of?" asks the nursery rhyme, and it answers its own question: "Snips and snails and puppy-dog's
tails; / That's what little boys are made of." This is the one love that is
never tainted, is always simple and pure.

From Hero to Antihero

In early-twentieth-century dog fiction the canine hero was very much in
evidence, from Albert Payson Terhune's misnamed "rabbit-hearted

collie giant" Hero who, needless to say, earns his brave name by story's end, to the more orthodoxly heroic Lad and Wolf. ("Here Lad lived out his sixteen years of staunch hero-life and of d'Artagnan-like stature"; "You will remember reading, a year or so ago, in the newspapers, of Wolf's hero-death".) Reginald Cleveland's *Cop: Chief of Police Dogs*, is another typical example of the breed.

By mid-century the dog hero had become enough of a cliché to merit parody. In 1958, in the heyday of the television *Superman*, an action pilot called *Superpup* was pitched, though never (alas) sold or aired. It was to feature the exploits of Bark Bent, otherwise known as Superpup, a reporter for the *Daily Beagle*. Bark and the other characters were all to be played by (human) actors dressed as dogs. Meanwhile, heroic superpups in the real world continue to chase down and apprehend criminals. "Doggone Heroes," proclaimed a headline in the *New York Daily News*, describing the exploits of a woman and her 140-pound mastiff, Buz, who caught a mugger trying to flee by taxi and foot.

Some old-style dog heroes still appeal to the popular imagination—for instance, Balto, a black longhaired malamute who in 1925 mushed with his dog team through a blizzard to reach Nome, Alaska, with anti-toxin desperately needed to combat a diphtheria epidemic. A statue of Balto stands in Central Park in New York City, and in 1995 *Balto*, an animated feature film, was based on his dramatic story. The editors of *Dog Fancy* suggest that though "Balto was proclaimed the canine hero" who made it all possible, "the true hero" was the lead dog, Togo, who led the team over 340 miles of the 658-mile run. But without either dog, they concede, the Serum Run would probably have failed; "both Balto and Togo have earned their place in the Hall of Fame."

Film and fiction canines today, however, are often, like Flush, anti-heroes, who reflect the ambivalences of the age toward the concept of heroism. Two recent war pictures nicely illustrate the point, since both deal with cantankerous military officers out of step with their times.

In the Oscar-winning film *Patton*, the larger-than-life hero General George Patton (George C. Scott) loses his command of the Seventh Army because he has intemperately slapped a soldier (called in the film, in contemporary parlance, a "dogface"). Disgraced, assailed by the press and the public, forced by General Eisenhower to apologize to the troops, this heroic loner immediately acquires a dog—a little bull terrier he dubs William (played by a terrier who rejoiced in the name of Abraxas Aaran). William the Conqueror is the model Patton has in

mind (the Allies are about to commence their attack on Normandy), but
when William turns tail after being assailed by a diminutive Maltese
bitch named Abigail, Patton renames him in disgust: "Your name isn't
William—it's Willy."

Willy becomes the sign of what has happened to his master. Once
the proud masculine commander of troops in the field, he now finds
himself (like Willy) "feminized" and domesticated, reduced to addressing women on the home front. Willy accompanies him for the rest
of the film, tucked aboard a transport plane that smuggles Patton into
France, then riding in the jeep when the rehabilitated general is given
a new combat assignment, as head of the Third Army. The roller coaster
of heroism and disgrace, shrewd soldiering and inept lack of diplomacy
that renders Patton an anachronism and provides the "tragic" center-
piece of the film is neatly emblematized in his affection for this extremely ordinary dog. Attentive viewers may also note in Willy a
striking echo of another smooth-coated white dog briefly glimpsed early
in the film, this one tied by a rope to tank on a ruined battlefield in
Tunisia, desperately barking as the last jeep speeds away from the
scene—a bitterly economical sketch of the random miseries and victims of war. (*Patton* was released in 1970, at the height of hostilities in
Vietnam.)

At the end of the film, Willy is Patton's only consolation. Relieved
of the command of his beloved Third Army, the general says farewell to
his officers, then collects the eager dog and takes him off on a leash for
a walk across the fields. The film ends on this note of pathos and sup-
plementarity. It seems no accident that Willy is palpably ill-trained,
leaping up on people and straining at the leash. The general who
prided himself on training his soldiers to do their jobs rather than to
love him ends up with a canine companion who loves him and has no
notion of dog decorum. Without Willy, apparently a minor character,
this would be a very different film.

Twenty-five years later the story of Patton and Willy was deliber-
ately evoked in another war film that centered on the conflict between
old-style and new-style military men, the 1995 Tony Scott film *Crimson
Tide,* starring Gene Hackman as a crusty nuclear-submarine commander and Denzel Washington as his principled, "new Navy" executive
officer. Washington's role, like that of Karl Malden as General Omar
Bradley in *Patton,* is that of the reasonable, thoughtful—and compara-

tively bland—modern officer who comes up against (and ultimately re-places) an anachronistic, egotistical, and charismatic old-style hero. The echoes of *Patton* are strong and plainly intended; at one point, for example, the submarine captain (Hackman) engages his subordinate in a long discussion of Lippizaner stallions, one of which Patton rides in a key riding-for-a-fall scene in that film. Hackman has a dog, too (in this case a Jack Russell, the favored small-and-feisty-movie-dog of the nineties), who accompanies him on a review of the troops as they pre-pare to board ship, then walks the decks with him, urinating wherever it pleases, much to Washington's fastidious consternation. Clearly this is the one sustained, and sustaining, relationship in the captain's life; we learn that his marriage has failed. When Hackman, like Patton be-fore him, falls into disgrace through his own unrestrained actions and his refusal to follow Navy rules, he is confined to his cabin by Wash-ington, with the dog as his only company. At the film's close, when his resignation from the Navy has been accepted by a military tribunal, he collects the dog, on leash, from the sailor who has been minding him, and saunters off, like Patton, into the distance. The scene is a clear quotation from the earlier film.

In both *Patton* and *Crimson Tide* the little dog becomes the sign of the hero's fall as well as the "humanizing" grace note: the man who loves no one, the man who loves only war, also turns out to love this in-significant creature, whose very inconsequence (these are *not* hero dogs) underscores the necessity of the bond. Is the dog the man? Has he become a visibly "split subject," abject and hero in one? Maybe so. We could say, if we really wanted to, that the dog is his transferential object, or his love substitute, or his cultural fetish, but the plain fact says its best: he loves something, someone, who needs his love, who does not compete or contradict, who obeys some orders and flouts oth-ers, a companion whose very loyalty and occasional disobedience mark the difference between him and the general's or commander's other as-sociates.

Dog as antihero? Why not? The "antihero," a favorite interpretive concept for mid-century critics, was a way of revising the concept of heroism for a modern world beset by forces beyond the individual's control. "A protagonist who lacks traditional heroic virtues and noble qualities and is sometimes inept, cowardly, stupid, or dishonest, yet sensitive," as one literary reference book sums it up. The protagonists of Kafka and Dostoyevsky, Joyce's Leopold Bloom and Joseph Heller's Yossarian are antiheroes. One particularly powerful example of the ambivalent canine antihero appears in Mikhail Bulgakov's 1925 *The Heart of a Dog*, a parable of the Russian Revolution, in which a stray dog, befriended by a wealthy Moscow professor and surgeon, is implanted with the testicles and pituitary glands of a man: "The whole horror of the situation," observes one onlooker, "is that he now has a *human* heart, not a dog's heart. And about the rottenest heart in all creation!" But he is only venal as *man*, not as *dog*. In fact in his canine persona his gratitude to the professor, whom he regards as "the great, the powerful benefactor of dogs" is the crowning irony of this mordant comic fable about what it might mean to be human. The sensitive dog of the last decades of the twentieth century may—at least in some quarters—be replacing the sensitive man, that briefly imagined icon of seventies feminism.

Anatomy of the Dog Tale

There are several popular modes of canine biography and autobiography, each revealing in what it says about the literary genre as well as about human-dog relations. We might call them, after their human fictional models, the Dickensian, the Wordsworthian, and the picaresque, though to this traditional array we will need to add the as-told-to celebrity biography, like *Millie's Book* ("as dictated to Barbara Bush") and *Sandy, The Autobiography of a Star.*

John Steinbeck's *Travels with Charley* and Lars Eighner's *Travels with Lizbeth* may be regarded, perhaps, as examples of the doggy picaresque. The structure of the traditional picaresque novel, a series of loosely connected episodes detailing the adventures of "a peripatetic rogue of 'loose' morals" in which the hero, or picaroon, "need not be a man" but "may be a woman or an animal," is obviously ideally suited to the description of a dog's life. The "sidekick" aspect of the picaresque (Don Quixote and Sancho Panza; Huckleberry Finn and Jim the runaway slave) is also relevant: Steinbeck and his poodle Charley and Eighner and his random-bred Lizbeth swap "master" and "servant" roles from time to time, the supposedly dependent dog often—like Sancho and Jim—exhibiting greater wisdom, practicality, or "humanity" than his or her putative owner. The canine picaresque is, more often than not, an account taken from life, and functions as something like a double portrait. Thus, for example, Thomas Mann's *A Man and His Dog* casually alludes to his "picaroon forays" with his dog, Bashan.

The "Wordsworthian" mode of dog biography is really the story of the author's lost childhood, as remembered through the nostalgic medium of the dog: "The coarser pleasures of my boyish days, / And their glad animal movements all gone by" (Wordsworth, "Tintern Abbey"), a mode that might also be described as "Intimations of Immortality from Recollections of an Early Dog." Willie Morris's *My Dog Skip* is a case in point. The affable, baseball-playing Skip is really a genius loci, a spirit of place—and, indeed, of time. "In that place and time," writes Morris, "we began driving our parents' cars when we were thirteen years old; this was common practice then, and the town was so small that the policemen knew who you were, and your family."

Driving through town with Skip in his old four-door green DeSoto, Morris would look for a group of old men outside the Blue Front Café and "get Skip to prop himself against the steering wheel . . . while I crouched out of sight under the dashboard." Inevitably one of the men would shout, "Look at that ol' dog drivin' a car!" Morris used the same ploy outside the general store and the church. "That sudden bucolic hush and quell remain unforgettable for me," says Morris, "as if the very spectacle of Old Skip driving that green DeSoto were inscrutable, celestial, and preordained."

Similar adventures take the author and his dog fishing, to the local cemetery at night ("There was something in the very air of a small town in the Deep South then, something spooked-up and romantic, which did funny things to the imagination of its bright and resourceful boys"), to the radio to listen to Hitler giving a speech ("I never knew a dog so down on Hitler") and so on; Skip the dog, historically real though he may have been, functions as a placeholder for the author's recollections of early childhood.

The "Dickensian" mode is perhaps the most familiar to aficionados of the dog tale: here can be included the loyal, brave, and suffering dog heroes of London and Terhune and their many followers and imitators in fiction and film today. The typical narrative includes a dog wrenched by theft, accident, or change of ownership from a happy home to a life of suffering and servitude, and his or her triumphant and (here we must say it) dogged return, despite what seem insuperable obstacles, to health and contentment. Sometimes (though not always) the dog returns

to the long-lost original master; in other cases he or she is adopted by a
kind individual or family. This is a broad plot outline, at once sentimental and sensational, that encompasses works like *The Call of the
Wild*, *Lassie Come Home*, and *Bob, Son of Battle*. "Dickensian"
episodes—like picaresque or Wordsworthian ones—can be embedded
in dog narratives of a mostly different spirit, as in the case of Flush,
Elizabeth Barrett's pampered spaniel, and his travails at the hands of
mercenary dognappers. Contemporary dog films like *101 Dalmatians*
and *Beethoven* also clearly draw upon this pattern of expectation and
reversal: Cruella de Vil, whose name suggests both the devil and the
wicked city, is a parody Dickensian villain.

I am using the term "Dickensian," rather loosely, to describe one
kind of dog book, one morphology of the dog tale. By that term I meant
to imply that the dog suffers losses and cruelties at the hands of society
just as, in several of Dickens's novels, a child does: the best (human)
example here is probably *Oliver Twist*. But *Oliver Twist* also contains a
dog story—the story of Bill Sikes's faithful dog, whom Sikes at one
point tries to destroy when he himself becomes a fugitive from justice.

> The dog, though. If any descriptions of him were out, it would not
> be forgotten that the dog was missing, and has probably gone
> with him. This might lead to his apprehension as he passed along
> the streets. He resolved to drown him, and walked on, looking
> about for a pond; picking up a heavy stone and tying it to his
> handkerchief as he went.
>
> The animal looked up into his master's face while these
> preparations were making; whether his instinct apprehended
> something of their purpose, or the robber's sidelong look at him
> was sterner than ordinary, he sulked a little farther in the rear
> than usual. . . .
>
> "Do you hear me call? Come here!" cried Sikes.
>
> The animal came up from the very force of habit; but as Sikes
> stooped to attach the handkerchief to his throat, he uttered a low
> growl and started back.

The unfortunate dog, after wagging his tail pacifically, finally flees, only
to rejoin his master in a London thieves' den. Having escaped death
once, he dies tragically nonetheless when Sikes, fleeing an angry
crowd, accidentally hangs himself from a rooftop. "A dog, which had

lain concealed till now, ran backwards and forwards on the parapet with a dismal howl, and collecting himself for a spring, jumped for the dead man's shoulders. Missing his arm, he fell into the ditch, turning completely over as he went; and striking his head against a stone, dashed out his brains."

The pathos here is unmistakable; the dog is loyal to the end, even to the miscreant who has killed Nancy and has tried to kill him. Readers of the book often point to Bill Sikes's relationship with his dog as the one humanizing element in his character: "The only rudiment of a redeeming feature he possesses is a kind of affection for his dog."

Charles Dickens's literary use of the dog as a provisional shorthand sign of "kindness" in an otherwise unredeemable villain, is, in fact, quite characteristic of one strand of Victorian "humane" thinking. As historian Harriet Ritvo points out, "the Victorian critique of 'inhumanity' . . . confounded two missions: to rescue animal victims and to suppress dangerous elements of human society," while it equated kindness to animals with Englishness. Victorian children's fiction saw to it that bullies came to a bad end: "Kindness to animals was a code for full and responsible acceptance of the obligations of society, while cruelty was identified with deviance"—and often with foreigners or with the undisciplined, uneducated lower classes.

But the most exemplary and influential of nineteenth-century sensational dog life stories should probably be described, for reasons historical and circumstantial, as Stowean rather than Dickensian. Although largely ignored by today's young readers of the dog book, this American classic is remembered with great fondness by an older generation. It is a book that took part in, if it did not actually incite, a small but important social revolution.

The Uncle Tom's Cabin *of the Dog*

The publication of Anna Sewell's *Black Beauty: The Autobiography of a Horse* in 1877 had drawn public attention to the plight of maltreated horses, and was hailed by the president of the American Humane Society as "the *Uncle Tom's Cabin* of the Horse." Sixteen years later a book called *Beautiful Joe* aimed to revolutionize awareness of the mistreated dog. Written by Canadian (Margaret) Marshall Saunders, *Beautiful Joe* told, in the genial and "humane" voice of the dog, a story of suffering and redemption. In 1923 a third book, Hungarian Felix Salten's *Bambi: A Forest Life*, completed the move toward humane education, adding wildlife to the horse and the dog as creatures worthy of human empathy and protection—and commending itself, like *Black Beauty* and *Joe*, to children as well as to adult readers.

Beautiful Joe is dedicated to George Thorndike Angell, "President of the American Humane Education Society, the Massachusetts Society of the Prevention of Cruelty to Animals, and the Parent American Band of Mercy," the same man who had compared *Black Beauty* to Harriet Beecher Stowe's landmark novel. And significantly, *Beautiful Joe* begins by evoking the American institution of slavery. If it is not quite the *Uncle Tom's Cabin* of the dog, its ambitions are clearly in that direction. In the naming of "beauty," however ironically, in its title, it cites, as well, Sewell's novel, its "autobiographical" predecessor—for *Joe*, too, is "An Autobiography," spoken by the voice of anthropomorphized, and decidedly humane, subject:

> My name is Beautiful Joe, and I am a brown dog of medium size. I am not called Beautiful Joe because I am a beauty. Mr. Morris, the clergyman, in whose family I have lived for the last twelve years, says that he thinks I must be called Beautiful Joe for the same reason that his grandfather, down South, called a very ugly colored slave-lad Cupid, and his mother Venus.
>
> I do not know what he means by that, but when he says it, people always look at me and smile. I know that I am not beautiful, and I know that I am not a thoroughbred. I am only a cur.

The connection between *Beautiful Joe* and *Black Beauty* was clear in the minds of both the Humane Society—which awarded it a publication prize in 1893—and the eponymous "author," Joe himself. Hezekiah Butterworth, representing the committee of readers for the Humane Society, introduced the volume, and he, too, invoked *Black Beauty*:

> The wonderfully successful book, entitled "Black Beauty," came like a living voice out of the animal kingdom. But it spake for the horse, and made other books necessary; it led the way. After the ready welcome it received, and the good it has accomplished and is doing, it followed naturally that some one should be inspired to write a book to interpret the life of a dog to the humane feeling of the world. Such a story we have in "Beautiful Joe."

Joe has his own way of putting things; by his account it is his idea to co-author the story, inspired by Sewell's example and the effect of *Black Beauty* on his own kind mistress:

> I am an old dog now, and am writing, or rather getting a friend to write, the story of my life. I have seen my mistress laughing and crying over a little book that she says is the story of a horse's life, and sometimes she puts the book down close to my nose to let me see the pictures.
>
> I love my dear mistress; I can say more than that; I love her better than any one else in the world; and I think it will please her if I write the story of a dog's life.

Joe's story is indeed Stowean—or Dickensian—in its outlines, though his time of suffering is short. Born in the stable of a cruel milkman, he is abused from the beginning. His siblings, condemned as ugly and un-salable, are cruelly put to death before their mother's eyes, and Joe alone escapes, for no reason that he can see. His mother subsequently dies of grief and maltreatment. Joe at first wonders why she doesn't run away from her master, but soon concludes that the answer, inexplicably, is love: "Cold and savage as he was, she yet loved him, and I believe she would have laid down her life for him."

As the year-old pup is mourning her, the milkman walks up and kicks him; in the subsequent scuffle Joe bites his master in the ankle, and is, for his pains, savagely mutilated, his ears cut off close to his head, his tail cut off close to his body. In the aftermath the bleeding puppy is rescued and taken to the home of his benefactors, the Morris family, with whom he comes to live for the rest of his happy life, in the company of two other dogs, a cat, a talking parrot, a guinea pig, and a series of canaries—the ultimate humane home.

The sad early life of Beautiful Joe, which he himself says he is re-luctant to discuss, occupies only the opening pages of the book, which goes on to tell the stories of various rescued or acquired animals and their human masters, to describe a children's humane organization called the Band of Mercy, and to urge, by example and precept and—in Joe's own last words—"Boys and girls, be kind to dumb animals, not only because you will lose nothing by it, but because you ought to."

The phrase "a dog's life" appears twice—once, as we have seen, de-scribing Joe's own tale, and once, with what seems inadvertent appropriateness, in its usual proverbial sense ("most farmers lead such a dog's life"). In a book in which words like "doggedly," "doggerel," and "sheepish" appear in stylistically naive contexts, and in which an old gentleman can be described, without irony, as "pawing the floor with impatience," less may be here than meets the eye. The effect is not that of a modernist or postmodern narrator wittily punning on his own condition, as in the case of Thurber's dogs or Peter Mayle's Boy, but rather suggests—and this is in a way the point of *Beautiful Joe*—that the condition of "dumb animals" and the condition of their human "masters" is, or ought to be, the same. In 1893 Hezekiah Butterworth made the point explicit:

> The story speaks not for the dog alone, but for the whole animal kingdom. Through it we enter the animal world, and are made to see as animals see, and to feel as animals feel. . . .
>
> Such books as this is one of the needs of our progressive system of education. The day-school, the Sunday-school, and all libraries for the young, demand the influence that shall *teach* the reader *how* to live in sympathy with the animal world; how to understand the languages of the creatures that we have long been accustomed to call "dumb."

As the author of a contemporary memoir for another beloved dog would put it, "when at last the tide has turned, and human and humane are convertible terms in the treatment of animals," the life of a dog, "one so well-deserving and who so amply repaid affection, if it may not adorn a tale, is worthy to point a moral."

Whose Life as a Dog?

The title of the 1985 Swedish film *My Life as a Dog* has had something of a life of its own; the movie is frequently invoked, in a jokey way, as some fictive or celebrity dog's "favorite." Actually the film, set in the fifties in Sweden, is both charming and sad, and would hardly be any dog's favorite, I think, if the plot were told. The young boy at the film's center has a mother who becomes seriously ill, so that the family is dispersed, and he winds up, lamenting his missing dog, with an uncle in a country village. The dog has been "put in a kennel"—which is to say, destroyed, a fact that the audience suspects from the outset but that the boy learns only quite belatedly. Over the entire film there hovers like a dark ghost the boy's phantasmatic passion for, and periodic visions of, the Russian space dog Laika, who is linked to both the dying mother and the unwillingly abandoned pet dog, and who also, quite clearly, is a double for the boy. At one point the boy crawls on all fours in his uncle's kitchen, barking, and his frequent reveries about Laika form a kind of leitmotif for the film as a whole.

In November 1957 Laika, a random-bred dog of middle size, became the first living earth-creature to travel into space. Photographs of her smiling face in its helmetlike harness and of the network of wires that tracked her responses appeared in newspapers around the world, and millions of well-wishers followed her journey in *Sputnik 2* (or, as Ed Herlihy of Movietone News archly dubbed it, *Muttnik*). It was soon clear, however, that she would not return. She barked, floated weightless in space, ate food from a dispenser, and, after a week, when the air in the cabin ran out, she died.

In a moving poem dedicated to Laika, "First the Dog," the distinguished Polish poet Zbigniew Herbert tested the ironies and outrages:

> so first the dog honest mongrel
> which has never abandoned us
> dreaming of earthly lamps and bones
> will fall asleep in its whirling kennel
> its warm blood boiling drying away
>
> but we behind the dog and second
> dog which guides us on a leash
> we with our astronauts' white cane
> awkwardly we bump into stars
> we see nothing we hear nothing

Laika, a veteran of earlier rocket tests, had been chosen, it was said, because of her "even-temperedness." Did she ever realize, I wonder, that she had been betrayed by those she trusted?

In any case, why send a *dog* into space? Monkeys or other primates are more closely related to humans, and the United States chose primate precursors for its space travelers: Abel and Baker, two small monkeys, and Enos, a chimpanzee. But the Russian physiologist Vasel Parin explained the choice of Laika: as a student of Ivan Pavlov, he considered the dog to be the "best friend" of the scientific community. Furthermore, because of Pavlov's laboratory, Russian biomedical researchers knew more about the dog than about any other animal. Laika, the "even-tempered" female random-bred, became the successor to Pavlov's famous laboratory dogs, and a figure of pathos and lonely heroism to millions—including the Swedish filmmaker and his child star.

Pavlov's Dogs

"Pavlov's dogs" were said to salivate at the sound of a bell; they became, in my childhood at least, rhetorical figures for the conditioned reflex, the automatic response. We didn't think much—indeed, perhaps at all—about the dogs themselves. They had become figures of speech, conformists, followers, yes-men.

Here is Ivan Pavlov's own description of one of his dogs, a dog that puzzled his researchers until they came up with an explanation for its "peculiar behavior":

> It was evidently a very tractable dog, which soon became very friendly with us. We started off with a very simple experiment. The dog was placed in a stand with loose loops round its legs, but so as to be quite comfortable and free to move around a pace or two. Nothing more was done except to present the animal repeatedly with food at intervals of some minutes. It stood quietly enough at first, and ate quite readily, but as time went on it became excited and struggled to get out of the stand, scratching at the floor, gnawing the supports, and so on. This ceaseless muscular exertion was accompanied by breathlessness and continuous salivation, which persisted at every experiment during several weeks, the animal getting worse and worse until it was no longer fitted for our researches. For a long time we remained puzzled over the unusual behavior of this animal. We tried out experimentally numerous possible interpretations, but though we had had long experience with a great number of dogs in our laboratories we could not work out a satisfactory solution of this strange behaviour, until it occurred to us at last that it might be the expression of a special *freedom reflex*, and that the dog simply could not remain quiet when it was constrained in the stand.

The dog wanted its freedom—that was what was wrong with it. Having identified the "freedom reflex" Pavlov and his researchers set out to overcome it "by setting off another against it—the reflex for food." Before long the dog began to eat all its food on the experimental stand. "At the same time the animal grew quieter during the course of the experiments: the freedom reflex was being inhibited." Pavlov concluded that, although William James did not even include this reflex in his enumeration of the human "instincts," it was very powerful: "one of the most important reflexes, or, if we use the more general term, reactions, of living beings."

Such descriptions of how to transform a "friendly dog" into one "no longer fitted for our researches" in order to study "reflexes" about which nothing has ultimately been understood are painful to read, however important the research may have been for modern theories of human—and animal—behavior.

The investigation of the physiological bases of psychological behavior is currently once again a key area of inquiry for psychologists, many of whom now regard figures like Freud as mere curiosities only fit, perhaps, for study in departments of literature. Pavlov's starting point was, he said, Descartes's idea of the nervous reflex. Descartes had established the idea of the animal as automaton, a machine rather than a kind of "person" with what we would call "feelings" as contrasted with simply physical "feeling." But in his last years Pavlov attempted to make some links between his researches on dogs and conclusions that might be drawn between animals and humans, especially in his exploration of "two forms of neurosis in man—in the pre-Freudian terminology *neurasthenia* and *hysteria*"—and the degree to which they could be correlated with the behavior of his experimental dogs. That is to say, he saw his work as beneficial to an understanding of the human condition, mental and social as well as physical. Why then does the very language in which he describes his experiments seem so chilling to (at least my) human ears?

"In all the cases which have . . . been described," he concludes in the last of his series of lectures, "what is most striking is the extremely characteristic passive self-protective postures of the animal. When I recall a large number of experiments performed one after another and year after year it is hardly possible not to conclude that at least in most cases what is known in psychology under the names of 'fear,' 'cowardice,' or 'caution' has a physiological substrate in a state of inhibition of the nervous system."

Fear, cowardice, caution, freedom—all these emotions and desires could be identified, in the dog, as physiological traits. Could Descartes's notion of the dog as machine be seen, not as a dividing line between human and animals, but rather as a common bond? What was the applicability of Pavlov's experiments on dogs—inducing in them what we might well regard as entirely appropriate states of "fear" and "cowardice"—to human beings?

Pavlov's findings were resolutely materialist and mechanical, a physiological and not a psychological explanation of behavior, despite his use of psychological terms like "neurosis." The reflexes he studied were produced under laboratory conditions rather than observed in the course of an ordinary "dog's life." If we contrast this Pavlovian notion of the conditioned reflex with a developmental narrative derived from Freud's case histories, we can see something of the implications of each for the comparative study of human and dog life stories.

Coming of Age in Dogdom

The psychoanalytic story of *human* development is often, in essence, the story of sexual awareness and a coming to sexual maturity. Developmental narratives about human beings focus on key transitional moments: the separation from the mother; the discovery of sexual difference; the Oedipus complex and castration; the oral, anal, and genital phases of sexual organization; the entry into language and the social world beyond the dyad of mother and child.

What is the developmental narrative of the dog? To mention these human scenarios is to realize that, although they are all in some way present in a dog's life, their sequence and importance (or lack of importance) is both so different from ours and so closely intertwined with ours as to call into question both the human-dog analogy and—more significantly—the inevitability of the stories we like to tell ourselves about *human* development.

Freud posited a continuum of "normal" human development from the oral to the anal to the mature genital phase. Separation from the mother, so crucial in a human baby's life, is, say ethologists, dog trainers, and novelists alike, an early and complete severance in the life of a dog. (Though Jack London's White Fang frets that his mother does not recognize him after a year, this is an entirely "anthropomorphic" worry.) A puppy is separated from the mother, more often than not, at the moment of its adoption into a *human* family. Training manuals are full of advice to owners about suitable chew toys, feeding routines, and bedding, as well as sage counsel about how to lay down the law as top dog, or "alpha," in the new relationship. For many house dogs, the on-set of sexual maturity is signaled by, not the *fear* of castration, but cas-tration *tout court:* the dog is "altered," "fixed," or "neutered"—which is not to say that, in emotional or even social terms, he or she becomes an "it." This is often an emotional crisis for the *human* involved, and especially for some men, who identify all too readily with their about-to-be-castrated pets.

Love, as we know, is made up partly of identification and partly of desire. Nowhere is the problem of "identification" more accurately recorded than in the reluctance some dog owners (mostly male) have to altering or neutering their dogs (mostly male). "My husband just couldn't face it," said the owner of Barney, a handsome male golden re-triever I met on a walk one day. Barney's canine companion, a female puppy just beginning to find her feet, was, however, destined to be spayed. In his memoir, *The Dogs Who Came to Stay,* George Pitcher, who adopted a stray female dog he named Lupa and her son Remus, ad-dresses the question:

> Since there is an enormous over-population of cats and dogs, many millions of unwanted animals being put to death each year, Ed and I considered it a moral duty to have Lupa spayed, but male chauvinism or—much more likely—neurotic fear of castra-tion kept us from even entertaining the idea of having Remus al-tered. The thought of Remus without his testicles would have struck me as quite horrible. If we had actually discussed the is-sue, I would probably have argued that to castrate Remus would be an act of mutilation and that it would change his personality, his very essence, in a terrible way, turning him into a docile, far less interesting animal. But then shouldn't I have had the same reservations about spaying Lupa? Yes, I must now humbly con-fess.

As the owner of two male dogs who were "altered" in their first year, I can testify that my own dogs, at least, are completely "interesting" and far from docile. But I find the word "altered" itself intriguing: do dogs become "others," estranged from some notional true nature, when they undergo surgery to prevent reproduction? Humane societies and shelters campaign mightily against this sentimental identification of human sexual potency with animal fertility. But these passions run high. Anyone who remembers the bad old days of antifeminist rhetoric (and, indeed, the bad new days as well) might well recall the ultimate put-down for a powerful woman: "castrating bitch."

"Why," asks celebrated dog trainer Barbara Woodhouse, "are owners so hesitant about altering dogs?"

> A neutering operation does not adversely affect a dog's mind. There must be no ideas in the owner's head about denying the dog its natural pleasures; an ordinary dog doesn't get those "natural pleasures" unless it is a stud dog or belongs to a bad owner who allows it to wander. . . .
>
> After all, sex in a dog cannot be looked upon in the same way as sex in humans. . . . The mind of a dog doesn't look into the future if its sex organs are to be removed; it doesn't anticipate a loss of pleasure.

Woodhouse thus has some genial sport with the idea of the canine psychiatrist: "The dog . . . cannot answer questions as to whether his sex life is normal or whether he had unpleasant sexual adventures when young." Yet she herself makes use of one of psychotherapy's most misused terms: "oversexed." "An oversexed dog is a curse," she declares. "I say with all my heart that unless the owner of such a dog particularly requires it for show purposes, it should be neutered to make its life happy and that of its owners equally trouble free." And by "dog" here she means "male dog": "With female dogs this characteristic of being oversexed doesn't exist," says Woodhouse flatly.

Castration, then, is a human crisis experienced on behalf of the dog. Orality and anality, however, are for the dog not only stages but also perpetual conditions; though the puppy may chew things that an adult dog is trained not to touch, eating, chewing, fetching things in the mouth, and, of course, eliminating (being "exercised" or "walked") are the principal activities and gratifications of many a domestic dog's life. What humans and dogs have in common, then, is that they are both toilet-trained by humans. Does this account at all for human affection?

Though dog training manuals—meant to be purchased and read by humans—often translate dog phases into human ones (*Surviving Your*

Dog's Adolescence; Mother Knows Best; Dog Psychology; Good Dogs, Bad Habits), the dog's life is one of calculated *im*maturity: his or her ideal role is that of obedient companion, not free spirit. The dog (ideally) moves his bowels according to your walking convenience (one puppy-training guide suggests the use of glycerin suppositories to hurry him up if it's raining or you have someplace to go). Sexual encounters with other dogs are discouraged except for breeding purposes. Falling in love is something that happens only between human and animal, if it happens at all; unruly affections are out of bounds (and must sometimes be settled by costly court suits). It's a commonplace to say that dogs are "like children." Does this mean that they never grow up? Is there, ironically and perversely, something comforting about the fact that most dogs die at an age when children would start to leave home?

Human empathy with and for dogs has often turned into a kind of identification and transfer of properties or roles. Playwright Eugene O'Neill and his wife, Carlotta Monterey O'Neill, had a beloved Dalmatian called Silverdene Emblem, known to the family as Blemie. "Blemie," Carlotta once remarked, was "the only one of our children who has not disillusioned us." A Kansas researcher on human development and the family noted that children who had pets and interacted with them "tend to have significantly more empathy than children who don't," and a Minneapolis veterinarian who specializes in household pets observed that "during elementary school, children tend to treat a pet like a sibling," playing ball with the dog or house with the cat. But, cautions the director of the Delta Society, a national organization with headquarters in Renton, Washington, that studies interactions between people and animals, people who get pets for their children should not have grandiose expectations. "The dog won't necessarily be Lassie, and your child won't suddenly start cleaning his room."

Pavlov Revisited

As Elisabeth Roudinesco, a historian of psychoanalysis, explains, "Pavlov was not the founder of a new psychology; but his doctrine, which could be applied to human physiology, entailed a psychological representation of human behavior that excluded the notion of the unconscious, or, rather, dissolved it in a neurophysiological system." Yet in Pavlov's late work, undertaken in his eighties, as we have seen, he strove to put forward analogies between human and animal neuroses.

Since his mode of demonstration was the analogy, even his admirers grew cautious:

> Several fundamental questions arise. First, the reliability of the analogies. It is one thing to see a certain objective symptom in a dog or a patient but quite another to compare the objective manifestation in the dog with a psychiatric "disease entity" (if such there be). Our information of the latter and its diagnosis and naming rests more upon what we obtain and know about the subjective life of the patient than upon the objective manifestations.

According to Pavlov, "excitable" dogs become neurotic; "weak" dogs become depressed. And these "neuroses in dogs" should be "most naturally" compared with "neurasthenia in man."

"Pavlov is the greatest fool I know," remarked playwright (and vegetarian) George Bernard Shaw. "Any policeman could tell you that much about a dog." Whatever the truth of this rather characteristic Shavian pronouncement, it fell to Pavlov, in connection with his work on human and animal neuroses, to explain exactly who *could* tell you much about a dog. Surprisingly or not, it was—the dogs themselves. Here is Ivan Pavlov's fantasy of the dog on the psychoanalytic couch, answering his own rhetorical question, "With what does one deal in the dog?"

> One can conceive in all likelihood that, if these dogs which became ill could look back and tell what they had experienced on that occasion, they would not add a single thing to that which one would conjecture about their condition. All would declare that on every one of the occasions mentioned they were put through a difficult test, a hard situation. Some would report that they felt frequently unable to refrain from doing that which was forbidden and then they felt punished for doing it in one way or another, while others would say that they were totally, or just passively, unable to do what they usually had to do.

So the proof of the conditioned reflex comes in the "testimony" of the dog patients, as intuited, "in all likelihood," by Pavlov himself. "And so," he concludes, "what my associates and I have found with our animals are elemental physiologic phenomena," as well as "the prime and most fundamental basis of human neurosis." The mute testimony of the laboratory animals, some by his declaration "weak," or else, even if "strong," castrated (and thus given to "chronic pathological inertness") is given as evidence that they are prone to human conditions like "obsessional neurosis" and "paranoia." Thus the father of Skinnerian behaviorism comes, at the close of his career, to psychoanalyze his canine patients. In the end, Pavlov, despite himself, seems haunted by the psychological—and indeed by the imagined voice of the talking dog.

Talking Dogs

"It's always 'Sit,' 'Stay,' 'Heel,'—never
'Think,' 'Innovate,' 'Be yourself.'"

DEMETRIUS: Do I entice you? Do I speak you fair?
Or rather do I not in plainest truth
Tell you I do not [nor] I cannot love you?

HELENA: And even for that do I love you the more:
I am your spaniel; and Demetrius,
The more you beat me, I will fawn on you.
Use me but as your spaniel—spurn me, strike me,
Neglect me, lost me; only give me leave
(Unworthy as I am) to follow you.
What worser place can I beg in your love
(And yet a place of high respect with me)
Then to be usèd as you use your dog?
—Shakespeare, *A Midsummer Night's Dream*,
Act II, Scene i, ll. 199–210

R

Is the dog's letter, and hurreth in the sound; the tongue stroking the inner palate, with a trembling about the teeth.

Ben Jonson, *The English Grammar*

KEVIN (MICHAEL KEATON):	Should we speak the unspoken language of love?
JULIA (GEENA DAVIS):	You mean, the kind only dogs can hear?

Speechless (1994)

Who Is Sylvia?

"I love you." "Even when you hit me, I love you." "I think you're God." The tragically misguided testimony of a victim of spouse beating or child abuse? No. Rather, this is the joyous declaration of love in playwright A. R. Gurney's surprise hit play *Sylvia*. And it is, of course, Sylvia who is speaking. Sylvia the dog, that is, played to tail-wagging perfection by a crimp-haired Sarah Jessica Parker in ordinary jeans and ragged sweater, a figure whose entry in full sniff and high-spirited bark ("Hey! Hey! Hey!") was greeted by the audience at the Manhattan Theatre Club with delighted smiles of recognition.

The audience had come to the theater in full knowledge of the canine impersonation to be exhibited there; I wondered, fleetingly, what it might otherwise have made of Parker's exhaustive, obsessive nose-to-the-furniture inventory of the onstage apartment. Street person? Wild child? Mental patient? But we *knew:* all was well. Sylvia was a dog.

And not just any dog—a dog brought home by Greg, who is in the midst of what used to be called a midlife crisis, and introduced to his wife, Kate, who finds Sylvia a stray distinctly without charm. "I think you're prejudiced against dogs," he says. "I'm not prejudiced," she retorts. "When I was a girl, I read the Albert Payson Terhune dog books cover to cover. I watched *Lassie* on television."

Despite these impeccable canophile credentials, however, Kate does not want Sylvia moving in. And in a way she's right: Sylvia has become the other woman. When she returns from the groomer resplendent in pink leggings and kneepads (for Sylvia's wardrobe is, like Sylvia herself, drawn from the vocabulary of human rather than canine style), Sylvia is beautiful in Greg's eyes. And—best of all—she loves him, loves him uncritically, and shows her gratitude at every turn. How can a wife compete, especially when her own career is burgeoning and her husband's is apparently at a standstill?

Kate has an exciting new job as a teacher of Shakespeare, and it doesn't take a literate audience long to recall that "Silvia" is the heroine of the one Shakespeare play (*The Two Gentlemen of Verona*) that features a key and comic scene between a man and a dog. In Shakespeare's play, Launce the clown has been instructed to give his dog Crab "as a present to Mistress Silvia, from my master." In Gurney's play, Kate wouldn't have Sylvia as a gift. Sotto voce references to classic "dog" texts from *Two Gentlemen* to *Lassie* to Terhune's *Lad: A Dog* recur throughout the text, culminating in a classic farewell scene. Sylvia is to be given away to a nice family in the country so Greg and Kate can go to England on Kate's fellowship (it has not escaped Kate's notice that English law requires foreign dogs to be quarantined for six months before they can enter the country). An aghast and sarcastic Sylvia, told that she'll adapt easily to a new master, tells Greg to "read the *Odyssey* sometime." Sylvia's parting (and Parthian) shot in this scene, "I'll have to depend upon the kindness of strangers," is pure Blance DuBois/drag queen, complete with a brave toss of the head and an ironic backward glance.

Ultimately, of course, Kate relents and Sylvia stays.

New York Times critic Vincent Canby described *Sylvia* as "critic-proof . . . at least for anyone who has ever owned a dog, loved a dog, wanted to wring a dog's neck or wishes the dog would take a long weekend. . . . Forget Lassie, Lad, Rin Tin Tin, Benjy, Asta and ever-reliable old Nana. I've never seen a dog portrait in films or on the stage that quite matches the truth and wit of Ms. Parker's performance as the part-Lab, part-poodle Sylvia."

But none of Sylvia's named canine precursors, not even J. M. Barrie's Nana, actually *spoke*. They barked, whined, nudged, pointed, pushed, pulled, and generally shaped up their human charges, who were often reduced to feats of interpretation ("What, Lassie? What is it, girl? What are you trying to tell us?"). The wittiness of Gurney's play, and one of the secrets of its success, is in letting the audience hear what it longs to hear: the voice of the talking dog.

Much of the play's charm comes from the conversation between Greg and Sylvia, conducted in human language, though occasionally punctuated, at times of high dog emotion, with "Hey! Hey! Hey!" ("Out? Did I hear 'out'?" croons Sylvia in high ecstasy.) Kate, of course, doesn't speak to Sylvia or hear her speak, and (therefore?) inevitably decides that therapy will be the answer to Greg's problems. "You seem to suggest that he has actually fallen in love with Sylvia," notes the marriage counselor, an aggressively androgynous personage (played by the same actor who plays Kate's female friend and Greg's male acquaintance from the dog run at Central Park.) "Do you think there is anything physical in his relationship with Sylvia?"

"A man and his dog. It's a big thing," one of Greg's dog-owning friends counsels. "Women sense it. They nose it out. My wife feels very threatened by it." Sylvia's fidelity to Greg, unquestioned and unquestioning, does not prevent her from having a fling in Central Park with Bowser, the handsome stud from across the way. But that's just sex; with Greg it's love. He asks if she liked her former owner as much as she likes him, and she replies, teasingly, "How do you know it was a guy?"

Playwright Gurney is noted for his analysis of "the American Protestant psyche," and at times his play calls to mind the old joke about how you can tell the bride at a WASP wedding: "She's the one kissing the golden retriever." "Gurney's Notion of a Very Different Ménage à Trois," read the *Times* headline. In a show-stopping triple rendition of the song "Ev'ry Time We Say Goodbye," Sylvia, left behind in the apartment and curled up on the forbidden sofa, torches her way through her yearning for Greg's return, while Greg and Kate, separating at the airport, sing reprises; Greg misses Sylvia; Kate, as she boards the plane, realizes that she will miss Greg. Greg is the man in the middle, torn between a new love and an old one, wishing that they could somehow get along.

Sarah Jessica Parker's model for Sylvia, she said, was "Matthew's dog, Sally," who belonged to the actor Matthew Broderick, with whom Parker was living. Sally "is madly and hopelessly in love with Matthew. They have a terrific love affair," Parker noted. Broderick himself saw the resemblance, in both directions: "It was an odd feeling. It was like seeing my dog on stage, because she reminded me so much of Sally.

And then I came home and saw Sally and thought, 'Wow, she's acting just like Sarah.'"

Broderick's devotion to Sally was reiterated at the Drama Desk Awards for 1995, when, watching play director winner Gerald Guiterrez bring his dog onstage to share the award, Broderick, who won the award for best actor in a musical, bemoaned the fact that he hadn't brought his dog, too. And when actress Jan Hooks replaced Parker in the role of Sylvia, she, too, credited a dog as her inspiration. Of Frank, her three-and-a-half-year-old German shepherd, Hooks said, "That dog has taught me as much about love as anybody. I said to him, 'I hope I do justice to your species.'"

Sylvia is hardly the first or the only talking dog to captivate audiences and readers. The 1967 musical *You're A Good Man, Charlie Brown,* based on the Charles M. Schulz comic strip, featured Bill Hinnant as an alternately joyous and discouraged Snoopy. The first character to come onstage in *Can You See Me Yet?* (1977), a play by Canadian Timothy Finley set in an asylum for the insane, is a man called Doberman who thinks he's a dog. But the success of Gurney's play is a symptom of modern longing: a longing for perfect communication, a longing for unqualified love. In an age when the conversation between men and women is analyzed in books with titles like *You Just Don't Understand* (and social relations between the sexes are parodied in self-help volumes like *How to Make Your Man Behave in 21 Days or Less, Using the Secrets of Professional Dog Trainers*), it is perhaps inevitable that interspecies conversation, between "man" and his proverbial "best friend," has become fantasized and idealized.

"Eloquent with Things They Can Not Say"

In a poignant tribute to the beauty of canine communication, Helen Keller, herself blind and deaf, wrote:

> The charming relations I have had with a long succession of dogs
> results from their happy spontaneity. Usually they are quick to
> discover that I can not see or hear. Considerately they rise as I
> come near, so that I may not stumble. It is not a training but love
> which impels them to break their silence about me with the thud

of a tail rippling against my chair, on gambols round the study, or news conveyed by expressive ear, nose, and paw. Often I yearn to give them speech, their motions are so eloquent with things they can not say. Truly, as companions, friends, equals in opportunities of self-expression, they unfold to me the dignity of creation.

"Man himself cannot express love and humility by external signs, so plainly as does a dog, when with dropping ears, hanging lips, flexuous body, and wagging tail, he meets his beloved master." So observed Charles Darwin, resisting the attempts of his contemporaries to dismiss such signs as mere "instincts." They were no more so, he declared roundly, than "the beaming eyes and smiling cheeks of a man when he meets an old friend. Dogs, Darwin said, exhibited affection to their masters by rubbing against them, by licking their hands and the face, by "lower[ing] their ears in order to exclude all sounds, so that their whole attention may be concentrated on their master," and even by "grinning"—a practice he documents by reference to literature (William Somerville's "The Chase") as well as to the observation of nature ("Sir W. Scott's famous Scotch greyhound, Maida, had this habit, and it is common with terriers"). Communication, in other words, was effected by gesture, demeanor, and action. But Darwin did not claim that dogs spoke, or even that they thought.

Another chronicler of human-dog communication, novelist Jack London, ardently disclaimed any intention to endow his protagonists with "human understanding," or his narratives with human allegory: "I have been guilty of writing two animal stories—two books about dogs," he insisted. "The writing of these two stories, on my part, was in truth a protest against the 'humanizing' of animals, of which it seemed to me several 'animal writers' had been profoundly guilty. . . . [T]hese dog-heroes of mine were not directed by abstract reasoning, but by instinct, sensation, and emotion, and by simply reasoning."

London was, he said, a Darwinist, faithful to "scientific research"—not, as his critics claimed, a "nature-faker." But though the narrator of *The Call of the Wild* does periodically deny the quality of dog "reason" ("Not that Buck reasoned it out. He was fit, that was all, and unconsciously he accommodated himself to the new mode of life") the appeal of the book is, precisely, in its invitation to "identify" with the dog; in fact, by allowing Buck an "unconscious" the author directly invokes, even as he seems to resist, the concept of canine consciousness.

But unconscious accommodation is not an activity only of dogs; London himself, his daughter reports, described the powerful human allegory of his story (the fact that by describing dogs it seemed to describe the tensions and loyalties in human life) as a fortuitous accident. "I was unconscious of it at the time. I did not mean to do it." Nevertheless, it is for their "humanizing" of dog consciousness that London's books are often remembered by affectionate and loyal readers.

The Call of the Wild is the prototype of the dog adventure narrative in our century, a novel whose very title suggests the ambiguous function of language. Buck, the canine hero, half St. Bernard, half Scotch shepherd, is the book's supervening "consciousness," and it is to him that are ascribed such behaviors and emotions as thinking, understanding, "imagination," "surprise"—and love. "Buck felt vaguely that there was no depending upon these two men and the woman" is a not-untypical phrase. He has no human language, but his beloved master reads speech in his silence: when Buck "sprang to his feet, his mouth laughing, his eyes eloquent, his throat vibrant with unuttered sound, and in that fashion remained without movement, John Thornton would reverently exclaim, 'God! you can all but speak! '" All-but-speech may be better than real speech, especially when it is mutual: "Often, such was the communion in which they lived, the strength of Buck's gaze would draw John Thornton's head around, and he would return the gaze, without speech, his heart shining out of his eyes as Buck's heart shone out."

The Call of the Wild tells the story of a domestic dog who adapts to the wild. London's second dog novel, *White Fang*, reverses the pattern of wild and tame, tracing a wild cub's life among men. Rescued, like Buck, from a cruel human owner, White Fang repays the favor by saving his master's life when Weedon Scott breaks a leg: "White Fang knew the meaning of 'home,' and though he did not understand the remainder of the master's language, he knew that it was his will that he should go home." Once home he is desperate to communicate with Scott's wife and family:

> His throat worked spasmodically, but made no sound, while he struggled with all his body, convulsed with the effort to rid himself of the incommunicable something that strained for utterance. . . .
>
> "He's trying to speak, I do believe," Beth announced.

At this moment speech came to White Fang, rushing up in a great burst of barking.

"Something has happened to Weedon," his wife said decisively. . . .

White Fang ran down the steps, looking back for them to follow. For the second and last time in his life he had barked and made himself understood.

Human needs makes for *dog* speech.

In 1919 Lad of Sunnyvale, Albert Payson Terhune's paragon of colliehood, "began to 'talk.'"

> To the Mistress and the Master alone did Lad condescend to "talk"—and then only in moments of stress or appeal. No one, hearing him at such a time, could doubt the dog was trying to frame human speech. His vocal efforts ran the gamut of the entire scale. Wordless, but decidedly eloquent, this "talking" would continue sometimes for several minutes without ceasing; its tone carried whatever emotion the old dog sought to convey—whether of joy, of grief, of request or of complaint.

Shortly thereafter, having survived the dogfight of his life, Lad lifts his bandaged head and tries "to tell the Mistress the story of the battle. Very weakly, but very persistently he 'talked.' His tones dropped now and then to the shadow of a ferocious growl as he related his exploits and then scaled again to a puppylike whimper."

By describing these growls and whimpers as "talk" Terhune emphasizes what he elsewhere calls "the *human* side of a dog"—"brains, fidelity, devotion"—though characteristically none of his humans display these traits to any reliable degree. The gift of "talking"—introduced, we might note, in conjunction with the pathos of the old (and then the wounded)—dog, here gratifies through reversal the *human* wish to be understood.

The Helpful Animal

The phenomenon of perfect and instantaneous canine communication, so dear to the hearts of animal-story writers, is easy (and fun) to parody. "*Lassie* was my favorite show," says comedian Andy Andrews. "We watched it every week, but we never could figure it out. We never could figure out how a dog would understand everything the people would say, and how the people would understand everything the dog would say."

Did you ever notice how Timmy would talk to Lassie? "Lassie, Lassie, go get Mom and Dad and tell that I am down by the beaver pond and I am stuck under a pine tree. It is a loblolly pine tree, not the long-leaf variety. They are on the north forty, Lassie, not the south forty, but the north forty, on the red tractor. Do you understand? Now go, Lassie, go!"

And Lassie would take off. She would be getting across that field, and Ruth and Paul would see Lassie coming and automatically know, "Here comes Lassie, looks like trouble."

Lassie would get up there and they would say, "What is it, Lassie, what is it, girl?

"Woof!" That would be all Lassie would say, but Ruth would respond in a very excited voice, "Oh my God, Paul, Timmy is down by the beaver pond stuck under a loblolly pine tree!"

How did they know? I never did figure that out. I had a collie and I could never even teach him to say "Woof," much less communicate to my parents when I was in trouble. If he knew the difference in pine trees, he never told me.

Writer Benjamin Cheever offers a similar, tongue-in-jowl account of the skills of Rin Tin Tin: "O.K., Rinty, if you bark once, that means we should head for the stockade. If you bark twice, I should go on alone, and come back with help." These examples may seem like witty exaggerations, but a random viewing of old *Lassie* episodes produced this gem: Mother (trapped by fallen tree): "Lassie, do you remember the C-clamp that the trapper brought? Go get it." Needless to say, Lassie did. As if in response to this convention, a *New Yorker* cartoon by Danny Shanahan (reproduced on p. 13) depicts first a drowning man crying "Lassie! Get help!!" and then a voluble and gesturing Lassie on the analyst's couch.

It is interesting to note that these fifties dog vignettes, whether on television or in the movies, employ the old theme of the "helpful animal" familiar from mythology and romance.

In ancient Greek mythology a dog was the companion to Asclepius, the god of medicine, and in one version of the myth a dog suckled him. Sacred temple dogs are mentioned in inscriptions on the temple of Asclepius in Epidaurus. Anubis, the jackal-headed god, functions as a "helpful animal" in the Egyptian myth of Isis and Osiris. Fools and court jesters, often associated with the so-called natural man, were frequently accompanied, in pictorial representation and in court practice, by dogs. "Again and again in fairytales," writes C. G. Jung, "we encounter the motif of helpful animals. These act like humans, speak a human language, and display a sagacity and a knowledge superior to man's. In these circumstances we can say with some justification that the archetype of the spirit is being expressed in human form."

The hero of medieval romance was often accompanied by a dog who served as guide, guardian, or rescuer. And the dog, traditionally a guardian of the threshold (think of Cerberus, the triple-headed dog of the Greek underworld and of Dante's Hell), can also protect those who wish to *cross* a threshold. St. Christopher, the patron saint of travelers, is pictured in the Greek Orthodox tradition with a dog's head.

For a good modern example of the helpful animal as talisman and protector, we might consider Toto, Dorothy's little dog in *The Wizard of Oz,* who makes the journey with her to the world of Technicolor and magic, provoking the now-classic, often parodied observation, "Toto, I think we're not in Kansas anymore." (The Wicked Witch of the West clearly recognizes Toto's talismanic powers; hence Margaret Hamilton's immortal line "I'll get you, my pretty, and your little dog, too.") The dog, sometimes described by Jungians as "psychopompos," conductor of souls, both eases and naturalizes the transition from one place to another. Lassie, like Toto and dozens of other fictional dogs, often accompanies a young owner to a new world; in the *Lassie* film of the nineties, she helps a skateboarding, Walkman-festooned city boy adjust to life on a rural farm. As trivial as these examples may seem, they are indicative of a pattern. The modern taste in dog stories reflects, whether consciously or not, a familiar trope from myths and fairy tales.

As readers both literary and psychoanalytic have always realized, such transitions are personal and psychic, as well as geographical. In Jungian analysis the helpful animal, a crucial aspect of the theory of archetypes, was interpreted allegorically, which often meant that the dog—or the dog's dogginess—disappeared, transformed into an aspect of the human being.

Jungians often associate the dog with the instincts ("The dog [on a tarot card] appears to be trying to communicate something. The Fool seems to be in such close contact with his instincts that his animal side literally guides his steps"). Whether taken to indicate the instincts or the superego, the body or the mind, the dog is often viewed as a human's complement. Lassie and Rin Tin Tin, responsive, loyal, and communicative to a fault, are prime examples of the helpful animal in modern popular culture. Rather than representing the "instincts" indicated by the Jungians, they seem sometimes to function as superego and conscience—another form of guide. The Jungian analyst Marie-Louise von Franz writes that "of all the animals, the dog is the most completely adapted to man, is the most responsive to his moods, copies him, and understands what is expected of him. He is the essence of relationship."

Lest we consider the dog as helpful animal to be only a charming fiction of folklore or an allegorical cliché, however, it is worth considering the several invaluable forms this canine helpfulness takes in the modern world. Every day service dogs, companion dogs, and search-and-rescue dogs work with and for humans, bringing the literary helpful animal uncannily to life. There are Seeing-Eye dogs, hearing dogs, and dogs trained to help disabled persons by picking up and fetching objects, turning on light switches, and opening doors. Pet therapy for the elderly and for autistic and mentally disturbed or depressed persons has become a recognized form of health care. Rescue dogs and police dogs assist in tracking, patrol, drug detection, and search efforts.

The concept of the guide dog originated in Germany during World War I, in part as a way of assisting blinded soldiers. The aptly named Buddy, a female German shepherd trained in Switzerland, became the first Seeing Eye dog in the United States, partnered with Morris Frank, a blind teenager who learned of the program through an article in the *Saturday Evening Post*. Dorothy Eustis, the article's author, who had invited Frank to Switzerland to work with Buddy, later returned to her native United States and founded the Seeing Eye.

The heroic action of Lyric, the dog who dialed 911 to save her mistress, was a clear instance of the modern helpful animal. Assistance dogs, typically Labradors and other retrievers, often rescued from shelters, can be trained over about a year to perform a hundred tasks, from turning on lights to helping pull their owners out of chairs and bathtubs. A study published in the *Journal of the American Medical Association* was the first actually to quantify the benefits of dog owning for persons with disabilities. Surveying twenty-four disabled persons who had assistance dogs, and twenty-four others who had not yet received them, the authors found that over a period of eight years people with disabilities could save $50,000 to $90,000 that would otherwise be paid to human care attendants. The dogs documented in the study helped disabled people with more than with their work lives. Five participants in the study got back together with their spouses after getting assistance dogs, and one who was divorced got remarried. One man with multiple sclerosis said his wife joked that he would never have gotten married if it hadn't been for his dog, who proved a lively conversation-starter. Paul Spooner said his yellow Lab, Klister, also helped him win bets, by picking up wagered dollar bills from the floor.

A young girl named Melissa reported that Cashew, her golden retriever, was her best friend. "He brings me my dolls and he is always picking up my shoes. He turns off the lights when we leave the room to go for a walk and pulls me in my wheelchair. He is fun to go shopping with, which I could never do before."

How close the helpful animal remains to its origins in myth and folklore may perhaps be seen in the disputed account of the two stray dogs who were said to have kept alive a boy with Down syndrome. The ten-year-old boy wandered away from home and was lost for three days in the Ozarks' single-digit weather. He was found, his family reported, when a horseman heard barking and discovered the boy under the protection of two dogs. "The dogs took him in as if they were his mother," said the local sheriff. "They probably curled up next to him and kept him warm, warm enough to stay alive." The boy's parents said they were planning to adopt the two strays, whom they described as "God's angels." Two months later the county prosecutor in Cassville, Missouri, declared it a tale too good to be true and hinted that "there was criminal activity involved." But the sheriff was unconvinced, and the heroic tale of two angelic dogs had clearly captured the public imagination: the family sold their story to a Hollywood producer for an undisclosed sum.

Other contemporary versions of the helpful animal include the dog as traveling companion, a canine version of the "buddy film" so dear to Hollywood moviemakers. The "travels with . . ." motif gives the dog the role of running commentator and double, often gifted with philosophical distance from the foibles of the humans he accompanies. John Steinbeck's dog Charley, a standard poodle, says "Fft." Is this "talking"? "He is the only dog I ever knew who could pronounced the consonant *F*," says Steinbeck. "The word 'Fft' usually means he would like to salute a bush or a tree." Sometimes "Fft" means Charley is hungry. Sometimes it means he's irritated with Steinbeck being Steinbeck. "Fft" is an all-purpose sound, for all intents and purposes mimetic of dog utterance rather than human utterance—the obverse, we might say, of the Nestlé puppet dog Farfel's yawning, humanoid "Chaaaw-klit!" (It's ironic, incidentally, that this is Farfel's catchword, since chocolate is poisonous to many dogs.) But Steinbeck, who makes Charley not only his travel companion but a more woebegone alter ego (down to the prostate problems that afflict poodle rather than master), is philosophical about Charley as philosopher:

> I tossed about until Charley grew angry with me and told me "Fft" several times. But Charley doesn't have our problems. He doesn't belong to a species clever enough to split the atom but not clever enough to live in peace with itself. . . . I've seen a look in dogs' eyes, a quickly vanishing look of amazed contempt, and I am convinced that basically dogs think humans are nuts.

The occasion for this reverie is a reflection on racial tension in the American South circa 1960. Steinbeck has arrived in Texas and Louisiana, where Charley, a black poodle riding in the front seat of the truck, is often "mistaken," to the accompaniment of much ribald laughter, for a Negro passenger—"Thought you had a nigger in there." A kindly southerner seeks to enlighten Steinbeck on local mores:

> "Suppose your dog here, he looks a very intelligent dog—"
> "He is."
> "Well, suppose he could talk and stand on his hind legs. Maybe he could do very well in every way. Perhaps you could invite him to dinner, but could you think of him as people?"
> "Do you mean, how would I like my sister to marry him?". . .
> "I'm only telling you how hard it is to change a feeling about things."

The similarity of this gambit to Dr. Samuel Johnson's notorious witticism about a woman preaching will strike many readers: "It is not done well, but you are surprised to see it done at all." The dog on its hind legs, talking, becomes a dismissive sign of inferiority. "Could you think of him as people?" asks Steinbeck's interlocutor rhetorically.

Charley, who "doesn't even know about race" and "once fell in love with a dachshund, a romance racially unsuitable, physically ridiculous, and mechanically impossible," becomes in his master's eyes a paragon of liberal sentiment and romantic love: "He loved deeply and tried dogfully." Is this a less demeaning comparison than Johnson's, or the helpful southern gentleman's? Hard to say. Steinbeck means well, or means to mean well, by his doggy parable. But Charley, by *not* talking, is able to rise above these petty human frailties, and not just on his hind legs, either.

The familiar paradox is again becoming clear: the wish for dog speech is a wish to hear what we would like to hear, whether it is "I love you" or "Love one another." When Charley does "speak," it is to confirm Steinbeck's own anomie in this imagined dialogue:

> "What's the matter, Charley, aren't you well?"
> His tail slowly waved his replies. "Oh, yes. Quite well, I guess."
> "Why didn't you come when I whistled?"
> "I didn't hear you whistle."
> "What are you staring at?"
> "I don't know. Nothing I guess."
> "Well, don't you want your dinner?"
> "I'm really not hungry. But I'll go through the motions."

"Come in up on the bed, Charley. Let's be miserable together" is Steinbeck's rejoinder. They have been too many places, driven too many miles, seen—or sniffed—too many sights and smells. It is time, he thinks, to head home. This is the helpful animal twentieth-century style, a psychological comfort rather than a physical guide.

But none of these undoubtedly helpful animals "speak" in the strict sense of the term. Rinty's version of Morse code, Lassie's succinct "Woof," and Charley's "Fft" stand in place of speech.

Do dogs understand human language? Do they have a language of their own? To quote one of the first questions asked (strangely enough) by human parents of human infants, "What does the doggie say?"

Dumb and Dumber, or,
You Just Don't Understand

Marshall Saunders's pioneering *Beautiful Joe,* written in the voice of a dog, is emphatic about the eloquence of "dumb animals." Under a photograph of the author and her dog used as a frontispiece to a modern edition is inscribed, in what appears to be her handwriting and with her signature, the legend "Open thy mouth for the dumb." "A child has a voice to tell its wrong," Joe's new young mistress tells his rescuer, who wonders what the use might be of punishing his former tormentor, the cruel milkman. "A poor, dumb creature must suffer in silence; in bitter, bitter silence." And, she insists, the master's cruelty is likely to extend to human beings: "If he is bad enough to ill-treat his dog, he will ill-treat his wife and children."

Beautiful Joe, published in 1894, was intrigued with the problem of animal speech, importing into the narrative—and into the Morris household—a talking parrot who has been coached to know the names of all the members of the family:

> I had never heard of such a thing as birds talking. I stood on the table staring hard at her, and she stared hard at me. I was just thinking that I would not like to have her sharp little beak fastened in my skin, when I heard someone say "Beautiful Joe." The voice seemed to come from the room, but I knew all the voices there, and this was one I had never heard before, so I thought I must be mistaken.

Once the source of the sound is pointed out to him, he is embarrassed, or, as he says, "sheepish": "I had never heard a bird talk before, and I felt so sheepish that I tried to get down and hide myself under the table."

When the Massachusetts Society for the Prevention of Cruelty to Animals changed the name of its magazine from *Our Dumb Animals* to *Our Animals* it was responding, in large part, to the vulgar sense that "dumb" meant without intelligence rather than without voice. But in allowing for animal intelligence, a category of cognition until recently "actively discouraged, ridiculed, and treated with hostility," the new title also opened the door, or rather the sound waves, to the concept of animal speech.

What do we mean when we invite, or command, a dog to speak?

"Stand in front of your dog holding his favorite dog biscuit in front of his face," suggests dog trainer John Ross in the aptly named *Dog Talk:*

—Give him the command *"Sit."*

—Give him the command. *"Speak."* If he sits there looking at you with a blank expression on his face, repeat the command.

—Your dog may perform every behavior he knows. Continue to say *"Speak."* You may even try barking at *him* a few times. Chances are good that your dog will eventually bark at you out of frustration.

—As soon as he barks, praise him enthusiastically and let him eat a piece of the biscuit.

These point-by-point instructions, filed under "Speak!" in a section on "Movie Tricks," are *not* precisely what we tend to mean by animal speech. My dog Wagner will "speak" in this fashion if you say "Wuh" to him; sometimes he actually barks, at other times he just moves his mouth and puffs his cheeks. He seems to be provoking me to do the same; it's a kind of play. Ross had a dog that did that, too, so I suppose it is a fairly common dog response to human invitation.

Wagner has also perfected the art of canine throat-clearing, producing a sound that is not a bark but a polite little verbal hint. "I might consider going outside," it could be translated, or "I think you may have inadvertently forgotten to put water in my bowl," or "Have you noticed that it's getting near dinner-time?" Situated somewhere between the petitionary and the subjunctive, this extraordinarily eloquent utterance—all produced by the identical syllable intoned with just the right touch of deferent insistence—never fails to elicit a prompt and appropriate human response. The door is opened, the bowl is filled, the dog food rattles into the dish. I think he must think he is training me well.

Do dogs speak? And do they understand human speech? One of my favorite dog cartoons of all time is a little diptych from Gary Larson's *The Far Side* in which an owner addresses a dog. The owner's remarks are given in two adjacent panels: "What we say to dogs" and "What they hear." In the first panel the owner, accusatory finger outstretched, declares: "Okay, Ginger! I've had it! You stay out of the garbage! Understand, Ginger? Stay out of the garbage, or else!"

This is what the dog hears: "blah blah GINGER blah blah blah blah blah blah blah blah GINGER blah blah blah blah blah . . ." The dog listens to a paragraph in which all he can understand is his own name. In this brilliant account are encapsulated all our hopes and fears about understanding, and being understood.

But *how* does Ginger listen? Sympathetically? Imperturbably? Patiently? Ginger's face, like the face of the Thurber dogs of whom he (or she?) is surely a relation, gives no sign. Even the enunciation of the name can have significance, as Thomas Mann pointed out his affectionate account of his dog Bashan:

> I am happy to interrupt my literary occupation in order to speak and play with Bashan. I repeat—to speak with him. And what do I find to say? Well, the conversation is usually limited to repeating his name to him—his name—those two syllables which concern him more than all others, since they designate nothing but himself, and thus have an electrifying effect upon his entire being. I thus stir and fire his consciousness of his ego by abjuring him in different tones and in different degrees of emphasis to consider the fact that he is called Bashan and that he *is* Bashan. By keeping this up for a short time I am able to throw him into a state of veritable ecstasy, a kind of drunkenness of identity.

"Probably you only hear vowels," speculates W. H. Auden in a wonderful poem called "Talking to Dogs" (dedicated to the memory of "Rolfi Strobl, Run over, June 9th, 1970") "and then only if / uttered with lyrical emphasis, / so we cannot tell you a story, even / when it is true."

For trainer John Ross real "dog talk" means human communication with the dog. Ross notes that certain words become familiar to dogs through unvarying repetition, words like "come" and "stay"; but since "dogs cannot think or act like humans," while "most humans can think and act like dogs," he instructs the dog owner to "view the world through a canine point of view. . . . It is your job as the trainer to learn *dog talk*." The very *in*ability of the dog to talk often, it is claimed, gives rise to what Freud would call the overestimation of the object: owners "impute kind and noble thoughts to a pet and view them as confirmed in the animal's clever responses to its owner's body language," producing what Ross aptly terms a "mutually satisfying interaction founded on mutual miscomprehension."

"Do you chat casually with your dog in private?" asks another dog training manual. "Are you embarrassed to be heard talking to it in public?" Too bad if you are, because "the more a dog is talked to, the more responsive it becomes to verbal control." It's not the case that dog commands need to be limited to single words ("Come"; "Fetch"; Sit"). "The talked-to dog has no trouble expanding his vocabulary to include such things as 'Let's go home and have dinner,' 'Get your feet off the gearshift,' . . . or 'Go into the kitchen and lie down.'"

When I tell my fitfully obedient golden retriever Yofi "Go to the kitchen," he goes. But does he "understand" what I am saying? As in the old "look-say" method of reading instruction (in which the child looked at the drawing of a quadruped labeled HORSE and read, triumphantly, "Pony!") he does and he doesn't. He gets the idea, even if he doesn't in fact recognize the words. Does "kitchen" mean anything to him outside of the phrase, "Go to the kitchen"? I doubt it. But he knows perfectly well what a kitchen is: it's the place where he waits for us when we're out, and the place where he gets fed. As for Wagner, the phrase he recognizes most plainly is "Let's go watch the news." For some reason he loves the television evening news, even when there are no dog stories on the air. "News" for him probably has no independent meaning; but "Let's go watch the news" sends him running to the TV set, no matter where we are when I say it.

"It's Okay to Talk to Your Dog," says radio pet show host Warren Eckstein, who has worked with the animals of celebrities like Lily Tomlin, Al Pacino, Kathie Lee Gifford, and David Letterman.

By now, I know what you're thinking. "This guy is nuts! Talk to my dog, indeed! Aside from sit, stay, and heel my dog doesn't or won't understand a word I say."

That couldn't be further from the truth! Look at it this way: Your dog talks to you. He barks, he growls, he whines. He communicates his pleasure when he wags his tail while greeting you at the door or when he licks your face in an obvious show of affection. And what dog hasn't nudged family members under the dinner table in an effort to get a few tasty morsels?

All of these are forms of communication, so why shouldn't you communicate back? In fact, why not try this: Ask him in your sweetest voice "You wanna go for a walk?" or "Do you want your dinner?" I'll bet you a bag of dog chow that his ears will go up, that he'll cock his head, look you straight in the eye, and even wag his tail in agreement. In fact, many of us have to spell words such as "out," "cookie," and "bath" when conversing with other people, lest we unnecessarily excite our pets. And even then they often understand. I've actually had clients who resorted to using

a second language around their dogs, but after a while their per-
ceptive pooches caught on. Who says dogs don't understand us?

Stanley Coren's *The Intelligence of Dogs* includes a glossary of over
sixty terms his own dogs understand, from "Away" and "Back" (used in
the car to send the dog from the front to the back seat) to "Who wants a
cookie?" and "X-pen" ("Wait by the exercise pen"). Then there are
words like "bath" that produce unintended, and undesired, responses.
Likewise a century and a half ago Elizabeth Barrett Browning was convinced that her dog, Flush, fully understood human language, a fact she
regarded "as a family faculty; since it never appeared to me, nor does
it to others, one common to dogs as dogs."

> My Flush clearly understands articulate language—only I think,
> at least I have thought, that it is rather particular words &
> phrases, which he understands, than the construction & modifi-
> cation of language. "Dinner, "cakes," "milk," "go downstairs,"
> "go out," everybody's name in the house, "go & kiss Miss Bar-
> rett," "kiss" (abstractedly)—"kiss the hand," "kiss the face,"—
> my Flush understands & applies all that as well as Dr. Johnson
> cd. have done—yes, all that—& a great deal more."

On another occasion, writing to Hugh Stuart Boyd, she described Flush
"lying with his head on one page folios while I read the other. (Not *your*
folios—I respect your books, to be sure). Oh, I dare say, if the truth
were known, Flush understands Greek excellently well."

But comprehension is not the sexy issue in dog language, though
any dog owner will have a few favorites of his or her own. Rather it's
utterance: What does Spot say? As with "Ma" and "Pa" and other
human baby sounds, so with dog "speech": each nationality has its own
transliterations. In a charming poem called "Praise of a Collie" Norman McCaig says of a diminutive canine friend:

> Even her conversation was tiny:
> She greeted you with *bow*, never *bow-wow*.

"Bow-wow," "woof-woof," and "arf-arf" are English and American dog
sounds, but German dogs say "Wau-wau," Chinese dogs "Wung-wung,"
Spanish dogs "Jau-jau," French dogs "Ouah-ouah," and Israeli dogs
"Hav-hav." Coren offers a second glossary of "dog vocalizations," broken down into specific "Barks," "Growls," "Other Vocalizations"

(whimpering, sighing, howling, panting, moaning) and "Signals and Gestures" (with tail, ears, eyes, mouth, body, and paws). Thus, for example, an "undulating growl" means "I'm terrified. If you come at me, I may fight or I may run," and a yawn ("probably one of the most misunderstood dog signals") is not a sign of boredom, as with humans, but instead a sign of stress": "I'm tense, anxious, or edgy right now."

"Let's take a quick look at the world as our dog sees it," invites professional dog trainer Carol Lea Benjamin.

> Dogs don't use their senses in the same way that we do, nor do they communicate with words as we do. Dogs often communicate with their urine or feces, a fact every owner of an adolescent dog should understand. And last, as you take a peek at how your dog views things, I hope you are reminded that your dog is not a little person in fur. He is as different from you and me as an extraterrestrial might be. This makes it all the more amazing and wonderful that we can learn to communicate with each other.

Fortified by this advice (*had* I been thinking of my dogs as little people in fur?) I found Coren's vocabulary of signs thoroughly interesting and enlightening, on the Inuit-language-has-many-words-for-snow principle; once he delineated all his dogs' barks, growls, and snuffles, I began to hear them in my own and other dogs.

Of course there is variation within breed, as well: Susan Conant's wonderful dog mysteries, featuring a pair of Alaskan malamutes, remind readers that malamutes "Woo-woo" rather than bark. Conant's dog-loving detective, Holly Winter, was born to her breeder parents on the same day two of their golden retriever bitches produced a total of seventeen puppies. Holly was the eighteenth. "I've often had the feeling that a human puppy must have been a surprise to [my parents] Buck and Marissa," she observes. "They must have been stunned when I began to utter words. Buck still considers speech to be some peculiarly advanced form of barking." Holly herself has two "woo-ooing" Alaskan malamutes, but she has no difficulty in translating from the malamute. "If malamutes could speak English, what they'd say is 'Me, too!' 'Me, too!'"

René Descartes, equating language capability with intelligence, denied that animals had either; nor did they have consciousness, he thought, or souls. The animal was a machine, whose cries were not expressions of emotion: "The animals act naturally and by springs, like a watch." No animal was capable of "arranging various words together and forming an utterance from them." Nonetheless, Descartes himself had a little dog, Monsieur Grat, whom he took for solitary walks. His contemporary Madame de Sévigné, who doted on her own dog, made short work of the philosopher's theories ("Machines which love, which prefer one person to another, machines which are jealous . . . come now! Descartes never thought he could make us believe that!") but the Cartesian view prevailed among many behaviorists down to the present day. The question of whether dogs have souls is one that has preoccupied many dog owners and dog lovers, as we shall see. (Of course, early philosophers and theologians wondered whether *women* had souls, too.)

Most people do not long for a colloquy with a collie on the topic of Kant's third critique. Our desires are more basic—as basic as we imagine the dog's to be. If a dog could speak, what would we want it to say? Probably "I love you." Or "Thank you." Or "Is there anything I can do for you today?" The familiar joke about human narcissism—"But that's enough about me. Let's talk about you. What do *you* think about me?"—is no joke when it comes to the human-dog interchange. The two most dreaded words of early childhood speech, "No!" and "Why?" are happily absent from the dog's vocabulary, though both, especially the first, may be indicated by obstinate (in)action.

Yet human investigations, from ancient myth to modern science, have persisted in trying to imagine and supply language to, or for, dogs.

Look Who's Talking

Novelty recordings with significant sales in recent years have included *Live from the Pound* (dogs barking to Beatles tunes) and a pair of Yuletide specials, Top Dog's *Howliday Favorites In Dog!* and Jingle Dog's *Christmas Unleashed* which includes the "Jingle Bells Boogie," dogs barking "Jingle Bells" (arf-arf-arf; arf-arf-arf, etc.) over a boogie background. Nor is the singing dog merely a creature of popular culture. In 1983, pianist and composer Kurt Nurock's *Sonata for Piano and Dog*, a chamber work in four movements, was performed by Nurock and dogs Emily and Sasha at the Carnegie Recital Hall. (A howling success?)

"Singing dogs" records have existed at least since the fifties. But fifties "talking dogs" tended to exist only in fiction, or in cartoons. Modern-day Hollywood has beefed up the canine fare. Max McCarter, the Jack Russell terrier of the film *The Mask*, is described by director Chuck Russell (no relation) as "an extraordinary verbal actor." Like others in the cast invited to redub fluffed or indistinct lines, Max was brought in at the end of the picture to "rerecord his squeals, snorts and indignant yelps." But is this really "talking"? Like Rin Tin Tin's communications or the "talking" of Terhune's Lad, the matinee idol of an earlier, reading culture of juvenile fans, Max's expressiveness is in the ear of the auditor. But other canine film stars have been furnished with voice-over human language. A recent pack of dog movies, like *Homeward Bound* (1993), *Fluke* (1995), and *Look Who's Talking Now* (1993), have featured the ventriloquized voices of humans playing dogs. The golden retriever, the cat, and the bulldog who are the featured players in *Homeward Bound* have the voices of famous, and recognizable, human actors. When Shadow the golden retriever worries audibly about his boy owner, Peter, he does so in English, in the voice of Don Ameche, not in whimpers or yelps. The title of *Look Who's Talking Now*, a remake of *Lady and the Tramp* with animal rather than animated actors, tells its own story: Danny DeVito is the voice of Rocks the mutt; Diane Keaton is the voice of Daphne the elegant standard poodle. *Fluke*, a somewhat less successful venture in the same genre, casts Matthew Modine as the voice of the eponymous hero, and Samuel L. Jackson as the voice of the older, more experienced and streetwise Rumbo.

Babe (1995), the story of a pig adopted by a farm family of dogs, featured sophisticated animatronics that allowed the film's creatures to "speak" by moving their mouths, thus conflating the techniques of animation and voice-over that had heretofore been the most frequently alternatives for talking-dog films. Fly, a resourceful border collie, mothers the orphaned Babe along with her own litter of puppies, and her maternal advice is all the more appealing for being delivered, quite credibly, from her own mouth. Likewise, when Rex, the farm watchdog who is a reluctant convert to Babe's feckless charm, goes in desperate search of a password that will allow the pig to herd sheep at a local dog trial, his quest is made more poignant and more comical by the visible "conversation" that appears to take place between them.

Jokes about language, a topic addressed earnestly by philosophers and psychologists, are not infrequent in these films: in *Look Who's Talking Now* the rambunctious mutt Rocks is sure his name is "No!" because that's what is constantly being shouted at him, and there is a wonderful little scene in which the poodle Daphne and the little girl Julie are each convinced that they are training each other ("Daphne, paw." "Julie, paw.") The same mutual misprision takes place in *Homeward Bound: The Incredible Journey,* where the effect, as so often in dog films, is one of pathos. When at the close the aged and sore-footed Shadow finally limps onto the scene, there is a joyous reunion between dog and boy, and it is Shadow's voice we hear: "Oh, Peter, I worried about you so. Peter, you're okay."

It's striking to note that the book version of *The Incredible Journey,* published in 1961, hardly anthropomorphizes the dogs and cat at all. Although the three animals have names (the bull terrier is called Bodger, the golden Lab Luath, and the Siamese cat Tao), once they leave human territory for the wild the narrative merely refers to them as "the old dog," "the young dog," and "the cat": names become important again only in the human-animal reunion scene, when the masters think wistfully of their missing pets. (The battered Bodger, triumphantly limping home, is accorded only on the penultimate page his classy official monicker, "Ch. Boroughcastle Brigadier of Doune.") Nor do these animals think—much less speak—aloud. The children so prominent in the film are mere props, parentheses of plot, in the novel, and though the traditional love theme sounds in a phrase like "an indistinguishable tangle of boy and dog" the book is admirably spare throughout, leaving the gushing and mourning, such as they are, to the human caretakers the animals meet in the course of their travels.

The closest the narrative gets to voice-over/voice-under is tactful description: "The young dog, their gently worried leader, had found his charge again. He could continue with a lighter heart." In the novel "the young dog" is the Labrador, the old one the bull terrier; the film reverses the roles, turning the bull terrier (a.k.a. "pit bull") into a lovable American bulldog with the name of Chance, and dubbing the retriever Shadow, emphasizing the pathos of his fragile seniority and his fidelity. "A gaunt, stare-coated shadow of the beautiful dog he had last seen," says the novel, providing what is perhaps the textual source of the dog's film name, as it describes the "strange, inarticulate half-strangled noises that issued from the dog when he leaped at his master" at the final homecoming. But strange, inarticulate half-strangled noises, though they may do for Frankenstein's monster, will not accommodate the sentiments necessary for this reunion. Thus Hollywood, with predictable but (or "and"?) powerful effect, supplies the voices. "Oh, Peter, I worried about you so." The worry, please note, is on the dog's side. See—they care about *us*.

The talking dog as a literary genre long predates the era of animation and voice-over. Perhaps the most famous single example is the droll motto penned by Alexander Pope and inscribed on a dog's collar:

> I am his Highness' dog at Kew;
> Pray tell me, sir, whose dog are you?

(The "Highness" in question was Frederick, Prince of Wales.) Pope's witty couplet makes "dog" a figurative term equivalent to "servile attendant," reversing the power relations between reader and read; condescending to read the collar, the courtier finds himself, as in an oracle's prophecy, already inscribed there. To this polite canine inquiry there can be no effective human reply.

Mark Twain's equally famous adoption of canine speech makes a different, but related, political point: "My father was a St. Bernard, my mother was a Collie, but I am a Presbyterian. That is what my mother told me; I do not know these nice distinctions myself." So much for what the twentieth century calls "identity politics."

Indeed, the talking dog is often an ironic commentator on the state of human progress, as attested by an impressive series of dog stories and novels. O. Henry's short story "Memoirs of a Yellow Dog" begins, "I don't suppose it will knock any of you people off your perch to read a contribution from an animal. Mr. Kipling and a good many others have demonstrated the fact that animals can express themselves in remunerative English, and no magazine goes to press nowadays without an animal story in it." "Nowadays" was 1906; the tale the "yellow dog" has to tell is that of his, and his master's, emancipation from the rule of an oppressive woman (the master's wife, who has dubbed her dog Lovey—a name ultimately changed to the more acceptably masculine Pete). "I led a dog's life in that flat," complains the author, recording his futile attempts to communicate with the hapless and henpecked "biped."

> I looked up at him and said, in my way . . . "You ought to be thankful you're not a dog". . . .
> The matrimonial mishap looked down at me with almost canine intelligence in his face.

"Why, doggie," says he, "good doggie. You almost look like you could speak. What is it, doggie—Cats?"

Cats! Could speak!

But, of course, he couldn't understand. Humans were denied the speech of animals. The only common ground of communication upon which dogs and men can get together is fiction.

In Mikhail Bulgakov's *The Heart of a Dog* it is precisely the fact that the dog *talks* that allows him to cross the boundary between dog and man. In this version of *Faust* and *Frankenstein* for the Soviet era, the hapless, nameless stray begins as the story's narrator, speaking "dog": "Ooow-ow-ooow-owow!" is the novella's first "word," and the dog goes on to muse, in indirect discourse ("It takes a lot to keep a good dog down") until he is adopted, and named, by the wealthy professor who will change his life. But after his operation, when he is implanted with the organs of a man, he begins to speak words like "taxi," "liquor," "evening paper," and every known Russian swear word, and before long the "talking dog" has the appearance, appetites, name, and language of a man—with violent results disastrous for those around him. "Because he talked?" the professor says skeptically to the police. "That doesn't mean he was a man." But the law inclines to think otherwise, at least until the dog reverts to dog-consciousness and the "warm, comfortable" life of a domestic pet.

Shakespeare's Dog, a novel by Leon Rooke, is written in the voice of the dog, Hooker, who speaks a kind of Elizabethan dog English (cognate to dog Latin?): "Woof-woof, grr and growl . . . take this and that, demented beast, thou feast of a cesspool!" "Agh and etch (blech and blah), you piddler, you leaf-sniffing pooch!" "Blech and blah, woof and rar—oh you mangy huffers with pig's feet for brains." Hooker is contemptuous of Anne Hathaway ("my master Two Foot's kicksy wicksy, the noxious Hathaway") and of the literary aspirations of his master, Will. Written from the same household-retainer perspective as *Lord Byron's Doctor,* or the legendary *Lincoln's Doctor's Dog, Shakespeare's Dog* affords a cur's-eye (and curbside) glimpse of the world: "I remember once, talking with Will and him saying dogs were lower than the low, I'd pointed out even Aristotle had noted favorably the link between dog and man: how each shed his teeth similarly and had a single stomach that daily required replenishment. 'Who?' he'd said—and taken out his pen to write it down. 'Aristotle who? What's he done?'"

A wisecracking and cynical scoundrel who is given to citing Proust, Sartre, W. C. Fields, and other assorted experts on human behavior, Peter Mayle's dog Boy, the protagonist-speaker of *A Dog's Life* (1995), is a stray of no particular breed adopted by Mayle and his wife at their home in Provence. Boy's irreverent memoirs—very much in the same tone as those of O. Henry's Pete if we allow for some natural differences in literary taste over the course of ninety years—end with some helpful "Notes on the Human Species" and the perhaps inevitable bromide "To err is human, To forgive, canine." In the chapter "The Art of Communication" our hero lays things on the line: when a fulsome neighbor lady gushes, "Don't you wish he could talk," he rejoins to the reader, "The fact is, I have no need to talk. I can make my feelings and wishes perfectly clear to anyone who has the most rudimentary powers of observation." Everyone important understands Boy—his owners, the neighbors, the local tax collector. "I may not talk, but I like to think that I am one of the great communicators. I have a manly and distinctive bark, an eloquent sniff, a squeal of horror that serves to discourage any attempts at grooming," as well as "a most expressive snore" and a growl that is a "model of menace." Furthermore, Boy is a (self-described) master of body language, "the key to it all." "The supplicant paw, the vibrating tail, the fixed and loving gaze, the shudders of rapture—these speak louder than words when used by an expert." *A Dog's Life* is calculated to appeal to two audiences: those who like dogs, and those who might like light satire about human foibles. In a relatively humorless age we have again permitted dogs to be our humorists.

Two best-selling children's books by Susan Meddaugh, *Martha Speaks* and *Martha Calling,* were inspired, says the author, by her seven-year-old son's artless query "If Martha-Dog ate alphabet soup, would she be able to talk?" In the books, Martha does just that, beginning with gossip and small talk that can only be called catty ("Lassie is not all that smart") and proceeding, after the novelty wears off, to irritate her family with her chattiness and lack of social tact. Later Martha discovers the telephone and enters a contest offered by a local radio station, winning a vacation weekend for herself and her family at a no-dogs-allowed resort. How to account for Martha's popularity? Says the author, "Children who have dogs—and I suspect grown-ups too—wonder what their dog would say if it could talk."

But it sometimes seems as if the dog can hardly get a word in edgewise. *The Quotable Dog,* a "treasury of observation on our canine companions," does not in fact quote dogs but human "dog lovers," and *Unleashed*, a volume of "poems by writers' dogs," though it is described as "full of canine inspiration," afford the writers, not the dogs, an opportunity to express themselves. "An attempt at translation," say the editors, Amy Hempel and Jim Shepard; "it comes from watching a dog and believing we can interpret what we see." Many of the poets in *Unleashed* in fact grapple with the problem of language, from Birch, who complains that his owners pronounce his name with obscure meaningfulness ("At times they say it like *Walk.* / At times they say it like *Bad.* . . . Watch their eyes. . . . Foreign language") to Skipper, whose "Complacencies of the Fenced Yard" tests the regularity of canine tetrameter ("*Huh*-huh *huh*-huh *huh*-huh *huh*-huh") to Heather McHugh's "My Shepherd" (not ascribed to any named canid) who remarks—or rather, as she says, "rebarks"—of an aficionado of the frankfurter, "He loves paw-long hot-men." Perhaps the most poignant is the account, by a dog named Scout (now owned by writer R. S. Jones), of his adoption from a shelter:

> You paused outside
> to look into my cage.
> I tried to play it right
> wanting to catch your eye
> with a shy glint in my own,
>   a soft bark,
> that said, "Choose me,"
> in a canine grammar
> I hoped you'd understand.

The anxieties of communication revealed, or "interpreted," in these charming poems are doubled: the dogs, through their owners, worry about being let out to relieve themselves, about castration, about (human) sexual rivals, about fetching, about food. These are anxieties it is easy to share, as is the commonest one of all: the anxiety about love. "God I love my master," says one. "Of all the dogs I have the best master / What a great master." Whose anxiety, and whose adoration, is being comically paraded here?

Of course, dog-loving poets have often tried to imagine what goes on in the minds of their dogs. Thom Gunn uses a conceit similar to that of the poets in *Unleashed* when his "Yoko" muses on a summer walk in sultry New York with the person he describes as "my leader, my love."

He laps from the toilet bowl, leaps upon his leader, and roams with him into the world of old and new smells, pissing on a garbage can, finding his own smell ("well that's disappointing / but I piss there anyway"), and locating on this occasion a dried old turd that is not only "so interesting . . . a gold distant smell like packed autumn leaves in winter" but also a timely prompt, "reminding me of what I have to do," while "My leader looks on and expresses his approval." The spirit of "Yoko" is very much the spirit of Gurney's *Sylvia,* a love poem from a dog to a man—ghost-written by the man: "I care about him more than anything."

Sotto Voce

While the dog in literature is often asked to embody the fantasy of perfect devotion, a slightly more ironic—not to say cynical—voice is sometimes heard in cartoons. "Do you want to handle this or should I?" asks one dog of another in a Michael Maslin cartoon, as they take note of a cat strolling down the street. In two of the cartoons reproduced in this book, human language comes under critical scrutiny. Three dogs chatting under a tree commiserate about thoughtless human clichés: "Speaking personally," says one, "I haven't had my day, and I've never met any dog who has." And a pair of dogs imagined by cartoonist Peter Steiner lament their owners' narrowness: "It's always 'Sit,' 'Stay,' 'Heel'—never 'Think,' 'Innovate,' 'Be yourself.'" In these cartoons we never "see" (and in the animated versions, never hear, except as a series of incomprehensible musical toots) adult speech, although child characters appear to hear and comprehend it.

And then there's the lingua canina or meet-them-on-their-own-turf version, in which humans bark at dogs. "Woof woof woof woof woof woof," offers a weary-looking businessman as he enters his apartment, and his dog, curled up on an easy chair in front of the television, retorts, "Knock if off, will you, Tom? I've had a lousy day."

In the realms of cartoon and advertisement, where dog speech is usually to be found, the result tends to be comic rather than terrifying. A confident dog accompanied by a solemn man with a briefcase addresses his master: "From now on, Ted, I will speak only when adequately represented by counsel." A retriever pads into the living room and remarks to his owners, "Once again I find myself in the rather awkward position of having to ask one of you for a biscuit."

Other cartoon and comic book dogs think, rather than speak. Snoopy's "speech" is actually "thought," conventionally indicated in standard comic-strip form by a cloud over his head. This allows him, periodically, the position of analyst and critic, offering a sardonic punch line to human foibles. (One of the mutual benefits of this division between "human" and "animal" in Schulz's strips is that each party gets to feel superior to the other.) When, for example, Charlie Brown tells him Lucy's bark is worse than her bite, we see Snoopy reflecting, "I hate those expressions."

But Snoopy, a versatile canine star, is not limited to this genre of thought-speech. Periodically he fancies himself a writer, of novels, memoirs, or biographies, and the strip pictures him typing on top of his doghouse. (In another version of the dog at the typewriter, a Robert Mankoff cartoon depicts a dog defending his species honor by typing, "The quick brown *dog* jumps over the lazy *fox*.") " 'Beagle Press' has asked me to write my autobiography," exults Snoopy at one point, and at another, despairing of rejection slips, he produces a potboiler called "A Love Story" under the pseudonym of Erich Beagle. So Snoopy communicates either in thought or in "print" (a serif-adorned font different from the ordinary lettering used in the strip to indicate speech).

Snoopy, of course, is not the only dog whose dream is to produce an autobiography. The Bush family dog, Millie, made *The New York Times* best-seller list with *Millie's Book*, which began, "My name is Mildred Kerr Bush and I came to live with the Bush family on February 13, 1987." (Purebred springer Millie notes that "the Kerr part of my name has caused me great embarrassment. Some people who just hear the name think that my name is Cur not Kerr.") The book was officially billed "as dictated to Barbara Bush," and all proceeds were to be donated to "The Barbara Bush Foundation for Family Literacy." Whether one of the goals of the foundation was to help other aspiring canine authors to learn to read and write was never made fully clear.

The connection between dogs and literacy recurs in a recent full-page ad for the National Center for Family Literacy, where a portrait of a golden retriever is framed by the words, "To 12 million adults this is an ad about a dog. Actually, it's an ad about literacy." The pathos of the ad lies in its placing of the illiterate adult in the same position as a dog, unable to read the marks on the page. A more upbeat version of the same theme comes in Robert Urich's endorsement for a premium dog food: "He Can Sit, Roll Over, Beg, Play Dead and Even Sing, But He

Couldn't Read an Ingredient Label If His Life Depended On It." ("Do
your dog a favor and read a few dog food labels," counsels the ad.
"Don't play tricks on your dog.")

Virginia Woolf's Flush expressed wonderfully this dog's-eye view of
the mystery of reading and writing:

> Flush was at a loss to account for Miss Barrett's emotions. There
> she would lie hour after hour passing her hand over a white page
> with a black stick; and her eyes would suddenly fill with tears;
> but why? . . . there was no sound in the room, no smell to make
> Miss Barrett cry. Then again Miss Barrett, still agitating her
> stick, burst out laughing. . . . What was there to laugh at in the
> black smudge that she held out for Flush to look at? He could
> smell nothing; he could hear nothing. There was nobody in the
> room with them. The fact was that they could not communicate
> with words, and it was a fact that led undoubtedly to much mis-
> understanding. Yet did it not also lead to a peculiar intimacy?

When dogs do speak to humans, the effect *is* uncanny.

A television commercial for a product called Bush's Baked Beans
(no relation to Millie) featured a complacent young man in an armchair,
accompanied by a handsome young golden retriever. "Roll that beautiful bean footage," commands the man, clearly a scion of the founder's
family, and the camera obediently pans a series of tempting dishes.
When the man declares that his exclusive family recipe is safe, since
he has "shared the secret with only one other soul, and he's not talking," right on cue, the golden retriever speaks: "R-r-roll that beautiful
bean footage."

"Uh-oh," says the young man.

Here the "dumb animals" joke is on the human owner, whose "secret," like that imparted by King Midas's barber to the reeds, improba-
bly becomes general knowledge against all "natural" expectation.

The r-r-r in "r-r-roll" is a reminder of the mimetic or imitative aspect of human "dog speech." Imitated dog sounds (woof! grrr!) are often used as examples of onomatopoeia, in which human words try to
imitate what they signify. This crossover between dog sounds and human sounds can go in both directions. In John Ross's book *Dog Talk*,
the all-purpose "correction" is the sound "NHAA!" which is meant to
duplicate the growl with which the mother dog chastises her young
pups.

From now on, your "NO" should be "NHAA." Loud is not as important as deep and tough-sounding. The tone should sound like a growl. You are imitating dog language. When a dog tells another dog to stop doing whatever he is doing, he growls. He does not say "Bad dog" or "Stop it." He growls. I have heard trainers use the word "Fooey." Think of how ridiculous this is. Have you ever heard a dog tell another dog "Fooey"?

Something strange, in fact, seems to happen to human language upon prolonged exposure to stories about dogs. "Randolph Gets Ruff," proclaims a headline in *The Boston Globe* introducing a story about a town ordinance against barking dogs. (Randolph is a town, not a dog.) "Unpoopularity" was cited by *The National Law Journal* in a story about a "pooper-scooper" law in Portland, Maine. And another article in the same journal was entitled "No 'Flea Bargaining.'" Millie Bush mentions casually her experience "posing for *Vanity Fur,* the stylish fashion magazine for dogs and cats." Then there are the titles of Susan Conant's popular dog-lover's mysteries: *Ruffly Speaking, Paws Before Dying, A New Leash on Death.* And when *The Washingtonian* declared Millie Bush "Ugliest Dog," Senator Bob Dole, among others, sprang to the springer's defense, issuing a press release in the name of his own dog, Leader: "Let's make no bones about it," said Leader, the *Washingtonian* article was an "arf-front to dogs everywhere."

In his essay "The Power of Pets," Richard Klein accounts for (and exemplifies) the phenomenon this way:

> To pun in succession while speaking, say, to a president would surely be considered a faux-paw. . . . But does the subject [of pets] invite a form of linguistic playfulness, a sign that the tone is being dropped down to a level more appropriate to the topic? . . . The punning tells you that the writer doesn't take this entirely seriously—this assumed responsibility to report on the state of our pets.

Klein, as we have noted earlier, goes on to protest this lack of seriousness, and to warn us that the humanization of animals may lead to an animalization of humans, particularly in the realm of capricious killing. But it seems to me that, in the case of puns, the exchange of properties between humans and animals is happening not on the level of behavior but on the level of language: a pun is "the lowest form of humor" precisely because it uses words as sounds, just as, in onomatopoeia, animal sounds are heard as words. Both figures involve an utterance in which the meaning follows the lead of sound. This is what canine utterance and human utterance have in common. The pun, in other words, is acting out the ideal of a sound shared equally between two meanings, which becomes, in a sense, a meaning shared between two species.

High Fidelity

But doesn't all this fantasizing about dog speech cover over the rather obvious fact that what we love about dogs is the fact that they *don't* speak? "Can Your Dog Talk?" asks an advertisement in *Dog Fancy* magazine, only to answer its own question. "Unfortunately, dogs can't talk, which means you don't know how they feel. Like people, dogs also suffer from arthritis." The ad goes on to urge the merits of a product called "Arthritis Care for Dogs," dubbed by the manufacturers a "deep penetrating 'doggy Ben-Gay'"—that is, a canine version of the kind of pain reliever routinely peddled to (human) viewers of the evening news. Do we really want our dogs to talk so we can hear them kvetch? Or is their silence, by contrast, golden? "The leading distinction between dog and man," Robert Louis Stevenson wrote, "is that the one can speak and that the other cannot." Yet while the absence of the power of speech hinders the dog from philosophical speculation, still "his silence has won for him a higher name for virtue than his conduct justifies."

"I don't believe human beings would love animals as well, if they could speak," muses the wise and experienced Beautiful Joe. No need to worry that they'll talk behind our backs (they're never catty), or criticize our weight, or complain about their unhappy puppyhood to their future analysts—although the dog in therapy is starting to become a theme in *New Yorker* cartoons, as witness a recent Barsotti sketch in which a recumbent dog tells his note-taking canine analyst, "They moved my bowl." This may give a whole new meaning to the enterprise of keeping the dog off the couch.

Emily Dickinson, herself a poet of reticence, makes many telling remarks about the superiority of canine silence over human speech. "Shunning Men and Women" because "they talk of Hallowed things, aloud—and embarrass my Dog," she preferred the society of Carlo, "a

Dog—large as myself—that my Father bought me" and whom she called "my mute confederate." "I think Carl[o] would please you," Dickinson wrote to her friend and mentor Thomas Wentworth Higginson. "He is dumb, and brave." "They are better than Beings—because they know—but do not tell."

They know—but do not tell. . . .

"He knew that he was saying to me all that love should say," wrote the Symbolist playwright Maurice Maeterlinck about his bulldog puppy, Pelléas, whom he remembers "sitting at the foot of my writing-table, his tail carefully folded under his paws, his head a little on one side, the better to question me, at once attentive and tranquil, as a saint should be in the presence of God." Maeterlinck uses the language of utterance to describe a nonspeaking speech: "He was there, studying, drinking in all my looks; and he replied to them gravely, as from equal to equal . . . he knew he was saying to me all that love should say."

But how does the writer "know" what the dog "knows"? Maeterlinck's pleasure in the message is ensured by his complete control of its interpretation. Pelléas's questions, replies, and declarations, so perfect in their comprehension of the master's desires, are all, of course, the master's construction. The dog's eloquent speech in fact consists of listening.

When pet and wildlife expert Roger Caras chose to call his own book on dogs *A Dog Is Listening* (in deliberate contrast to an earlier volume, *A Cat Is Watching*) he drew attention to that quality which, perhaps above all, dog owners cherish in their pets.

It is not accident that one of the most commercially successful images of the faithful dog is the trademark on RCA Victor label: a little fox terrier with his head cocked, listening to a gramophone, with the motto "His Master's Voice." James Merrill's poem "The Victor Dog" takes that image as its point of departure. "The little white dog on the Victor label / Listens long and hard, as he is able."

Merrill's poem does not give the dog a name: "The Victor dog" for him is, rather, a quality of attention. But the "little white dog on the Victor label" has long been known to his legions of admirers and collectors as Nipper, a black-and-white fox terrier born, it is said, in Bristol, England, in 1884, and immortalized in a famous painting by his master, Francis Barraud, in 1899. Nipperie, as Nipper memorabilia is known, is now a major collectors' industry whose subjects range from Nipper paperweights (1900) and cigar cutters (1901) to Nipper lampshades (1924), mirrors, crockery, cufflinks, bookends, clocks, doll houses (1924), floor covering and curtain material (1935), postcards, shop signs, stained glass, salt-and-pepper sets, and Nipper statues small and large, including one on the roof of a building in Albany, almost twenty-six feet high.

A store exclusively dedicated to Nipper and Nipper brand products was opened on Oxford Street in London by Sir Edward Elgar in 1921. During World War I Nipper, patriotically transformed into an English bulldog, peered out from a gramophone trumpet to frighten away a spike-helmeted dachshund on a poster supporting the war effort. (A pun on "Victor"?) A pub in London's West End was renamed "The Dog and Trumpet" in his honor in 1973. And Nipper's bones, exhumed from his original burial site at Kingston-upon-Thames by EMI Records in the fifties, were reinterred in 1984 at 77 Clarence Street, Kingston, Surrey—now the site of a branch of Lloyds Bank.

Thus does the human business of communications technology honor the image of the perfect receiver.

They Know, but Do Not Tell

The human fascination with withheld knowledge has often led to the depiction of the dog as philosopher. In Franz Kafka's "Investigations of a Dog," Descartes's anthropocentrism is turned on its head. "When I reflect on it," meditates the narrator, "I see that dogdom is in every way a marvellous institution. Apart from us dogs there are all sorts of creatures in the world, wretched, limited, dumb creatures who have no language but mechanical cries; many of us dogs study them, have given them names, try to help them, educate them, uplift them, and so on."

Kafka's elegant parable presents the dog as philosopher, trying to explain the mysteries of dog culture. The first-personage protagonist, whose experiences are mystical as well as practical, ponders such puzzles as why, after diligently scratching and watering the ground, the dog finds that his food comes from above. "I began to enquire into the question: What the canine race nourished itself upon." He generates maxims about dog society that tacitly reflect upon the state of the human sciences: "Anyone who has food keeps it to himself; that is not selfishness, but the opposite, dog law"; "the mother weans her young ones from her teats and sends them out into the world: 'Water the ground as much as you can.' And in this sentence is not almost everything contained?" "All knowledge, the totality of all questions and all answers, is contained in the dog."

The investigator's persistent questioning produces a larger question, one "before which all smaller ones sink into insignificance": "How long will you be able to endure the fact that the world of dogs, as your researches make more and more evident, is pledged to silence and always will be?" And this question in turn elicits a meta-question, the philosophical touchstone of the investigator's argument, the problem of his own unique consciousness: the canine philosopher meditating upon canine philosophy. "Was I really so alone in my enquiries, at the beginning and up to now? Yes and no. It is inconceivable that there must not always have been and that there are not today individual dogs in the same case as myself. . . . Every dog has like me the impulse to question, and I have like every dog the impulse not to answer."

Another view of the consolations of canine philosophy is provided by Virginia Woolf's account of the mirror-gazing Flush, once again disconcerted by his own image. In this scene, Flush falls prey to the fleas of Italy, and Mr. Browning clips him:

> As Robert Browning snipped, as the insignia of a cocker spaniel fell to the floor, as the travesty of quite a different animal rose round his neck, Flush felt himself emasculated, diminished, ashamed. What am I now? he thought, gazing into the glass. And the glass replied with the brutal sincerity of glasses, "You are nothing." He was nobody. Certainly he was no longer a cocker spaniel. But as he gazed, his ears bald now, and uncurled, seemed to twitch. It was as if the potent spirits of truth and laughter were whispering in them. To be nothing—is that not, after all, the most satisfactory state in the whole world? . . . Anyhow, settle the matter as he might, there could be no doubt that he was free from fleas. He shook his ruff. He danced on his nude, attenuated legs. His spirits rose. So might a great beauty, rising from a bed of sickness and finding her face eternally disfigured, make a bonfire of clothes and cosmetics, and laugh with joy to think that she need never look in the glass again or dread a lover's coolness or a rival's beauty.

> . . . The true philosopher is he who has lost his coat but is free from fleas.

The brief invocation of a famous scene from Dickens's *Bleak House,* when Esther Summerson contracts smallpox and all the mirrors in her house are covered so that she will not see her own disfigurement, is highly typical of Woolf, as is the lightning-quick shift of tone from elegiac pathos to epigrammatic wit. Flush, vainglorious, ashamed, and reflective, becomes by turns a beautiful woman, a penurious male (human) philosopher—and a dog.

The connection between philosophy and loss is made parodically apparent in a poem entitled "Missing: A Dog's Doggerel," in the collection *Unleashed.* Meditating on his recent castration ("I'm somehow altered"), the dog narrator concludes,

> Perhaps they've made me human.
> It's how humans seem to me.
> Seeking, looking, searching
> For what can never be.

Whether what is missing is a coat (and its troublesome fleas) or the apparatus of canine masculinity, these doggy meditations, scripted by humans, equate the consciousness of loss with both humanity and philosophy. Do we flatter ourselves when we imagine that our dogs' inner lives center around us? Was Francis Bacon right to suggest that man was the dogs' God? Or is the orthographic inversion (dear to children learning to spell, as well as to witches casting spells) more to the point? In any case, however we may interpret them, dogs are ultimately ineffable: we hear them, they hear us, but is either one of us ever sure what the other understands? Blah, blah, Ginger. Bow-wow, Timmy. Yet we are somehow sure they know. As W. H. Auden wrote in his late poem "Talking to Dogs,"

> Being quicker to sense unhappiness
> without having to be told the dreary
>   details or who is to blame, in dark hours
> your silence may be of more help than many
>   two-legged comforters.

If the dog somehow stands for a human fantasy of communication, the nature of that fantasy is far from simple. Opaque and transparent, other and same, talking and mute, the dog stands in for the very complexity of human desire. Like the approval-conveying maternal face beaming at an infant, the dog offers us nonjudgmental recognition. Like the new baby, dogs offer us their needs and their bodies. With them we can innocently regress—we can babble, handle excrement, express affection. But we can also be master, dominate, require submission. The fantasy of the talking dog provides an object lesson in the pleasures and dangers of projection. "The fact was that they could not communicate with words," observes Virginia Woolf about Flush and Miss Barrett, "and it was a fact that led undoubtedly to much misunderstanding. Yet did it not also lead to a peculiar intimacy?" Precisely because our dogs cannot speak, we are able to hear—with uncanny and uncanine skill—what they have to say.

Unconditional Lovers

Drawing by Mort Gerberg; © 1991 The New Yorker Magazine, Inc.

Millie, the young Springer, is sitting beside me, head in my lap as I type, practicing the "spaniel gaze." At sixteen months she's already got it down. The spaniel heart is warm. The soft spaniel eye brims with love. If ever the world's diplomats and arms negotiators learn the spaniel gaze there will be peace on earth.

—Larry Shook, *The Puppy Report*

The eyes of a dog, the expression of a dog, the warmly wagging tail of a dog and the gloriously cold damp nose of a dog were in my opinion all God-given for one purpose only—to make complete fools of us human beings.

—Barbara Woodhouse, *No Bad Dogs*

"Love, genuine passionate love, was his for the first time. This he had never experienced. . . . love that was feverish and burning, that was adoration, that was madness, it had taken John Thornton to arouse." A come-hither excerpt from the back cover of a torrid work of gay fiction? No, this is Jack London's *Call of the Wild*. The "he" of the passage is London's dog hero, Buck, and John Thornton is his new master, the man who has saved his life in the Klondike.

The love between them is described in the most erotic, if innocent, of terms. Thornton "had a way of taking Buck's head roughly between his hands, and resting his own head upon Buck's, of shaking him back and forth, the while calling him ill names that to Buck were love names. Buck knew no greater joy than that rough embrace and the sound of murmured oaths, and at each jerk back and forth it seemed that his heart would be shaken out of his body so great was its ecstasy." When Buck is asked to win a bet for his master by pulling an impossibly heavy load, Thornton urges him on by whispering in his ear. "'As you love me, Buck. As you love me,'—was what he whispered. Buck whined with suppressed eagerness." And when—inevitably—the bet is won, the crowd recognizes the intimacy of the moment between man and dog, and "drew back to a respectful distance, nor were they again indiscreet enough to interrupt."

In London's *White Fang*, which traces the opposite path, a wild wolf-dog's transformation into domesticity, we find the same insistence on the word "love." White Fang, having first come to live with Grey Beaver the Indian and then been sold to the contemptible Beauty Smith, has been rescued by Weedon Scott. To White Fang all men, however cruel, are "gods," but it is only in his relationship to Scott that "*like* had been replaced by *love*."

> But White Fang was not demonstrative. . . . He had never barked in his life, and he could not now learn to bark a welcome when his god approached. He was never in the way, never extravagant nor foolish in the expression of his love. He never ran to meet his god. He waited at a distance; but he always waited, was always there. His love partook of the nature of worship, dumb, articulate, a silent adoration.

The "evolution of *like* into *love*"—a significant phrase for a novelist so often associated with Darwinism—is elaborated in a chapter called "The Love-Master." White Fang learns to "snuggle"; he "romps" with the master; unwolflike, he wags his tail. The term "love-master" is unself-consciously used for the remainder of the novel as the wolf-dog's chosen term for the man he loves. Despite, or rather because of, London's contention that he is not a "nature-faker" who anthropomorphizes his canine heroes, this emphasis on the transforming power of love is striking. To allegorize this as a tale about strictly human affairs is to lose much of its affective power.

White Fang's brief (and offstage) encounter with a female collie on Scott's California ranch makes him the father of puppies, who tumble about him in the novel's last scene, but there is no question about the place of "love" in his life—or in the book. Love—without quotation marks, though sometimes italicized for emphasis—is something a dog feels for a man.

And something a man or a woman feels for a dog. George Pitcher remembers the beloved English setter of his childhood: "I have a snapshot of Joe and me at the Jersey shore. It is 1937 and I am twelve years old: there I am in my bathing suit, grinning, Joe standing on his hind legs with his forepaws in my hands. The top of his beautiful black-and-white head just reaches my skinny chest. It is evident that we are mad about each other."

And here is the Czech Milan Kundera on the feeling that his character Tereza has for her dog, Karenin, a gift to Tereza from her chronically unfaithful husband-to-be, Tomas:

> The love that tied her to Karenin was better than the love between her and Tomas. Better, not bigger . . . given the nature of the human couple, the love of a man and woman is a priori inferior to that which can exist (at least in the best instances) in the love between man and dog.
>
> It is a completely selfless love: Tereza did not want anything of Karenin; she did not ever ask him to love her back. Nor had she asked herself the questions that plague human couples: Does he love me? Does he love anyone more than me? Does he love me more than I love him? . . .

And something else: Tereza accepted Karenin for what he was; she did not try to make him over in her image; she agreed from the outset with his dog's love, did not wish to deprive him of it, did not envy him his secret intrigues. . . .

Then too: No one forced her to love Karenin; love for dogs is voluntary.

We may notice that Kundera gives us the human's-eye view, where London's point of view is that of the dog. What is therefore remarkable is the fact that the unconditional completeness of love is expressed from *both* sides. The dog completely loves the man; the woman completely loves the dog. "The love between dog and man is idyllic," reflects Kundera's narrator, because "dogs were never expelled from Paradise."

"Love" is a term that is often used by children, and sometimes by adults, to describe their relationships with beloved pets. "I love dogs so much that I want to marry one," declared a five-year-old I encountered when I was walking my own dog. Her elders looked tactfully away, as if she had said something improper. (My own response was equally unacceptable, I'm afraid—all I could think was, "You can't have this one, he's *mine*.")

The fact is that we are as a society quite comfortable with *children* who say they "love" dogs. But when *adults* say they love their dogs— and we do all the time—an alarm bell can go off if their description of that "love" seems to embody too much of the romantic or even parental phrasing reserved for other humans. It's one thing for nuclear family units, where the dog completes the set. It's another— sometimes—when the dog occupies a central emotional place in a "nontraditional" family: a family of two (person and dog) or even of three (when the persons are a married couple with no children, or partners of the same gender). In the first case the human is sometimes said to be "compensating" for the absence of a spouse or partner. In the second the "compensation" is for the absence of a child. Dogs, it seems, must be substitutes or supplements. Only when the person or family doesn't seem to "need" the dog does it become unproblematic to say we "love" it.

The idea that the dog was a love substitute rather than a fit love object is at least as old as Plutarch, who tells a reproving anecdote:

Caesar once, seeing some wealthy strangers at Rome, carrying up and down with them in their arms and bosoms young puppy dogs and monkeys, embracing and making much of them, had occasion not unnaturally to ask whether the women in their country were not used to bear children; by that prince-like reprimand gravely reflecting upon persons who spend and lavish upon brute beasts that affection and kindness which nature has implanted in us to be bestowed on those of our own kind.

These ancient dog owners are like the women in P. D. James's futuristic novel *The Children of Men,* who wheel pet dogs or dolls in their baby carriages because no one any longer gives birth to human children. Notice that the pet-lovers are "strangers," outsiders to Rome; Caesar's "not unnatural" rebuke identifies human-family values to the Roman state. The zoologist James Serpell observes that "This view of pet-keeping as a 'gratuitous perversion' of natural behaviour has been reiterated time and again throughout history and, nowadays, it is most often expressed either by means of caricatures of postmenopausal women and poodles or by a general tendency to regard people's relationships with their animal companions as absurd, sentimental and somewhat pathetic. As the psychiatrist Aaron Katcher points out, 'we are taught to despise the sentimental, to think of it as banal or as a cover for darker hidden emotions.'"

Thus Konrad Lorenz warns against allowing love of animals to *replace* love of humans, calling such a preference "ethically dangerous" and a "moral danger." "The human being who, disappointed and embittered by human weakness, removes his love from mankind and bestows it on dogs and cats is committing a grave sin, a repulsive social perversion." This is the language of the official English translation of Lorenz's *Man Meets Dog,* dating from 1955. A more recent translation of the same sentence is less pussy-footing about the particular "perversion" intended: "Anyone who, disappointed and embittered by human failings, denies his love to mankind in order to transfer it to a dog or a cat, is definitely committing a grave sin, social sodomy so to speak, which is as disgusting as the sexual kind."

Lorenz, the Nobel Prize–winning ethologist often praised—as those who study animal behavior so often are—for his "warm humanity" and "deep sympathy for the human condition," has a decidedly limited view of the kind of humans that deserve this "deep sympathy."

He describes the overbreeding of dogs "like the Pekinese and the pug, with which childless women express their need for love and affection. It is, of course, a sad side effect that these poor dogs are also usually overfed and made neurotic." Like their owners, he (just) forbears to say.

Women with affectionate bonds to dogs are, much more often than men, treated by therapists and the media as compensating for some sort of absence in their lives. Thus former film star Brigitte Bardot, who heads a Paris-based animal-rights foundation, some years ago announced that she intended to be "no longer an image, a physique, a sex symbol, but a spokeswoman for animals." Yet this powerful and influential woman is twitted by some for choosing to love animals "because she had been so let down by men." Comic writer Cynthia Heimel spends hours trying to find homes for abandoned or abused dogs. Asked by an interviewer whether she would choose men or dogs if she could only have one or the other, Heimel replied, "No contest! I don't want to wipe out half the planet, but I think it's just a personal affinity I have. I always screw it up [with men], but I'm incredibly good with dogs. We're much more in tune. I have seven dogs. It's a slightly dysfunctional family."

Lorenz is willing to condescend, when necessary, to the truly emotionally needy: "Of course it is harmless and legitimate for a lonely person, who for some reason or other is deprived of social intercourse, to procure a dog to assuage an inward longing to love and be loved, for it is a fact that one no longer feels alone in the world when there is at least one being who is pleased at one's return home." As in the equally dismissive passage we have already noted in which he describes the small dogs "with which childless women express their need for love and affection," Lorenz here makes a clear if inexplicit divide between the emotionally healthy and the desperately compensating individual. He himself, of course, is part of the first group (indeed, perhaps, their pack leader), which allows him to prescribe remedies for the unfortunate souls in the second.

Yet the dog, it would seem, can occupy and reveal many dimensions in human emotional and sexual development. The "developmental fallacy" in our common descriptions of dog love, as a way station rather than an end point, devalues passions that are among the most strongly felt, and establishes without critique a "norm" of maturity and adulthood. Rather than thinking of these either as subordinate to some idealization of a purely human bond, or as sequential, as a succession of phases leading to the supposed attainment of a "maturity" that would leave them all behind, perhaps we can think of the dog as something that permits us to *keep* them all—to retain all these dimensions as an emotional and physical reservoir of fantasy and possibility.

Part of the problem of "loving" a pet is based on the human model invoked by the word "love." Do we love dogs the way we love erotic partners or spouses? Or do we rather love them the way we love children—or even, as some have implied, as masters "love" their servants or their slaves? Dr. Samuel Johnson remarked that love of dogs produced a (presumably satisfying) feeling of superiority and contempt. Do we "love" dogs not only because they "love" us, but because the power relation between a human being and an inferior loving subject is intrinsically pleasurable? Is caninophilia an erotics of dominance?

A point of view liberated, just for the moment, from conventional assumptions about "love," "sex," and the nature of desire might thus come around to seeing that the conundrum of "loving your dog" raises, for the human animal, some fascinating philosophical questions about what we mean by these frequently invoked terms. In *human* society, why should it be the case that love and sex are presumed to be part of the same relationship, attached to the same person? Men—and, much less frequently, women—go to prostitutes; men and women both, inside marriage and outside it, may "stray" or have casual (or meaningful) sexual relations with persons whom they do not love. Conversely, many people find that the person they love is no longer—if he or she ever was—the person they most desire. Does the dog shed any light on these human conundrums?

Man and Dog Together

George Pitcher and Ed Cone, two Princeton professors who share a house, adopted a stray female dog and one of her seven pups. Lupa and Remus became the emotional center of their lives, and the central figures in Pitcher's touching account, *The Dogs Who Came to Stay*. "The feelings that Ed and I had for Lupa were paradoxical," writes Pitcher.

> On the one hand, we loved her and cared for her as parents love
> and care for their child. But on the other hand, she was also, for

us, a mother figure. I'm not quite sure what that means, but I'm certain it's true. Part of what it means, I think, is this: we felt that as long as she was there, we were in some inexplicable way, if not exactly safe from harm, then at least watched over and generally speaking okay.

"One of the problems that had driven me to psychotherapy," Pitcher adds with the disarming frankness that marks the book throughout, "was a crippling inability to feel and express genuine affection or tenderness. Lupa cured me of that."

It took him a while to woo the stray's affection, since she had apparently been harshly treated on the streets. But when, after patiently leaving food for her and her puppies over time, Pitcher finally got her to wag her tail, "all my defenses were instantly swept away." He thought to himself, "I'm yours forever!" Remus, the male pup, also helped. When he put his front paws on Pitcher's knee, his master-to-be was flooded with "the knowledge that I had been chosen." And when Ed met the puppies, "he was as smitten by them as I was," Pitcher reports. Unsurprisingly, the book's jacket flap calls this "a true love story that gave a man back feelings he thought were lost to him forever and immeasurably enriched his life," noting also that the book "describes the joys of man and dog together."

Woman's Best Friend

Dogs and Their Women, a book of striking full-page photographs and text, was conceived as a way of telling "another side to the story," of focusing directly on the "emotional bond" and the "special relationship" between female dog lovers (of all ages) and the dogs that share their lives. One of the book's purposes is to refute the persistent belief solemnly intoned by a dog owner in A. R. Gurney's play *Sylvia*: "A man and his dog is a sacred relationship. What nature hath put together let no woman put asunder."

"Growing up in the fifties," note the authors, "we watched 'Rin Tin Tin' and 'Lassie' on television and *Old Yeller* at the movies, all of which depicted relationships between boys and dogs. And dogs have always been 'man's best friend.'" Convinced from their own experiences that "the combination of a dog's unconditional love and loyalty and a woman's nurturing invariably results in a deep emotional attachment," they set out to illustrate their belief that "women's unique bond with their dogs honors them as equals." The dog is not a Peter Pan–youthful *self* but a reliable *other.*

This is the unabashed language not only of love but of a certain era of feminism, and the mini-narratives the book has to tell are as various as the women and girls pictured within it. Dogs are partners, companions, sisters, caretakers, rescuers of their owners (Ursa the Newfoundland dives into the water to save a boat in high seas), rescuers of others (Bear, a search dog, travels around the world with Marcia Koenig to look for people lost in the wilderness). "In prison time is endless, yet with a dog to love, time has meaning," notes a woman prisoner. "Some people thought I was tough—but little Billy didn't, he knows my heart." The accompanying photograph is of a serious-looking woman in jeans and checked shirt, holding the leash of one of the smallest, solidest little dogs I've ever seen. Notice that the book's title insists that ownership, if it exists at all, is by dog of woman, not by woman of dog. "I don't consider the dogs as my pets," writes one contributor, pictured with her three beautiful animals. "It's more that we're all fortunate to be sharing one rocky road."

In a way *Dogs and Their Women* reflects three different strands of feminism: the "women's ways of knowing" school, which holds that women and girls do things differently from men, and that the problem is getting those different ways to be more valued; the culturalist school, which contends that supposed gender differences in aptitude and behavior are actually the result of historical differences in social treatment and educational opportunity, so that men and women are intrinsically more alike than different; and the "fish without a bicycle" school, which suggests that it is condescending to talk of women *needing* men to complete or fulfill their lives: a woman without a man will do just fine, thank you, whether she is on her own, with another woman, or in a women's community. The dogs in *Dogs and Their Women* are matched with independent-minded women who live interesting lives, some with men, some with women, some with canine but not human partners. What they all have in common is "love."

Paula Bennett writes of her dog, Topper, that when she was thirteen and a half and "desperately unhappy" "he was the only thing I loved. And just as important, he was the only thing that loved me." Jo Giese reports that she "replaced a six-foot Swedish husband with a five-pound dog," a Yorkshire terrier named Framboise. At Christie Fajkowski's wedding in the woods, her dog, Oboe, was "maid of honor, flower girl, best man, and the one who gave me away" ("All this—just for a chance to kiss the bride!"). Jeri Wagner, posing with Sasha, quips, "People tell us we look more like sisters than like mother and daughter." Jane Kelley displays a photo (taken with her terrier, Busby) from her campaign for town clerk in Hampton, New Hampshire. "I was going to have him fixed," she confides, "but discovered a perfect heart-shaped freckle on his weenie. I felt it was a sign that he is a lover and decided to leave him alone." Jokey and serious, eloquent and epigrammatic, these stories, some just a sentence long ("Never lonely," reads one caption for a picture of a woman and two black Labs seated on a pier and gazing out to sea) are all moving, in their own ways.

Human, All Too Human

If dog "love" sometimes verges toward, or even into, what might be called petophilia, such occasions are very much the exception. Far more often it is the dog who represents the "pure" and unambivalent relationship *in contradistinction to* human-all-too-human narratives of erotic complexity and ambivalence.

Novelist and short-story writer John Cheever, whose journals provide a fascinating record of his lushly transgressive bisexual *human* affections, pays what is perhaps the most wholehearted homage in his pages to one of the Cheever family dogs, a black Labrador named Cassiopeia and known as Cassie, whom he describes succinctly as "the old dog; my love."

"The introduction of love in our relationship," he writes, "came that day at Welton Falls. The stream was swollen and knocked her off her feet, and rolled her down a little falls into a pool. Then, when we returned, I hoisted her up in my arms and carried her over while she lapped my face . . . with this her feelings toward me seemed to deepen." He describes "her role as a confidant during some quarrelsome months," when he, his wife, and his daughter each "would take her into the woods and pour into her ears . . . complaints."

Cassie appears to have been a typical "Cheever story" character. Her master offers the following unforgettable portrait:

That she enjoyed men very much and was conspicuously indifferent to women. That her dislikes were marked and she definitely preferred people from traditional and, if possible, wealthy origins. That she had begun to resemble those imperious and somehow mannish women who devilled my youth: the dancing teacher, the banker's wife, the headmistress of the progressive school I attended. There was a genre of imperious women in the twenties whose hell-for-leather manner made them seem slightly mannish. They were sometimes beautiful, but their airs were predatory and their voices were sometimes quite guttural.

"When I was alone and heard her wandering through the house," he says, "my feelings for her were of love and gratitude; her heavy step put me to sleep."

I Love a Lassie

The last Cheever dog was a golden retriever bitch unexpectedly called Edgar (she was originally named Tara, but Cheever thought this an unsuitable name for a dog). The novelist tended to refer to Edgar as "him," as his daughter reports, "altering the pronoun to go with her new name."

As we have seen, the female dog in Kundera's *The Unbearable Lightness of Being* likewise has a male name, Karenin, and is always described with a male pronoun, even when "his" menstrual cycle is under discussion. This cross-naming is not, presumably, a result of the Tom / Tomasina problem ("I thought it was a male, but she's having kittens") legendarily encountered with cats. Male and female puppies are clearly distinguishable at birth (though Millie, Barbara Bush's springer spaniel, seemed to think Mrs. Bush couldn't tell them apart). If there's a reason, it's probably that human love for dogs is bisexual—that dogs occupy an emotional place that is not determined by sex, or gender.

Lassie herself, of course, has always been played by a male dog, a fact noted by Homer Dickens, author of a book on drag in the movies, when he dedicated the volume to "Pal and his male descendants, who successfully impersonated Lassie to a generation of moviegoers." The cross-casting of Lassie has been variously explained as a necessary fact: female collies shed when they go into heat, and so are less reliably beautiful; Lassie would look more heroic if she (i.e., he) were bigger, so the greater size of the male is an advantage; the original casting call produced a more charismatic male than the females who tried out for the part. On one TV show Lassie gave birth ("quite a trick for a male dog"); sponsor Campbell's Soup instigated a contest to name the pups, who were then given to the winners. (In another piece of cross-gender Lassie trivia, the name "Timmy" was chosen for Lassie's boon boy companion because it was the name of show owner [and former child actress] Bonita Granville's *mother*.) Fellow movie star "Benji" was a bitch, whose gender-crossing was outed by a disappointed White House Millie, hoping for romance: after a day of eager expectation, she says, "I discovered the awful truth, Benji turned out to be an aging [twelve-year-old] female."

Transitional Objects

In choosing human partners, we tend to regard a beloved person's gender as part of the reason we fall in love with him or her. We are attracted to men or women (or both). With children, there is (at least in theory) no such gender barrier. We have terms of endearment, languages of love both for boy children and for girl children, and to a certain extent those terms are carried over into our affectionate relations with dogs. But the dog occupies an emotional territory which is not quite that of the child, nor yet that of the (human) lover.

"Human beings fall for other human beings," Midas Dekkers observes. "And if they occasionally fall for an animal, they are attracted by the animal's human features. What attracts the dog lover is not the doggishness of a dog . . . but its human qualities—faithfulness, gratitude, patience in waiting for its master." That these "human qualities" are seldom found in humans may in part account for the overdetermined nature of the love expressed for the pet. "No human being has such an entreating expression as a basset hound, no human being is as loyal as his dog."

If the imaginary space of sexual and emotional fantasy has its origin in that most fundamental of infantile experiences, the love of a transitional object, could the versatility of the dog arise from its similarity to the beloved blanket, teddy bear, or doll?

Among the various dolls and teddies belonging to a child, there
may be one particular, probably soft, object that was introduced
to the infant at about ten, eleven, or twelve months, which the infant treats in a most brutal as well as a most loving manner, and
without which the infant could not conceive of going to bed; this
thing would certainly not have to be left behind if the child had
to go away; and if it were lost it would be a disaster for the child
and therefore for those caring for him or her. It is unlikely that
such an object would ever be given away to another child, and in
any case no other child would want it; eventually it becomes
smelly and filthy and yet one dare not wash it.

This is psychiatrist D. W. Winnicott's definition of what he calls a
transitional object, the first "not-me" possession, linking the "perceived world" to the "self-created world." The first such object, perhaps, was the mother's breast; another common example is the baby's
blanket. What Winnicott catalogues as transitional phenomena—"the
use of toys, of auto-erotic activities, of bedtime stories and nursery
rhymes"—are part of the child's mechanism for adjustment. "The best
that can happen for any one of us," he wrote, "is that there shall have
been sufficient overlap of external reality and what we can create. We
accept the idea of an identity between the two as an illusion." These
clinical observations, intended to help emotionally deprived children
to attain the state of self-sufficiency Winnicott perceived in healthy
children, are extremely suggestive. They try to account for a crucial
imaginative and emotional space which is neither wholly self nor
wholly other, a space in which every individual learns to love.

Into this transitional arena comes the dog, fantasy companion, link
between self and other, erotic trigger: soft, alternately loved and bru-
talized, becoming, eventually, smelly and filthy, an ordinary object
which is, by reason of the significance attached to it, absolutely necessary and unique. The word "puppy" itself comes from French *poupée*,
doll, and in the history of dog breeding many types of dogs have been
produced to resemble puppies their whole lives.

It is no accident that an entire class of dogs is called toys. As Roger
Caras observes, "These are the knickknacks of the dog world. Some,
like the Italian greyhound, the Pomeranian and the toy Manchester terrier, have been reduced in size to be toy companions, while others
evolved that way from early toy stock. These are really working dogs,

but their work is to please, amuse, help their owners battle loneliness. Their task is to be needed and they virtually always are needed wherever they are found."

"The toys," notes dog expert Caras, "are stunning little dogs that exhibit one of the domestic dog's most endearing charms: they never grow up. They remain tiny children for as long as they live and that gives purpose to the lives of the people who own them. To laugh at a toy is to laugh at human emotional needs. These are among the most skilled therapists in dogdom."

The Love of His Life

No less a specialist in *human* sexual behavior then Alfred Kinsey was said to have believed "that a man might fall passionately in love with his dog, and that the affection could be returned in kind." Consider now this description of a relationship that flourished in the 1940s and 1950s, just when Kinsey was issuing his *Reports.*

> I don't believe there was anything special about her, except that she was rather a beauty. In this context it is not she herself but her effect upon me that I find interesting. She offered me what I had never found in my sexual life, constant, single-hearted, incorruptible, uncritical devotion. . . . She placed herself entirely under my control. From the moment she established herself in my heart and home, my obsession with sex fell wholly away from me, my single desire was to get back to her, to her waiting love and unstaling welcome. . . . I sang with joy at the thought of seeing her. I never prowled the London streets again, nor had the slightest inclination to do so. On the contrary, whenever I thought of it, I was positively thankful to be rid of it all, the anxieties, the frustrations, the wastage of time and spirit. It was as though I had never wanted sex at all, and that this extraordinary long journey of mine which had seemed a pursuit of it had really been an attempt to escape from it. I was just under fifty when this animal came into my hands, and the fifteen years she lived with me were the happiest of my life.

The voice here is that of the brilliant novelist and writer J. R. Ackerley, and the beloved he writes about so feelingly is his Alsatian dog,

Queenie, also known to his readers as the title character in Ackerley's *My Dog Tulip* and as Evie, the desirable (and well-named) bone of contention in the novel *We Think the World of You.*

"Seldom has a loved animal—seldom has any lover—been so completely rendered in literature," wrote Felice Picano of *My Dog Tulip.* Ackerley's own quest for the elusive Ideal Friend, "the One, the Charmer, the Long Sought-For & Never Found Perfect Friend to Be, instantly recognizable, instantly responsive, the Destined Mate," whom he imagined as a heterosexual working-class man, thus culminated in his relationship with a female dog. More than one longtime associate evinced consternation that Ackerley had wound up, as he says, not with a boy but with a bitch.

Given the evident strength of his passion, and the sexual adventurousness of his early life, it is perhaps not surprising that Ackerley's friends were curious about the specific nature of his relationship to Queenie, a dog E. M. Forster coolly described as "that unnecessary bitch."

> One of my friends, puzzled by the sudden change in my ways, asked me whether I had had sexual intercourse with her. It may be counted as something on the profit side of my life that I could now receive such a question intelligently. I said no. In truth, her love and beauty when I kissed her, as I often did, sometimes stirred me physically; but although I had to cope with her own sexual life and the frustrations I imposed upon it for some years, the thought of attempting to console her myself, even with my finger, never seriously entered my head. What little I did for her in her burning heats—slightly more than I admitted in *My Dog Tulip*—worried me in my ignorance of animal psychology, in case, by gratifying her clear desires, which were all addressed to me, I might excite and upset her more than she was already excited and upset.

Ackerley, like Konrad Lorenz and Elizabeth Marshall Thomas, writes of seeking a "husband" for his beloved Alsatian bitch, and of supervising her various attempts at "marriage." In his tone, however, we hear not the idealization of a human institution but a commentary on its folly. Tulip's first suitor, Max, had "never been married before," and when Tulip is brought for a "formal introduction to her betrothed," the mutual inexperience of the pair proves disastrous.

Then the recently married owner of a male dog confides to Ackerley that he has been wondering if his dog "mightn't settle down better if I found *him* a wife, too." But this courtship is likewise doomed to failure, as is the suit of the aristocrat Mountjoy, whose owner, Mrs. Tudor-Smith, was "frightfully keen on the marriage," but who turns out to have a physiological problem that impedes the sexual act. "Mountjoy's owners . . . , who had never offered him a wife before, were totally ignorant" of this fact, Ackerley notes with some quiet pleasure.

In any case, Tulip clearly prefers her master: "When she had me back to herself, [she was] in her most disarming mood, and as soon as we were home she attempted to bestow upon my leg and my overcoat all the love that the pusillanimous Max had been denied." And as for Ackerley: "I felt, indeed, extremely sympathetic toward Tulip's courtiers," he confides. "(I would have been after the pretty creature myself, I thought, if I had been a dog.)"

When a young female veterinarian diagnoses the cause of Tulip's chronic misbehavior in the doctor's office she speaks of self-evident truth that nonetheless comes as a surprise to both master and reader:

> "Tulip's a good girl, I saw that at once. You're the trouble."
> I sat down.
> "Do tell me," I said.
> "Well, she's in love with you, that's obvious. And so life's full of worries for her. She has to protect you to begin with; that's why she's upset when people approach you: I expect she's a bit jealous, too."

In Ackerley's novel *We Think the World of You* the dog, Evie, is the central figure in not one but two erotic triangles, and the risible as well as poignant triangulation that inevitably developed among Ackerley and his human and animal dependents is exemplified in a note left by his sister Nancy at the time of her (apparent) attempted suicide. "She seems to have been jealous of your wife as well as your aunt," a police constable told Ackerley. He explained that he was not married, and the constable persisted: "Well, another woman is mentioned. Someone called Queenie."

The novelist Rosamond Lehmann said of *My Dog Tulip* that it was "the only 'dog book'" she knew "to record a human-animal love in terms of *absolute equality* between the protagonists." "It is necessary to add that she is beautiful," Ackerley says of Tulip in the early pages of that book. Affectionately recording some of Tulip's foibles, he remarks without emphasis that "the events I have related took place many years ago when she was young and a shade irresponsible, and our love was new."

"Love" is the word invariably used by both Ackerley and his friends to describe his and Queenie's relationship. Indeed, part of Forster's discomfort was his conviction, shared by a large proportion of the post-Freudian population, that "people love animals because of sex-repression." The spectacle of an adult person, male or female, whose chief emotional ties are with a pet animal tends to elicit from many observers responses ranging from pity to condescension. The frequently heard "substitution" theory, the idea that love for a dog (or other pet) is a sign of failure rather than success in emotional or erotic relations, is often linked to a kind of pity or contempt, and is directed, more often than not, toward women and gay men.

But Ackerley almost suggests that, on the contrary, sex with men was a substitute for or a forerunner of love for a dog. The point is perhaps not to argue about whether dog love is a substitute for human love, but rather to detach the notion of "substitute" from its presumed inferiority to a "real thing." Don't all loves function, in a sense, within a chain of substitutions? For Freud, the original object is the parent, and all nonincestuous loves are then substitutes for the love that has become taboo. For Winnicott, as we have seen, the first "not-me" object can be a thumb, a blanket, a teddy bear, or a nursery rhyme. We learn to love by loving, and it is a long, indeed, in interminable process. To distinguish between primary and substitutive loves is to understand little about the complexity of human emotions.

The Freudian Dog

Lorenz's condescending dismissiveness and Forster's notion of "sex-repression" are part of a simplified Freudian interpretation of developmental stages. In Freud's own life and family, however, the questions of dog love was more complex and far more interesting.

"A lot of rubbish has been spoken about the psychoanalyzing of dogs in the modern world," declares "walkies" "dog lady" Barbara Woodhouse in her book *No Bad Dogs*. But the relationship between dogs and psychoanalysis is a long, honored, and indeed foundational one.

Wolf, a black Alsatian, was Freud's gift to his daughter Anna in 1925, the same year that his student Jeanne de Groot, a Dutch psycho-analytic trainee, became engaged to Hans Lampl, a suitor Anna (and her father) had rejected. "Lampl got his Jeanne and Anna got her Wolf," joked a gossip columnist for a Vienna newspaper. The equation was not unjust.

Freud, Anna Freud, and Lampl had once formed an uneasy triangle in which the suitor Lampl eventually dropped out (Anna wrote to her father after the end of the romance "to confirm our judgment of him from last year and to rejoice that we judged correctly"). Was Wolf a Lampl substitute? Or was he that which enabled Anna Freud not to leave her father? The two Freuds, Sigmund and Anna, began to develop a dog family of their own. (That the first dog was called Wolf has, in view of Freud's writings on the "Wolf Man," a certain satisfying crossover dimension between animal and human.)

In 1927 Freud was presented with a chow, Lun Yug, by Anna's friend Dorothy Burlingham. This first chow died in an accident some fifteen months later, and was shortly replaced by another, the beloved Jo Fi (also spelled Jo-Fi and Yofie) A succession of chows became in his later years his closest companions.

As Freud aged, as his children married and left home, and as he suffered a series of family bereavements (his precious daughter Sophie; his beloved grandson Heinerle, Sophie's younger son) the dogs began to occupy more of his time and attention. "Wolf . . . has almost replaced the lost Heinerle," he wrote to Jeanne Lampl–de Groot. But as soon became clear, it was as much a matter of transference as of substitution.

In an essay on transference love, written long before he actually had a dog, Freud described the restraint necessary for the analyst in terms of an analogy.

> For the doctor, ethical motives unite with the technical ones to restrain him from giving the patient his love. . . . He must not stage the scene of a dog-race in which the prize was to be a garland of sausages but which some humorist spoilt by throwing a single sausage on to the track. The result was, of course, that the dogs threw themselves upon it and forgot all about the race and about the garland that was luring them to victory in the far distance.

Freud's analogy, which restages the story of Atalanta (the tale of how a fleet-footed woman lost a race and became a wife), also recalls a letter he wrote to Sandor Ferenczi cautioning him against kissing and having sex with his patients, a practice Freud describes as part of Ferenczi's analytic "technique." Here is Ernest Jones's translation of Freud's letter:

> A number of independent thinkers in matters of technique will say to themselves: why stop at a kiss? Certainly one gets further when one adopts "pawing" as well, which after all doesn't make a baby . . . and soon we shall have accepted in the technique of analysis the whole repertoire of . . . petting parties, resulting in an enormous increase of interest in psychoanalysis among both analysts and patients.

"You have compelled me to be quite blunt," he concluded—an instance of Freud calling a dog a dog.

For Freud, the household dogs offered a new and gratifying preoccupation at a time when he was becoming increasingly impatient with the competitiveness and perceived disloyalties of his human disciples. "What Freud prized in his dogs," Anna observed, "was their grace, their devotion and loyalty; what he often commented—as a marked advantage in comparison to people—was the absence of any ambivalence. 'Dogs,' as he used to say, 'love their friends and bite their enemies, quite unlike people who are incapable of pure love and always have to mix love and hate in their object relations.'"

On his birthday, May 6, the dogs—assisted by Anna and others in the household—presented him with gifts, and decked themselves in bows and ribbons for the occasion. (This scenario is captured in some Freud family home movies, in which the dogs appear with poems tied around their necks. In these films Anna Freud is clearly more interested in the dogs and their gifts than in the human members of the psychoanalytic community gathered to place tributary bones at the master's feet.)

But the dog was not merely an ornament; she was a part of the process (the "petting cure"?). "The dog would sit quietly at the foot of the couch during the analytic hour," writes Freud biographer Peter Gay. How quietly she sat, however, is a matter of some small dispute. Anna Freud says that "Yo-Fie . . . patiently participated in all analytic hours," but Freud's son Martin suggested that Yofi helped Freud determine when a session was up by unfailingly beginning to stir at the end of the hour. And the poet H.D., who was in analysis with Freud, recalled that "I was annoyed at the end of my session as Yofi would wander about and I felt that the Professor was more interested in Yofi than he was in my story."

When Yofi became pregnant, "the Professor" remarked that if there were two puppies, one would go to the owners of the sire, "but if only one, 'it stays a Freud.'" So in a way Freud himself was the real father of the imagined chow pups. He had at one time promised a puppy to H.D.'s lover, Bryher, whose nickname was Fido, but only a single puppy survived of that litter and Freud, as promised, kept him. Perhaps H.D. was right in her suspicion that his interest in Yofi competed with his interest in her.

Freud distinguished the "narcissistic" personality (preoccupied with self) from the "anaclitic" (preoccupied with others—from a Greek word meaning "to lean on," an attribute that many dog owners will recognize as appealingly characteristic of their own pets). A Freudian chart may prove illuminating for our assessment of the roles assigned in human culture to person and dog. "A person," says Freud, may love:

(1) According to the narcissistic type:
    (a) what he himself is (i.e., himself),
    (b) what he himself was,
    (c) what he himself would like to be,
    (d) someone who was once part of himself.
(2) According to the anaclitic (attachment) type:
    (a) the woman who feeds him,
    (b) the man who protects him,
        and the succession of substitutes who take their place.

Notoriously, Freud associated the narcissistic personality with women, criminals, and cats. A glance at the attributes of the anaclitic type, given to loving the feeder and protector, will suggest a possible role for the dog. This is not to say that no dog can be a narcissist—many, perhaps most, at least occasionally are. (Flush, as we saw, spent hours in front of the mirror. Dog shows are prime exhibit spaces for extroverted, crowd-pleasing performers. And my dogs certainly love a compliment.) In fact these "types," like gender roles and other identifications in

Freud, are best understood as positions within a structure rather than as immutable social or psychological roles. Anyone—person, dog, or cat—can love, and be loved, "narcissistically" *and* "anaclitically"; it is not a matter of either-or, but of relationship. Nevertheless, the notion of the dog as other-directed, capable of "complete object-love of the attachment type," is highly recognizable to anyone who reads dog books or knows dog owners. This is what we describe, often with so much wistfulness and yearning, as the dog's capacity for "unconditional love."

Sex and the Single Dog

"Surely you didn't think you were the first?"
Courtesy of Michelle M. Barbera. Cartoon first seen in *Dog Fancy*

I am not a dog-lover. To me, a dog-lover is a dog who is in love with
another dog.

—James Thurber

What happened between Bowser and me is over and done with. It
was just a fling, Greg. Just a dumb, silly fling.

—A. R. Gurney, *Sylvia*

Walking the Dog

The association of dogs with human sexual immorality has a long
history.

Four hundred years ago the Puritan John Rainolds, in his
The Overthrow of Stage-Playes (1599), argued that one reason the theaters should be closed was that they fostered transvestism, immorality,
and same-sex desire, making men into "dogs." Citing as his authority

Deuteronomy 23:17–18 ("There shall be no whore of the daughters of Israel, nor a sodomite of the sons of Israel. Thou shalt not bring the hire of a whore, or the price of a dog, into the house of the Lord") Rainolds insisted that "hee, who condemneth the female hoore and male, and, detesting speciallie the male by terming him a *dogge*, . . . might well controll likewise the meanes and occasions whereby men are transformed into dogges." As Sigmund Freud, whom we have already seen to be a dog lover, observes, "It would be incomprehensible . . . that man should use the name of his most faithful friend in the animal world—the dog—as a term of abuse if that creature had not incurred his contempt through two characteristics: that it is an animal whose dominant sense is that of smell and one which has no horror of excrement, and that it is not ashamed of its sexual functions." Despite these animadversions, however, both the imagined fact of human/animal sexual encounters and the actual fact of such encounters have been part of human culture and language, West and East, high and low, for hundreds of years.

One of the many slang meanings of the word "dog"—besides (for example) a pistol, a promissory note, a slow horse, the moon, or a venereal disease—is the male sexual organ. The sly innuendo of Rufus Thomas's rhythm-and-blues song "Walking the Dog" (a slang term for sex) was underscored in the Rolling Stones' 1964 rendition with the help of suggestive dog-call whistles and the reiteration of the bouncy refrain "If you don't know how to do it, I'll show you how to walk the dog." Another blues song invites the addressee to "Play with Your Poodle." In the seventeenth century "dog" could mean penis, testicle (= dogstone), dildo, or even "The *Womans Privity*," and "to dog" could mean "to copulate on all fours."

Capitalizing on the double meanings of many canine-related terms, a recent book entitled *How to Make Your Man Behave in 21 Days or Less, Using the Secrets of Professional Dog Trainers* offers advice (complete with illustrations depicting human males) to women who are looking for a man ("Do not lose the leash until you're completely confident of your established bond," "Always say *no* clearly," "Does size matter?" and "One of the dog's favorite games is: where can I hide my big bone?")

Ancient literature not infrequently mentioned sexual congress between humans and dogs. The third-century Roman author Aelian reported that "hounds are said to have assaulted women, and indeed it is reported that a woman in Rome was accused by her husband of adultery, and the adulterer in the case was stated to be a hound") and "such testimony in the ancient writers," one commentator reports, "boosted similar tales during the Renaissance." Such as the episode in the late sixteenth century when "A Damsel of *Tuscany* . . . caused her self to be covered by a Dog." A piece of Royalist propaganda concerning sexual relations between a dog and an elder's maid," in this case an "abominable Mastive," was an item of gossip still being retailed by John Dryden in 1682.

Spaniels, already celebrated for their servility ("I am your spaniel . . . use me but as your spaniel," says Helena to Demetrius in *A Midsummer Night's Dream;* Julius Caesar speaks of "base spaniel fawning," and the ironic Petruchio of *The Taming of the Shrew* names his spaniel Troilus because of the breed's legendary uncritical attachment to love objects) were also singled out as sex toys; in the late eighteenth century brothel visitors were said to come to a house of pleasure "just to kiss the *part* where *pleasure* lies, Like *spaniels lick the centre* of all joys." The most frequently described canine sexual partners, however, were not mastiffs but lapdogs, whose name described not only their privileged place, but sometimes their imagined function.

As usual, our modern age, which prides itself on its sexual frankness, turns out to be much more inhibited than some earlier centuries. Sir Philip Sidney's famous sonnet sequence, *Astrophel and Stella* (1581–1583), contains an entire sonnet (Number 59) describing the poet's sexual envy for his lady's dog because of its place in her lap, and Thomas Lodge's *A Fig for Momus* (1595) makes the same observation. Edward Ward's "Panegyrick upon my Lady *Fizzleton's* Lap-Dog" of 1709 notes that the lady "Kindly rewards the little Four-legg'd Beau, / For secret Service he performs below," and Robert Gould's 1682 satire on women, *Love Given O're*, links lapdogs and dildos as providers of women's pleasure in their private apartments: "Where flaming Dil———s doe inflame desire, / And gentle Lapd———s feed the am'rous fire: Lap-d———s! to whom they are more kind and free, / Than they themselves to their own Husbands be."

The altar of the goddess Dildona in Samuel Cock's *Voyage to Lethe* of 1756, is adorned with "the Branches of the *Dildo* tree . . . and with the Tongues of Lap-dogs." It should not escape our attention that a lot of these poetic fantasies are male fantasies about the insatiable sexuality (and sexual duplicity) of women. But the "dog days" of summer, when—according to folk wisdom—the heat of the Dog Star, Sirius, was added to that of the sun, were thought to inflame sexual desire in both women and men.

In late-nineteenth-century Paris, certain *maisons de tolérance* specialized in exhibitions of women having sexual intercourse with dogs. For these French cathouses, the Great Dane—a fashionable society dog—and the Newfoundland—which abounded in the suburbs—were the preferred canine performers. Police reports confirmed the existence of dogs specially trained to take these roles. Nor is this a sexual fantasy confined to the historical past. Dogs have had a long history of bit parts (bite parts?) in pornography. American porn star Linda Lovelace describes the film *A Dog Loop* in her autobiography, *Ordeal,* and French actress Sylvia Bourdon offers a chapter called "Une Vie de Chien" in *L'Amour est une Fête.*

"The dog's penis was smaller than a man's, and the actual fucking was over almost before it began, but the sensation was unimaginably erotic—no, not erotic, pornographic," confesses the narrator of Laura Reese's 1995 erotic thriller, *Topping from Below,* describing a sexual encounter with a Great Dane name Rameau. Rameau is named for the lazy, sensual social parasite in Diderot's character sketch *Le Neveu de Rameau* ("Rameau's Nephew"), a work invariably described as a "biting satire" on contemporary society.

In today's comparatively repressed and workaholic world, when the laptop has replaced the lapdog as the favorite portable object for many women and men (and a computer program called Golden Retriever fetches data for Mac users on command) it is perhaps worth noting that the lapdog, now described as a "minidog," has been making a comeback among the rich and famous. *People* magazine reports that for celebrities "minidogs" like the Chihuahua, the Maltese, and the Yorkshire terrier have become "Man's Best Accessory," and woman's, too. Portable pups in prominent places have been carried aboard Greek yachts, hot-air balloons, and the Concorde by media stars from Joan Rivers (Yorkie Spike) to Debi Mazur (toy poodle Dolores) to Madonna (Chihuahua Chiquita). As pop culture analyst Faith Popcorn, the owner of a tiny Japanese chin, explained, "It's lonely at the top." The dogs "don't know how famous you are. They truly love you."

So eighteenth- and nineteenth-century sex fantasies about the dog have turned to twentieth-century love fantasies about the dog. And what else is new? Love seems a lot harder to come by, and hold onto, these days, than sex.

Love, Doggy Style

"We are not made for each other," remarks bestiality expert Midas Dekkers. "A woman who actually mates with her dog is in for a surprise: she may be unable to detach herself from the dog." Dekkers adds that "the greatest danger to the woman arises if there is any panic as they are uncoupling." Literary corroboration for this fact, should any be needed, is provided by the Marquis de Sade's *Juliette*, where a "very big mastiff" named Lucifer who had mounted the heroine attempts to withdraw, causing the adventurous Juliette considerable pain in the aftermath of her pleasure.

Perhaps for this reason—though morality, taboo, and practicality are also involved—most human-dog sexual encounters, like those human-animal couplings elevated to the status of mythology by the ancient Greeks, remain on the level of fantasy. Madonna cavorts with a delightedly wriggling dog in the pages of her picture book *Sex*. And one of Nancy Friday's subjects in *My Secret Garden*, recalling a time when, at the age of fifteen, she wandered downstairs for breakfast in an empty house completely naked, had an encounter with the family dog:

> He started to nuzzle up and sniff me (he was only a young dog, not very well trained and a bit stupid). I suddenly realized the dog had this huge hard-on, and he kept trying to climb up me. I think I was fascinated and I kept stroking him. Half of me wanted to let him—let him do what? At that age I didn't really know what he'd do—and the other half was ashamed. But God, it was a strong impulse, to close my eyes and let his nose go where it would. I have always wondered what it would have been like if I hadn't got on with my breakfast.

Nor is this woman the only one Friday interviewed who fantasized about a canine partner. Several other respondents contribute their own inventive scenarios. As Friday remarks, "dogs bring a very important, blameless quality to fantasy: it's never your fault, or the dog's either, really." Furthermore, she adds, "Rover is a more perfect gentleman than most: he'll never look surprised at something you may ask him to do, never make you feel ashamed, and will never, never talk. Is it surprising then that of all animals, dogs star most frequently in female sexual fantasies?"

Midas Dekkers's point of view is that of an empathetic enthusiast. "A dog regards all the members of the household as fellow dogs," he observes.

> It is a pleasant duty for a male dog to service the members of his household from time to time, certainly if he has no access to a bitch in heat. On these occasions something pinkish flops out of the abdomen and is rubbed against one's legs, or with the impertinence native to dogs, against the legs of your visitors, which are firmly gripped by the dog's front paws. Giggling politely or otherwise ignoring it is fairly pointless, punishment only increases the animal's frustration, and dog lovers maintain that politely rejecting the animal's advances is a more appropriate response. Unless one really enjoys them, that is. With some adjustment it is not difficult to exchange the leg for a more appropriate part of the body and actual mating can ensue. Mostly, however, things do not reach this stage and the dog is most commonly used for cunnilingus. Dogs have an ideal tongue for the purpose, and can be taught it, like so many other tricks. As a reward something edible can be applied to the appropriate spots, or the dog can be masturbated as a return favor. Every dog is a potential lapdog.

Whatever one's view of this aspect of the human-dog bond, Dekkers's invocation of the Emperor's-new-clothes-syndrome seems apt. "In spite of the dangling penises and the cries of females in heat, the eroticism of our dogs and cats is completely ignored. With these darlings we adopt the role not of lover, but of master or mistress." For example, he says, picture a "respectable lady taking her dog, a Great Dane, for a walk. We are so familiar with it that it no longer strikes us as odd that what we are actually looking at is a woman walking along with the huge prick on a lead." This is a formulation clearly and mischievously intended to provoke. Perhaps we should rather congratulate ourselves on the fact that we do not notice dog nakedness as nakedness (a Great Dane, with a flat coat, is much more "naked" in this sense than a Newfoundland or a Great Pyrenees). After all, the fashion for dog cover-up clothing, like the "clothing" worn by cartoon animals, covers virtually everything *except* the area of the sex organs. (Daisy and Donald Duck wear upper-body costumes, and are "naked" without them, but their lower bodies are bare.) Contrast this with familiar Renaissance depictions of Adam and Eve after the fall, where "nakedness" clearly involves a recognition of the private or taboo nature of the genitals. A friend of mine offers a provocative counterexample, however. The owner of a large, handsome, shaggy dog, she finds that whenever he slips out of his collar or has it removed to be groomed she has a vivid sense of him as being "undressed"—a sensation she admits to finding sexy.

Yet if canine nakedness goes unnoticed by passing humans, what might human nakedness be to a dog? Consider the use of the dog to bare the human bottom in the ads for Coppertone suntanning lotion. In a book called *Child-Loving*, James Kincaid has discussed the erotic appeal of the *child* to the adult viewer, but he relegates the dog to a footnote, from which any suggestion of bestiality is rigorously absent:

> For pure erotic longevity, nothing has been able to top the blond child in the Coppertone ad, the one whose pants are being yanked down from behind* so as to expose a chubby bottom fully and who reacts to the exposure with a becoming blush and with no attempt whatever to cover herself.
>
> *By a dog, to be sure, a cute little puppy. That makes it all very "innocent," conveniently so; we are invited to look our fill, without risking anything messy, like arrest.

While *Child-Loving* deftly identifies signs of pedophilia in the Victorian age and in our own, it seems not to occur to Kincaid that a dog (a puppy!) could be anything but innocent. Two recent parodies of those ads have replaced the "innocent" girl with a far-from-innocent grown man: first rap singer and Calvin Klein model Marky Mark (known for his underwear ads) and then actor Jim Carrey (celebrated for his role in the film *Ace Ventura, Pet Detective*). The pants-pulling pup remains the same, though his (or her?) breed can vary from version to version. Marky Mark, photographed by Annie Leibovitz, was presumably chosen because of his reputation as a "rap singer" whose underwear was always showing, while Carrey, as pet detective, was famed for his "talking buttocks" routine. (There is a joke in here somewhere, since "pet" means "fart" in French. The antics of the Pet Detective recall a highly

successful vaudeville entertainer in nineteenth-century France, Joseph
Pujol, known as "Le Pétomane," who played tunes and blew out can-
dles with his anus at the Moulin Rouge.) The Carrey parody of the original ad adorns the cover of *Rolling Stone* magazine, in a photograph by
Herb Ritts, but things get more ambiguous in the image accompanying
the profile of the actor inside. There, a scratched and bleeding Carrey
lies on his back, dominated by the same fluffy black dog, now snarling
at the camera. A shred of Carrey's red bathing suit lies in the fore-
ground. If this is not exactly a sex scene, the suggestion of kinky dominance games is surely not far away.

Heavy Petting

In *Sexual Behavior in the Human Male* (1948), and a few years later in
Sexual Behavior in the Human Female (1953) Alfred Kinsey forth-
rightly discusses both the phenomenon of sexual "petting" ("physical
contacts which involve a deliberate attempt to effect erotic arousal")
between male and female humans and the frequency of "animal contacts," that is, sex between male or female human beings and animals,
barnyard or domestic.

With an observation I particularly cherish for its lack of affect—always a hallmark of the Kinsey style—America's pioneer sex researcher
noted that "petting provides somewhat fewer orgasms than nocturnal
emissions, and only animal intercourse is less important as a source of
outlet."

Petting and animal intercourse. Why does the word "petting" im-
plicitly join these two activities, which common usage so rigorously
keeps apart? Why is petting *called* petting? What, if anything, does it
have to do with pets?

Petting, it turns out, was in Kinsey's time largely a middle- and
upper-class activity, more prevalent among the college-educated than
among those without higher education. "Petting is the particular activity which has led many persons to conclude that college students are
sexually wild and perverted," he says. It marks a conflict of values "between two systems of mores. . . . With the better educated groups"—
says Kinsey—"intercourse versus petting is a question of morals. For
the lower level, it is a problem of understanding how a mentally normal
individual can engage in such highly erotic activity as petting and still

refrain from actual intercourse." "Petting," says historian Paul Robinson, "is a word that has virtually disappeared from our sexual vocabulary."

On the question of "animal contacts," Kinsey has this to say: "No biologist understands why males of a species are attracted primarily, even if not exclusively, to females of the same species." "There is a considerable literature on this subject, but it needs to be analyzed with caution because so much of it is anthropomorphic, arriving at the sort of interpretation that a human intelligence would expect to find if intraspecific mating were the only possibility in nature."

In other words, people have resisted the idea of cross-species mating, for "anthropomorphic" reasons.

But in fact, Kinsey reported, there were "increasing" instances of cross-species mating or attempted mating "with individuals of totally distinct and sometimes quite remote species," including mankind. (A fascinating footnote in his volume on the human female records sexual activity attempted "between animals of gross morphologic disparity, including female eland with ostrich, male dog with chicken, male monkey with snake, stallion with human, chimpanzee with cat, and cow with human.") "In light of the above, it is particularly interesting," he says in his typical mild-mannered way, "to note the degree of abhorrence with which intercourse between the human and animals of other species is viewed by most persons who have not had such an experience."

Yet animal contacts, as Kinsey shrewdly observed, have had a long and honorable history in sexual *fantasy life*—which is to say, in high culture and popular culture as well as in pornography. Human females (Kinsey never says "women") have long featured in those foundational cultural fantasies we call folklore and mythology: "Females have sexual relations with bears, apes, bulls, goats, horses, ponies, wolves, snakes, crocodiles, and still lower vertebrates." "Classical Greek and Roman mythology," he points out, "had accounts of lovers appearing as asses, Zeus appearing as a swan."

Thus, and not for the first time, behavior that appears (in practice) as a primary violation of boundary between humans and animals turns out to be (in figure) foundational to received notions of "culture" and civilization. Not only the ancients found these couplings attractive; in the modern literary canon "Leda and the Swan" is taught to every college student—as, indeed, is *A Midsummer Night's Dream*. These images of cross-species sexual encounters are among the texts on which we found our culture.

Now, Kinsey, as I have said, was a zoologist (his early research was on the gall wasp). His evaluation of behavior was based upon what had precedents among animal species, and not on what was prescribed, or proscribed, by religion or the church, and his "naturalism" was, in Paul Robinson's phrase, "responsible for a good deal that humanists found objectionable in the Reports."

"The elements that are involved in sexual contacts between the human and animals of other species are at no point basically different from those that are involved in erotic responses to human situations," Kinsey wrote. (What he calls in his section on "Techniques in Petting" the "French kiss or soul kiss, in the college parlance," for example, is traced to the activities of the reptiles, birds, and mammals.) He therefore "found it entirely credible," as Robinson notes, "that a man might fall passionately in love with his dog, and that the affection could be returned in kind."

Kinsey asked twenty thousand Americans how often they had had sex with animals. His genius as an interviewer lay in this kind of formulation: not "Have you ever had sex with animals?"—a question guaranteed to produce adamant denials—but "how often," and under what circumstances. Eight percent of men, and 3½ percent of women, acknowledged that they had had some carnal knowledge of an animal, either in the farmyard or in the home. Part of the explanation for this may be social and demographic; in the forties "nice girls" (and, to a much lesser extent, "nice boys") didn't have sex (with human partners) before marriage; adolescence being what it is, "nature" took its course. And there were, of course, more farms and barns and fields of livestock in proximity to the general population than there are now.

"A fair number of city boys," Kinsey reported, had sexual relations with animals, and "some of this is had with household pets, particularly with dogs," though more was with farm animals encountered on visits during vacation periods. For boys, "masturbation," he reported, "may be either on the male or the female animal, but it is most common with the male animal, particularly with the male dog." (Kinsey, typically, did not flinch from calling such male-male cross-species contact "homosexual," though he noted that since most boys didn't think of it that way, they felt no conflict about it.) Furthermore, he insists that "in some cases the boy may develop an affectional relationship with the particular animal with which he has his contacts," and drew a parallel between such affection and that felt by "persons, everywhere in our society, [who] become considerably upset at the loss of a pet dog or cat which has been in the home for some period of time." As for the dogs, they, too, may form attachments. "On the other side of the record, it is to be noted that male dogs who have been masturbated may become considerably attached to the persons who provide the stimulation; and there are records of male dogs who completely forsake the females of their own species in preference for the sexual contacts that may be had with a human partner."

The popularity of the dog was more striking among women than among boys and men. Of the women who told Kinsey and his researchers that they had made love with an animal, nearly three quarters (74 percent) said their partner was a dog. (This finding, that "the majority of female contacts with animals are had with dogs," was confirmed by more than half a dozen experts, including Havelock Ellis and the German sexologist Magnus Hirschfeld.) Among the tabulations subsequently prepared by the Kinsey Institute, and not included in the original *Reports,* was one entire table (Number 399) itemizing, for both males and females, "Type of Sexual Contact with Dogs." Most women had restricted themselves to stroking and touching the animal's sex organs; only one in the study had had actual coitus with an animal. Midas Dekkers reports that various accounts by psychiatrists, sociologists, and other sex researchers attest to the "preference" of women for dogs over other nonhuman animals: "The psychiatrist Von Maschka knew a woman of forty-five who confessed that 'as a result of her very passionate temperament [she] had engaged in sexual activities with her pet dog'"; another psychiatrist reported that one of his patients was "a maid, who was caught in the act while she was allowing herself to be mounted like a bitch by a dog on all fours," and Ronald Grassberger, who studied Austrian court proceedings from 1923 to 1965, notes that "the few cases in which a woman has been sentenced because of immorality with animals . . . concerned exclusively sexual contact with dogs."

Such activities are usually classified as perversions. The author of a book rather tendentiously titled *Female Sex Perversion: The Sexually Aberrated Woman as She Is,* declared in 1935 that a woman who had trained her dog to give her sexual pleasure was unquestionably "abnormal," since "in every community there are opportunities for normal cohabitation. Any woman, virtuous or lewd, can always find a man for sexual congress however plain she may be."

The Johns Hopkins University sexologist Dr. John Money reported that a female patient of his had "almost casually . . . mentioned that she had had intercourse with the dog of the house." Although she had been in therapy for years, she had not thought to describe this fact of her life before "because she thought that the doctors would not understand anything about it." She would, she said, "sneak dogs in the house" even after she was married, although she thought that "if anybody would catch me . . . I would be ruined for life."

Happy Hunting

One of the most notorious versions of the woman-and-dog sexual scenario was incorporated into Xaviera Hollander's 1972 best-seller, *The Happy Hooker*. Published with an author's note assuring the reader that "the events in this book actually happened," *The Happy Hooker* told the story of a young, beautiful woman who was "the most famous and successful madam in New York City." Among the tales of sexual hijinks among the rich and famous (as well as some raunchy incidents of prison life) was the encounter of the highly sexed author with a South African German shepherd.

Hollander was visiting her stepsister and her husband, who lived in an "exclusive outer suburb of Johannesburg," complete with servants, swimming pool—and dogs. Nonetheless she was lonely and bored; at home in Amsterdam she was used to regular sex, and "there didn't seem to be any unattached males around except for the servants, whom," she says, "I wouldn't consider quite apart from the fact that there is a penalty of nine months' imprisonment in South Africa for crossing that kind of color line."

> One day as I was lying by the pool thinking I would go ape out of horniness, I became aware of the big German shepherd lying restless by my side. This dog had embarrassed me the first five days after my arrival by following me everywhere and sniffing at my legs. He apparently has a nose for sex so at this point, where I could no longer be choosy, I decided that—bizarre or not—my first South African lover would have to be him.

Once she determined, by manual stimulation, that the dog was indeed a willing partner, Hollander sought privacy for the two of them in her brother-in-law's study and locked the door behind them. The dog, "a young, strong animal," was a satisfactory partner, and indeed in some ways (for this experienced woman) a familiar one: "His eyes were looking at me with an old, but somehow familiar, give-it-to-me doggie expression." Securing her own pleasure, she did not neglect his, partly out of a sense of fairness and partly out of "clinical" curiosity, after which he "gave me an apologetic look, conked out, and went straight to sleep. Not the most touching love scene," the Happy Hooker concludes, "but at least all parties to the action were happy, temporarily."

The seventies, many readers will recall, were an era of supposed sexual license and experimentation, the time of the "sexual revolution" and the "zipless fuck." Hollander's narrative return to an old and popular brothel genre, the prostitute's exhibition with a German shepherd, fits in nicely between her amateur encounters with lesbianism and group sex and her move into the professional world of sex for pay—all equally conventional, from a literary point of view.

The Happy Hooker sold well around the world, and in 1987 a revised edition was published in Britain, boldly announcing on its cover that "although this frank sexual shocker raised eyebrows on first publication—Xaviera didn't tell all!" Purchasers of the new, revised edition would finally get to read the whole story, including "what modesty forbade" the first time around. An epilogue to the new book describes Hollander's transition from prostitute and madam to expert: "Now, having written more than a dozen books and having been invited to participate in international congresses of sexology, lecture at universities and appear on many TV panels, I am treated seriously as someone whose experience makes a valuable contribution to the understanding of sexual problems."

Yet in this new, finally unexpurgated account, something has been not added (as one might expect) but rather omitted. Hollander's visit to South Africa is still included in the new, happier *Hooker,* together with her account of why she declined to make advances to the servants and an anecdote, which originally followed the dog story, of how she was approached sexually by the seven-year-old son of her hosts. But the two pages describing her seduction of the German shepherd are gone.

Nostalgic former readers will search in vain for this little episode, which apparently was too strong for the tastes of the late eighties in

Britain, however "advanced" they may have been proclaimed to be. The "frank sexual shocker" in fact retreats, rather than advances, on the question of human-animal eroticism. Was this a necessary corollary of Hollander's new respectability? Or was it, as her epilogue seems (with unconscious wit) darkly to hint, a sign of the swing back of the pendulum, when "the hounds of Puritanism" were "once more baying for blood"?

Animal Nature

Of course it's not only women who tell tales—or tails. In his autobiographical memoir, *Secret Life*, Michael Ryan describes having sex with the family dog. *Secret Life* is an explicit account of the author's sexual life, beginning with the declaration that "every sex addict has his own thing." Ryan chooses the word "molest" and its various derivations as his epigraph. In the book he chronicles his experiences with women, with men, with students, with pornography, with the neighbor who molested him when he was five years old. But when journalist James Atlas wanted to characterize the "climate of unbridled candor" that marks the current mode of literary confession, he zeroed in on the ultimate taboo: "There's no rule—not even an ethical one—to prevent the poet and former Princeton professor Michael Ryan . . . from revealing that he had sex with his dog."

Writer, social critic, and iconoclast Paul Goodman once necked with a "handsome mongrel dog, part shepherd" at a party in New York. As his friend George Dennison recalls the event, Goodman, by that time forty-six and the author of twenty books, was at loose ends at the party, which was given by Gestalt therapist Allison Montague. "There were no intellectuals. The young actor he was waiting for arrived with a woman. And it seemed that all the young men had come with women." Goodman, seated on the floor, was greeted by the dog, who went up to him and wagged his tail.

> Paul took its head caressingly in both hands and spoke to it. There was self-pity in his voice, but also admiration and outright gratitude. "Yes, my darling," he said, "you're the prettiest one here." The dog licked him, and Paul licked him back, and for a full twenty minutes they exchanged kisses. The voices in the room fell silent, started up, fell silent. The two red tongues

touched again and again, and Paul opened his mouth to the dog's tongue.

He meant to offend the human company. It was an effective display of contempt. But much more than that could be seen. The longing expressed by his open mouth was real, and was disquieting, as of something beyond placation. His affection for the dog was real, too; his fingers liked its fur, and he welcomed the closeness.

The dog, which belonged to his host, was summarily dragged away and locked (alone) in a bedroom. "But Monty," Goodman protested to Montague. "It's *my* dog, Paul," the Gestalt therapist replied.

Dennison speculates that for Goodman this performance was in part an act of will, the will to "overcome the squeamishness, that is, the way of life, and the entire tradition of that way, that appeared in those other faces" at the party. "The didactic burden of his display with the dog was obvious: if you would affirm and not suppress your animal nature, etc., if you would be as direct as this dog instead of wasting life in idiotic avoidances, the world would be more practicable, and I not so alone." But this measured and distanced view of a "didactic burden" soon shifts into an earlier moment of personal recollection.

> When my younger brother was three or four, [writes Dennison,] he and the family bulldog were much enamored of each other. One night my father could bear it no longer, and said, "stop kissing the dog on the mouth." But the kissing went on. My father grew angry and sent my brother up to bed. Ten minutes went by. They heard his footsteps coming down the stairs, and then he stalked into the room, both fists clenched, and made for the dog shouting. "I don't care! I love Skippy and I'm gonna kiss 'im on the mouth!"

"There really was a child like that alive in Paul," the affectionate chronicler observes.

For Goodman, a lively, transgressive intelligence, combative, multitalented, bisexual, and complex, the eroticism of the man-dog boundary seemed compounded of simple pleasures and not-so-simple ones. His editor and literary executor, Taylor Stoehr, collecting previously unpublished Goodman works, notes that "he had suppressed just those stories that no one would have printed anyway, no publisher was likely to touch"—like "love-making during menstruation, with newsboys, or collie dogs!" In a piece appropriately called "The Continuum of the Libido," Goodman's narrator reports that "he found he was in love with his mother-in-law's collie-dog Tippy," and "cheerfully" sets out for the kennels where he "got himself a beautiful and desirable mongrel bitch, which he cajoled and used."

> And how was he to place himself on a level, and on a basis of mutual desire, with the poor dumb frightened animal, lost as to the meaning of the pain imposed on her? by what new authority? for what cause? . . . His eyes filled with tears as he petted the frightened bitch. Tears also for himself as he contemplated the gulf, yawning for so long a time, between himself and this desire.

"It was necessary to crowd his attention into the olfactory sense: to sniff and smell," he reports, "Indeed, as he did so, a new world unfolded within him, of obscure reminiscences soon becoming sharply precise, tho not to be readily expressing in our visual language, and of organic longing. And his mouth at the same time began to water, and licking and sniffing became one longing. 'This is of course mere infantilism,' he thought, from so far off! but he clung to the beast, being thereby almost free and perfect in desire."

Not only hypothetical publishers but many actual readers may find themselves "squeamish" in the face of this erotic narrative. It is a record of "longing" and "desire," themselves always ultimately inexplicable. The narrator's conclusion, perfectly consistent with this argument for human erotic freedom, offers a naturalizing of the most transgressive claim of all: that in loving a dog he is, somehow, obeying the will of God:

> "Eia!" he thought with joy, "I could never thus apparently quit human reason, law, and freedom—for men are only free in the intelligible world—in order to be almost free and perfect in desire with this beast in a world of bodily odors, if I were not also submissive to my absolute Creator. I should not dare to lie with a dog; but I, like few, am on His side! I have set *my* father so high in heaven that here I have every license and no fear. [What a stratagem!] Yet I am compelled, too; for I *must* not fear or dare to deny myself in any way.

TOP: *Alice and Louis,*
March Avery, 1994.
BOTTOM: *Double Portrait,*
Lucian Freud, 1988–90.

Family Values

CLOCKWISE FROM TOP: Lassie's human family, the television cast (clockwise from Lassie): Timmy (Jon Provost), Ruth Martin (June Lockhart), Uncle Petrie (George Chandler), and Paul Martin (Hugh Reilly). The family that prays together stays together: Lassie, Timmy, and Ruth in the seventh year of their long-running television series. Lassie's canine family, including Lassie Jr. and Pal, the star of the original film. Lassie (Pal) brings Roddy McDowall his schoolbooks (and they're not even dog-eared): the most famous publicity photo from *Lassie Come Home*, 1943.

Home Is Where the Dog Is

Photographs by Robin Schwartz

FROM TOP: *Couple on a Mattress, 1984; Strays on Car, 1987; Hoboken Lady and Her Dogs, 1983.*

Talking Dogs

FROM TOP: A good listener: Nipper (the RCA Victor dog) cocks an attentive ear. Francis Barraud's painting *His Master's Voice* was rejected by the Royal Academy in 1899, and later became world-famous. Farfel, the floppy-eared spokesdog for Nestlé "chaaaw-klit!" from 1956 to 1966, with stage companions Danny O'Day (*left*) and Jimmy Nelson. "Who is Sylvia, what is she, that all our swains commend her": Sarah Jessica Parker played top dog in A. R. Gurney's 1995 comedy *Sylvia,* with Charles Kimbrough as her adoring master. Bill Hinnant as Snoopy (here in his alter ego as the World War I flying ace) in *You're a Good Man, Charlie Brown,* 1967.

Dog Stars

CLOCKWISE FROM TOP LEFT: Beethoven and Missy (she's the one with the bow). Lady and the Tramp. Cruella DeVil connects the dots in *101 Dalmatians*. Shadow, Chance, and Sassy run for home in *Homeward Bound: The Incredible Journey*. Not in Kansas anymore: Dorothy (Judy Garland) and Toto in *The Wizard of Oz*.

🐾

A Dog and His Boy

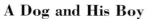

CLOCKWISE FROM TOP LEFT: Rin
Tin Tin and Rusty (Lee Aaker),
from the 1950s television show.
Dickie Moore and Pete the Pup,
featured players in Hal Roach's
"Our Gang" comedies. *Paul and
His Dog*, photograph by Nadar
(Gaspard Felix Tournachon), circa
1865. Tintin and Milou. Krypto
and Superboy.

Eminent Canines

CLOCKWISE FROM TOP LEFT: *Lord Gristle:* Contemporary artist Thierry Poncelet reinvents an old satirical art form. *The Connoisseurs,* Sir Edwin Landseer, 1867: One of England's most famous dog painters scrutinized by his subjects. *Keeper—From Life:* Emily Brontë's 1838 tribute to her beloved companion. A portrait of Boatswain, Lord Byron's dog, by Clifton Thompson, 1803: Declaring in his epitaph that Boatswain, a Newfoundland, possessed "all the virtues of man, without his vices," Byron asked to be buried with him. The statue of Greyfriars Bobby, Candlemaker Row, Edinburgh: This icon of canine fidelity kept watch by his master's grave for fourteen years.

Doggy Style

FROM TOP: *Back East,* photograph by William Wegman, 1988. *Jonah and Lypsinka at POWARS [Pet Owners with AIDS Resource Service] Benefit,* photograph by Robin Schwartz, 1995. Look-alikes on parade at the Massachusetts Society for the Prevention of Cruelty to Animals' Walk for the Animals, Boston, 1995.

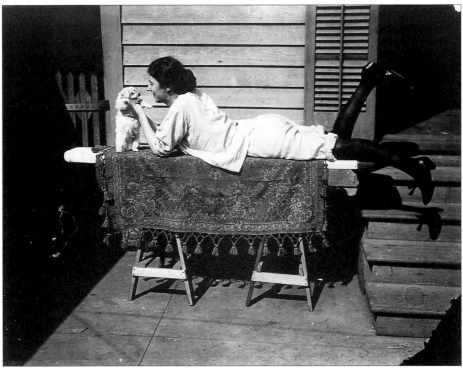

Hot Dogs

FROM TOP: Marky Mark caught with
his pants down by Annie Leibovitz.
Untitled (Storyville Portrait), photograph by E. J. Bellocq, circa 1912:
a New Orleans prostitute and her
dog. *Nude with Dog*, Gustave
Courbet, 1861–62.

Dogs of War

CLOCKWISE FROM TOP: Laika, the Russian space-dog. Byrd dog: Igloo, a fox terrier, with his commander, Richard Byrd. World War I recruiting poster. Salvo, a member of the British "Parapup Battalion," descending by parachute in World War II. Monument to the unknown canine soldier, Hartsdale Canine Cemetery, Hartsdale, New York.

Sleuth Hounds

CLOCKWISE FROM TOP: The dog as perpetrator: *The Hound of the Baskervilles,* 1939. As witness: Kato, Nicole Brown Simpson's Akita, who barked at the murder scene; photograph by Annie Leibovitz, 1995. As detective: Asta, with fellow sleuths Nick and Nora Charles (William Powell and Myrna Loy), in *Song of the Thin Man,* 1947. As cop: *Pete, Hoboken K-9,* photograph by Robin Schwartz, 1993. As mastermind: Alfred Hitchcock and Sarah, photograph by Philippe Halsmann, 1974.

Political Animals

CLOCKWISE FROM
TOP LEFT: Herbert
Hoover and King Tut.
Winston Churchill
and bulldog.
Lyndon Johnson
and Yuki.
FDR and Fala.

FROM TOP:
Richard Nixon and
Checkers.
Millie Bush.
Queen Elizabeth II and
corgis Heather, Buzz,
Foxy, and Tiny.

Longtime Companions

CLOCKWISE FROM TOP LEFT: Sigmund Freud
and chow puppies, 1933. J. R. Ackerley
and Queenie, 1950s. Eugene O'Neill and
Blemie (Silverdene Emblem), Beacon
Farm, Northport, Long Island, 1931.
Marie Bonaparte (Princess George of
Greece) and Topsy, late 1930s.
Helen Keller and Kenzan-Go, 1955.

🐾

The Paragon
of Animals

CLOCKWISE FROM TOP: *Man Ray Contemplating Man Ray,* photograph by William Wegman, 1978. Sigmund Freud in 1931, sitting for a bust by sculptor Oscar Nemon, while Lün, his last chow, looks on. *Self-portrait 1988,* Robert Mapplethorpe.

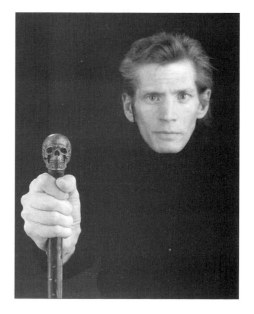

Photographs
by
Bruce Cratsley
ABOVE:
*Gertie in
Angel's Arms,*
1991.
RIGHT:
*Ms. Muffit,
Chez Moi,*
1986.

Philip Rahv rejected this story for *Partisan Review* in the early forties and, as Taylor Stoehr remarks, "because the character in the story
in fact made love to his dog," Rahv "spread the rumor that Goodman
himself practiced bestiality. 'Goodman? he fucks dogs!' This calumny
and its source got around," Stoehr reports, "and became a joke among
Goodman's friends."

The first-person version of "Continuum" was written in Chicago in
1938; in 1942, suitably transformed into a novel now called *Don Juan,
or, the Continuum of the Libido,* and bereft of its disconcertingly "blas-
phemous" conclusion, it was put into the mouth of the novel's titular
character, who offers these observations as part of a public lecture on
his own erotic continuum. The new format affords Goodman a chance
to pull his punches a little; thus when the Don declares his passion for
Tippy, the novel form allows him to report that "some in the audience
were shocked," and when he describes his acquisition of the "beautiful
and desirable mongrel bitch" they are "profoundly shocked." Don
Juan's assertion that sex with a dog rendered him "almost free and perfect in desire" is met with mixed approval and disapproval from the
crowd, who are now themselves described as erotic animals: "Some
barked like dogs, some crowed like roosters. One man flapped his arms
like the Eagle that bore Ganymede aloft; and a woman was lowing like
Pasiphaë." Ganymede was the boy lover of Jupiter, who transformed
himself into the eagle; Pasiphaë, the mother of the Minotaur, had intercourse with a white bull. Goodman, like Kinsey, sees the comedy and
the irony in the myths that ascribe "bestiality" to the gods.

Paul Goodman's erotic imaginings, like his erotic experiences, test
the boundaries of public taste and tolerance. The saga of Tippy the collie and the kennel dog acquired in her stead opens up areas of cross-
species contemplation that many "dog lovers" will find alien and
repugnant, and that some will surely regard as nothing but animal
abuse. That Goodman himself sought to link such images to the loves of
the Greek gods suggests that he was serious about the idea of a "continuum of the libido," and that he sought to uncover, in the unconscious
of literature and myth as well as of his readers, traces of the same transgressive wish. "These stories are not strictly autobiographical, and you
must not take them literally," cautions Stoehr. "But that doesn't mean
they aren't interesting!" He adds that the Goodman family generally
had a dog, "the last of which had the same name as his [Paul's] daugh-

ter, and so was called 'Daisy Dog.'" The editor's or publisher's opti-
mistic observation, that "Goodman's own campaign in the Sixties for a
more permissive attitude toward sexuality has helped relax censorship
and make his book publishable at last," seems itself, sadly, a little
dated in view of more recent political impulses toward censorship.

As Goodman makes clear, the appeal/repulsion of bestiality is the
appeal/repulsion of transgression. What Dennison called the "didactic
burden" of Goodman's "display with the dog" concerned the experience of crossing a forbidden line—taking the pleasures of the body
past repression, past morality, even past humanity. As the narrator of
Topping from Below puts it, "The taboo nature of the act aroused me immensely."

Breeding

*"The Father Belonged to Some People Who
Were Driving Through in a Packard."*

Flush knew before the summer had passed that there is no equality among dogs; some dogs are high dogs; some are low. Which, then, was he? No sooner had Flush got home than he examined himself carefully in the looking-glass. Heaven be praised, he was a dog of birth and breeding! . . . When about this time Miss Barrett observed him staring in the glass, she was mistaken. He was a philosopher, she thought, meditating the difference between appearance and reality. On the contrary, he was an aristocrat considering his points.

—Virginia Woolf, *Flush*

There are two kinds of dogs, for, some are well-bred, others low-bred. The well-bred, indeed, are silent and free from guile; the low-bred are ill-tempered and fond of barking. So it is with women: the nobles are artless, silent, and lovers of solitude; the ignoble to be sure are loud and roamers in the streets.

—*Speculum Laicorum,* thirteenth century

I like a bit of mongrel myself, whether it's a man or a dog; they're the best for every day.

—George Bernard Shaw, *Misalliance*

"We are glad you have a Dalmatian," wrote Eugene O'Neill to a friend in December of 1942. "They are much more sensible than any other breed of dog I know—and I've known many breeds. Unlike the English Bulldog or bull terrier, for example, or the French poodle, or the German Gestapo dog, they never drool or yap or whine about the white dog's burden of Empire, or their supremely rational culture, or the enlarged yard space due to a superior race of mutts. Unlike the Irish Wolfhound, they don't bay beautifully at the misty moon about 'the cry of the hounds on the hills of old Ireland.' I never heard Blemie [the O'Neills' Dalmatian] mention Dalmatia except as a certain section of land where his ancestors happened to be when they were born. And, of course, Dalmatians are not only superior to other dogs, they are like all dogs, infinitely less stupid than men."

O'Neill's charming paean to the virtues of the Dalmatian romps briskly through the list of human nationalist foibles in praise of his own dog, Blemie. Part of the appeal of his mocking antinationalist account comes from that fact that "Dalmatian," as a dog breed, functions as the equivalent of a dead metaphor. The average admirer of the Dalmatian may think "Firehouse" or "Coach dog" or "Cruella de Vil," but he or she does not usually think "Adriatic coast," any more than the wearer of Bermuda shorts thinks, when donning them, of the island of Bermuda. The same is true for numerous other breeds from the Newfoundland (or "Newfie") to the Weimaraner, both likewise named for their places of origin.

But breed names often do preserve, or even instate, clichés of "national character" that date from another century or another era (have I mentioned that Dorothy Parker's dog's name was Cliché?). Thus the indomitable and obdurate Scottie, the frivolous "French poodle" with its stylish clip, the "English bulldog" (and its equally pugnacious Yale equivalent) all survive as cartoon species, often quite unrelated to the actual nature of the dog breed in question. Indeed, the case of Handsome Dan, the Yale bulldog mascot, might remind us that the competitive emotions of a certain kind of nineteenth-century "nationalism" have devolved, these days, upon rival sports teams and their emblems. Young fans who know nothing about the natural world will speak in expert tones about beasts like the Nittany Lion and the Wolverine.

Sometimes the breed names themselves are both picturesque and literary: the Dandie Dinmont, for example, a terrier breed known since the early eighteenth century, gets its name from a farmer in Sir Walter Scott's 1815 novel *Guy Mannering* who had six of the otter-hunting terriers: Auld Pepper, Auld Mustard, Young Pepper, Young Mustard, Little Pepper, and Little Mustard. Some breed designations go as far back as John Caius's sixteenth-century *Of English Dogges.* Caius, describes the Skye terrier, for example, as "brought out of barbarous borders from the uttermost countryes northward . . . which, by reason of the length of heare, makes showe neither of face nor body." Popular with early English monarchs, the Skye (whose breed motto, according to the Skye Club of Scotland, is "Wha daur meddle wi me") continued to be a favorite with royals and nobles. Queen Victoria admired them; Sir Edwin Landseer painted them, and today's Skye fans note that there was a time when "a duchess would almost be ashamed to be seen in the park unaccompanied by her long-coated Skye."

The Bernese mountain dog comes originally from Berne, Switzerland (though a friend of mine persists in calling them "Béarnaise mountain dogs," as if they were covered with sauce). The Chinese crested, with hair only on the head, tail, and feet, was known in earlier times as the Chinese ship dog and the Chinese royal hairless. Perhaps appropriately, this "naked" breed was popularized in the 1950s in the United States by Gypsy Rose Lee.

The bichon frise, descended from the barbet or water spaniel, was first called barbichon, then abbreviated to bichon. Dating from antiquity and popular in Spain and Tenerife in the Middle Ages, the dogs were rediscovered by Italian sailors on their voyages and brought back to Europe as the "Teneriffe" or "bichon." There they lived a double life: as the aristocratic favorites in the courts of Spain and of Francis I and Henry III of France—and later as the organ-grinder dogs of popular street fairs and circuses in the nineteenth century. "Bichon frise" ("curly-haired bichon") is a modern name, dating from 1934. In short, behind every dog breed we find an ethnography and a social history as well as a genealogy—the story of its life in culture as well as its genetic descent.

"Dogs reflect the culture in which they live," note the authors of a book on genetics and the social behavior of the dog.

> In the Middle East there are essentially only three kinds of dogs: salukis used for gazelle hunting in the deserts, large herding dogs used by Kurdish shepherds to protect their flocks from wolves, and mongrels which chiefly act as scavengers in the cities. By contrast, in modern France, where dogs are chiefly used on farms, there are some seventeen breeds of shepherd and stock dogs. In England, where hunting has been a popular sport in all classes from as far back as the Middle Ages, there were in 1959 twenty-six recognized breeds of sporting dogs. We can think of human social change as providing the opportunity for the phenomenon of canine adaptive [change].

The authors, behavioral geneticists whose research spanned thirteen years, go so far as to see canine genetics not only as a reflection but even as a predictor of human evolution. "Dogs have gone through some four thousand generations since their domestication while man has gone through only four hundred," they note. "These facts suggest a hypothesis: the genetic consequences of civilized living should be intensified in the dog, and therefore the dog should give us some idea of the genetic future of mankind, always assuming that there are no radical new changes in the condition of human living." Precisely because of its shorter life span and its long-term relationship with human society, the dog, these scientists suggest, may be "a genetic pilot experiment for the human race."

Human friends of the dog may regard this prediction with eagerness or with trepidation. But one thing seems certain: Whether or not dogs can tell us our genetic future, they can certainly tell us a lot about our past and present.

Studs

In 1873 the English Kennel Club was founded in London, and the first volume of its *Stud Book*, listing dogs exhibited since 1859, appeared the following year. The purpose of the club, as historian Harriet Ritvo indicates, was to regulate public dog shows, which had fallen prey to various kinds of cheating since their inception in 1859. The members were, by their own account, to be "true sportsmen . . . who breed to win and to whom pecuniary questions are of no moment." In other words, questions of *human* class and breeding were at issue. In 1884 dog fanciers in the United States followed suit, founding the American Kennel Club in New York and compiling the first American *Stud Book*.

From time to time in classic English detective stories bluebloods like the friends of Dorothy Sayers's Lord Peter Wimsey inquire about whether someone is "in the Stud Book." The stud books Wimsey's aristocratic friends have in mind are not compilations of animal genealogies but Burke's or Debrett's Peerage (or, more properly, *Peerage, Baronetage, Knightage and Companionage*) listing all the titled personages of the realm. The United States equivalent would be the *Social Register*. ("Peer" is one of those curious words that has achieved antithetical sense over time; it presumably once meant "equal," as in many contexts it still does, but a "peer of the realm" is, like Orwell's famous animals, more equal than others, and sits among the lords rather than among the commons.)

Artist Thierry Poncelet's dog portraits—produced, as we have noted, by painting dog faces onto old paintings of human aristocrats—are quite clearly a commentary on this whole business of genealogy and pedigree. In their wing collars and cutaways, or lace fichus and brooches, with human arms and hands still extending from their sleeves, Poncelet's pooches are wittily grouped into classes: artists and aesthetes, tycoons and grandees, royals and bluebloods, Don Juans and femmes fatales, swashbucklers and athletes, explorers and visionaries, cads, rotters, and rogues, persons of great affairs, denizens of the demi-monde, and—inevitably—(uniformed and bemedaled) dogs of war. Bruce McCall's accompanying text teases out the subtleties: the bon vivant Edward "Coupe" de Ville, in black tie with the head of a boxer, is described as "a dazzling amateur pugilist." Companion portraits of Carlo and Carlene, the Dancing Clumbards, picture a pair of setters credited with introducing teatime London to the Step'n'Fetch and dazzling a royal audience at a "command performance" with "the bobbing syncopation of the Down Boy, Down Boy Rag." "Carlo (born Rover) and Carlene (née Trixie) had hoofed their way up from the small-time, delivering slippers and pipes in Birmingham." The volume's title, *Sit!*, puns on pet and portrait discipline to emphasize the analogies—and the disjunctions—between human and dog. What is chiefly noticeable in the portraits, however, is the immense dignity of the animal faces—and the occasional ludicrousness of the trappings of human wealth and position.

The world "pedigree" is used both of persons and of animals, and originally merely means a line of ancestors, from the resemblance of a crane's foot (Anglo-Norman *pie de grue*) to the lines on a genealogical chart. Such is the social difference between humans and animals, however, that all persons can have "pedigrees"—in theory at least—but only purebred animals do. "Lineage," which means direct descent from a particular ancestor, is more likely to be used for people. But here is a chart of "Lassie's Lineage":

Stage Name	Call Name	Trained by
Lassie I	Pal	Rudd Weatherwax
Lassie II	Lassie Jr., son of Pal	Rudd Weatherwax
Lassie III	Baby, son of Lassie Jr.	Rudd Weatherwax
Lassie IV	Mire	Rudd Weatherwax
Lassie V	Hey Hey	Rudd Weatherwax
Lassie VI	Boy, son of Hey Hey	Rudd Weatherwax
Lassie VII	The Old Man	Rudd Weatherwax
Lassie VIII	Howard, great-great-great-great-great-great grandson of Pal	Robert Weatherwax, son of Rudd

As with the kings of England, the dignitaries in this line have both official (state or stage) names and unofficial (personal or call) names. (King George VI, for example, was known as "Bertie" until his accession to the throne, and his brother, the former Edward VIII, was "David."). We may notice that the Weatherwax (human) line runs parallel to the Pal (dog) line, though it is, of course, shorter.

Meanwhile the word "stud" itself has, at least in some circles, become a kind of sexual compliment; "He's a real stud" is perhaps this century's earthier version of the Victorian or Edwardian "dog." On daytime television in the 1980s and 1990s a program called *Studs* offered young women a choice of three attractive men to date, based on their sexy double-entendre answers to a series of apparently banal questions.

Canine Victorians

All dogs are snobs, says Robert Louis Stevenson. "It is hard to follow their snobbery among themselves; for though I think we can preserve distinctions of rank, we cannot grasp what is the criterion." We are ignorant of "the real life of dogs, their social ambitions and their social hierarchies. At least, in their dealings with men, they are not only conscious of sex, but of the difference of station." Furthermore, Stevenson concluded, "the true dog of the nineteenth century is in love with respectability."

And so, of course, were his masters. For Victorian society, as Harriet Ritvo observes, "the elaborate divisions of dogs into breeds and classes and of individuals into precisely ranked hierarchies within those classes seemed to imitate and thus endorse the stable, rigidly hierarchical social system represented by the human upper orders." At the same time, however, the reasons for awarding a prize to one dog rather than another, since they were based upon arbitrarily chosen "prize" qualities, undercut this idea of natural superiority and substituted for it a competitive principle of the marketplace. A long or short nose; a broad or narrow head; a straight or curling tail; a parti-colored coat; blue merle in collies, red "dapple" in dachshunds—color patterns involving a dominant gene, producing dark blotches against a lighter background of the same color. "Sometimes qualities were valued only because they were unusual or difficult to produce. The prizewinning pedigreed dogs of the late nineteenth century seemed to symbolize simply the power to manipulate and the power to purchase— they were ultimately destabilizing emblems of status and rank as pure commodities." Thus Victorian dog fancy, as it evolved as a middle-class pursuit, became, again in Ritvo's words, "an index of [the Victorians'] paradoxical willingness aggressively to reconceive and refashion the social order in which they coveted a stable place."

French dog breeding was somewhat less culturally anxious, according to historian Kathleen Kete: "The business of breeding was not taken very seriously and unlike in Britain not linked to microdivisions within the social scale. French attitudes toward the physical characteristics of breeds were cavalier and, to the British mind, frivolous." The French were more cosmopolitan than the British, less provincial in their exhibitions: "Most French dog shows were held in the capital—

beginning in 1865, on the Cours-la-Reine, Champs-Elysées—and favored [high] society canophilia." The Société centrale pour l'amélioration des races des chiens en France (the "Centrale"), dominated by titled aristocrats, took over the management of dog shows (*expositions canines*) in the 1880s, confirming the link with high society.

It was, however, not in the shows but in the dog-care handbooks, according to Kete, that "the construction of French breeds took place." Amateur readers at home in Paris encountered "the 'moral' qualities of a breed" in "a sketch or story, a fictive signature that fixed the type as distinctly as did body size, color, or shape of ears and tail," for "it was the idea of the breed, not its supposed use, that mattered." Mountain dogs in Paris did not climb mountains; sheepdogs did not herd sheep. But the romantic tales of their adventures colored the owner's choice. In short, the "characteristics" of dogs developed through an imaginative set of associations—with Renaissance history, with (human) lifesaving, with the medieval past—that dog owners then (re)appropriated for themselves. "The identification of owner with pet was a function of image that the pet acquired, however arbitrarily that meaning came about." Dog fancy, in other words, came about through the creation of a *chien de fantaisie*. Feminized, deanimalized, and infantilized, dressed in clothing that matched his mistress's costumes in color and style, the nineteenth-century Parisian dog, whether poodle, Newfoundland, greyhound, or St. Bernard, had a couturier, a hairdresser, and a rigorous diet intended to subdue beastly impulses from sex to breaking wind. "The clothed pet was a double, a doppelgänger, a personalized expression of control."

It is easy to be amused by these "bourgeois" affectations of a previous century—until, like Flush, we look into the mirror. One hundred years later pet beautification, couture, and merchandising are again in the ascendant among pet owners of all classes and many nations—nowhere more vividly, in fact, than in the United States. But the story of the dog as a measure of human society begins much earlier.

Mixed Breeds

The idea that dog hierarchy, dog culture, and dog society offer a pattern for human status and degree is famously articulated by Macbeth in his rather testy reply to the First Murderer. In the face of Macbeth's evident scorn the Murderer protests his own "common humanity":

FIRST MURDERER: We are men, my liege.
MACBETH: Ay, in the catalogue ye go for men,
As hounds and greyhounds, mongrels, spaniels, curs,
Shoughs, water-rugs, and demi-wolves are cleipt
All by the name of dogs.
                                        Macbeth, Act III, scene i, ll. 90–94

That the society of dogs could be seen as a model for the society of humans in the English Renaissance is also clear from John Caius's treatise *Of English Dogges,* published in Latin in 1570, translated in 1576. (The English translator warned against those who would "snarr and snatch at the English abridgement, and tear the Translator, being absent, with the teeth of spightfull envye"—"there eloquence is but currishe.") In *De Canibus Britannicis,* Caius, a Humanist, physician, and cofounder of Gonville and Caius College at Cambridge, describes at least six main varieties of dogs: greyhounds, true hounds, bird dogs, terriers, mastiffs, and shepherd dogs. All dogs are not alike. From the pointer to the lapdog (pet of "daintee dames" and "wanton women") to the messenger dog who carries letters in his collar, they have their classes, their proper occupations, their social roles.

Since "Caius" is the pseudonym Shakespeare's Duke of Kent chooses for himself when he goes underground to follow King Lear, first onto the heath, and later to death, the name itself serves in effect as a kind of shorthand sign-word for "dog." Exhibiting the fidelity and loyalty for which (some) canines were already celebrated, the disguised Duke reproaches Lear's cruel daughter Regan with "if I were your father's dog, / You should not use me so." As for Lear, he anticipates, in his invective, Macbeth's catalog of dogs: he calls the insolent servant Oswald a "mongrel," a "cur," a "whoreson dog." Kent is a good dog. Oswald is a bad dog. Here, too, breeding tells.

Virginia Woolf quotes Sir Philip Sidney's *Arcadia* (1580) on the question of class and breeding among dogs: "greyhounds, Spaniels and Hounds; whereof the first might seem the Lords, the second the Gentlemen, and the last the Yeoman of dogs," and goes on to note some crucial differences between the species:

If we are led thus to assume that the Spaniel followed human example, and looked up to Greyhounds as their superiors and considered Hounds beneath them, we have to admit that their aristocracy was founded on better reasons than ours. Such at least must be the conclusion of anyone who studies the laws of the Spaniel Club. By that august body it is plainly laid down what constitute the vices of a spaniel, and what constitute its virtues. . . . The merits of the spaniel are equally clearly defined. . . . The spaniel that exhibits these points is encouraged and bred from; the spaniel who persists in perpetuating topknots and light noses is cut off from the privileges and emoluments of his kind. . . .

But if we now turn to human society, what chaos and confusion meet the eye! No Club has any such jurisdiction upon the breed of man.

In fact, says Woolf, "If there had been a Man Club corresponding to the Spaniel Club in existence" at the end of the eighteenth century, nothing would have prevented Flush's first owner, Dr. Mitford, "from being branded as a mongrel man unfitted to carry on his kind. But he was a human being. Nothing therefore prevented him from marrying a lady of birth and breeding, from living for over eighty years, from having in his possession several generations of greyhounds and spaniels and from begetting a daughter." It was that daughter who gave Flush to Elizabeth Barrett.

In the same year in which *Flush* was published, 1933, the new Oxford English Dictionary recorded some significant meanings for the word "mongrel."

The offspring of two different breeds of dog. Chiefly, and now only, a dog of no definable breed, resulting from various crossings. Applied to persons as a term of contempt or abuse (Cf. *cur*). *Obsolete.*

A person not of pure race: the offspring of parents of different nationalities, or of high and low birth. Chiefly in disparaging use.

In the following year, 1934, British liberal historian and educator H. A. L. Fisher would write, firmly, "Purity of race does not exist. Europe is a continent of energetic mongrels."

Species, Race, and Physiognomy

Charles Darwin used the word "race" to describe hereditary varieties of domestic animals and plants. "When we attempt to estimate the amount of structural difference between the domestic races of the same species," he wrote,

> we are soon involved in doubt, from not knowing whether they are descended from one or several parent species. This point, if it could be cleared up, would be interesting; if, for instance, it could be shown that the greyhound, bloodhound, terrier, spaniel, and bulldog, which we all know propagate their kind so truly, were the offspring of any single species, then such facts would have great weight in making us doubt about the immutability of the many closely allied natural species . . . inhabiting different quarters of the globe. I do not believe, as we shall presently see, that all our dogs have descended from any one wild species.

(That debate, indeed, continues today: witness Konrad Lorenz's questionable distinction between "Aureus" dogs and "Lupus" dogs, supposedly descended, respectively, from the fox and wolf.)

"A dachshund dog is as different from a St. Bernard bitch as a rabbit is from a calf," writes Midas Dekkers,

> and nevertheless he mounts her. How is it that a pug can allow itself to be crushed or impaled by a mastiff? How is it that they are able to see something of themselves in the other dog? How far apart must you breed two dogs before they reject each other as alien? It is as though dogs are anxious to bridge the gaps that human beings create between the breeds as quickly as possible by means of the weirdest crosses. A pedigree dog is a bundle of hereditary characteristics which can bark. People maintain those breeds, dogs want to be rid of them. This is not very difficult for a dog, because it simply does not know whether it is small or large; a dog has no sense of proportion. It is not its dimensions which give it its identity as a dog, but its smell.

In the nineteenth century the word "race" was regularly used as a term for genus; thus we are told, for example, in an affectionate dog biography from 1875, that "Max was of Newfoundland breed, born of illustrious parents . . . his father a noble specimen of the race." Robert Louis Stevenson observes that his little Skye terrier, though handsome enough in his master's eyes, does not seem to appeal "to the ladies of his race." In France, Maurice Maeterlinck used "race" the same way in

characterizing *Our Friend, the Dog:* "He loves us not only in his consciousness and his intelligence: the very instinct of his race, the entire
unconsciousness of his species, it appears, think only of us, dream only
of being useful to us." The word "race" sounds odd in modern American ears when applied to the dog. It may even suggest uncomfortable
analogies to the assumptions of self-satisfied "owners" in other times;
slaves and personal servants ("my man"), too, were assumed to be unquestionably, gratifyingly loyal—and silent.

A "scientific" determination that certain physiognomic features
predisposed a human individual to crime or intellectual brilliance or
generosity was used around the turn of the century, as is now quite generally acknowledged, as part of a campaign of racial and ethnic discrimination. Charts and statistics describing the ideal relationship of
eyes, nose, and shape of the head were supposed to indicate the difference between good breeding and bad breeding.

Thus, for example, Francis Galton, a cousin of Charles Darwin and
the founder of the modern theory of eugenics, created in the 1880s
composite photographs of Jewish schoolboys in order to produce what
he described, in remarks made to the Anthropological Institute, as the
"typical features of the Jewish face." A German anthropologist, Hans F.
K. Gunther, used Galton's photographs to interpret what he called the
"sensual," "threatening," and "crafty" gaze of the Jew. Racial "types"
of this sort were said to govern individual behavior. Physiognomy, the
"art" of judging human character from facial figures, became for a
while part of the "scientific" apparatus of social hygiene. In the same
way the Italian criminologist Cesare Lombroso explored the physiological links between body shapes, profiles, handedness, and a pre-
disposition to crime, and similar observations were made about
African-American features by other investigators. Such "scientific" ex-
planations based on physical appearance inevitably began to be popularized, and many laypersons developed their own opinions about head
shape, nose shape, personality, and character.

In ironic response to this tendency the October 1919 issue of Frank
Crowninshield's *Vanity Fair* ran an article called "How to Read Character at Sight," testing out the character types disclosed by "canine
physiognomy." Nine photographs of the faces of dogs of distinctly dif-
fering breeds were offered in evidence, together with "analyses" of
their facial—and "racial"—characteristics. The breeds were not identified by name; the reader had to supply his or her own expertise. Thus

an English bulldog is described as a "concave-vital type. Should not be argued with. Shaves neck. Extended tongue indicates adenoidal trouble and signifies inability to see two sides of a question. Should go on to stage and play detective or politician parts." The head of an Airedale is labeled "Nordic type. Suffers from hay-fever. Easily imposed upon, but is given to brooding over insults in private. Believes that the time has come when the proletariat should have a chance." And a large full-face photograph of a St. Bernard is captioned "Plodder type. Lacks imagination, but would do well as a city magistrate. Wears a stiff-bosomed shirt every day and wheezes when he laughs." These send-ups are not especially funny, but the design of the whole piece calls attention to the foolishness of reading character in the (canine) face. Yet in fact these stereotypes, or ones very like them, continue to exist in the characterization, or mischaracterization, of dog breeds. And, indeed, of persons, as "typified" by race.

A *Mann* and His Dog

Thomas Mann's affectionate memoir *Herr und Hund* (*A Man and His Dog*), published in Germany in 1918, offers a meditation on the human resonances of canine breeding. Mann's dog Bashan, the subject of the novelist's recollections, is a "peasant," or, in the unforgiving typology of a local veterinary hospital, a "bastard setter."

> Bashan cannot really claim to be a setter such as are described in books—a setter in accordance with the most meticulous laws and decrees. . . . To be sure, one of his rather arbitrary glories— the colour of his hair—might also appear a dubious point to those who rate racial laws higher than the values of personality. . . . But what odds?—setter or pointer or terrier—Bashan is a fine and handsome animal.

Bashan's predecessor in Mann's affections, it appears, was an aristocrat—"a Scotch collie, a harmless, somewhat weak-minded aristocrat" by the name of Percy—and the late Percy is vividly contrasted to the virile, sprawling Bashan. Though Bashan's "manner of sitting is a bit peasant-like, a bit uncouth," and "his shoulder-blades twisted like a yokel's," "the expression of his face, an expression of reasonable cheerfulness, proclaims the fine masculinity of his moral nature, which is reflected physically in the structure of his body." His chest, his haunches, his legs, all his parts "proclaim a brave heart and much virile virtue—proclaim peasant blood—hunting blood. . . . He is a bonafide setter—if you must know—even though he may not owe his existence to some snobbish bit of blue-blooded inbreeding."

Throughout the brief memoir Mann returns to this comparison: "Bashan enjoys perfect mental health, whilst Percy, as I have already intimated, was—as is not uncommon with dogs of blue-blooded pedigrees—a perfect fool his whole life long, crazy, a very model of overbred impossibility." Bashan has "simple and popular ways"; "the enunciation of his emotions remains within the bonds of common sense and a sound earthiness without ever touching the limits of hysteria—limits which Percy often transgressed." But just as you might begin to conclude that Mann has espoused, in full, all the clichés of antisnobbism, he reverses himself, to acknowledge that Percy had some virtues, and Bashan some faults:

> Bashan, you must know, is somewhat crude, like the common people themselves, but like them, also soft and sentimental, whilst his noble predecessor combined more delicacy and possibilities of pain with an incomparably prouder and firmer spirit, and despite his silliness, far excelled that old yokel Bashan in the matter of self-discipline. It is not in defence of an aristocratic cult of values that I call attention to this mixture of opposite qualities, of coarseness and tenderness, of delicacy and resolution, but purely in the interests of life and actuality.

If not human, all too human, Bashan is earthy, all too earthy, easily given to sentimentality "in contradistinction to the impervious Percy." He is, in fact, a creature of blood and soil, a dog uncannily linked to the very terrain, the landscape along the river, the hunting ground that he traverses with his master: "for there is a strange affinity between this and the person of Bashan." Fully half the memoir is thus given over to a description of this suitable match between dog and hunting-ground, "the aboriginal and original vegetation," the "huge patriarchs of the willow."

Whether Mann is consciously satirizing or unconsciously reproducing the prevailing German dialogue about folk culture and nativity here, the timeliness of his reflections in 1918, just after the war, accentuates the sense that *human* "breeds" and "races" were, in some quarters, to be compared, contrasted, and eugenically controlled.

Though Bashan was no aristocrat, that was perhaps in some eyes preferable. Virile, masculine, native to the land, master-loving and peasant-awkward, Bashan is a figure whose "person" is directly contrasted with the effete and sensitive foreign aristocrat, Percy, who perishes of a disfiguring skin disease. As an allegory of contemporary politics *A Man and His Dog* is artlessly affective, whatever its intentions—and without in the least undercutting the emotional appeal of the double portrait it limns.

Tell Me Where Is Fancy Bred?

Just as I am unable to think of any great intellectual who physically approaches anywhere near to an Adonis, or of a really beautiful woman who is even tolerably intelligent, in the same way I know of no "champion" of any dog breed which I should ever wish to own myself.

—Konrad Lorenz, *Man Meets Dog*

The technical term for "the art or practice of breeding animals so as to develop points of conventional beauty of excellence" is "fancy," sometimes in a combining form indicating the species: pigeon fancy, cat fancy, dog fancy. To be "in the fancy" is to be a member of the club of dog breed enthusiasts. "I was beginning to suspect that Joy did not belong to the fancy," speculates the heroine of a dog mystery when she discovers that an acquaintance is more concerned about human accommodations than canine ones. *Dog Fancy* is the name of one leading dog magazine. Another, *Dogs USA*, published annually by Fancy Publications Inc., contains full-page advertisements that describe the particular selling points of a dog or bitch for breeding purposes. The dog (or bitch) is posed in a striking manner, and the advertisement contains blurbs from satisfied former customers—or, one presumes, their owners.

A typical ad looks like this:

Chantal's Bouviers Proudly Announces . . .

some spectacular litters. Fabulous bloodlines and Fabulous Colors. Brindles, Grays, Blacks and Fawns, Specializing in the Ultimate "Fawns."

Sired by Ch. Chantal's Maxx, brother of the well known Polar Bears and son of Cover Girl bred to Ch. My Serasue (WKC Breed Winner 1990) out of Ch. Pio and Ch. Jeraphi.

Top European Bloodlines Imported Directly from Belgium
Also 5 generations on premises

For those who appreciate the TRUE French/Belgium [*sic*] bloodlines

or like this:

The American Polish Owczarek Nizinny Club, Inc.
(APONC)
presents

"SKI," a charming representative of the Polish Lowland Sheep-dogs bred in America of Polish stock.

These robust little sheepdogs, once prevalent herders on the lowlands of Poland, have adapted well to life in the New World. Ideally suited to families, PONS are trustworthy, faithful and de-voted to all their "flock," while instinctively suspicious of strangers. Their compact size (17"–20") luxurious non-shedding coats that come in all colors, and their merry dispositions distin-guish the Polish Owczarek Nizinny as a thoroughly delightful companion dog.

or like this:

Cottonkist Coton de Tulear

Known in Europe as "the Anti-Stress/Anti-Depression Dog," possessing a clownish and affectionate personality, this charm-ing rare breed is the perfect loyal companion. Pictured above is our own Champion Cottonkist Macaroon. . . .

or like this:

Be Loved
Own a Shar-Pei

or like this (accompanying a full-page color photo of seven puppies in a red wagon with three young adult dogs perched below):

Right for you?
I'm an Ibizan Hound. . . .

> Short on hair, long on legs,
> medium to large size.
> For best all around dog
> I take home the prize. . . .

and so on through five verses of what can truly be called doggerel.

The word "fancy" also means fantasy, illusion, or capricious preference; "fancy" and "fantasy" were, until fairly recently, the same word, derived from the Latin *phantasia* and from Middle English "fantsy," imagination or fantasy. Dog breeding is thus, in part at least, a fantasy of perfect forms, or what in dog lingo is called "the standard"—the measurement by which a perfect specimen, according to the American Kennel Club or any competing authority, may be judged. "Standard," then—a word that in ordinary parlance is often taken to mean "average"—comes to mean ideal.

> The standard portrays what, in the minds of compilers, would be the ideal dog of the breed. Ideal in type, in structure, in gait, in temperament—ideal in every aspect. Thus, the standard is not the representation of any actual dog, but a concept. It is against this concept that a dog show judge must measure every competitor of that breed. The dog most closely approaching that idea in the judge's determination, is the dog that wins.

This information is provided by the American Kennel Club at the beginning of its official publication, *The Complete Dog Book*, which then goes on to list "the official standard" (familiarly known as the "standard") for all registered breeds. A dog that exemplifies the standard in all respects is known in the fancy as "typey," a word that has connotations miles removed from "typical." "Type," according to an AKC-approved glossary of dog-related terms, is "the characteristic qualities distinguishing a breed, the embodiment of a standard's essentials." But the most intriguing term I gleaned from AKC publications is the word used to describe "the process of posing the dog's legs and body to create a pleasing profile." "Stacking" is what this seductive posture is called. Next time you hear or read that some voluptuous human being is "stacked" ("very well built in the sexual sense; having an attractive body") bear in mind that the term probably originated in a dog show.

The standard describes the ideal attributes of the breed under a variety of headings: "General Appearance"; "Size, Proportion, Substance"; "Head"; "Neck, Topline, Body"; "Forequarters"; "Hindquarters"; "Coat"; "Color"; "Gait"; and "Temperament." As might perhaps be expected, sections of "the standard," especially the entries under "Temperament," would make wonderful raw material for novelists of human affairs. The English cocker spaniel is "merry and affectionate, of equable disposition, neither sluggish nor hyperactive, a willing worker and a faithful and engaging companion." The golden retriever is "friendly, reliable, and trustworthy. Quarrelsomeness or hostility towards other dogs or people in normal situations, or an unwarranted show of timidity or nervousness, is not in keeping with Golden Retriever character." The expression of the chow chow is "essentially scowling, dignified, lordly, discerning, sober and snobbish, one of independence."

"Sweetness of temperament is the hallmark of the Newfoundland," that favorite dog of the Romantics and pet of both Byron and Emily Dickinson; Byron's moving epitaph for his Newfoundland, Boatswain, is duly quoted. "The Alaskan Malamute is an affectionate, friendly dog, not a 'one-man' dog." The popular toy breed Shih Tzu, originally bred in China, is summarily accounted for: "As the sole purpose of the Shih Tzu is that of a companion and house pet, it is essential that its temperament be outgoing, happy, affectionate, friendly, and trusting toward all."

"Properly clipped in the traditional fashion and carefully groomed, the Poodle has about him an air of distinction and dignity peculiar to himself." The "ideal" German shepherd is "stamped with a look of quality and nobility—difficult to define, but unmistakable when present." As for its temperament, "the breed has a distinct personality marked by direct and fearless, but not hostile, expression, self-confidence and a certain aloofness that does not lend itself to immediate and indiscriminate friendships." (Yet it may be well to note here that the German shepherd was the only breed I could find in the *Complete Dog Book* for which it seemed expressly necessary to say that among its show faults leading to disqualification were not only "cropped or hanging ears" and an "undershot jaw" but also "any dog that attempts to bite the judge.")

Even these pedigreed dogs have family values, or at least values within the family. *The Complete Dog Book* praises the boxer ("with family and friends, his temperament is fundamentally playful, yet patient and stoical with children") and the weimaraner; the latter "is accustomed to being a member of the family and he accepts the responsibilities which that entails." Unlike whom? Other dogs? Or other family members?

And what about the dog sometimes wrongly identified in the newspaper as a "pit bull"? The AKC is explicit in its defense, ascribing its public-relations problems to human faults rather than canine ones. The American Staffordshire terrier, known earlier in England as "the Bull-and-Terrier Dog, Half and Half, and at times Pit Dog or Pit Bullterrier," and in America from 1870 as "Pit Dog, Pit Bull Terrier, later American Bull Terrier, and still later as Yankee Terrier" is described, elaborately and carefully, as exceptionally "game" but not, or not only, "a fighting machine": these dogs "should not be held in ill-repute merely because man has been taking advantage of this rare courage to use them in the pit as gambling tools." In fact they are "docile," get along well with other dogs when trained to do so, and "easily discriminate between strangers who mean well and those who do not." They "are flashy-looking and attract much attention on the show bench." They also, the AKC comments finally, and with an evenhanded affect that borders on the deadpan, "have another characteristic that is unusual: when they are sold, or change hands, they accept their master in a comparatively short time." Is this a good thing or a bad thing? I suppose it depends upon whether you are the new "master" or the old one.

Best of Opposite Sex

The judge then finishes the breed judging by selecting a Best of Opposite Sex to the Best of Breed.

—American Kennel Club Dog Show Rules

The AKC began as an exclusive club—and, moreover, not surprisingly, as a men's club. Dog detective-story writer Susan Conant points out that it wasn't until 1974, almost a hundred years after its founding, that the AKC began to accept women delegates. "The Ladies' Dog Club had to send a man." The exclusivity of the club, the question of breeding, was not entirely then a matter of purebred *dogs*. As Conant's detective, Holly Winter, explains, in her dog-centered family "I grew up thinking that Emily Post was a woman hired by the American Kennel Club to write its human obedience regulations."

But which does a *dog* "have"—sex or gender? Anthropologists and other analysts of culture have tended to reserve "sex" as a term describing biological categories, and to use "gender" to refer to social or cultural categories. On this view, dogs (and bitches) have *both* sex and gender, since they have both biological and cultural attributes that lead to their discussion, and indeed their typification and discrimination, along "sexual" lines.

Here is the AKC *Complete Dog Book* official standard for the chow chow: "There is an impression of femininity in bitches as compared to an impression of masculinity in dogs." And for the German shepherd: "Secondary sex characteristics are strongly marked, and every animal gives a definite impression of masculinity or femininity, according to its sex."

Or consider this account, from a 1936 book on dog owning designed for the general reader. The question under discussion is whether to buy a male or female dog.

> The one great disadvantage to the bitch as a pet is the nuisance of her bi-annual periods when she must be restrained and kept away from the collected group of males in front of the house. These periods last from two to three weeks, and it is usually simpler and cleaner to send the bitch away to a boarding kennel until she has ceased to be attractive to other dogs. Unless she is watched, a careless owner will not only call down the curses of every owner of a male in the vicinity upon his head, but will also find a pretty mess of mongrels tucked away some morning. Spaying, of course, removes this trouble if properly done, but it is not usually to be recommended as it may often produce obesity and nervousness. If spaying is to be done, it is best performed before the bitch is six months of age. There is seldom any excuse for castrating a male, and if the purchaser wishes a dog which will not feel the sexual urge he had better buy a spayed bitch. If a bitch has not been spayed, there is the chance that she will grow fractious and disagreeable in her later years unless she has been allowed to perform her natural function and to have a litter of puppies.

Anyone interested in trying to distinguish between "sex" and "gender" as categories of analysis is advised to underline in red pencil all the "sex" references in the above passage, and in blue pencil all the "gender" ones. The book's author, a man, does have a kind word to say for bitches despite these caveats: choosing one as a pet "merely means that she must be away from the household for a short period twice a year, and that is a small enough matter for which to sacrifice the advantages of temperament and behavior which plead so highly for a bitch as the ideal pet."

More than forty years later both the tone and the message had changed, somewhat. A guidebook written in 1980 by Roger Caras, now the president of the ASPCA, advised that "bitches do *tend* to be a little softer, and this is more true of some breeds than others. . . . Many females tend to have a 'bitchy' look, and that is often less attractive than the broader, heavier, 'doggy' or masculine look," though Caras adds that "that is *not* a rule, however, and some of the most magnificent show dogs seen every year are bitches." As for spaying and altering, he recommends it for both males and females. "It is more expensive to spay a bitch than it is to alter a male. (Spayed and altered dogs cannot be shown, but if dogs are not intended for the show-ring, then your life and theirs will be much improved by a little surgery.) Bitches that have not been spayed can be messy when they come into heat twice a year, and they tend to attract a lot of stray males to your front yard." Caras does not, however, suggest sending female dogs away from home at this time, despite their messiness. And he does note that if you are hoping to breed your dog, you should remember that "it is the bitch that has the puppies." Dog trainer Carol Lea Benjamin notes that since there is no knowing precisely when a bitch in heat will accept a male dog, "an intact female should be kept away from intact male dogs for the entire three weeks. The bitch may exhibit erratic behavior during her heat period in addition to the adolescent difficulties" common to both males and females.

The Monks of New Skete, in their classic book *How to Be Your Dog's Best Friend*, also grapple with the sex and gender question. "Females are often more resilient, smaller than males, and more easily trained at an earlier age." Although "the fabled weight gain of spayed bitches is more fantasy than fact, behavioral changes usually do take place," producing "mellowing," "more responsiveness, and better retention of commands." All in all, though, the Monks recommend males: "On the whole, males tend to be more high-spirited, more in command of the situation, and in spite of their size—from the smallest poodle to the majestic shepherd—they have a manner of being aware of who they are and where they are, and not just what belongs to them. . . . Pleasing their owners becomes almost their reason for being. . . . Male dogs have much to relate to the owner who takes the time to listen." Sex, or gender?

The no-nonsense Barbara Woodhouse offers some of the same facts with a different spin on them: "Everyone who has a lot to do with training of dogs can't help noticing that females are far easier to train than males. The reason is that, except when she is 'in heat' or in the throes of a pseudo-pregnancy, a female's attention is not disturbed by matters of sex. . . . A bitch is better-tempered than a male dog on the whole, for the fighting instinct for supremacy over other dogs is not so prevalent."

As has so often been the case in our consideration of the dog in modern culture, these examples from dog handbooks illustrate as much about *human* foibles and attitudes as they do about their ostensible subject. Both sex and gender are discussed in the passages here quoted, and the usefulness of both terms—as well as their "cultural" implications—is, I think, fairly clear. The human slang use of "bitch" unavoidably if unintentionally inflects some of these utterances, like Caras's use of the word "bitchy" to mean "characteristic of the female dog." Since the word "dog" is currently rather out of fashion as gendered slang there would be no point in saying that a man's behavior was "doggy." (Will headline-grabbing performers like Snoop Doggy Dogg change that?) But language is part of culture—is, indeed, as many theorists have contended, the translucent (not transparent) medium of culture itself. How we feel about canine dogs and bitches is going to be affected by how we feel about human "bitches" and human "dogs," and vice versa.

Name That Dog

Old Possum's Book of Practical Cats, the T. S. Eliot volume later turned into a long-running musical, began with a poem called "The Naming of Cats." But what of the naming of dogs? Here's what the AKC advises. "Name choices are limited to 25 letters. Consider the name choice carefully. A dog's name may not be changed once it is registered." (Bad news for Robert Louis Stevenson, whose beloved—and ill-behaved—Skye terrier was called Woggs, Walter, Watty, Woggy and finally Bogue by his doting owners.)

"No Arabic or Roman numerals may be included in name choices" (forget about naming your Chocolate Lab "Super Bowl XXIX," or your boxer "Friday 13"), though "AKC reserves the right to assign a Roman numeral," presumably if the name you want is already taken. Thirty-seven dogs of each breed can be given the same name, "and many common names, such as Spot, Snoopy, Lassie, King, etc., are fully allotted." Sensibly, the AKC reminds dog owners that "the longer and more unique the name chosen, the greater the chances for approval," and points out that "the easiest way to lengthen a name is to incorporate your surname, for example, 'Smith's Spot' instead of Spot." This is undoubtedly sage advice, but the chosen example is deceptively brief. In these days of hyphenated marriages, and in a nation which is still a melting pot for family names if not for cultures, you are as likely to wind up with a name much longer than the disyllabic "Smith's Spot." Some examples from a recent dog show: Penywyd N'Fairwd's Inherit the Wind (a weimaraner); Paris Diablesse Maybe I Will (a whippet). In practice, many show dogs incorporate the names of their breeders, kennels, or ancestors: Ch. Chaotic Bigtree's Home Brew (a briard); Chickadee's Goodnite Irene and Ch. Charisma Five O'Clock Shadow (both black cocker spaniels). As the unfailingly helpful AKC handbook points out, however, this is not the name you have to bellow out the back door at dinnertime. "Remember that the dog's 'call name,' that is, the name he responds to, does not have to be the same as his registered name. If you name your dog 'Spot' and it is not approved, you may continue to call him 'Spot,' even though his registered name may be different." Out, damned Spot, is a lot easier to say than "Out, Riverside-N-Applecreek High IQ," the full name of one champion Dalmatian.

For those who don't show, breed, or perhaps even register their dogs, naming would seem to be a simpler activity. Entire books on dog naming, however, subcategorized by historical, biographical, physical, and comestible terms ("Here, Biscuit"; "Here, Chablis") stand on the shelves ready to assist you. (Without benefit to assist, one of my friends named her Westie "Shortbread" and her Cairn "Pancake"—both great names for feisty little dogs). As for my own: there's a story there, too.

Nietzschie was a dog I came to live with after he was already named. His name, spelled with an "i-e" at the end and pronounced "Nee-chee" (as indeed one vet seemed inclined to spell it) was a kind of a joke, arrived at because the owner wanted something that sounded like "peachy," by the rhyming-nonsense system ("Peachy" . . .

"Preachy" . . . *Nietzschie!*"). His owner is a literary critic, whose work deals with deconstruction, and therefore with philosophers like Friederich Nietzsche (no "i-e," and pronounced "Nee-chuh"). "Nietzschie" was thus in part a send-up of the tendency of academic dog owners to give their pets literary names. (Harvard Shakespearean Harry Levin's golden retriever was called Yorick, for example, after Hamlet's beloved childhood jester.) In fact, the critic Harold Bloom, meeting Nietzschie and his owner on the streets of New Haven, addressed the dog as "Rousseau," the other continental philosopher favored by deconstructors. (Bloom, as he cheerfully admitted, knew nothing about dogs. "Rousseau" is *not* an obvious dog name, although Freud has a joke about a Roux-sot, a dumb redhead, which some might see as a fitting moniker for a golden retriever.) Many humans who got to know Nietzschie during his magnificent twelve years of life figured that the owners must not know the proper pronunciation of his name (academics are like that) and pointedly addressed him as "Nee-chuh," a mispronunciation he shrugged off with his usual dignity.

When Wagner, a second golden retriever, was added to the household, it was clear that his name ought to have something to do with "Nietzschie"—but what? After days of shouting other golden-typical names at him—"Here, Midas"—we suddenly noticed that he never stopped wagging his tail. Since Friedrich Nietzsche had written against the music of the composer Richard Wagner (pronounced "Vahgner") the name Wagner for our golden puppy (pronounced "Wag-ner") seemed perfect. We always say that he's named for the nonstop action of his tail—and are greeted with raised eyebrows by intellectual dog owners who want to be sure we know they get the joke. They tend to murmur the philosopher's title (*Nietzsche Contra Wagner*) about as often as Professor Levin must have heard "Alas, poor Yorick."

As for Yofi, also a golden, he's named for Freud's beloved chows. Or for the Hebrew word "yofi," which means "beautiful" or "terrific!" or "great!" These punning double names are a source of some pleasure for us. And the dogs bear with us, and don't seem to mind.

Show-and-Tell

Brain, fidelity, devotion, the *human* side of a dog—these were totally ignored in the effort to breed the perfect physical ani-

mal. . . . The body was everything; the heart, the mind, the name-
lessly delightful quality of the master-raised dog—these were
nothing.

So declared Albert Payson Terhune in *Lad: A Dog*, published in 1919.
In a chapter pointedly called "For a Bit of Ribbon" Terhune describes
the Westminster Kennel Club's annual show at Madison Square Garden
as "an exhibition which to the beholder is a delight—and which to
many of the canine exhibits is a form of unremitting torture."

> In some kennels Airedales were "plucked." . . . In other kennels
> bull terriers' white coats were still further whitened by the harsh
> rubbing of pipe clay into the tender skin. Sensitive tails and still
> more sensitive ears were sandpapered, for the victims' greater
> beauty—and agony. . . . Ears were "scrunched" until their wear-
> ers quivered with stark anguish—to impart the perfect tulip
> shape, ordained by fashion for collies.

This is, of course, literary anthropomorphism of the most unashamed
kind. Partisans of the dog show counter that none of these grooming activities is painful, and that, as an enthusiastic show judge wrote in
1936, "Much of the public's pity for dogs on a show bench is wasted.
The average dog loves the excitement of a show and has a grand time."
Lad, it should be noted, despite his unhappiness at Westminster ("He
was magnificent—but he was miserable"), manages to win the Novice
and the Winners' classes on his first time out, despite the fact that he
looks unfashionably like an old-style collie. ("The up-to-date collie—
this year's style, at least," points out a collie breeder, patronizingly, "is
bred with a borzoi [wolfhound] head and with graceful small bones.
What's the use of his having brain and scenting power? He's used for
exhibition or kept as a pet nowadays—not to herd sheep.")

I have to admit that my own first experience as a dog show spectator was far more upbeat than Terhune's account led me to expect. As I
entered the parking lot it was clear that I was among dog people. License plates proclaimed van cargoes (or their owners) to be CH DALs
(champion Dalmatians), WEIMS 1 (weimaraners), TIBETN (Tibetan
hounds), and HOUND. A bumper sticker announced that one conveyance
was a "Rottweiler Express." Another archly declared, "Wife and Dog
Missing. Reward for Dog." The Eighty-fifth Annual Eastern Dog Club

Show (Unbenched) was under way. Supported by entities like the Tartan Gordon Setter Club, the Bernese Mountain Dog Club of Nashoba Valley, the Miniature Bull Terrier Club of America, and the Labrador Retriever Club of Greater Boston, the show attracted a huge number of observers and participants. Eighty-eight glistening golden retrievers competed for best of breed (none of them, I was glad to see, nearly as handsome—to my eyes—as the two ardent noncompetitors I had left snoozing at home). A snowdrift of Great Pyrenees ambled amiably around Ring Six, while a crowd gathered at Ring Nine to watch a demonstration by the K-9 Corps. "We look for a dog of courage," said the police spokesman earnestly, while Utz, a shepherd imported from Germany—as are many of today's police dogs—responded to his master's instructions in German by dutifully releasing the arm of a make-believe "perpetrator." Coincidentally or as a calculated effect of racial counter-stereotyping, the police dog handlers on this occasion were African-Americans; the "perpetrator" (another policeman in uniform) was white.

What was perhaps most striking to the neophyte dog-show attender was the relative absence of either sound or smell. No one barked; the decibel level was far lower than, for example, at a hockey game or even a tennis match. Dogs were taken out of the hall to be "exercised" on the frozen terrain. The rare call for bucket and mop, intoned with calm reserve over the public address system, was easy to miss in the elegant and dignified parades of champions and would-be champions. The human beings—surprise!—made more noise, and more mess, than the dogs. And made do with far less high-quality vittles. Not for the first time I wondered why nature had ordained that humans wear miscellaneous blue jeans and down parkas, rather than, say, a nice guard coat of hair.

My overall aesthetic observation (manifestly not that of an expert or a club member) was that some breeds of dog looked better singly, while others were especially fetching in groups. I admired the stylishness of the Great Pyrenees (my candidate for Best-Looking Dog When Seen in Groups) and the Newfoundlands, both large breeds in single colors. Likewise with the Samoyeds. The parti-colored dogs, from wirehaired fox terriers to (one of my favorites) Bernese mountain dogs, seemed somehow too much in batches; their gorgeous panoply of colors tended to vulgarize in the plural. The fox terriers looked like eager little wind-up toys, and the Bernese, so individually replete with splendor, seemed just a little "busy." One shar-pei handler kept trying to curl up her dog's recalcitrant tail; as soon as she had done so, it began to uncurl again. Another handler had been given her dog charge at the last moment, and complained irritably to a friend outside the ring, "She keeps *sitting* on me," by which she meant lapsing into the "sit" position (not climbing onto the handler's lap). Ideal comportment at home—at least *my* home—this posture is considered unsuitable for the show ring. I felt sorry for the eager-to-please dog (okay, it was a golden), and annoyed at the annoyed handler. But this, clearly, was show business.

An owner of big dogs myself, I was inclined at first to admire the large ones above the small. The giant schnauzers, an improbable and handsome crew; the briards, with stuffed-toy good looks in a jumbo size; the all-white Great Pyrenees and the all-black Newfies. To me the Chinese cresteds, hairless except for strategic poufs, looked like tiny but determined cheerleaders, with pompoms at foot and head. The Maltese all seemed to be *en femme*, with bows in hair and silky coats brushing the ground, and they traversed the diagonal runway like little Miss Americas in training. But some small breeds proved unexpectedly endearing; I fell in love with the border terriers, a breed I'd never noticed in the flesh (or the fur?) before. ("His head like that of an otter," with "eyes full of fire and intelligence," according to AKC standards.) In fact, a dog show turns out to be a three-dimensional dog encyclopedia, with or without the help of the books and videos available from the AKC booth. The American Kennel Club was itself, of course, a highly visible presence, as was a representative of the St. Louis Dog Museum, dispensing Wegman T-shirts, dog-tapestry handbags, and assorted canine stationery to the pre-Christmas crowd. But so, too, were the various rescue groups, breed- and non-breed-specific, including the local Yankee Golden Retriever Rescue Club, the Greyhound Rescue, and the Animal Rescue League of Boston.

Not all events in a dog show are breed-specific. Obedience and agility events are open to all breeds, including what the agility announcer called the "All-American," apparently the newest euphemism for mixed-breed or mutt. The agility events, reliable crowd-pleasers, are basically obstacle courses for dogs, laid out on a field of sodded turf with many fences and hurdles. The trainers run the course with their charges, shouting "Tunnel, tunnel" or "Over, over" at appropriate points, and gesturing firmly or desperately in the direction of the next obstacle. The trainers themselves tended to be quite diversely "All-American" in appearance, some tall and some short, some plump and some trim, and I couldn't help wishing for a latter-day James Thurber to capture the heterogeneous spirit of the event.

As for obedience, here, too, the mix of big and small made for a kind of earnest comedy; the officials were constantly resizing jumps and substituting miniature dumbbells for big ones, as each new competitor entered the ring. Winners, incidentally, were immortalized on film, the patient dog surrounded by smiling exhibitor and judge, often with a floral arrangement and a blue ribbon or prize plate in hand. The "Say 'cheese'" moment was achieved in what was clearly a traditional fashion: a photographer, armed with a rubber carrot or other squeaky toy, flipped this decoy into the air at the crucial moment, presumably causing the dog to look alertly in the right direction. The winning dogs had clearly been through these motions before, and behaved with dignified aplomb. More varied behavior was exhibited by the human participants.

What were the *class* markings of a dog show, I found myself wondering? Of course this will differ greatly from show to show (Westminster presumably is the Park Avenue of the American cycle; its official headquarters are, in fact, on Park Avenue) and from event to event. The show dogs all, of course, had distinguished appellations—and shorter "call names" (a Bernese called Champion Olympians Pegasus II, "more affectionately known as 'Kyle,'" was among those advertised as being "at stud to approved Bitches" in the Eastern Show catalogue). Some of the female judges were known by their married names ("Mrs. George Thompson" rather than "Jane Thompson"), a style I associate only with an earlier era or a certain social class. Late nineteenth- and early twentieth-century dog fancy was often a high society activity, led in America by such patrons as Geraldine Rockefeller Dodge, who built extensive kennels on her two-hundred-forty-acre New Jersey estate, Giralda, raised dogs of eighty-five different breeds, and commissioned a custom-design maroon Cadillac touring car (with eight doors) that would hold a dozen dogs in comfort and took three years to construct. But the sartorial style at the East Dog Club Show was latitudinarian for both handler and onlooker, and the general spirit "democratic" and generous. At one point I heard my own name being called on the loudspeaker, and was summoned to a booth; it turned out that I had over-paid for a bunch of cut-price dog books, and the stallkeeper, finding my name on the check, had gone to the steward to have me paged so he could refund my money. I can't recall another event, sporting or other, at which such a thing has happened, but the seller didn't seem to find his actions at all unusual.

Dog shows, of course, have a long history. The first modern-style dog show may have been that held in 1859 at Newcastle upon Tyne in England, which brought together some sixty entries, limited in breed to pointers and setters. A few years later, in 1870, a show of much larger scope and significance took place at the Crystal Palace, and by 1873 the Crystal Palace Show, sponsored by the newly formed Kennel Club, had a record of 975 entries, a remarkable expansion of popularity in so short a time.

Today there are six million dogs in Britain, some twenty thousand of which compete at the annual Crufts dog show, the premier event in British dogdom, before an audience of almost a hundred thousand people. Charles Cruft, an entrepreneurial pet food salesman representing the James Spratt Company, makers of biscuits for dogs, held his first show in 1886. In 1891 he had his great coup, persuading Queen Victoria to exhibit her collie and six of her Pomeranians. (All the Queen's dogs won prizes.) By the year of Cruft's jubilee dog show in 1936, ten thousand dogs were being exhibited.

"In a curious way," reported *The Guardian*, commenting on the annual event, "the dogs are secondary. 166 breeds are represented at Crufts, each one with its own subculture, but it is as much human as canine." Labels like "Manchester terrier" or "Gordon setters" are used as shorthand terms for the breeders rather than their animals, and "naturally, the owners take on the characteristics of the dogs"—border terrier people wearing casual sweaters and jeans, Afghan owners dressed to the nines. *The Guardian*'s reporter had some predictably catty things to say about the human-dog pairings under view, like "the gait that shows a wire-haired pointer to its best advantage does not necessarily do the same for its owner, particularly if it possesses a fuller figure and wears a trouser suit," where the ungendered owner ("it") is presumptively female, since a full-figured man in a trouser suit would, I assume, be not the exception but the rule. In general, however, his account falls into the dogs-and-mad-Englishmen or humans-will-be-humans school of dog reporting: "In the world of Dogdom it may still be an open question whether or not the pedigrees are getting barmier, but as far as the humans are concerned there can be no debate."

New York's Westminster Kennel Club Show has become a television favorite with people who love dogs, beauty contests, stars, and crowds. "A ribbon in Westminster," one spectator noted, "is akin to an Oscar, or an Emmy, or a Pulitzer—for the dog owners, if not the dogs." That the show may be viewed differently by dog owners and their dogs is hardly a new thought. Cosmetic surgery, nose-blacking, hair-dyeing—none of these are acceptable enhancements for beauty in the show ring, at least for dogs. "According to American Kennel Club regulations," quips Susan Conant's fictional detective, Holly Winter, it's "forbidden to exhibit dogs that have been 'changed in appearance by artificial means.' Unfortunately, the rule doesn't apply to handlers."

The Westminster show takes place each February, and to highlight the occasion in 1995 the *New Yorker* published a "profile" of a dog. Not just any dog, of course; this was Champion Hi-Tech's Arbitrage (how's that for a nineties monicker?), better known to his owner, his family, and now the entire *New Yorker* readership as Biff. Biff is a show dog (and a stud dog) who is about to begin a new career as "celebrity spokesmodel" for Pedigree Mealtime. Like other stars, he travels with a companion—in his case Brian, an English toy Prince Charles spaniel—and a bevy of human handlers. He possesses, it seems, two sets of parents, one canine, one human. He is said to have his (canine) father's head and his (canine) mother's body, but his personality (he's described by an admirer in the dog press as "very, very personable") comes, it seems, from his human progenitors. "He has my nature," says owner Tina Truesdale. "I'm very strong-willed. I'm brassy. And Biff is an egotistical, self-centered, selfish person. He thinks he's very important and special, and he doesn't like to share." "He doesn't take after me very much," says William Truesdale. "I'm more of a golden retriever."

An interesting flavor of cross-gender discourse creeps into the article—Biff's father was "a little feminine," says his owner, "he would have made an awesome bitch"—but this is nothing compared to the cross-species language deftly put in play by reporter Susan Orlean. "If I were a bitch, I'd be in love with Biff Truesdale," her article begins, in that technique of human/animal misdirection we have already noticed (we could call it bite-and-switch). "Biff is perfect. He's friendly, good-looking, rich, famous, and in excellent physical condition. He almost never drools. He's not afraid of commitment. He wants children—actually, he already has children and wants a lot more." If it weren't for the celebrity portrait accompanying the piece, Biff's species would have remained presumptively human, since it is unspecified until four paragraphs into the piece. Later, completing the switch, she will report "I pawed through his suitcase." Biff himself is clearly a stud in more than one sense, and for more than one appreciative audience; as William Truesdale remarks, enthusiastically, "He has a fabulous rear."

Social Clumber

The 1996 Westminster Kennel Club Show was the Club's one hundred and twentieth, the second-oldest continuously held sports event in America (after the Kentucky Derby, which is a year older). Advance betting was on a stylish Afghan bitch to win Best in Show. Indeed early editions of *The New York Times* (gone to press before the show's late-night conclusion) presumed she would win. "Just like a diva, she had a hairdresser hovering over her before she met her public," declared the *Times*. "For 45 minutes, he brushed, sprayed a mixture of water and conditioner, brushed, combed, and brushed again." This was another in the sleight-of-paw genre of "make the reader think you're talking about a person (not a dog)" articles so familiar in dog culture, as its next two paragraphs make clear:

> Meanwhile, she munched on sliced ham and bologna and sipped on ice water. Her nose bumped the ice cubes, but no matter. She was happy, and when her public got its first look at her, it cheered and oohed and aahed. Every time she moved, she pranced like Deion Sanders high-stepping into the end zone.
>
> She is Ch. Tryst of Grandeur, a 5-year-old, 50-pound black Afghan hound.

Once again, gendered language was front and center, as well as up close and personal. Tryst, the *Times* assured us, was "the height of femininity." Her male "handler/caretaker/hairdresser," who wore a sequined jacket in the show ring, said proudly: "She's everything a feminine Afghan should be. She's graceful and elegant, like a beautiful woman. That little glint in her eye lets you know she can be just as naughty as she wants to be." The seventy-one-year old male judge who selected

her as best of breed said she was "very exciting." Certainly in the ring
she behaved as if she were a seasoned beauty queen on the runway,
calmly showing off for her fans. Another dog reporter called her the
"glamour bitch" of the competition, and speculated that she "must
have thrown a hissy fit when trounced" by the eventual winner, who was
"accompanied by a woman in a rather plain day suit."

For Tryst, despite her glamour (and her Grandeur), did not in fact
win Westminster. Top prize went to Champion Clussexx Country Sunrise (known to his friends as Brady), a Clumber spaniel who, at the age
of four, was making his last appearance before retirement. The *Times*
had to remake its sports page. Brady represented not glamour but energy: "He stays in condition by chasing tennis balls and can hold three
in his mouth at once." But to Judge Roy Holloway he was "beautiful."

"Clumber Lumbers to the Top" and "Underdog Clumber Clambers
to the Top" quipped one newspaper's headlines. Unlike Tryst, who was
staying in a midtown hotel with an assistant handler, Brady slept, mod-
estly and democratically, in his crate in the Madison Square Garden
rotunda. "Now our defining dog is . . . a Clumber spaniel?" mused
columnist Vicki Croke. "It's like John Goodman winning Wimbledon.
A size 14 taking the Miss America crown. Or as though the classic TV
sitcom we all watched was 'I Love Ethel.' " Or *The Brady Bunch?* The
solid, stolid Clumber, ranked only 124th among 137 AKC breeds in
popularity, was clearly the dog of the moment—and the dog for the
needs of the nineties. If "the top dog at Westminster tells us about the
mood of our country," this was, perhaps, the event politicians should
have been watching instead of the Iowa primaries. A Clumber in the
White House?

The Clumber, once the favorite dog of England's King Edward VII
and his son George V, is "long, low, and rather heavyset," according to
Roger Caras, who served on this occasion as the deep and orotund
voice of Westminster. (In his capsule accounts of each breed, the eloquent Caras produced perhaps my all-time-favorite piece of inadvertent political correctness when he described the Rhodesian ridgeback
as "named for his country of origin, Zimbabwe.") A "fine, steady field
dog without enormous social grace," a "somewhat dour character," the
Clumber is a stocky spaniel who resembles a basset hound in body with
a St. Bernard–like head. "Those wanting the excitement of a canine pal
and fellow socializer," Caras wrote in his *Dog Book*, "may find this

breed less than ideal." But Brady's breeder insisted that Clumbers have "a royal air in attitude and spirit." And Brady, said his handler, actually loved the show ring. Indeed the handler, Lisa Jane Alston-Myers, the daughter of a well-known handler and a judge, and the wife of another handler, had a dog show pedigree of her own, as the Westminster television commentators noted throughout the evening. Her victory over the man in the sequined blazer was duly noted. And when she wept, she said it was because, with Brady retiring, she would no longer see him every day.

Whether or not Brady the Clumber had "enormous social grace" and "the excitement of a fellow socializer"—and it seems from both his demeanor and his fans that he did—the Westminster Kennel Club itself provided more than enough in the way of high-society occasions. Dachshund fancier Iris Love and gossip columnist Liz Smith gave a party at the Tavern on the Green in New York's Central Park for more than four hundred dogs and other guests. Their smooth-coated dachshund competed successfully in the ring, and another of Love's dachshunds, a young female named Arete, belied her classical name (which means "virtue") and delved into a chopped-liver mold—in the shape of a dachshund—on the buffet table. Love, described in a masterpiece of journalistic compression as a "socially prominent archaeologist," praised her dogs as "excellent archaeologists" in their own right, and very thorough investigators." One had helped her to measure the depth of holes at a dig in Turkey, and another slept protectively on the cashbox in her tent. Dachshunds, she told a reporter at the stylish annual "dog party," are "good strategists and very affectionate, although they can be a bit of the snob." Whether this meant that they do or don't socialize with Clumbers remained to be seen.

"But I Have That Within Which Passeth Show"

But not every breed fancier is a fan of dog shows. Novelist Donald McCaig, the vice president of the United States Border Collie Club and author of *Nop's Trials*, published a stinging *New York Times* op-ed piece about the American Kennel Club, which he accused of having a "single-minded show-dog orientation" that led it to ignore genetic problems in the breeds it registers. The AKC, reported McCaig, was begun in New York

> by a group of rich dog fanciers who didn't let any old mutt into their club; breed registries aspiring to join had to turn over spotless stud books (the records of all purebred matings within the breed) and produce an established conformation standard (what the dog should look like). Those breeds that didn't measure up, or whose owners didn't care to become vassals of the kennel club, were ignored and considered mongrels.

Yet today, McCaig charged the kennel club is preoccupied with hostile takeovers of breed clubs that don't want to join, like the Cavalier King Charles Club (whose members want to specify that breeders can't sell to pet shops or wholesale puppy mills, a practice the AKC refuses to condemn) or McCaig's own border collie group, which believes that "breeding the border collie for shows will inevitably ruin the breed's working ability." (That working ability, mythologized by the sheepherding dog mentors in the move *Babe,* has been put to ever new uses in modern life: in Mamaroneck, New York, border collies have been successfully used to herd messy flocks of Canadian geese out of the scenic harbor area.)

A pack of letters to the *Times* in response to McCaig's attack gave voice to all sides of this volatile issue. The AKC's communications officer pointed out that the club sanctions more "performance events" (hunting tests, retriever trials, obedience trials, field trials, and herding trials) than dog shows. "Of the 11,000 events the club sanctions each year, only 1,400 are all-breed conformation dog shows." Other correspondents urged that mutts be permitted to compete in obedience and other performance events and that border collies and Cavalier King Charles spaniels be accorded "the right of self-determination." One writer feelingly decried "the reprehensible state of affairs of the American Kennel Club," which had led, she claimed, to the "victimization" of her German shepherd by the breeding industry. The German shepherd has been bred for looks. As a result, the writer's dog was beautiful, but doomed to an early death from a condition caused by inbreeding. "Gorgeous, symmetrical coloring; championship, regal posture; an ancestral tree worthy of any European monarch. And an irreversible, deteriorating genetic disorder that drives my husband and me to tears."

"If close relatives mate for generation after generation in a community," writes dog sexologist Midas Dekkers, "inbreeding will result and aberrations will become chronic. In dogs all kinds of breeds have been created in this way. As a rule, pedigree dogs are less healthy than a mongrel chosen at random because the desired characteristics are almost always accompanied by undesirable ones: boxers are unable to bite very well, poodles have breeding difficulties, dachshunds have back problems. It is always dangerous to apply breeders' wisdom to human beings, but . . ."

Inbreeding in *human* family trees is associated with both the high and the low end of the social scale. The male heir of the Russian Romanov family developed hemophilia, a hereditary clotting disorder that afflicted members of Queen Victoria's extended family among the crowned heads of Europe. Meantime in the United States "the Jukes and the Kallikaks" became shorthand for the kind of regressive inbreeding that took place, it was claimed, among impoverished Appalachian clans. Yet inbreeding (and linebreeding) are intrinsic to the notion of the dog breed, the one forum in which the concept of developing a pure and exemplary "master race" is not discredited.

Equally dangerous to the health and welfare of the dog is breed overpopularity, which can lead to thoughtless dog ownership and to neglect. For example, when Disney wanted to remake the 1961 animated hit *101 Dalmatians* with live dogs, the British Dalmatian Club put the studio on the spot. Claiming that after the original movie was distributed Dalmatian puppies were heedlessly purchased and subsequently neglected, the BDC voted against participation in the project. Disney went ahead with an open casting call nonetheless. (Glenn Close, already certified as a thoroughbred bitch by *Fatal Attraction,* was a natural to play Cruella de Vil.) The same kind of dangerous overpopularity has affected a number of other breeds, from the collie to the cocker spaniel. So the market is often flooded with previously owned dogs with nowhere to go. Enter the dozens of breed rescue groups, from Airedale to West Highland white, who take unwanted dogs into shelters and try to find them new homes. For those who find the idea of one-breed shelters "exclusive" in a negative sense, breed proponents have an answer. "If every breed had its own rescue [organization] there would be a lesser burden on the shelters," says Susan Foster, codirector of the Yankee Golden Retriever Rescue. "We take some of the strain off the system by having placed seventeen hundred dogs."

Bad Dogs

When the Ohio legislature attempted to pass a vicious-dog statute in 1987, the act was initially intended to apply to all dogs regardless of breed, but lawmakers decided at the last minute to single out one breed of dog, the "pit bull." Breeders' associations and owners complained that any dog or breed can become a "bad dog," and that "bad dogs" were "manmade," a result of "human interference with the natural propensities of the animals to create excellent guard dogs, fighting machines, or whatever suits man's purpose." Viciousness was a human problem, not a canine one.

Opponents mounted constitutional challenges to the Ohio statue, claiming that the state was in effect mounting "a vendetta" to eliminate pit bulls entirely. One unintended and undesired result was that many dogs were given up for adoption so owners would not be liable for their actions; since they were not considered adoptable, most were destroyed. Others were abandoned by their owners, also to avoid liability, and ran loose—the opposite of what had been desired by the lawmakers. It was contended that in singling out pit-bull owners the statute failed to offer "equal protection." Since many dangerous dogs were not registered as belonging to *any* breed, they escaped calumny. Furthermore, since, as we have seen, the very definition of "pit bull" is in dispute, the law was also seen as impossibly and unconstitutionally vague: to whom (or to which dogs) did it in fact apply?

The "pit bull" had become what literary critics of a certain genre would call an "undecidable" figure: singled out for vilification by the law, yet not reliably identifiable as a breed. "Everyone knows" and "no one knows" what a "pit bull" is. Everyone knows, and no one knows, that "they" are dangerous.

"Pit bull" ordinances adopted by Dade County, Florida, and Denver, Colorado, "define" the "pit bull" in interesting ways. The Dade County ordinance, for example, stipulates that "the term 'pit bull dog'" will refer, for legal purposes, to a dog that "substantially conforms" to AKC standards for American Staffordshire terriers, or Staffordshire bull terriers, or to the United Kennel Club standard for American pit bull terriers. But if the dog in question does not conform to the standard because of "technical deficiencies" it can still be called a "pit bull dog" for legal purposes, and if a veterinarian, zoologist, animal behaviorist, or animal control officer says it's a pit bull this declaration "establish[es] a rebuttable presumption." Since, as a book on dog law points out, the term "pit bull" is "actually generic," when a dog is "determined" by a designated expert to be a "pit bull" it often, in effect, becomes one.

The demons as well as the darlings of dogdom have changed over time. A California insurance company recently refused to renew one family's homeowners' insurance because they owned a Doberman pinscher, a breed the company condemned as having "aggressive tendencies." Local dog organizations said the company had missed the point, branding a breed rather than an individual dog as vicious. "We have a very serious problem with anyone who proclaims that a breed is vicious," declared the president of the California Federation of Dog Clubs. "It's dog racism."

Self-described "animal poet" Vicki Hearne tells a particularly moving story of the way in which human racism and its social effects crossed over into a court case involving a supposed "pit bull," Bandit, whom she rescued from legal "execution" in Connecticut as a dangerous dog. Bandit had belonged to an elderly black man from Virginia named Lamon Redd, who had complied with a judge's request that he build an expensive fence and doghouse to contain his supposedly menacing pet. Nevertheless, Bandit had been reapprehended by the law and now stood in danger of being killed. When Mr. Redd rose at a hearing to testify for him, here is what he said:

> All the ladies in the neighborhood like him. Not just the colored
> ladies. The white ladies like him, too.

Hearne was shocked and sickened by what was revealed by this tactic of defense. "Mr. Redd is from Virginia," she explains, "where the racism is fairly straightforward. When you have straightforward racism, then the fact that the white ladies liked the dog is straightforwardly evidence in the dog's favor. . . . Mr. Redd's plea didn't work, but his was the only fully relevant remark anyone made at that hearing. 'The white ladies like him, too.'"

If today's bête noir is the "pit bull," yesterday's—or, at least, yesteryear's—was the German shepherd. "I have no wish to enter into the controversy about German Shepherds," wrote a dog breeder and judge in 1936.

Such superstitions as that of their wolf origin have long since been exploded. For some time the country could not have enough of them, and enormous numbers were imported, bred, and sold. Some unscrupulous breeders, in their haste to cash in on the profits to be made, undoubtedly sold many poor and vicious dogs, and there was a great rise of backyard breeding. . . . Many are still seen on the streets, exhibiting clearly a cross of alien blood, and often these mongrels have given the breed a bad name by a general surly air, a vicious shyness, or unprovoked attacks.

"Thus," he concluded, "it has come to the point where the average person has had instilled in him a real distrust of the breed." Like the collies ruined by the popularity of *Lassie,* German shepherds were doubtless overbred as a result of the film and radio (and later, television) popularity of Rin Tin Tin.

The "wolf" legend is also described by *Cop: Chief of Police Dogs,* itself a curious mixed-breed book, part children's story, part album of international champions, which extols the excellences of the shepherd dog. (The children's book is illustrated with color sketches, the factual appendix with formal posed photographs of "International Champion Donar von Overstolzen, Sch.H.," "International Champion Asta von Kaltenweide, Sch.H.," and their fellows). "All sorts of silly stories concerning [the shepherd's] 'wolf ancestry,' 'wild blood,' 'natural ferocity,' and other non-existing traits, have become current," reports the author, who wants to assure the reader not only that these claims are untrue, but that the shepherd's nature is "very nearly the exact opposite of the wolf nature: faithful where the wolf is treacherous; courageous where the wolf is cowardly; intelligent . . . where the wolf is sly." Fans of the wolf will be surprised at this account of an animal today reckoned both intelligent and courageous, but clearly *someone* must be the Bad Dog in any moralizing bestiary. "Police dog" is also seen as a potential slur, despite the praise that is heaped on properly trained canine protectors. (And anyone who remembers Bull Connor's dogs, used to resist desegregation in the American South, may greet the image of the shepherd as a "police dog" with mixed emotions.)

"German," of course, was also once a problem; in British parlance the shepherd became an "Alsatian" to liberate it from unwelcome political associations during the war. Eugene O'Neill, as we have noted, referred in passing to the "German Gestapo dog." Interestingly, Konrad Lorenz, who was born in Vienna and served as a physician in the German Army during World War II, calls his own shepherd dogs "Alsatians." He shares—in 1955—some of the qualms expressed in earlier decades: "Some of the nervous and vicious show specimens that have earned a bad name for this breed in England have already evolved temperaments which deviate so far from the ideal as to put them in an entirely different category from the genuine working Alsatians." Typically, Lorenz's view is not without some gender attitudinizing: "The matter becomes serious when fashion, that silliest of all silly females, begins to dictate to the poor dog what he has got to look like." He goes on to "deplore" the mental and physical "degeneration" of some of his favorite breeds, including the chow and the Scottish terrier: "If one looks at old pictures, which in the case of English dog breeds can be found dating back to the Middle Ages, and compares them with pictures of present-day representatives of the same breeds, the latter look like evil caricatures of the original strain."

"Alsatians," explains Barbara Woodhouse matter-of-factly,

> will hate men or women instinctively if thought transference comes from an owner with a similar dislike. So many women own Alsatians to show their superiority over their fellow men and women. They like big guard dogs, and the big guard dog . . . easily develops a dislike of the sex its owner wishes to contemplate. Corgis do the same. I have particularly noted it in these two breeds, partly because they are highly intelligent breeds and telepathy is very marked.

For Woodhouse this is a matter of both nature and culture; she recommends conditioning, perhaps even a "'dog-sitter' of the hated sex," since "this sex hatred is not a breeding fault." As her title insists, there are no bad dogs.

Top Dogs

The "pit bull," as Vicki Hearne points out in defense of the allegedly "dangerous dog" Bandit, was once a *favored* breed in the United States. Pete the Pup of *Our Gang* was a lovable pit bull terrier. President Theodore Roosevelt had a pit bull in the White House, and a celebrated war poster of 1914 represented the countries in conflict during World War I in terms of national breeds. "Germany is a Dachshund, France a French Bulldog, Russia a Borzoi, England an English Bulldog. America is a Pit Bull Terrier, wearing Old Glory around his neck."

What is the "American" dog today?

The American Kennel Club periodically offers statistics on which breeds of dog are most favored by owners. "The Rottweiler is the guarddog-of-the-moment," says the AKC vice president for communications, and the second most popular purebred in the United States. "But as popular as these dogs become, they never displace the number-one dog, which for the past few years has become the Labrador, the quintessential family dog. So you have the most friendly dog at the top, followed by a guard dog. That's some incredible yin and yang." The "Rottie," as its fans like to call it, has traditionally been favored by men, but apparently more and more women have been taken by its charms. "It's the ideal dog for a woman living alone in the city," notes one happy owner. "Everybody gets out of my way when I walk down the sidewalk with Honey; it's like the parting of the Red Sea."

Good Dog! "The Consumer Magazine for Dog Owners" offered information about breeds that had recently fallen out of favor. Cocker spaniels, the favorite pet of the 1940s, were first replaced by poodles, then overbred, creating "dogs with fear problems or standoffish personalities." Cairn terriers have dropped in popularity since 1990 (Dorothy's Toto was one, but *The Wizard of Oz* isn't shown as much as it used to be), and the keeshond, the otter hound, the chow chow ("May look like a woolly bear but can be rude and nasty"), and the petit basset griffon vendéen ("Americans can't remember the name") have all declined. How reliable these figures are seems a little open to question, since many dog owners, like me, acquire dogs with "papers" and never bother to register them, since they don't intend to show or breed them. What's as interesting as the data is the popularity of the topic: *Good Dog!*'s list of neglected breeds made it into *Time* magazine, with a page of irresistible pictures, a stylish lead ("Who's up, who's down in the world of pedigreed dogs") and a winning headline ("Man's Not-So-Best Friends").

By another kind of reckoning, it could be said that the most "American" dog in the country's cultural imagination is the mutt (aptly called "All-American" by an agility trial announcer at the Eastern Dog Club

Annual Show). In one sense every child dreams of owning Lassie. But in American cultural fantasy life, whatever dog the individual or family may own, the real American hero is the mutt—or mongrel, or cross-bred, or random-bred. Like the cowboy and the self-made man, the mutt represents resilience, ingenuity, energy in overcoming obstacles—and without any undesirable human extras. As Mark Twain wrote, "If you pick up a starving dog and make him prosperous, he will not bite you. This is the principal difference between a dog and a man." Tramp of *Lady and the Tramp* is one example of this "new breed," Willie Morris's dog Skip was another, and their number has been legion. (O. Henry's yellow dog, Twain's talkative cross-breed, and so on.) When Comet, a handsome golden retriever who appears in the television series *Full House*, was chosen as the star of the movie *Fluke*, where the plot called for Fluke to be a mutt, he was transformed into a "mixed-breed" by clipping his fur and dyeing it a deeper brown with vegetable coloring.

Perhaps the most eulogized of movie mutts has been Old Yeller, star of the 1957 Disney film of the same name. Described in the film's ballad theme song as a lop-eared mongrel of uncertain ancestry, Yeller is a homespun American hero, not much to look at but in heart and courage the best dog in the West. "Yeller, come back Yeller . . ." urges the chorus (which I found myself joyously yodeling for days). "Come back Yeller" was the "home" theme once again, now seamlessly blended with the western frontier: home on the range. And once Yeller has sacrificed himself to save his human family, his son Young Yeller is there to carry on the family tradition. Young Yeller, clearly the image of his father, lop-ears and all, is now characterized as a handsome puppy whose "family tree" is "plain to see." In short, in one generation (rather than the AKC's statutory three) the Yeller family has achieved a kind of pedigree. But theirs is a pedigree with a difference, the proud lineage of the self-made dog.

Most enterprising movie mutts are male, like Yeller, Tramp, and Rocks. Their romantic alliances with purebred females are one ticket up the social ladder. Other mutts get their family values from human rather than canine associates, but here, too, a lone male stray seems more socially acceptable than a female (even when, as in the case of Benji, he's *played* by a female). Despite constant reminders about the unhappy fate of unwanted random-bred dogs (*"No random-bred dog should ever be permitted to reproduce,"* says Roger Caras firmly. "Millions must be destroyed every year for the want of homes") there is the hope that an undistinguished dog may distinguish himself, or herself, by sheer merit rather than championship lineage. A feature of certain thirties films involving rivalries between *human* bluebloods and scrappers, the perpetual heartstring tug between the purebred and the mutt is a tried-and-true American "success story."

Underdogs

Humans have taken to describing their own behavior in terms they have learned from books on dog training. An "alpha male" in dog parlance is the leader of the pack, acknowledged and deferred to by the other dogs; the term is derived from the leadership of wolf packs in the wild. Dog owners are urged to become the alpha, or pack leader, with respect to their own dogs. "How large a pack leadership problem you have with your dog is largely determined by two factors: (1) how dominant your dog's personality is and (2) how assertive you are as an individual. . . . If you have a dominant dog and you are inconsistent, extremely indulgent, and a nondisiciplinarian, you may have a big problem convincing your dog that you are the pack leader." If this sounds like a sound bite from *How to Succeed in Business,* that's probably not far from the truth. "Top dog" is an informal term describing the person of a group who seems to have the most prestige or authority, especially as a result of some kind of competition. (It may also have a sexual connotation, since the "top dog" mounts the others as a show of dominance, regardless of the sex of the "under dog"). "Underdog" itself has become so much part of the language of human competition, whether in sports or in politics, that we often forget the "dog" embedded in the term. An "underdog" these days may be someone regarded as at a disadvantage, and the competition can be of a general nature ("getting ahead") as well as of a specific one (the championship game). Here, too, the metaphor comes from puppyhood, from the fact that each puppy has a position in the hierarchy of the litter. "The biggest, toughest, and loudest puppy . . . became 'top pup.' The more submissive puppy, who accepted being bitten and growled at, assumed a lower rank in the pack." Americans have traditionally regarded themselves as "rooting for the underdog" even when they also proclaim "We're Number One." (In national stereotypes consistency is the hobgoblin of little minds.) The runt of the litter, like his or her fairy-tale counterpart, Cinderella, is often the hero of many of our favorite dog stories.

"Two of my best friends are dogs of a whirling mélange of ancestry," wrote Dorothy Parker in the forties. "They are short in the paw, long and wavering in the body, heavy and worried in the head. They are willing, useless, and irresistible. Nobody ever asks their breed. 'Oh, look at the Thurber dogs,' people say."

The "Thurber dog," a somewhat spaniel-y, somewhat bloodhound-y beast capable both of great (apparent) complacency and great (apparent) emotion, was a cherished feature of *New Yorker* cartoons. Unlike other "new breeds" (the cockapoo, the Labradoodle) the Thurber dog, a "lovable, vulnerable, bewildered canine of indeterminate breed," came to symbolize, to readers and ultimately to the artist himself, a canonical (or caninical) version of Everydog. Hundreds of admirers named their own dogs Thurber, while the flop-eared dog, the mercurial cartoonist's favorite doodle, was increasingly regarded as an autobiographical sketch: "the saddened artist as canine, in a perpetual cry for help, hoping for sympathy, affection, and understanding." James Thurber's portrait of the artist as a young (or middle-aged) mutt became one enduring image of the rite of passage from tentative boyhood to tentative manhood, a four-pawed parable of muddled masculinity and fireside self-esteem.

The tension between hierarchical order and self-creation noted by Harriet Ritvo in Victorian society has only intensified in late-twentieth-century America. On the one hand, the mutt represents the dream of the "self-made dog" at its most aggressively democratic; on the other, capitalism's fascination with "57 varieties" of everything from ketchup to automobiles makes the proliferation of new and ever more improbable breeds of dog inevitable. "Heinz dog," after all, has today become common slang for "mutt."

Dog Law

The dog and man at first were friends;
    But when a pique began,
The dog, to gain some private ends,
    Went mad, and bit the man.

Around from all the neighbouring streets
    The wondering neighbours ran,
And swore the dog had lost his wits,
    To bite so good a man.

The wound it seemed both sore and sad
    To every Christian eye;
And while they swore the dog was mad,
    They swore the man would die.

But soon a wonder came to light,
    That showed the rogues they lied:
The man recovered of the bite—
    The dog it was that died.
           —Oliver Goldsmith, "Elegy on the Death of a Mad Dog"

When a dog bites a man, that is not news, because it happens so often. But if a man bites a dog, that is news.
           —John B. Bogart

Call Him "Dog" Pound?

Roscoe Pound, dean of the Harvard Law School from 1916 to 1936, once jestingly proposed "canine jurisprudence" as a fit companion to the existing fields of medical jurisprudence, dental jurisprudence, and the like. In Pound's view dogs had two duties: "to abstain from biting" and "to abstain from barking."

These "duties" still remain for the domestic dog. But a hundred years later, when canine jurisprudence is no longer an urbane joke but rather a significant body of law applying to country and city canines, a third "duty" has perforce been added: "to abstain from fouling the footpath." Under the heading of "biting," "barking," and "pooping," statutes and ordinances attempt to control the behavior of dogs. Or is it the behavior of their owners?

In any case, dog law is no longer merely a twinkle in a learned law professor's eye. The history of canine jurisprudence in the northeastern United States, for example, extends from 1791, and laws regulating dogs have been amended numerous times in this century. A Boston animal rights lawyer explains that he has made a career of defending dogs, especially those condemned to death or banishment for causing injuries to people. In 1992 *Dog Fancy* magazine produced a "Special Legal Issue," including provocative articles entitled "Laws about Dogs: What They Are, How You Can Change Them"; "Dealing with Dog Bites"; and "Write a Will that Includes Your Dog," as well as information on a "British Dog Ban" and the challenging question of "Off-Leash Freedom—Is Your Dog Ready?"

"Bone up on your knowledge of canine behavior," urged *Dog Fancy*'s editor, noting that "so much legislation concerning animals is being enacted" that dog ownership, once viewed as "a right that couldn't be taken away," was now becoming a privilege, and one that could disappear if owners were not vigilant. Britain, "that nation of dog lovers," had recently banned the import, sale, and breeding of the American pit bull terrier, Tosa Inu, Dogo Argentino, and Fila Brasileiro. San Mateo County, California, had enacted legislation regulating the breeding of dogs and cats that was "spawning copy-cat legislation across the country." In short, it was time for dog owners to sit up and take notice.

In New York City dog owners and the Park Enforcement Patrol are periodically at odds about whether dogs should be permitted to walk (or run) free. "When you give an inch, they take a lawn," said Parks Commissioner Henry J. Stern, who keeps his golden retriever, Boomer, firmly leashed. But pressure groups like You Gotta Have Bark in Prospect Park and the Urban Canine Conservancy in Central Park have lobbied for greater access to the city's wide open spaces. "Let Rover rove!" they cry. Plans are afoot to seek permission for a spacious dog run in the Sheep Meadow, paid for by a dog food company in exchange for "a tasteful bronze plaque." Meantime, park rangers ticket those scofflaws—and their name is legion—who contend that "canine happiness is a greater good."

The response to a newspaper account of this controversy, and to a subsequent endorsement of "canine liberation" in the parks by Elizabeth Marshall Thomas, was vociferous, ranging from "Park officers should be equipped with dart guns, and the pound should charge $500 to retrieve a pet" to "Parks and other public places were created for all Americans, be they bare of behind or covered with wool, two-footed or four-footed. The latter have faithfully served our country alongside the former in war and peace, and therefore deserve to share fully in the freedom they helped to preserve." Dog owners wrote to complain that they alone were singled out by park rangers ("Have you ever seen a skater get a ticket? A litterer? A graffiti artist or a kid doing damage?"), a birdwatcher complained that loose dogs endanger the city's "wild avifauna," and the president of Floral (Friends and Lovers of Riverside Area Life) pointed out that his group fostered cooperation between "dog owners and non–dog owners" in fixing up Riverside Park. The division of the world into these two basic categories, those who own dogs and those who don't, struck me as particularly felicitous for a more canine-centered planet—especially in view of another letter on the same page that pointed out that dogs in Holland (for example) attend weddings and funerals, since "they are considered members of the family, with all the rights and obligations that status confers." What was clear was that the dog owners and non–dog owners all had strong views, anecdotes, and grievances; the *Times*, in a highly unusual allocation of space, devoted its entire letters column to the topic, printing seventeen letters in all, under the urbane heading "Sunday in the Park with George, Rover and Spot." Major elections, budget battles, and acts of God have often made do with less.

Indeed, not content with vox populi, the paper itself weighed in with an editorial a few days later, conceding that "the dog owners do have emotion on their side," but supporting the city's "rationality" in requiring leashes on pets, at least during prime time. (The Parks Department, in what the *Times* proudly called "a very New York–style accommodation," had made it clear that it wouldn't enforce the leash law before nine A.M. or after nine P.M.) As the editorial also pointed out, this is old news for New York dogs: in her novel *Real Estate*, Jane DeLynn reported the melancholy sensations of a dog named Jack when confronted with a similar crisis, in the neo-Orwellian tones befitting a canine world turned upside down:

> "One day, just like that, the unspeakable had occurred. . . . He looked around; other dogs were on their leashes too. Great sadness there was in the park that day. Jack was still brought near and allowed to sniff other dogs, but the rituals of teeth-baring and attacking were almost instantly cut short; there was no running and demonstrating of hunting skills; worst of all, there was none of that camaraderie of dogs being off together with other dogs, away and separate from humans."

"Dog Laws Unleash Owner Anger," announced an article chronicling a similar dispute in Boston between lovers of lush park lawns and lovers of the animals who roam them. To require his dog to be leashed at all times, said one dog owner, is "tantamount to cruelty." In response to local attempts to enforce the leash law, he and his fellow activists formed a procanine group called Bark Up, resolved to perform acts of civil disobedience like letting their dogs run off the leash. Opponents claimed that not only parklands but local children were at risk: "These aren't terriers we're talking about," said the proprietor of a nearby day-care center. "These are Great Danes and Rottweilers and German shepherds. They're accidents waiting to happen."

Dog owners, of course, take a slightly different view of where accident-proneness may lie. In the park where I used to like to run my dogs, bicyclists and in-line skaters complained of dogs as hazards. Walkers sans pets are more vulnerable to the roller-rights crowd, with their self-confident cries of "On your left!" "On your right!" shouted as they whiz by. But from leash laws to noise abatement to custody and inheritance, the laws regulating dogs—and their owners—have begun more and more to mark the limits of "freedom" in an increasingly urbanized, and litigious, society. Some of these may seem frivolous, and others self-evident and fundamental. It depends, as always, upon whose "rights" are in question.

Consider the following entirely typical newspaper report:

Used to be, when town dog officer Richard Bustard answered a complaint about late-night barking, the most he could do was issue a toothless lecture appealing to the neighborliness and vague principles of pet etiquette.

But no more. Randolph now has a barking law with some bite.

The characteristically tongue-in-jowl style of this opening paragraph suggests that, though the article appears on the first page, readers may find its content both comic and trivial.

In many regions of the country, indeed, dog barking has been regarded as a social nuisance. A Little Rock, Arkansas, ordinance specifies that dogs are not allowed to bark after six P.M. and that husbands are not allowed to hammer after the same hour. But if "Man bites dog" is, proverbially, news, what can be said about "Man barks at dog"? A Portland, Maine, police officer cited a man named Johnny Mathis (not the singer) for barking at Zedo, a police dog, a little after one in the morning on a Saturday night. Zedo barked first, Mathis said in his own defense: "I had stopped barking, and the police still arrested me."

The Poop Perplex

"Picking up after your dog," as it is euphemistically called (picking *what* up? one doesn't say) is a way of life in Cambridge, Massachusetts, where I live. I never leave the house with the dogs and without plastic bags; in fact virtually no outer garment I own lacks an emergency stash. There are pooper-scoopers galore on the market, from the Dispoz-a-Scoop ("environmentally friendly because they are biodegradable," "perfect when walking your dog") to the Poopscoop with Spade (or Rake) to the scissorslike Sanitary Scooper. For the pet owner on the go, however, Baggies, however environmentally unfriendly, are convenient, cheap, and quick.

"Watch Your Steps," warned the *Boston Globe* with predictable jocularity, announcing a police crackdown on nonscooping poop perps who violate the city's 1979 scooper law. Efforts to expand Boston's enforcement team and add a "pooper detail" had, said an official, been "one of the things that fell through the cracks." "We haven't caught anybody yet, not red-handed," lamented the captain of the Code Enforcement Police, while another spokesman noted: "You have to see the dog in motion and someone without utensils." When dog owners see police officers hovering they "break out their doggie bags." Some city residents, complaining that dogs "performed" on their lawns with impunity, urged the possibility of a citizens' arrest, but this can be dangerous: the chairwoman of the streets and sidewalks committee of the Beacon Hill Civic Association reported that she had almost been punched by a man she asked to clean up after his dog. Among the creative excuses offered by delinquent dog owners was one man's suggestion that he was letting the dog feces "cure" before he picked them up.

So much for Boston. But similar scoop laws are on the books, whether or not they are scrupulously enforced, around the country. "Dog droppings have become a scourge, a form of environmental pollution no less dangerous and degrading than the poisons that we exude and dump into our air and water," declared the New Jersey Superior Court in 1971. A New York statute was (unsuccessfully) challenged by Orthodox Jews on the grounds that it interfered with the free exercise of religion, since the instruction to clean up after your pet would require them to work on the Sabbath. Guide, hearing, and service dogs (and their owners) are exempt from pooper-scooper laws in many places, including New York and San Francisco, which didn't prevent a San Francisco cop from forcing a blind woman to clean up after her dog. She sued for damages from emotional trauma, and won.

A French lawmaker's proposal for an annual dog tax to defray the huge sums spent annually in cleaning streets and parks was met with outrage by the dog-loving populace of France, where nine million dogs live in a nation of fifty-eight million people. (A task force of specially designed motorized vehicles scoops the poop on Paris boulevards.) Germany has a similar tax, apportioned locally, that amounts to about forty dollars per dog.

In Britain, where "fouling the footpath" has long been politely discouraged, a debate in the House of Lords centered on the question of whether the dog owner was littering when his dog produced droppings.

> *Lord Hesketh* (Minister of State, Department of the Environment): The offence of littering requires a person to drop, deposit, or leave litter. In the case of dog and other animal droppings it is clear that the person in charge of the animal does not do the actual dropping, depositing, or leaving, which is why the differential exists. . . .
>
> *Lord McIntosh of Haringey:* I must congratulate the minister. To stand up with a straight face and make that statement about the difference between droppings from a dog and droppings by the individual in charge of the dog requires some nerve.

In point of fact this is an issue of agency (or, in this case, perhaps, an agency of issue) of a kind very similar to others we will be considering under the "canine jurisprudence" heading. Here then is the scoop on the Poop Perplex: Is a dog a free agent or an aspect of his owner? Are the dog's droppings the master's droppings?

Petimony

The proposal that dogs be treated more like children than like property has been mentioned by one self-help book on dog law as a "radical departure from traditional law" which was "extremely unlikely to happen soon." But despite this sanguine prediction, dog custody and "petimony" cases are becoming regularly more common, as divorces continue to affect pet owners—and their pets. In Atlantic Beach, Florida, a judge granted a woman and her Labrador-shepherd mix, Bruiser, thirty dollars a month in pet support from the woman's ex-husband. In New York City, lawyer Eleanor Alter, who had represented Mia Farrow in her custody dispute with Woody Allen, reported that some of her wealthy clients include dog custody among their prenuptial stipulations. "I did one prenup with nine pages just on the joint-custody issue of their Dandie Dinmont terrier," Alter told *The New York Times*. "One party had primary custody, but the other had visitation rights. If the dog was bred, the one without custody had first pick of the litter; and then there was the question of what to do when the primary custodian went away on weekends—kennel or temporary transfer of custody?" The Dandie Dinmont is a hunting dog said by Sir Walter Scott to "fear naething that ever cam' wi' a hairy skin on't." But does it suffer from separation anxiety?

"Like so many divorced men, Ben Miller now picks up Bruce, aged five, every Friday evening from his ex-wife in the suburbs of New York and returns the collie on Sunday," reports dog observer Midas Dekker. A legal proceeding in another divorce case produced a court judgment that the female plaintiff "was in the best position to care for the afore-mentioned dog and that the wife is therefore awarded custody of the dog, with reasonable visiting rights for the spouse." The divorcing part-ners were determined to act in the best interests of the dog: "We are both determined that he suffer no adverse affects from being the prod-uct of a broken home." As part of their agreement, they pledged to re-sist "brib[ing] his affections with showers of tasty treats, fancy dog apparels [sic] or extended bouts of fetch-the-stick."

In a different but related ruling, a dog's double life was officially sanctioned by the law. Ginger, a shepherd mix belonging to one Mass-achusetts couple, had wandered away from home, been injured, and found a new life with a second family eleven miles away. The family initially tried to find Ginger's original owners, but through various agency glitches it took three years for them to get together, by which time Ginger had become Teddy and was regarded by the second set of owners as their own dog. Despite the fact that the statute of limitations had elapsed, the judge decided to split both ownership and medical ex-penses down the middle. "It's crazy," said the attorney for Ginger's original owners. "They spent $4,000 [in legal fees] for a 14-year-old mongrel. The judge was settling for the benefit of the [couples'] kids."

In the Dog House

Dog law also finds its way into the real estate pages, where "No Pets" provisions by landlords have made things increasingly difficult for would-be renters. At one branch of the Massachusetts Society for the Prevention of Cruelty to Animals, shelter workers said the principal reason that pets were given up for adoption was, as a placard attached to each cage declared, "Landlord won't allow." In 1994 19 percent of all animals given to the MSPCA for adoption were surrendered because landlords wouldn't rent to pet owners, a 5 percent increase over the previous year. Published reports that pet owning was beneficial to senior citizens and persons with disabilities led to a provision, in the Americans with Disabilities Act of 1990, that private landlords "make reasonable accommodation" for disabled persons with pets—a guideline so vague as to provoke considerable argument between landlords and potential renters. The MSPCA, meanwhile, began a program to help persons with AIDS keep their pets in any kind of housing. "It really poses a hardship," said the organization's director of animal welfare. "This is their lives." She meant, I think, the humans' lives—or maybe both.

The One-Bite Law

Law students in first-year torts classes all learn about the "one-bite law," which every textbook tells them is a misnomer.

> One of the common misconceptions that has developed about the law of animals is that every dog is entitled to one free bite. It is clearly true that once a dog has bitten, the owner will be on notice of its dangerous propensities and therefore strictly liable in the event that it bites again. It does not follow, however, that the converse of the proposition is true, as the dog which has not bitten may well have given its owner notice in some other way of its dangerous propensities.

One self-help guide for dog owners note that so-called dog-bite statutes are, likewise, not just laws about biting, but rather laws that cover all dog-inflicted injuries. The book provides a helpful chart, state by state ("State Name / Bites Only? / Other Provisions") and also points out that the term "vicious" in dog-liability language can mean virtually anything that implies that the dog might be a danger to someone, even overfriendliness. In this way I learned that, as the owner of two large and rambunctious golden retrievers, I might be said to harbor, according to the common law, two dogs of "vicious propensity." This strikes me as one of the more Orwellian facts about dog law. On the other hand, I also learned that my homeowners' policy probably covers damage from dog bites (or, presumably, excessively friendly leaps and bounds), though it, too, will probably have a "one-bite rule" that permits subsequent cancellation or a "canine exclusion."

"Dangerous" and "vicious" have legal meanings in dog law. A dangerous dog is one who without provocation has engaged in menacing behavior; a vicious dog is a repeat offender, who has menaced or injured before. As we have noted, breed-specific laws, banning breeds like the German shepherd, the Doberman pinscher, or the "pit bull" have been legally contested by groups like the American Dog Owners Association, the American Kennel Club, and the United Kennel Club. As *Dog Fancy* pointed out, such laws "unjustly penalize dogs with no history of viciousness" because of their putative heritage. "Who wants to condemn a family pet to death just because of its breed? And who is going to testify that this particular dog is, without a doubt, the breed in question?"

In a Michigan case a dog who lunged at a man on his owner's command was found to be a "dangerous weapon" within the meaning of a statute describing felonious assault: "any person who shall assault another with a gun, revolver, pistol, knife, iron bar, club, brass knuckles or other dangerous weapon. . . . shall be guilty of a felony." The owner had been suspected of stealing steaks; the dog (perhaps sympathetic to the theft?) when called by name or told to "go get 'em," got 'em. The question addressed in a law review article was whether, because of the use of the dog, the crime had escalated from simple assault to felonious assault. The defendant had claimed that the dog was an "animate instrumentality" and not a "dangerous weapon." Was a dog, could a dog, be, a "weapon"—usually defined as an *inanimate* object?

The dog was a German shepherd, assumed because of its breed to be large and fierce. "Might a docile German Shepherd be characterized as a dangerous weapon?" asked the author. "We are not told." What about a guard dog, left unattended? The issue is of interest because it asks a question about the dog's independent identity and his (or her) identity as an "instrumentality" of his owner.

Nor is this a new question, though some of the answers may seem novel. Four hundred years ago, in 1595 in the city of Leiden, a dog bit a child so severely that the child died. The dog was sentenced to be hanged, and its body "dragged on a cart to the Gallows field" where it should "remain hanging from the gallows to deter all other dogs." The court record assured readers that the conviction "emerged by the prisoner's own confession made by him without the use of torture or iron shackles." (The child "had a piece of Meat in its hand" when the dog bit it, but the court apparently did not regard this as an extenuating circumstance.) The law in this case was described as a deterrent, the punishment as a fierce warning, the "prisoner's own confession" self-evident testimony that justice had been done. No record exists of any owner's liability—nor, indeed, of any owner.

In the Pen

From 1991 to 1994 the nation's newspapers reported the continuing saga of Taro, the "death row dog." Accused of attacking a ten-year-old girl, and condemned to death under New Jersey's "vicious dog law," Taro was supported in his defense by the state legislator who had sponsored the law. Describing the injury as "a family matter that should never have gotten this far," the lawmaker called the order to execute Taro "as ridiculous as it is unbelievable." The child, Brie Halfond, was injured at a party at the home of her aunt and uncle. Legal authorities said Taro bit her; family members said the dog swiped at her with a paw, causing her lip to bleed, when the girl provoked it with a drumstick.

The case attracted worldwide attention. Actress and animal lover Brigitte Bardot wrote to New Jersey's governor, James Florio, asking that Taro be released. The Japanese government, noting that the dog was an Akita, a Japanese breed, offered to take him, and a Kenyan businessman began organizing support in Africa on his behalf. *People* magazine ran a story headed "Ready for a Milk-Bone Last Meal?" The borough of Haworth (population 3,400) spent about $60,000 in legal fees on the case, and the dog's owners, $25,000. The county spent some $18,000, including the cost of keeping Taro in jail.

In December 1993, the matter reached the New Jersey Assembly floor, where legislators, describing Taro as, alternatively, a noble reincarnation of Lassie and a crazed spiritual descendant of Stephen King's Cujo (and, in one cross-species account, a "vicious" dog who was "not going to change its spots"), debated the pros and cons of a clemency recommendation. Taro, it seemed, had a record: he had killed one dog and severely injured two others. In January the State Supreme Court spared his life until March 1, by which time an appeals court was due to consider his sentence.

New Jersey's newly elected governor, Christine Todd Whitman, was said to be eager to find a nonlethal solution, and later in the month she acted, reversing, by executive order, the forfeiture ruling that had allowed the dog to be seized three years previously. The cost: Taro was to leave the state permanently. Until that time no New Jersey governor had ever granted executive clemency in any kind of case, and Whitman's aides were insistent that this was not clemency ("There is no clemency for anything other than a two-legged creature") but another legal remedy to the problem.

Predictably, adoption offers poured in from around the globe. "The phone rings all day, every day," said Taro's owner, Lonnie Lehrer. "It's really heartwarming to get all this stuff." Offers included money (in one case a quarter of a million dollars), space (213 acres in West Virginia for Taro to roam on), and love. Even astrologer Jeanne Dixon saw Taro in her stars. Thousands of cards and letters arrived at the Lehrer home, some containing cash, others signed with paw prints. Germany, England, Japan, and Kenya were among the nations represented. The Lehrers turned down $10,000 from a Japanese television station for the right to film their reunion. Taro, said Lehrer, is "going to go to a loving family who cares about the dog, not the celebrity." And there was another criterion: the Lehrers wanted to be able to visit him. On February 10, 1995, with much fanfare, Taro was released from the Bergen County Jail Annex, whisked into a sedan owned by the K-9 Corps of the county sheriff, and driven off to a new life in Pleasantville, New York. "This is like moving John Dillinger," complained the warden, but Lehrer declared it "a great day to save a life."

In some quarters, however, the transplanted Taro was as welcome to the neighborhood as a convicted child molester. Within a month the Village of Pleasantville passed a resolution asking New York Governor Mario Cuomo to convey to Governor Whitman the village's "strenuous objection to the terms of the 'pardon' granted to the owners of the dog Taro," and a Jersey legislator who had opposed the governor's action quipped that "Once Taro gets his true nature back, they may have to change the name of Pleasantville to 'Not Pleasantville.'" Lonnie Lehrer, visiting Taro in his new environs, declined to say exactly where the dog was living. "Right now, he is just going around thanking everyone who helped him, paying his respects."

The Dog as Detective

While much of canine jurisprudence treats the dog as a potential law-breaker, it is equally common to find the dog on the side of law enforcement. Search-and-rescue dogs are trained to find missing persons by smell. It takes a year to eighteen months to train a search dog. The best breeds for this work, it is claimed, are hunting dogs such as Labs and golden retrievers, herding dogs such as German shepherds and border collies, and working dogs such as Doberman pinschers and Rottweilers. The same breeds ("large dogs with an aggressive but not hostile demeanor") are used for narcotics detection. They are usually acquired from pounds, from private donors, and from the SPCA. Bomb-sniffing (or "explosives detection") dogs and their handlers investigate bomb threats, suspicious packages, airport security breaches, and terrorist incidents. Within a period of three months, reported the *FBI Law Enforcement Bulletin,* Cliff, a two-year-old German shepherd, had "apprehended 6 felons, including an escaped murderer; completed 14 drug searches; participated in 12 public demonstrations; and searched 5 buildings, resulting in the capture of a burglar." But such efficiency sometimes creates image problems. The Kansas police department where Cliff worked was concerned about the need "to reassure citizens, especially the children, that police dogs were not vicious, uncontrollable creatures with gnashing teeth." Their solution? They created a series of K-9 trading cards featuring Cliff performing a variety of his detective exploits.

The police search dog is one of today's canine media heroes, replacing the more family-oriented amateur sleuth Lassie and the versatile Rin Tin Tin. Rinty, who began his screen and radio career as a veteran of the German army in World War I, was converted by television in the fifties to a survivor of a nineteenth-century Indian raid who subsequently became a private in the U.S. 101st Cavalry, and finally reappeared in a Canadian TV series of the eighties as a member of a twentieth-century police department. Reno, the highly decorated dog sergeant of the 1995 action film *Top Dog,* accompanies an initially skeptical, kickboxing Chuck Norris on his rounds, sniffing out bad guys, drugs, and high explosives, while amiably snacking on jelly doughnuts between assignments. "Good collar, Reno," snickers his friend, a woman detective, after the dog gets his man. (All things con-

sidered, this was a dog joke almost worth sitting through the film to get.)
In an increasingly familiar populist gesture of dog filmdom (see *Fluke*
for another example), Reno was constantly referred to as a "mutt," but
he appeared to this viewer to be a briard, a French breed (described as
"a heart wrapped in fur") known for its excellent war record. "Reno,"
incidentally, may be a backhanded compliment to the female U.S. attorney general, though the film's credits listed that as the canine actor's
actual name.

There are also, of course, amateur detectives in the dog world, canine snoops who act on hunches, who (to use an apt phrase) rightly or
wrongly "feel it in their bones." When Ted Kaczynski, the man suspected of being the Unabomber, was apprehended in Montana, a
neighbor noted that he had long been an object of suspicion to the local dogs. "All the dogs hated him," said the neighbor. "They'd chase
him, bark at him, growl at him when he walked or rode his bike. I had
to call them off him."

One sign of the idealizing transfer of properties from human to dog
has indeed been the popularity of the fictional figure of the dog as detective. Detectives from Dupin to Holmes and Poirot have been seen as
models of human intelligence at work. When it is the dog that does the
detecting, whether in mystery novels like those of Susan Conant or
Melissa Cleary ("starring Jackie Walsh and her crime-solving shepherd, Jake!"), in classical stories of Holmesian dogs that do or don't
bark in the night, in the "Thin Man" stories and the role of the little terrier Asta, in television shows like the popular cartoon Scooby-Doo, or
in works like Stanley Coren's *The Intelligence of Dogs* or Vicki Hearne's
"How to Say Fetch," questions of dog intellect and dog intuition are set
up to reflect upon human capacities and incapacities. The canine sense
of smell, for example, is far keener than the corresponding sense, and
dogs can hear things inaudible to humans. Does the dog act alone, in
concert with a human partner, or does it compensate for human physical or intuitive limitations?

"Bloodhound" has become a cliché synonym for "detective," and
with good cause. The fabled bloodhound Nick Carter "picked up a trail
that was 105 years old and followed it to a subsequent conviction," and
this record from the early part of the twentieth century has since been
more than doubled. "Several specimens have followed human quarry
for more than 50 miles, and one led the detectives 138 miles—all with
success." Whether the breed's name comes from its ability to track the

smell of blood, or from its aristocratic bloodlines, has been amicably disputed.

The Dog as Accomplice

Sometimes the dog is used as an unwitting accomplice, and/or victim, of a crime. Consider the case of the female English sheepdog who arrived on a flight from Colombia with five pounds of cocaine surgically implanted in her abdomen. The wholesale value of the drugs was estimated at $50,000. Packed in ten condoms each the size of an orange, the cocaine was discovered by a veterinarian who X-rayed the dog after its emaciated and lethargic state aroused the suspicion of customs inspectors. The grey-and-white dog, nicknamed "Coke" ("as a joke," he explained) by the veterinarian who rescued her, made what he called a miraculous recovery. She had not eaten in about two weeks, was weak, depressed, and very thin, and would have died, the doctor thought, had the foreign objects not been removed from her body. Dozens of callers wanted to adopt the dog after reading her story in the newspapers, but the agents preferred to keep her. Renamed Cokey by customs agents, she became a mascot at the U.S. Customs Service's Canine Enforcement Training Center in Virginia. The smuggler went to prison for three years.

Bullseye, a mongrel dog used as a lookout by two burglars in Northumberland in England, refused to budge when the owner of the house returned. Police decided that he might lead them to the suspects, and he did, earning plaudits from the London newspapers and dozens of offers of adoption. The lucky winners were John Paul Getty II and his wife, Victoria, who had their new charge picked up at the Newcastle Dog and Cat Center and delivered to their home. "When the driver turned up, we offered him tea," said Mrs. Getty to the London *Daily Telegraph.* "Bullseye was going crazy in the office next door, and left his calling card on the floor."

The Dog as Motive

But dogs have also featured as the *causes* of crime, in fiction and in life. In a lively modern mystery set in an English town, Robert Barnard describes the puzzling murder of a local churchwarden, by profession a veterinarian. Is the cause religious strife in the parish? No, as it turns out. The victim is murdered because he believes in Britain's dog quarantine laws and has realized that a neighbor's dog is in the country illegally. Unwilling to put her dog in a kennel for six months, the murderess kills the vet on the spot—and is promptly given a short sentence by a dog-loving judge, "who arrives at the Court each day in his limousine, with his two poodles in the back seat." The police superintendent in charge finds the motive surprising ("They say there aren't any new ones, but that *is* a motive I've never come across"), but the veterinarian's wife, who is also the story's narrator, sets him right. "The motive was love," she says. "She murdered for love."

Witness for the Prosecution

In a late Agatha Christie novel the murder of one elderly sister by another who takes her place is detected by Hercule Poirot through the actions of a dog.

> "There was also the evidence of the dog—"
> "The dog—what did the dog do?"
> "The dog bit her. The dog was said to be devoted to its mistress, but in the last few weeks of her life, the dog turned on her more than once and bit her quite severely."

The dog ("a very intelligent dog . . . More intelligent perhaps than the police were") has discerned the substitution. "The dog knew—he knew by what his nose told him."

One of Sherlock Holmes's most famous adventures turns on the testimony of a dog. Silver Blaze, a celebrated racehorse favored to win the Wessex Cup, has disappeared from his stable, and his trainer has been tragically murdered. Who is responsible for the crimes, and how are they connected? The crux of detection, a superb example of Holmes at his most didactically enigmatic, occurs in a conversation with the police inspector assigned to the case:

> "Is there any point to which you would wish to draw my attention?"
> "To the curious incident of the dog in the night-time."
> "The dog did nothing in the night-time."
> "That was the curious incident," remarked Sherlock Holmes.

Somewhat uncannily, in view of events that would occur a century later, the man initially accused bore the name of Simpson. "I had grasped the significance of the silence of the dog," Holmes tells his faithful dogsbody, Dr. Watson. "The Simpson incident had shown me that a dog was kept in the stables, and yet, though someone had been in and had fetched a horse, he had not barked enough to arouse the two lads in the loft. Obviously the midnight visitor was someone whom the dog knew well." The reason the dog did nothing was that it recognized the intruder. The horse thief was the horse's own trainer; the "murderer," acting in justified self-defense, was Silver Blaze.

The question of what the dog did in the nighttime, and whether it recognized its owner, became a key element in the evidence against O. J. Simpson, accused of the brutal murder of his wife Nicole. The dog in question was Nicole Brown Simpson's Akita, named Kato after the family lodger and friend Brian "Kato" Kaelin, though afterward renamed Satchmo by O.J.'s family. On the night of the murder, Kato's "very loud, very persistent barking" and his "plaintive wails" drew the attention of neighbors to the condominium site. One neighbor, Steven Schwab, was taking his own dog for a walk when he saw the Akita on the loose. He noticed blood on its paws and testified that it followed him and "would howl at every house we passed. It would stop and bark down the path." Schwab gave the dog to another neighbor, Sukru Boztepe, to keep for the night. Boztepe testified that he took Kato for a walk to calm him since the dog was "acting so nervous," and that the dog was "getting more nervous and pulling me harder" until he stopped at Nicole Simpson's home and gazed down the dark walkway. At the end of the path lay the body of Nicole Brown Simpson.

Lacking human eyewitnesses, prosecutors sought to persuade the jurors that the barking of the dog could establish within minutes the time of Ms. Simpson's and Ronald Goldman's deaths. The phrase "plaintive wail," uttered by a third neighbor, screenwriter Pablo Fenjves, became a keynote of the case, what a reporter described as a "truly memorable phrase, one that simultaneously captures the sadness beneath the circus, undergirds the prosecution's case and offers a morsel of poetry amid the cop talk, Californiaspeak and legalese."

Lead prosecutor Marcia Clark's "eyes lit up," according to Fenjves, when he first spoke the phrase "plaintive wail," and prosecutors insisted that he use it in his testimony. "That's a very important phrase," said prosecutor Cheri Lewis, so Fenjves used it again on the witness stand. It was as if only the dog could tell the truth, the whole truth, and nothing but the truth.

In the O. J. Simpson trial, Nicole Brown Simpson's dog was a key witness. He barked, later, at the scene of the crime, but why was he silent earlier? Did he know or recognize the murderer? If "the dog did nothing in the nighttime," that "nothing" was significant because it meant he knew the criminal and did not regard him as an intruder. Or, in the words of a blues song, "How Come My Dog Don't Bark (When You Come Around)?" In the blues, the "crime" is stolen love rather than murder, but the role of the dog is the same: sentinel; guardian; even arbiter of values. Once again dog nobility and fidelity stand over against human frailty. The loyalty we idealize, and that we signally miss in stories of betraying husbands or accused spouse-killers, is emblematized in the dog, who is at once witness, detective, constable, and judge.

Dog World, a monthly magazine with a readership of sixty thousand, assigned its own reporter to the Simpson case, covering the Kato angle. "If he could, I believe this dog would have rung doorbells," said reporter John Cargill, himself the owner of an Akita. *Dog World*'s editor concurred, emphasizing the importance to dogs of Kato's "testimony": the barks were "a real-life example that dogs are capable of more than we typically give them credit for." Cargill, speaking long before the verdict, had his own view of the case and its potential outcome: "If there are dog owners on that jury, O.J. and his defense team are in a big heap of trouble."

Indeed dogs, as many noted, were all over the Simpson case, since Rosa Lopez, a potential defense witness, was also prepared to offer evidence based on what she saw when she was out "walking her employers' aged, arthritic golden retriever." Yet another dog walker would later contradict her evidence, earning a chuckle from three (perhaps dog-owning?) jurors when he said the length of his walk was variable, "depending upon what the dog was doing." "Barking," noted a reporter, "is one of the street dialects in transient and reclusive Brentwood, a neighborhood where the residents stick to homes and cars and just about the only pedestrians are dog walkers. At that, one is more likely to know the name of the pet than of the person at the other end of the leash." "Will this be a case of the wail tagging the dog?" inquired a headline, perhaps inevitably.

Limousine driver Allan Park's attorney, his mother, was credited with saving the life of a pit bull terrier sentenced to die for killing another dog in Orange County eight years before. "Everyone and his dog is writing a book" about the trial, said a Los Angeles lawyer representing one hopeful author. His figure of speech turned out to be unwittingly accurate, according to an editor at Dove Books, which has published a number of Simpson-related volumes: at least two persons claiming to have communicated telepathically with Kato the dog offered to publish what they knew. Dog language seemed to be catching. At one point Marcia Clark declared of Simpson defense attorney Robert Shapiro, "Mr. Shapiro barks and expects everyone else to sit."

Nuthin' but a Hound Dog

Conan Doyle's other famous canine tale, "The Hound of the Baskervilles" (1902), presents the dog not as witness—nor, indeed, as detective or perpetrator—but rather as weapon in an uncanny and macabre story of murder for inheritance. The "Hound," with its spectral footprint and phosphorus-induced fire breathing, was a natural script for a horror film, and at least five versions have made it to the screen, from Basil Rathbone's definitive 1939 classic to Paul Morrissey and Dudley Moore's 1977 parody. (Mystery novelist Dorothy Sayers also borrowed liberally from the story's love plot to create, in *Clouds of Witness*, her own version of a passionate relationship between a rural femme fatale and an amorous aristocrat among the fens.)

But what the attentive *reader* of this Sherlock Holmes mystery will detect that the film versions are likely to omit is the trail of "dog" clues that, either by playful purpose or by what literary critics call unconscious "textual effect," mark the language of Conan Doyle's tale. Virtually the first thing Holmes deduces in the case is the benign presence of a pet dog (not the bogey-hound of the title), whose toothmarks on its master's stick—"too broad in my opinion for a terrier and not broad enough for a mastiff"—lead swiftly to a more precise diagnosis: "It may have been—yes, by Jove, it *is* a curly-haired spaniel." Watson, reliably, is dumbfounded ("My dear fellow, how can you possibly be so sure of that?") until Holmes reveals the process of his deduction: "For the very simple reason that I see the dog himself on our very door-step." This same logic of the self-evident seems to have amused Conan Doyle throughout the crafting of his tale, for the trace, track, or spoor of the phantom "dog" haunts the entire written text, leaving its mark over and over again, overtly and subliminally, on nouns, verbs, and metaphors of human action.

Over and over again we hear that our heroes have been "dogged" by humans: "I have ample evidence that you are being dogged in London" says Holmes; "A stranger then is still dogging us, just as a stranger dogged us in London," Watson ruminates, and later, "It was I, then, and not Sir Henry, who was being dogged by this secret man." Sir Charles Baskerville, the previous heir, has fallen apparent victim to the gigantic hound. Was it the mysterious manservant who had been "the last who had seen Sir Charles alive, and the first to dog the new heir when he returned to England"? Watson wonders. But shortly he will change suspects, turning his attention to the sinister Stapleton. "It is he who dogged us in London?" he will inquire, artlessly.

"It may possibly re*cur* to your memory," Holmes prompts Watson drily about a detail in his characteristic summation. Whether intentional or accidental, this almost comic re*cur*rence of the dog in the verbal texture of the narrative is the "masterful" tactic of the tale itself, and one of the causes of its uncanny effect upon the reader. "His nerves were so worked up," says Mortimer of his murdered neighbor, Sir Charles Baskerville, "that the appearance of any dog might have had a fatal effect" upon his heart. However terrifying the actual "hound of the Baskervilles" may be, it is the *human* animal—in this case another Baskerville heir in disguise—that is truly dangerous.

The Dog as Victim

Political scientist Jean Bethke Elshtain reports that in her research on women and war she came upon accounts of dogs used by the U.S. military in Vietnam for activities like scouting, mine detection, sentry duty, and drug detection. "Evidently, many of these dogs were killed rather than returned home, since it was feared their military training ill-suited them for civilian life." This is the flip side of the Dickin Medal, which honors canine heroism under fire. We have already noted the story of the Russian space dog, Laika, sent on a pioneering mission for the good of humanity from which it was not proposed that she return.

Mystery writer Susan Conant tells—again in the voice of her dog-owning heroine, Holly Winter—a similarly bleak story about the abandonment and destruction of an entire group of sled dogs that had accompanied Admiral Richard Byrd to Antarctica:

> Ninety-seven dogs left Wonalancet, [New Hampshire,] or maybe only ninety-five. No one seems to know for sure. At least four died on the way to Antarctica. No one kept count, but about twenty-six surviving pups were born in Little America, which makes about a hundred twenty-seven dogs. . . . Some died in dogfights. Some froze to death. At least twenty-five were killed and fed to their teammates. Of the seventy-seven still alive at the end of the expedition, seventeen were shot, and only sixty taken on board the ship.

Conant's novels often center on the detection of dog abuse: *Bloodlines* takes on the appalling conditions in puppy mills, where female dogs are kept in unspeakable conditions while they give birth to litter after litter. *Dead and Doggone* uncovers a disturbing story of laboratory experimentation on stolen and deceptively acquired dogs (criminal researchers answer "Free to good home" ads from loving dog owners who need to give up their pets).

The extraordinary effectiveness of Conant's dénouement is produced in part by the fact that Holly's *own* dog Rowdy has been taken and may already be maimed or dead. When Holly enters the laboratory she encounters a roomful of caged dogs who have been operated upon to remove their bark, but who are "voicelessly trying their barkless best to greet me."

> One large dog in a small cage at the far end of the room retained his voice. The sight of him gave me courage. The sight of my own dog always does.

In the Talking Dogs chapter we saw the degree to which voice, or the fantasy of canine speech, "humanizes" a dog in the human mind. These eerily *silent* dogs, trying to bark in greeting "or maybe even to signal my presence," are the sign of a borderline, not between human and animal, but between humanity and the inhumane. "You don't seem to understand. I bought these animals," protests the researcher.

> "They aren't animals," I said. "They're dogs."
> He couldn't seem to understand that I wasn't kidding.

"You're making a fool of yourself," he said. "I paid for every one. Researchers have to. There's no law against it."

"There's no law against it." The ardor of Conant's detective, and the splendor of her two malamutes, Rowdy and Kimi, provide what is almost surely more passionate ammunition for the humane cause today than any amount of promotional "literature" from action groups. This is the politics of that other kind of literature, imaginative writing, at its best. Though the tone of Conant's dog books for the nineties could hardly be more different from *Beautiful Joe*'s, her detective novels focus attention on the powerful and generous passions that bind dog lovers and their dogs (and, indeed, the dog lovers' lovers: Holly's boyfriend is a vet).

It isn't only medical research or exploration that uses dogs and may injure them; it's also sometimes sport. Some greyhound trainers have been known to mistreat dogs who can't run fast enough to win. In Arizona alone—and Arizona is just one of eighteen greyhound-racing states—hundreds of dogs have been reported over the last few years starved, battered, mutilated (to prevent identification by tattooed numbers), and bludgeoned to death. Greyhound rescue groups are kept busy finding new homes for abandoned racers and dogs who never made it to the track. But even a more idealized sport, like long-distance "mushing" in Alaska, has generated energetic opposition.

The Iditarod Trail International Sled Dog Race, an endurance test for humans and dogs that covers 1,049 miles of Alaskan terrain between Anchorage and Nome, has inspired much media coverage since its inception in 1973. Known as a sport in which women can—and do—beat men, mushing has become popular worldwide, and Susan Butcher, a four-time winner of the race, has become an international celebrity.

Yet the Humane Society of the United States and other animal-rights groups have now begun to describe the Iditarod as harmful to the health of the dogs that run it. Twenty-one sled dogs have died on the trail since race records began to be kept in 1990, and the guess is that they died in greater numbers in earlier years. Of the approximately twelve hundred dogs who pull sleds each year (until recently, twenty to a team) one died in 1992, six in 1993, and one in 1994. After the deaths in 1993 both ABC Television and sponsor Dodge dropped their support, and in the following year Timberland, which had been a major race sponsor since 1985, not only discontinued its sponsorship but contributed $50,000 to an animal welfare group called PRIDE (Providing Responsible Information on a Dog's Environment). A representative from the Humane Society went on ABC's *Good Morning America* to announce that the Iditarod caused death and injury to animals.

Ironically, the dog that died in 1994 belonged to Susan Butcher, long praised for her insistence on humane treatment for sled dogs. Butcher's dog was named H.C. In an *Atlantic Monthly* account of the Iditarod crisis a new note of empathy creeps into the matter-of-fact reportorial prose once H.C. is given a name. To name her is, indefinably, to confer "personality," and virtual personhood, so that "what killed H.C." becomes a concern, not only of the medical and investigatory personnel, but also of the reader.

Is the Iditarod a sport or a cruel human entertainment? "Sled dogs love to run," concluded *The Atlantic Monthly.* "It is incumbent on their human guardians to ensure that they run into health rather than death." Once again "love" becomes a crucial factor in human-dog relations, but in this case it is a "love" not only *for* the dogs but *in* them, a love not directed at persons but at pleasures, at what used to be called nature.

Dog Chow

The word "chow" in English is said to derive from two different Cantonese words: *gou,* meaning "dog," and *zab,* meaning "food, miscellany," from the Mandarin *za,* "mixed." In America chowchow is the name of a pickle relish mixed with mustard; chow chow (often with capital C's) is a breed of dog, originating in China, with a dense coat and a blue-black tongue. And thereby hangs a tale.

In China some dog meat is a delicacy, and it is illegal to keep dogs as pets (though many are kept surreptitiously, and cherished). In parts of the United States it is illegal to eat dog meat, and dogs are the nation's favorite pet. One of the several early names for the stylish Chinese crested, an American dog show favorite, was the Chinese edible dog.

"Yes, we are still eating dogs in China. What's wrong with that?" wrote James Piao, who has lived in the United States for seven years, to *The New York Times.* "America has been a perfect country for me except for one thing: I missed having dog meat back home." Piao wondered why Americans, so avid in their consumption of beef, distinguish so absolutely between animal and animal. "Does one kind of animal enjoy more rights than another?" he asked. "I am not ashamed of eating dog. I have a different color of skin. I speak a different language and I come from a different cultural background."

"Dog meat," writes Vietnamese-born Andrew Lam, "is a passage to the homeland" for many Asian immigrants. "As they reminisce over what's lost in a life, they share the rare delicacies, daring to eat the loyal animal." In Vietnam, Lam explains, "dogs are both expensive to keep as pets, and useless. In a country hardened by famine and war, the dog is the first animal to be sacrificed when times are lean. Coming from such a pragmatic culture, the Vietnamese refugee is thus often baffled in America by the existence of training schools, pet cemeteries and even cosmetic surgery for dogs and cats." So the newcomer dares to defy American dietary customs, and, on occasion, to eat dogs. But the eating of dog meat is one marker of cultural difference that remains difficult for many Westerners to swallow.

The introduction into the California state legislature of a bill that criminalizes the eating of dog meat (or cat meat), while not outlawing the consumption of other pet animals such as the rabbit, pigeon, and turtle, was, many Vietnamese immigrants thought, a direct attack on the immigrants' regional and provincial customs. Citing Brillat-Savarin's famous culinary dictum, "Tell me what you eat and I will tell you what you are," Lam wondered whether "those of us who dare to keep that provincial part of our culture alive" are to be "treated as criminals for keeping some remembered part of ourselves alive in this new land."

The director of the Korea Animal Protection Society reports that in anticipation of the 1988 Seoul Olympics, dog-eating was discouraged for reasons of international public relations, but that the practice was hidden from view rather then eliminated. "Dog farms are situated far out in the country in secluded territory, and 'dog soup' continues to be listed on restaurant menus but has been renamed 'strong man soup,'" since it is thought to enhance health and sexual prowess. Yet the International Fund for Animal Welfare, which used film footage of Korean dog and cat markets to raise funds for its coffers, has discontinued financial support of the KAPS, claiming that the footage showed abuses in *China,* and thus implying that eating dogs is no longer common in Korea. Animal-rights activist Brigitte Bardot urged South Korea to ban the sale of dog meat if it hosts the 2002 World Cup soccer championships, which will attract thousands of Western visitors.

"The domestic dog," zoologist James Serpell observes, "has become the Western equivalent of the sacred cow. Dogs are cherished and nurtured as man's best friend, and the idea of killing and eating one is virtually unthinkable. Yet, throughout much of the Near East dogs are reviled as symbols of all that is filthy and degraded, while in China, Korea and the Philippines they are cooked and devoured with enthusiasm."

As literary critic Marc Shell notes, "the pet emerged as the one essentially inedible animal" for Christianity, which had been an "omnivorous religion," not barring the eating of any food (unlike, for example, Judaism and Islam). The advent of pethood, or pet-keeping, "brought with it the feeling, amply illustrated in the literature, that it would be like ordinary cannibalism to eat a pet." This was, Shell contends, a new philosophical position for Christianity, and one that came from Protestantism. (Catholics, he says, "frowned upon pet owning—and also upon the practice of giving to animals 'Christian' names, or names 'appropriate' to human beings—because such practices tended to confuse the partly human Christ with the partly human Fido, or the Eucharist with pet eating.")

Arguing that pets "stand at the borderline between family and nonfamily" and "at the borderline between animal and nonanimal or between man and non-man," Shell suggests that this is why they are associated with both the taboo on incest and the taboo on cannibalism. But if "pets stand at the intersection of kin and kind" it is clear that this intersection is a major, and movable, crossroads, used by philosophers as well as anthropologists (or by anthropologists as well as philosophers) to define the very nature of "culture." In much children's—and adults'—literature, the wanton killing of dogs is itself a sign of inhumanity, and often, as we have noted, presages a genocidal plot. Yet, as Shell also notes, loving pets may function as an excuse for dehumanizing people: "Hitler anthropomorphized his pet dog—maybe his pet was the one being he 'loved'—just as he tried to dehumanize the Jews and Gypsies."

In the United States today the idea of eating pets produces a different kind of recoil or horror from the idea of having sex with them, but it is not unimaginable: thus the continued popularity of *Charlotte's Web*, in which Wilbur the innocent pig is rescued from the farmer's table by the ingenuity of a spider and her barnyard confederates. It is difficult to imagine, in America, a book about a *dog* being rescued from the stew-pot, since the privileged place of the dog in our cultural and affectional imagination ups the ante so considerably. In fact the film *Babe,* based on a 1983 novel, replaced Charlotte the spider as foster mother with a more cuddleable border collie, who teaches the piglet Babe not, like Wilbur, to do somersaults and look "radiant," but rather to herd sheep.

Where There's a "Will"

It is not only the question of edibility that activates the distinction be-tween kin and kind, but also the question of inheritance. If you are thinking of leaving money to your dog, think again. Dogs are property, and according to the law, property cannot own property. "Since prop-erty cannot inherit property, the dog will not inherit anything," cautions a popular handbook on dogs and the law in discussing the touchy ques-tion of wills. You can leave money to a friend for the care of your dog, and you can leave the dog as property to a friend, but courts will not honor a bequest to Bowser. Or so they say.

In England in 1985 tax accountants apparently advised Mr. Robert Beckman, an investment analyst, that William, an Old English sheep-dog, was not liable to pay taxes. The question came up because—with Mr. Beckman's investment advice—William had apparently done so well in the stock market over a period of eleven years that he was worth some one hundred thousand pounds. Both Beckman and William's owner, Beckman's former assistant Anthea Clift, insisted that the money was all William's, and that therefore no capital gains tax was ow-ing, since William was not a "legal entity." A commentator in a tax journal took up the challenge, arguing that the law indeed prohibited a dog from owning property, and citing case precedents. If William was not a "legal entity," nor yet a "person," according to the law, it might well be that William was not liable to tax. But in that case, neither could he own money. And since by their own insistence neither his in-vestment counselor nor his owner had any rights to the money it was clear, argued the commentator, that the money—all of it, not just the tax—belonged to the Crown.

In fact, dogs have not always been defined in the law even as prop-erty, since under English common law they had no value, and it was therefore not against the law to steal them. It took legislation both in

Britain and in the United States to make stealing a dog a crime. At one point in England, it was a felony to steal a dog's collar, and only a misdemeanor to steal the dog. Once a dog became defined as property, it followed, in some cases at least, that the animal was not protected against cruelty from its owner, who could in theory handle his or her property however he or she chose. Here modern activists may think of categories like spousal abuse and marital rape, which in some courts were until recently held to be private matters on similar grounds.

As Constance Perin points out, the fantasy of canine jurisprudence has today become a reality, though a reality with a conundrum at its center. What is a dog? Is it property or not? And if it is property, what kind of property can it be, since it has its own body, mind, appetites, and ideas, and can never be wholly controlled by its legal owner? Perin observes justly that "Dogs are and are not PROPERTY; just as dogs are and are not RELATIVES." Since this kind of "property" can travel on its own, it can't be fully "possessed." "But," as Perrin goes on to note, "differences between dogs as PROPERTY and as KIN and FRIEND go unrecognized legally. The law confers on them solely the status of CHATTEL, with the unintended effect of sanctioning their casual acquisition, minimal care, and abandonment."

But what *kind* of property is a dog, legally speaking? Basic property, like furniture or appliances, that must be replaced if damaged? Special property, with a value that may vary depending upon the amount of training and other expertise it has acquired? Or unique property, like real estate, that is not interchangeable with other items of the same kind, but is, in fact, irreplaceable?

When the owner of a golden retriever that died after frantically struggling to escape an overheated airline baggage compartment tried to recover damages for the dog's suffering and for his own mental anguish and loss of companionship, the court denied his claim, holding that the two-and-a-half-year-old Floyd was "property." There are no causes of action in New York or federal Second Circuit courts for an animal's suffering or for emotional distress on the part of his owner.

Hath a Dog Money?

The headline accompanying the story of William, the tax-evading sheepdog, was a Shakespearean tag: "Hath a dog money? Is it possible / A cur can lend three thousand ducats?" This must have seemed drolly apposite to the editors, though in giving the source—*The Merchant of Venice* I.3—they might have taken a moment to consider the context. For the speaker, of course, is the aggrieved Jew Shylock, reviled by the Christian Antonio for lending money at interest, and the term of revilement Antonio has chosen is "dog." "You call me misbeliever, cut-throat dog / And spet [i.e., spit] upon my Jewish gaberdine. . . . And foot me as you spurn a stranger cur / Over your threshold. . . . You call'd me dog." "I am as like to call thee so again, / To spet on thee again, to spurn thee too," replies Antonio.

Neither Jews nor dogs are well treated in this figure of speech, which stresses the "inhuman" image of the Jew. Words like "stranger" and "cur," here used to typify the dog as a homeless mongrel stray, resonate with the equally typical period accounts of Jews as homeless and stateless, of "mongrel" race and "cut-throat" tendency. The association of Jews with dogs was not only popular invective in the period, it also found itself into some aspects of the law. According to Midas Dekkers, the sixteenth-century Flemish jurist Joost de Damhoudere declared in his legal handbook that coitus between a Christian and a Jew was sodomy, and "a certain Jean Alard, who lived in Paris with a Jewess and had a number of children with her, was condemned for sodomy and burnt at the stake together with his girlfriend, 'since coitus with a Jewess is exactly the same as if a man were to copulate with a dog.'"

Since Shakespeare is amply capable of presenting quite other images of dogs, from cherished pets (*Two Gentlemen of Verona; Henry IV, Part I; The Taming of the Shrew; King Lear*) to hunting dogs (*A Midsummer Night's Dream*), "fawning greyhounds" (*Henry IV, Part I; Coriolanus*), and "dogs of war" (*Julius Caesar*), the use of "dog" in a stigmatizing context in *The Merchant of Venice* is not merely an index of early modern cruelty to animals, but rather a way of construing dog society, once more, as a model of human society. In other words, to take Antonio's choice of "dog" as an epithet as simply a sign of the treatment of *dogs* in the period is to miss both the irony, and the calumny, of the similar treatment accorded *persons* who were Jews.

None of this has anything to do with the comic tale of William the investing sheepdog. But it has a good deal to do with how the literal and the figurative intersect with each other to make what we call "culture"—and thus not a little, or at least one would hope, to do with the nature and purpose of law.

Can They Suffer?

In 1789, the same year as the French Declaration of the Rights of Man and of the Citizen, and of the drafting of the Bill of Rights amending the Constitution of the United States, the English philosopher Jeremy Bentham offered what is perhaps the most moving plea ever penned on behalf of the rights of animals.

> The day *may come*, when the rest of the animal creation may acquire those rights which never could have been withholden from them but by the hand of tyranny. The French have already discovered that the blackness of the skin is no reason why a human being should be abandoned without redress to the caprice of a tormentor. It may come some day to be recognized, that the number of the legs, the villosity of the skin, or the termination of the *os sacrum*, are reasons equally insufficient for abandoning a sensitive being to the same fate. What else is it that should trace the insuperable line? Is it the faculty of reason, or, perhaps, the faculty of discourse? But a full-grown horse or dog is beyond comparison a more rational, as well as a more conversable animal, than an infant of a day, or a week, or even a month, old. But suppose the case were otherwise, what would it avail? The question is not, Can they *reason?* nor, Can they *talk?* but, Can they *suffer?*

Behind Jeremy Bentham's ringing assertion, "The question is not, Can they *reason?* nor, Can they *talk?* but, Can they *suffer?*," we can, I think, hear a rhetorical echo of Shakespeare's Shylock: "If you prick us, do we not bleed? . . . If you poison us, do we not die?" With his appeal Bentham gave impetus to the campaign for animal rights that is still being waged today. A utilitarian who held that "the greatest happiness of the greatest number is the foundation of morals and legislation," Bentham extended the potentiality of "happiness" to animals, specifically to the dog and the horse.

Significantly, the analogy with the treatment of black persons by white persons was likewise being made by those proponents of animal rights who, like the British philanthropist William Wilberforce, were active in the abolition and manumission causes. As we have already noted, the founding of humane societies and the passage of humane legislation in the nineteenth century drew some of their energy from "autobiographical" accounts of animal mistreatment that became popular best-sellers: Anna Sewell's *Black Beauty* and Marshall Saunders's *Beautiful Joe*. *Black Beauty* was described as "a veritable bible of the animal protective cause," and, as has already been remarked, George T. Angell called it "the *Uncle Tom's Cabin* of the horse."

Uncle Tom's Cabin itself was attentive to the plight of *dogs*, which Stowe used both literally and figuratively to underscore the inhumanity of slavery. The slave George Harris is ordered by a cruel master to kill his pet dog, whom the master does not want to go to the expense of keeping. When George refuses and is whipped for his disobedience, the master kills the dog himself. Reporting this in sorrow to his wife, Eliza, George reminds her of his own lack of legal standing. "Don't you know a slave can't be married? There is no law in the country for that." Deprived of his beloved dog and about to be forcibly separated by the same master from his wife, George sets out for Canada in search of freedom. Later in the novel, when a white Southerner, Augustine St. Clare, buys the slave girl Topsy and presents her to his cousin Ophelia for "training," the offhand tone of his reference is chilling and its equation of slave and pet unmistakable: "'Here, Topsy,' he added, giving a whistle, as a man would to call the attention of a dog, 'give us a song, now, and show us some of your dancing.'" The slave was property; the slave had no human rights; the slave was treated, quite literally, like a dog.

A century later, a similarly jarring instance of the racist conflation of human and dog, seen through the eyes of a child, occurs in the novel *Sounder* (1969), a dog book often thought to be appropriate "for children" and made into a powerful 1972 film starring Cicely Tyson and Paul Winfield. A black sharecropper living in Louisiana during the Depression in desperation steals a hog to fed his wife and children. His son and the dog Sounder watch in fear as the sheriff's deputies come to take the father away. "Stick out your hands, boy," say the deputies, and the child imagines they must be talking to him. "Chain him up," says the sheriff, and the boy thinks they must be referring to the dog. In both cases, of course, it is the man—his father—they mean.

Racism here takes its language of abuse from both infantilization and animalization. Before the boy's eyes his father is stripped of humanity and manhood. The fact that the dog tries to join his master in the sheriff's cart, and is shot and maimed in just the same way that the father will later be maimed on the chain gang, merely completes this drama of identification and quiet heroism. Like many dog stories written "for children," this one is almost unbearable, at least to adults.

Humane Societies

As an early chronicle of the "humane movement" notes, "It was more than a mere coincidence that the humane movement in England and America followed so closely upon the abolition of human slavery." Parliamentary Acts of 1807 and 1833 outlawed first the slave trade and then slavery within the British Empire, and in 1809 Lord Erskine made a famous plea that animals were entitled to legal protection. Richard "Humanity" Martin accomplished the passage of the first effective animal-protection legislation in the world. "Martin's Act" was passed by Parliament in 1822, and the Royal Society for the Prevention of Cruelty to Animals was founded in 1824. In the United States the Emancipation Proclamation of 1863, in the midst of the Civil War, was followed in 1865 by the Thirteenth Amendment, completely abolishing and prohibiting slavery.

A year later, in New York State, Henry Bergh founded the American Society for the Prevention of Cruelty to Animals and saw through the state legislature a law that called for the punishment of any person convicted of neglecting, injuring, torturing, or killing an animal. Among the activities that attracted the Society's attention were dogfights, "which were then very popular with the scum of society and a certain class of wealthy 'sports.'" (It is in the context of such a fight that Jack London's White Fang is rescued and "freed" by his kindly new owner, Weedon Scott.) Any reader of today's daily newspapers will sadly recognize that dogfights, like cockfights, have not been completely eradicated; in a notorious 1995 case in the Dorchester section of Boston a pit bull died of violent slash wounds to its chest and stomach, and two small border collie puppies were severely injured. Bergh's law was the first in this country that made such contests illegal.

The supporters of women's suffrage also saw analogies between animal concerns and their own. In 1907 in Britain suffragists, trade unionists, and animal-welfare advocates banded together against London University medical students in a riot "triggered by the vivisection of a dog." (Antivivisection societies had existed in England since 1870, and in the United States since 1883, when the first U.S. group was founded in Philadelphia.) As for the rights of women: Jean Bethke

Elshtain notes that in the Western tradition of rational thought, "women were often located on a scale somewhere between 'man' and 'beast,' being deemed human but not quite rational." Dr. Johnson's famous remark, "a woman's preaching is like a dog's walking on his hinder legs. It is not done well; but you are surprised to find it done at all" is a typical rather than an exceptional estimate, though more memorably phrased than many. (Notice that even Johnson's talented dog is *male*.) And the vogue for pet-keeping in the Europe of the nineteenth century depended, as Kathleen Kete points out, on the "feminization" of dogs, regardless of their sex. Dogs were petted and coddled—or brushed aside—like fashionable women.

"With the emergence of the Western rationalist tradition," Elshstain argues, "animals lost the philosophic struggle." Descartes and Kant each had "dismissed out of hand the moral worth of animals," Descartes (as we have seen) because he held that animals were machines, devoid of consciousness or feeling, and Kant because, though he acknowledged that animals could and did suffer, he yet believed that they lacked self-consciousness, and thus could be made to serve human purposes. "So far as animals are concerned, we have no direct duties," he told his students in his lectures on ethics. "Animals are not self-conscious, and are there merely as a means to an end. That end is man." The nineteenth-century founders of "humane societies," attempting to reverse this trend, still tended to keep the focus on the benefits to humanity, regarding mistreated animals as objects of charity, pity, and condescension.

The "New Abolitionists"

In recent years this sentimental approach, while it has hardly disappeared, has been matched or countered by a more militant view. The "new abolitionists," as animal-welfare activists have sometimes come to call themselves, take the position that "animals, too, have rights, and that violating those rights constitutes oppression." They seek to close the gap between "human" and "beast" that has traditionally defined humanness as equivalent to abstract rational thought. Lawyers connected with the Rutgers University Animal Rights Law center, the only clinic of its kind in the United States, vigorously contest the idea that animals are, or could be, property. The clinic's founder, Gary L. Francione, and his wife, staff attorney and co-director Anna E. Charlton, have opposed the use of animals for product testing and supported student veterinarians boycotting surgical workshops that use healthy animals as subjects. They provided part of the defense strategy for Taro, the "New Jersey death row dog" pardoned by Governor Whitman in 1994, and Francione says his phone rings in the middle of the night with calls about dog-beaters in localities around the nation.

Much of the impetus for the present-day animal-rights movement has come from an influential 1975 book called *Animal Liberation: A New Ethics for Our Treatment of Animals*, by Australian philosophy professor Peter Singer, which held that what Singer called "speciesism" was analogous to racism and sexism. "If possessing a higher degree of intelligence does not entitle one human to use another for his own ends," he asked, "how can it entitle humans to exploit nonhumans for the same purpose?" Singer's eloquent and angry account disavows sentimentality: he begins his 1975 introduction with a telling anecdote about a woman who described her love for her dog and two cats while munching on a ham sandwich. "Cute" animals (the quotation marks are his) do not especially interest him. But he is not insensible to the rhetorical power of the cuteness factor, as the following passage will show:

> I am no more outraged by the slaughter of horses or dogs for meat than I am by the slaughter of pigs for this purpose. When the United States Defense Department finds that its use of beagles to test lethal gases has evoked a howl of protest and offers to use rats instead, I am not appeased."

In the course of claiming that horses, dogs, and beagles have no privileged place in his affections, or, indeed, in his moral convictions, Singer makes powerful rhetorical use of them. For those of you who *are* more moved by the plight of a beagle than by that of a rat, his sentence says, judge the strength of my feelings for all animals, even the most despised, by the strength of your own for endangered dogs. That the dog should be the chosen vehicle of this argument itself argues, quite powerfully, for the special place many people do accord to dogs.

A similar effectiveness had placed the dog at the rhetorical center of Voltaire's protest against the vivisection of dogs, rebutting the "mechanistic" view of Descartes:

> There are barbarians who seize this dog, who so greatly sur-
> passes man in fidelity and friendship, and nail him down to a
> table and dissect him alive, to show you the mesaraic veins! You
> discover in him *all the same organs of feeling as in yourself.* An-
> swer me, mechanist, has Nature arranged all the springs of feel-
> ing in this animal *to the end that he might not feel?*

Alexander Pope (who memorably penned that devastating couplet
for the collar of "His Highness' dog at Kew") ardently opposed the
practice of dissecting live dogs, maintaining that though power over
"the inferior creation" was given over to mankind, it was not therefore
permitted to us to mismanage that power. Both writers were decrying an
actual practice of the period. But both also wrote knowing that the dog
("who so greatly surpasses man in fidelity and friendship") had a special claim—call it rhetorical, call it political—on human identification. The passionate assertion that dogs could feel was in its way a plea
for *human* feeling in return. Peter Singer does the same thing in the
opening pages of *Animal Liberation* when he in effect uses the dog for
a hypothetical experiment to prove his point: "To most people . . . it is
obvious that if, for example, we stick a sharp knife into the stomach of
an unanesthetized dog, the dog will feel pain. . . . We cannot directly
experience anyone else's pain, whether that 'anyone' is our best friend
or a stray dog." In this case the uncited but familiar epithet "man's best
friend" binds the two polar terms, "our best friend or a stray dog."
Called upon to "prove" the existence of animal pain, Singer finds it effective to do so by instancing the particular animal many of his readers
will already accept as "someone" like themselves.

Today centrist groups like the Humane Society, the ASPCA, and
Cleveland Amory's Fund for Animals have been joined by newer, more
hard-line organizations like the activist Animal Liberation Front,
Trans-Species Unlimited, and People for the Ethical Treatment of Animals (founded in 1981 with the slogan "Animals are not ours to eat,
wear, or experiment on," and with a significant celebrity membership
including k. d. lang, the Indigo Girls, Michael Stipe of R.E.M., and
novelist Alice Walker). Some animal liberationists protest not only
against the eating of meat but also against the owning by (human) animals of (other, nonhuman) animals.

Inevitably these new groups have come in for their share of con-
demnation as animal extremists. One book on dogs and the law, dis-

cussing dogs as property, comments mildly that "it is not helping matters that animal rights activists are seeking to curtail or completely eliminate the breeding of purebred dogs." Dog trainer Vicki Hearne complains against the excesses of what she calls "humaniacs." A writer in a British newspaper observes dismissively that "there is a new school of ultras in the animal rights movement which holds that pet owning is inherently cruel, and that therefore the animals should not exist." And mystery novelist Susan Conant, once again in her fictional persona as dog writer Holly Winter, scathingly describes "a woman I'll call Lizzie Nopet, who was the head of a certain animal-rights group and the person whom the fancy most loved to hate" because of her "twisted vision of a dogless, catless, loveless future, a sort of Black Mass utopia in which domestic animals would return to the disease-ridden wild, thus abandoning us with nothing to pet and train except one another."

Debates about animal experimentation, animal welfare, and animal rights are heated, often involving the question of trade-offs between human and animal benefits. Is it worth experimenting on animals to save the lives of humans? To improve products for human use, even inessential products like cosmetics? Is there ever *any* justification for the use of animals—and especially "man's best friend"—for experimental reasons, as what we too readily call "guinea pigs"?

Ingrid Newkirk, co-founder and national director of PETA, cites Charles Darwin's observation that "the only difference between humans and other animals [is] a difference of degree, not kind." Says Newkirk: "If you ground any concept of human rights in a particular attribute, then animals will have to be included. Animals have rights." Peter Singer takes a more moderate line than PETA, suggesting that "experiments that serve no direct or urgent purpose" should be halted, and that attempts should be made to replace animal experimentation with other methods of research as soon as possible." One indicator of a change in attitude is the increasing use of the term "nonhuman animals" instead of just "animals." Thus Singer writes that "animal liberationists . . . see nonhuman animals as another oppressed group, suffering from blatant exploitation by a species that has unlimited power over another species."

The controversy about what is variously called "animal rights," "animal protection," and "animal welfare" continues in the public press as well as within these organizations, and shows no signs of abating. In

a *Newsweek* opinion piece a scientist who works in a biomedical research lab (and is a vegetarian) defended the two new studies on which
she was currently working, one of which might help to alleviate os-
teoarthritis in the elderly, and the other of which tested a drug that
might be beneficial in the treatment of AIDS. Both studies involved
dogs. "Let me tell you the extent of the 'cruelty' my dogs undergo," Jessica Szymczyk wrote with feeling. "In the first study they play with a lab
technician for an hour every day. The other experiment requires that
they drink a tiny amount of an extremely diluted drug . . . and have
some blood drawn. When I draw blood, the dogs are happy to see me
and they romp about like bouncy pups."

It is not true, she asserted, that all animals are euthanized at the
end of a study, and those that are receive the same kind of treatment by
a veterinarian as "your pet would in a veterinary hospital." Szymczyk,
who has fish, a pet mouse, a pony, a horse, and cats, and is "looking for
the perfect dog to complement my other companion animals," deplored
what she said was false information disseminated by animal-rights
groups: "I get angry when I hear the terrible things animal-rights
groups like People for the Ethical Treatment of Animals say about me
and my colleagues." But she has strong views of her own: "PETA, I've
read, envisions a future where I wouldn't be allowed to keep my pets.
And it considers a rat, a mammal, the equal of a child." Though she
stressed the fact that the medical advances help dogs and cats as well
as people, extending their life expectancy through research, her column drew the expected fire from critics who regarded such work, regardless of its supposed benefits to humanity, as inhumane.

What is the particular place of the *dog* in the new animal-rights ini-
tiatives? Note that Szymczyk was looking for the "perfect dog." Because of its particular pull on our emotions, and its special place in our
lives, the dog can function as the poster pet for channeling effective response. (As we've seen, concepts as diverse as literacy and computer
networks are regularly advertised with dog images, as are remedies for
headaches, muscle aches, stomach acid, and other ailments of middle
age that might prevent one from taking the dog for a walk.) The image
of lab technicians playing with the dogs every day, and of canine laboratory subjects greeting the researcher "like bouncy pups," is far more
emotionally affecting than any similar account of rabbits, rats, or mice.
Szymczyk faults PETA for placing equal value on the life of a rat and
the life of a child. But dogs occupy a strategic emotional middle ground.

They are in effect "poster creatures" for nonhuman animals, bringing the level of emotion down—or up—to a readily apprehensible level, bringing it *home*. When the lovable movie mutt Fluke is dognapped and taken to a lab where some product is tested by being dripped into his eyes, any audience will respond with anger and horror. When veterinary students are instructed to practice their surgical procedures on perfectly healthy dogs some of the students have organized in protest. Stories of dogs who have heroically—and often unwittingly—served human ends and then been abandoned or destroyed offer the most powerful kinds of argument: if it is a laboratory dog today, will it be *my* dog, or my *child*, or my *family*, tomorrow? Where is the line to be drawn around our own loyalties, our own affections?

(Best) Friend of the Court

In a famous court argument in 1870, attorney George Graham Vest, later to become senator from Missouri, defended the honor and glory of the dog, comparing his fidelity to man's ingratitude. The case was a suit for damages by the owner of a dog shot for trespassing, and Vest's moving account and high-flown rhetoric set the tone for more than a hundred years of sentiment.

> Gentlemen of the jury: The best friend a man has in the world may turn against him and become his worst enemy. His son or daughter that he has reared with loving care may prove ungrateful. Those who are nearest and dearest to us, those whom we trust with our happiness and our good name, may become traitors to their faith. . . . The one absolutely unselfish friend that a man can have in this selfish world, the one that never deserts him and the one that never proves ungrateful or treacherous is his dog. A man's dog stands by him in prosperity and poverty, in health and sickness. He will sleep on the cold ground, when the wintry winds blow and the snow drives fiercely, if only he can be near his master's side. He will kiss the hand that has no food to offer, he will lick the wounds and sores that come in encounter with the roughness of the world. He guards the sleep of a pauper as if he were a prince.
>   . . . . If fortune drives the master forth an outcast in the world, friendless and homeless, the faithful dog asks no higher

privilege than that of accompanying him to guard against danger, to fight against his enemies, and when the last scene of all comes, and death takes the master in its embrace and his body is laid away in the cold ground, no matter if all other friends pursue their way, there by his graveside will the noble dog be found, his head between his paws, his eyes sad but open in alert watchfulness, faithful and true even to death.

Here the fragility of human loyalty to human beings (friends, relatives, business associates) is unfavorably contrasted with the unconditional love and loyalty of the dog. The echoes of Shakespeare's *King Lear*, the quintessential play of human ungratefulness, are probably not accidental: the ungrateful children, the wintry winds tormenting the outcast, the willingness to kiss the hand that has no food to offer. Shakespeare's loyal Duke of Gloucester, encountering the mad king on the heath, exclaims, "O! Let me kiss that hand," and Lear replies, "Let me wipe it first; it smells of mortality." Lear decrying the cruelty of his daughters exclaims, "Filial ingratitude! / Is it not as this mouth should tear this hand / For lifting food to't?" "Mine enemy's dog," laments the true daughter, Cordelia, "Though he had bit me, should have stood that night / Against my fire."

The death scenario as attorney Vest imagines it, of the lonely master in "the last scene of all" with the faithful dog lying by his graveside, is, as we will see, a set piece of Victorian culture, epitomized in the legendary faithfulness of a dog called Greyfriars Bobby. But the fact that this speech was delivered in court (and later on the floor of the U.S. Senate) to a rapt and responsive audience suggests a powerful connection between canine nature and human nature, and thus between dog law and human law. The dog, Vest successfully implies, is not only "man's best friend," but also, in its moral superiority, something like a canine amicus curiae—literally, a "friend of the court"—a "person" invited to advise a court in a case to which he is not a party. The jury found for the bereaved dog owner, awarding twice as much in damages as had been requested, and Vest's argument is still quoted by judges today.

Dog Loss

Drawing by Chas. Addams;
© 1975 The New Yorker Magazine, Inc.

The old dog barks backward without getting up.
I can remember when he was a pup.
　　　　　　　—Robert Frost, "The Span of Life"

He's not the finest character that ever lived. But he's a human being, and a terrible thing is happening to him. So attention must be
paid. He's not to be allowed to fall into his grave like an old dog.
　　　　　　　—Arthur Miller, *Death of a Salesman*

Not long ago a retired colleague of mine gave a lecture in which
he quoted at length from the story of Argus's death in *The
Odyssey*. The faithful dog, having waited twenty years for his
master's return, was too feeble to do more than faintly wag his tail.
Abandoned on a dungheap, fed on scraps, he was a shadow of the

young dog he had been, but when he recognized Odysseus, he wagged his tail—and died. I felt the sting of tears in my eyes, and had to look away. When I looked up, I saw that my older colleague's eyes, too, were wet. He shook his head as if to clear it, and went on with his talk. It was one of the most intimate moments we had ever shared. But which "old dog" were we mourning, he and I?

Since the beginnings of Western literature, with the death of Odysseus' beloved Argus, the death of a dog has marked a moment of pathos and identification. Elegies and monuments to beloved canine companions echo the full range of their human equivalents. The proliferation of pet cemeteries and pet burial scenes in contemporary culture and in a novel like Evelyn Waugh's *The Loved One* tells us as much about human death and loss as about the role of the dog (and the pet) in human lives.

Love, death, and consciousness are concepts central to what we mean by "human." Yet the compelling paradox of our present-day society is that, in the stories we tell ourselves and each other, the stories with the most "human interest" are stories about dogs. Ambivalence, that besetting sin of so many human relations (compounded of too much hope, too much care, too much competitiveness, or too much identification) is, if not wholly lacking, then at least mostly so, in the relationships between people and their dogs.

The word "loss" itself has a double meaning when it comes to the dogs in our lives. "Lost Pets" is a standard classified advertising category describing not the deceased but the stolen or strayed. Signs describing "lost dogs" can be found on every community bulletin board, taped to telephone poles, tacked up in the grocery store. Often the photographs are heart-wrenching. Animal control groups and kennel clubs do everything they can to remind dog owners of how easy it is to lose a dog—and how easy it can be if you do the right things, to find your dog again. Tattoos, implanted microchips, dog licenses, strong leashes, good fences, firm training. And still, a dog can be lost. The beagle we had when I was ten was "lost." She was probably stolen (beagles were the height of fashion then in the town where I lived). Maybe she was hit by a car. We never found out, though I came home day after day to report that I had seen Bootsie in someone's yard, on someone's leash. My parents checked; it wasn't our dog. She was "lost," and she remained "lost," and I grieved for her a long time. It wasn't until I was an adult, and a pretty old adult at that, that I got another dog.

But "lost, strayed, or stolen" isn't really, of course, what people mean by "loss" when they say—in a phrase that has become so ritualized that it seems almost empty of meaning—"I'm sorry for your loss." People don't like to say "death." But dogs, like people, die and are "lost."

Our friends Ann and Charles had a beloved golden retriever whose name was Dylan. He served as unofficial greeter at the inn they own and run. Year after year guests, when they rebooked their rooms, asked about Dylan. He was a feature of the household, a part of the experience of being there. When Dylan died, Ann and Charles decided they didn't want another golden. Nothing would replace Dylan. But they still wanted a dog, and they got two, adorable PBGVs (petit basset griffon vendéens). Morgan and Tucker took over the yard and raced through the inn. They are much loved. But they do not replace loss.

Dog love and dog loss are part of the same story. Most people outlive their dogs—though there are poignant exceptions, some of which we will need to speak of here. But a dog's life expectancy is ten years, or twelve, or sixteen, depending on the breed. A child learns to love when he or she loves a dog; a child also learns to grieve. "It is strange how we buy our sorrow," writes J. C. Squire in a poem called simply "A Dog's Death,"

> For the touch of perishing things, idly, with eyes wide open
> How we give our hearts to brutes that will die in a few seasons.

There are differences, too, quite obviously, between losing a dog and losing a beloved human being. For one thing, when our dogs become old and ill many of us choose the day and time of their deaths. We "have them put to sleep." Always a painful decision, and a guilty one. But we feel guilt, I think, either way. Guilt that we survive. Guilt, as well as joy, that we have been so greatly loved.

On the death of his beloved black-and-white Newfoundland dog, Boatswain, the poet Byron wrote this epitaph on his grave:

> Beneath this spot
> Are deposited the remains of a being
> Who was possessed of beauty without vanity,
> Strength without insolence,
> Courage without ferocity,
> And all the virtues of man without his vices.

Byron's poem honoring Boatswain concludes with a ringing couplet: "To mark a friend's remains these stones arise; / I never knew but one, and here he lies." When he made his will, in 1811, Byron asked to be buried with Boatswain.

Frederick the Great of Prussia requested, as his dying wish, to be buried with his faithful dogs and his horse.

In the 1930s Maine governor Percival Baxter ordered the American flag lowered in front of all state buildings as a sign of public mourning for the death of his dog.

Are these signs of excessive grief, display, or personal power? Or are they, rather, indications of the special place in the human imagination that is reserved for the creature who is thought to provide, and to elicit, love without stint or measure?

"Max is dead, and many who loved the old dog will regret him and miss him sadly," begins a 1875 memoir of Max the Newfoundland written by an author who signs himself only as "his chief mourner." "Until the last he recognized the voices of those near and dear to him, and shook a farewell 'paw-paw' with his old master just before he died."

Maurice Maeterlinck's little classic of 1903, *Our Friend the Dog*, begins with a compact epitaph for the playwright's dog Pelléas, who died young: "I have lost, within these last few days, a little bull-dog. He had just completed the sixth month of his brief existence. He had no history. His intelligent eyes opened to look out upon the world, to love mankind, then closed again on the cruel secrets of death."

Of all paeans to the bond between dog and human, Maeterlinck's is among the most poignantly direct. The dog, he observes, "succeeds in piercing, in order to draw closer to us, the partitions, ever elsewhere impermeable, that separate the species! We are alone, absolutely alone on this chance planet; and amid all the forms of life that surround us, not one, excepting the dog, has made an alliance with us."

"The dog is really a privileged animal," Maeterlinck goes on to remark. "He is the only living being that has found and recognizes an indubitable, tangible, unexceptionable and definite god." This sentiment, echoing as it does Francis Bacon's seventeenth-century view of man standing, to the dog, "in stead of a God," underscores the sense of power and responsibility, as well as interdependence, that humans often feel for their dogs. And yet, being merely human, we all too often let them down.

> Carlo died—
> E. Dickinson
> Would you instruct me now?

This letter from Emily Dickinson to her friend and mentor Thomas Wentworth Higginson, quoted here in its entirety, records the death of Dickinson's cherished Newfoundland dog, Carlo. The spareness of the language, the directness of the appeal, and above all the eloquence of what is *not* said, all attest to the poet's grief. It was the first note she had written Colonel Higginson in eighteen months.

Carlo lived to a ripe age and died in 1866. As early as 1850 Dickinson had written playfully to another correspondent about the dog she called "my *Carlo*": "The Dog is the noblest work of Art, sir. I may safely say he is the noblest—his mistress's rights he doth defend—although it bring him to his end—although to death it doth him send!" His death— or her austere and painful notice of it—restored the correspondence between Dickinson and Higginson.

Carlo had been an early topic between them. When Higginson first inquired about her age, her books, and her companions, she mentioned among the latter "Hills—Sir—and the Sundown—and a Dog—large as myself, that my Father bought me." Small wonder that in 1869, three years after Carlo's death, Higginson could write to her that it was hard to understand how she could live so alone, with "thoughts of such a quality coming up in you & even the companionship of your dog withdrawn." When he invited Dickinson to visit him in Boston (apparently calling her "elusive" because she declined to go to see him) the poet in reply invoked the memory of Carlo: "Whom my Dog understood could not elude others," she wrote, describing herself in the third person. And in her next letter, again refusing an invitation to visit, she notes, simply, "I wish for Carlo."

For whom do we mourn?

The death of the beloved dog of childhood is often quite naturally the occasion for a double grief, since what is lost is both the canine companion and a sense of one's own youth and innocence. Thus, for example, Willie Morris's memoir *My Dog Skip* is framed by deliberate and overt nostalgic gestures, from the first chapter, "A Faded Photograph," to the last, "Going Away."

"I came across a photograph of him not long ago," the book begins, "his black face with the long snout sniffing at something in the air, his tail straight and pointing, his eyes flashing in some momentary excitement. Looking at a faded photograph taken more than forty years before, even as a grown man, I would admit I still missed him." The date is 1943, the author nine years old. Morris's narrative begins "when I saw him for the very first time," and ends with Skip's death. "I won a scholarship to England to complete my studies; I would be away three years. The day came when my parents had to drive me to meet the train East, where I would take an oceanliner. I knew I would never see Skip again." As this premonition suggests, the dog *is* childhood for Morris—childhood and America. Skip "lifted his head and looked at me, then put his head in my lap, nuzzling me with his nose as he had done the first time I had seen him as a puppy. I told him I had to go and that I would miss him. He looked at me again, and licked my cheek. 'Thank you, boy,' I whispered. Then I left without looking back." A month later the expected call comes from his parents: "'Skip died,' Daddy said."

Home, as we have seen, is where the dog is. For Willie Morris the dog Skip is a local habitation and a name. Mourning his dog in the streets of Oxford ("among the landmarks of the gray medieval town"), Morris traces a familiar transatlantic path, one marked by the footsteps of American expatriate writers like Henry James and T. S. Eliot. But unlike these transplanted American Englishmen, Morris will return. ("He lives," the author's note informs the reader, "next to Purple Crane Creek in Jackson, Mississippi, with his wife, JoAnne, and five cats, and his abiding memory of Old Skip.")

"Willie Morris takes us back to a Huck Finn America, a time when boys and dogs spent endless days in irreverent play and serious joy," declares the book jacket, offering up its own nostalgic view of home. The praise comes from Morris's friend Winston Groom, to whom *Skip* is dedicated. And Groom, best known as the author of *Forrest Gump*, created an American hero, not too bright but consummately faithful, loving, and joyously fleet of foot, who might be described as a human version of the dog as ideal companion. (It comes as small surprise to learn, from Morris's dedication, that "Forrest Gump" is in fact the name of the Grooms' dog.)

What is being remembered in *My Dog Skip*, and what is being mourned? As with Lassie, so with Skip and so many others: what is mourned is the author's own boyhood.

The dog of your boyhood teaches you a great deal about friendship, and love, and death: Old Skip was my brother.

They had buried him under our elm tree, they said—yet this was not totally true. For he really lay buried in my heart.

Today this degree of naked sentiment could perhaps only be exhibited in tribute to the death of a pet. And yet the real object of nostalgia, unsurprisingly, is the author's former self. The title of Morris's last chapter, as it turns out, refers to two kinds of "going away": the boy goes on to manhood, Oxford, and a career as a writer, the dog to death.

This capacity of the dog to offer us a way to mourn for our own lost beginnings is doubled by the dog's capacity to take upon himself or herself our present and future griefs as well. The loss of a dog may bring back other losses, at the same time that it is itself a profoundly painful event. Wallace Sife, author of *The Loss of a Pet*, tells the story of a widow in her late fifties who built a shrine in her apartment to her dead dog.

One of my patients was a widow whose dog died four years before she came to me. When the woman's husband died a few years earlier, she was shaken, but seemed to stand up well to the shock. The mourning period was brief and well handled. It was very important to keep up appearances for the neighbors.

She tried very hard to put on a brave face. All her attention and love now were focused on her dog, who reveled in this. . . .

When the dog died a few years later, she was overwhelmed by inconsolable grief and had to be hospitalized for a few days. After an intense period of mourning, which was never resolved, she tried to go about a normal way of life, but couldn't without the dog. She would not get another pet and as a result, her life became entirely devoted to the remembrance of her deceased dog. Her apartment was turned into a near shrine, with pictures draped in black, and the dog's toys and other memorabilia on prominent display. The pet's ashes and urn occupied the central focus of the apartment.

The woman continued this way for a few more years, in perpetual mourning and grief. After analysis, it turned out that much of this abnormal behavior was in response to a deep sense of guilt at not having grieved for her husband as much as she felt she was "supposed to." . . . There is a happy ending to this story, since she now is leading a normal life after wasting so many precious years.

It is not that the death of a dog does not, in itself, constitute a profound loss for a human being. But somehow, what is lost with the dog is a space for feeling, a space which draws into itself emotional energies from other, sometimes unacknowledged sources. This is true of famous people as well as of less-famous ones.

There is perhaps no more poignant version of this than the story of Sigmund Freud and Topsy. In the last years of his life, Freud collaborated with his daughter Anna in the translation of a remarkable little book by his pupil and benefactor, Princess Marie Bonaparte: *Topsy, the Golden-Haired Chow. Topsy,* written between March 1935 and June 1936, describes Bonaparte's distress at discovering a cancerous growth on the lip of her chow Teaupi or Topsy, and chronicles her X-ray treatments and her subsequent cure. The chapter titles are indicative of the style of the whole: Bonaparte's book is divided into two sections, "Topsy Is Ill" and "Topsy Is Healed," and the chapters include "The Sentence," "Poor Topsy!", "Topsy Beneath the Magical Rays" (that is, the X rays at the Curie Institute in Paris), "Respite from Things Human," and, perhaps inevitably, "Topsy and Shakespeare." In "Topsy and Shakespeare" the chow's indifference to literary fame is contrasted to the "illusion" of authors like Homer, Shakespeare—and indeed Princess Marie Bonaparte herself, who "strive[s] laboriously to trace vain signs on this paper" while Topsy "simply inhales the scented June air."

This contrast between human writing and animal living is a constant theme throughout *Topsy.* "The growth under Topsy's lip seems once more to be dissolving and disappearing," writes Bonaparte at one point. She may be "recovered in spite of my mournful poems. And I think that, up to now, it is only with ink and paper that she has been killed." When the news is good, she exults, "Topsy, Topsy, little healed dog, looking at you I am prouder to have almost magically prolonged your little life, than if I had written the Iliad."

But there is a comparison implicit in *Topsy* more compelling than that between Bonaparte and Shakespeare or Homer, and that is the comparison between Topsy and Freud. The "sentence" of oral cancer could only remind Marie Bonaparte, and doubtless her translators

Anna and Sigmund Freud, of the illness of the "master" Freud, likewise suffering from a tumor on the right side of the oral cavity, and likewise treated with surgery and X rays. In the last pages of the book
Bonaparte sees both herself as Topsy's savior ("Topsy who, thanks to
me, has probably recovered from a terrible ailment") and Topsy as a
"talisman that conjures away death" for her human owner.

In writing about Topsy, Marie Bonaparte not only found a way to express her own grief and fear about losing Freud, but also provided a
way for Anna and Sigmund Freud to "translate," displace, and work
through their own emotions. "Does Topsy realize she is being translated?" Freud teasingly asked Marie Bonaparte. As Freud's benefactor,
Bonaparte would also help to "translate" him from Vienna to London to
escape the Nazis. There it was Freud's dog who was imprisoned, temporarily, by the strict British quarantine laws. Freud visited his chow
faithfully in the state kennel throughout the summer and winter of
1938, a human fidelity much noticed and praised in the London Sunday papers.

Freud's emotional relation to his dogs continued to the time of his
own death. As Ernest Jones reports, "a distressing symptom [of his oral
cancer] was an unpleasant odor from the wound, so that when his favorite chow was brought to visit him she shrank into a far corner of the
room, a heart-rending experience which revealed to the sick man the
pass he had reached. The assurance Marie Bonaparte gave to Topsy,
that she would protect her from physical suffering, echoed a pledge
made to Freud by his doctor, Max Schur, as Freud reminded Schur two
days before his death: "You promised me . . . you would help me when
I could no longer carry on. It is only torture now and it has no longer
any sense." Schur fulfilled his promise, giving his patient morphia and
allowing him to die in peace.

Faithful unto Death

Dogs are not only the occasion for human grief; famously, they grieve
for their lost masters. Maybe one reason we mourn them so deeply is
that dogs themselves are reputed to be such good mourners: we mourn
for them as we would like to think they would mourn for us.

Like Freud, John Cheever was acutely distressed when his dog
seemed to sense his fatal illness. Returning from Memorial Hospital in
1981, where he had been diagnosed with cancer, Cheever found that

his golden retriever, Edgar, who had always slept at the foot of his bed, had removed to the living room to sleep. "Although none of us said it," writes Susan Cheever, "it was as if Edgar knew my father was going to die." Shortly Edgar herself was diagnosed with lung cancer. She died in March 1982; he died in June.

Willie Morris's dog Skip is a model mourner. When a starving kitten turns up at the Morris home Skip and his master adopt her, but despite their best efforts she shortly sickens and dies, and they bury her under the elm tree in the backyard. "For weeks Skip acted sad and strange." Morris's final leavetaking from the old dog takes place at the same spot, "not far from the grave of the little kitten we had buried those years ago," and a month later the place becomes Skip's own grave site, too.

In a poem by Wordsworth a little dog named Music is abruptly bereaved of her canine friend in the midst of a romp in the woods. When Dart the greyhound falls through the ice chasing a hare, "Music has no heart to follow" in the chase, for she is overtaken by distress. "A loving creature she, and brave! / And fondly strives her struggling friend to save." The poem goes on to describe her feelings and actions in terms for which "anthropomorphic" may be too weak a term:

> From the brink her paws she stretches,
> Very hands as you would say!
> And afflicting moans she fetches,
> As he breaks the ice away.
> For herself she hath no fears,—
> Him alone she sees and hears,—
> Makes efforts with complainings; nor gives o'er
> Until her fellow sinks to re-appear no more.

Music's fidelity is rewarded by the poet, who pens a "Tribute" to her after her own death. But it is a dog's faithfulness to *human* partners that has occasioned the most comment.

In another highly characteristic though little discussed Wordsworth poem called "Fidelity," written in 1805, a shepherd follows a dog into the mountains, puzzled by its presence in the wild landscape. The dog leads him to a spot where—as any reader familiar with Wordsworth's poetry might expect—the skeleton of a traveler lies. The poet's signature capital letters (Shepherd; Dog; Man; Discoverer; Traveller) mark the iconic and even allegorical nature of the event:

Not free from boding thoughts, a while
The Shepherd stood; then makes his way
O'er rocks and stones, following the Dog
As quickly as he may;
Nor far had gone before he found
A human skeleton on the ground;
The appalled Discoverer with a sigh
Looks round, to learn the history.

From those abrupt and perilous rocks
The Man had fallen, that place of fear!
At length upon the Shepherd's mind
It breaks, and all is clear:
He instantly recalled the name,
And who he was, and whence he came;
Remembered, too, the very day
On which the Traveller passed this way.

But hear a wonder, for whose sake
This lamentable tale I tell!
A lasting monument of words
This wonder merits well.
The Dog, which still was hovering nigh,
Repeating the same timid cry,
This Dog, had been through three months' space
A dweller in that savage place.

Yes, proof was plain that, since the day
When this ill-fated Traveller died,
The Dog had watched about the spot,
Or by his master's side:
How nourished here through such long time
He knows, who gave that love sublime;
And gave that strength of feeling, great
Above all human estimate!

The "he" (or rather, "He") of the final lines is of course God, Who
alone, says the poet, can account for the dog's survival without food,
and for his fidelity and grief.

As always in such poems there is a tendency to twin the mourner
and the mourned, to link the Discoverer with the fallen Traveller. In

Wordsworth's first "Essay upon Epitaphs" (1810) what is reserved to mankind is the consciousness of mortality and the recognition of death's inevitability. "The Dog or Horse perishes in the field, or in the stall, by the side of his Companions, and is incapable of anticipating the sorrow with which his surrounding Associates shall bemoan his death, or pine for his loss; he cannot pre-conceive this regret, he can form no thought of it; and therefore cannot possibly have a desire to leave such regret or remembrance behind him." In a way, such antici-patory consciousness—because it is supposed *absent* in the dog—is the cause of an even keener grief. How could the dog anticipate his master's dying, or his own loss? This, I think, is part of the poignancy of the relation between human being and dog: that we sense in dogs so much in the way of sympathy for our own moods, griefs, and losses— and that we are so powerless to explain loss, death, and sadness to them.

Her Sister's Keeper

When Emily Brontë died, her faithful dog, Keeper, walked "first side by side" with Mr. Brontë in the cortège behind the body, Anne and Charlotte following behind. Together with the other family members he came into the Brontë pew, and "sat quietly while the burial service was read." Then he took up his station outside her empty bedroom, and, for many days, he howled.

This affecting account of a dog's grief and propriety owes some-thing, doubtless, to the Victorian fashion in funerals. Following the lead of the bereaved Queen, who wore mourning for Prince Albert all her life, displays of elaborate mourning and of funereal sensibility were in vogue for much of the period. Keeper, whose very name seems so well to fit the requirements of his role, may have been influenced in his deportment by general expectations. That he accompanied Emily Brontë's father *at the head* of the procession certainly says something about both his place in the household and in Emily's affections.

Keeper was not the first Brontë dog. Grasper, a terrier, lived at Ha-worth in their early years (Mr. Brontë paid a dog tax starting in 1831), and his portrait was painted by Emily in January 1834. A family friend, Ellen Nussey, noted that "during [their aunt] Miss Branwell's reign at the Parsonage the love of animals had to be kept in due subjection. There was then but one dog, which was admitted to the parlor at stated times. Emily and Anne always gave him a portion of their breakfast, which was, by their own choice, the Old North Country diet of oatmeal porridge." And Flossy, a fat black-and-white curly-coated spaniel, was given to Anne Brontë by the Robinson children, for whom she was governess at Thorp Green, near York. But Keeper's role in the Brontë household, or at least in the Brontë mythology, was singular.

We do not, alas, have Keeper's own account of events. What we have instead is some letters, and the novelist Elizabeth Gaskell's celebrated 1857 *Life* of her friend Charlotte Brontë, in which Charlotte's strong "affection" for animals was contrasted with Emily's veritable "passion." "Some one speaking of [Emily] to me," writes Mrs. Gaskell, "in a careless kind of strength of expression, said 'she never showed regard to any human creature; all her love was reserved for animals.' The helplessness of an animal was its passport to Charlotte's heart; the fierce, wild, intractability of its nature was what often recommended it to Emily." Keeper, a mastiff, was a gift to Emily, and came accompanied by a warning: "Keeper was faithful to the depths of his nature as long as he was with friends: but he who struck him with a stick or whip, roused the relentless nature of the brute, who flew at his throat forthwith, and held him there till one or the other was at the point of death."

Emily Brontë soon had the opportunity to test both Keeper's fidelity and his rage, for the big dog had, it seemed, an inclination for the soft life, what Mrs. Gaskell calls his "household fault." He "loved to steal up-stairs, and stretch his square, tawny limbs, on the comfortable beds, covered over with delicate white counterpanes." The household remonstrated, and Emily announced that—despite the fabled ferocity of the breed—she would punish Keeper so severely, if he again transgressed, that he would never offend again. The stage was set for a confrontation between these two strong-willed creatures, and it came.

"Half triumphantly, half tremblingly" (the social dramatist is again Mrs. Gaskell) the parsonage housekeeper arrived to tell Emily that "Keeper was lying on the best bed, in drowsy voluptuousness." Charlotte "saw Emily's whitening face, and set mouth, but dared not speak to interfere; no one dared when Emily's eyes glowed in that manner out of the paleness of her face, and when her lips were so compressed into stone." Upstairs she went, alone, and came down, "dragging after her the unwilling Keeper, his hind legs set in a heavy attitude of resistance, held by the 'scuft of his neck,' but growling low and savagely all the time." (Modern dog owners will immediately recognize this intransigent canine attitude; if Charlotte is Mrs. Gaskell's authority here, as it appears, she was a good observer of dogs.)

The onlookers—Charlotte and Tabby the housekeeper—were silent, fearing to distract Emily's attention "from the enraged brute." But they need not have feared. "Her bare clenched fist struck against his red fierce eyes, before he had time to make his spring . . . she 'punished him' till his eyes were swelled up, and the half-blind, stupified beast was led to his accustomed lair, to have his swelled head fomented and cared for by the very Emily herself." And here Mrs. Gaskell produces the "moral" of this tale:

> The generous dog owed her no grudge; he loved her dearly ever after; he walked first among the mourners to her funeral; he slept moaning for nights at the door of her empty room; and never, so to speak, rejoiced, dog fashion, after her death. He, in his turn, was mourned over by the surviving sister. Let us somehow hope . . . that he follows Emily now; and when he rests, sleeps on some soft white bed of dreams, unpunished when he awakens to the life of the land of shadows.

Indeed, if Emily preferred animals to humans, Keeper "seemed to understand her like a human being," according to Ellen Nussey.

> Poor old Keeper! Emily's faithful friend and worshipper—he seemed to understand her like a human being. One evening . . . Keeper forced himself in between Charlotte and Emily and mounted himself on Emily's lap. Finding the space too limited for his comfort he pressed himself forward onto [a] guest's knee making himself quite comfortable. Emily's heart was won by the unresisting endurance of the visitor, little guessing that she herself being in close contact was the inspiring cause of submission to Keeper's preference.

The day before she died, Emily rose in the evening to feed the dogs— Keeper and Anne's spaniel, Flossy—despite her sisters' attempt to send her back to bed. Less than a year later Anne too was dead, and the dogs remained at Haworth. Charlotte wrote to Ellen Nussey that when she returned to the parsonage after an extended absence they seemed (quite naturally) to expect the two dead sisters to appear as well: "The dogs seemed in strange ecstasy. I am certain they regarded me as the harbinger of others, the dumb creatures thought that as I was returned, those who had been so long absent were not far behind." To her friend and publisher, William Smith Williams, she wrote that only the thought of her father "or some caress of the poor dogs" rescued her from loneliness and rebellion.

Keeper died in December 1851, three years after Emily and two after Anne. Charlotte, the surviving sister, recorded the event: "Poor old Keeper died last Monday morning, after being ill one night; he went gently to sleep; we laid his old faithful head in the garden. Flossy is dull, and misses him. There was something very sad in losing the old dog; yet I am glad he met a natural fate. People kept hinting he ought to be put away, which neither papa nor I liked to think of."

Mrs. Gaskell's sentimental eulogy for the animal she regularly described as "poor old faithful Keeper, Emily's dog" offers a fair portrait of dog love, and dog fidelity, revisiting her earlier account of Emily's conquest and capitulation: "He had come to the Parsonage in the fierce strength of his youth. Sullen and ferocious he had met with his master in the indomitable Emily. Like most dogs of his kind, he feared, respected, and deeply loved her who subdued him. He had mourned her with the pathetic fidelity of his nature, falling into old age after her death."

The moving saga of Keeper is a model for every dog lover—and every lover. Who would not want a mourner so faithful and so solemn, so true to his name?

Greyfriars Bobby

Of all cultural icons of canine fidelity, perhaps none has attracted so much popular attention as Greyfriars Bobby, who watched over his dead master's Edinburgh grave for fourteen years. Bobby was a Skye terrier, named after his owner's profession: John Gray (familiarly known as Auld Jock) was a Scottish policeman. When Gray died in 1858 and was buried in Greyfriars, an Edinburgh burial ground named for the Franciscan order, the two-year-old Bobby took up his vigil. The sexton tried to evict him from the churchyard each night, but he was befriended and fed by a number of local residents, including an innkeeper and a sergeant garrisoned at Edinburgh Castle. In 1861 Edinburgh officials, seeking to synchronize the region's disparate timepieces, decided to fire a cannon from the castle grounds at one o'clock each day. A famous sketch in *Good Words* magazine pictured the eager

Bobby waiting for the one o'clock gun, after which he would trot off to a nearby eating house for his midday meal, and then return to his vigil over John Gray's grave.

Bobby had friends but no official owner after Gray died, and therefore no dog license, so that under strict Victorian licensing laws he was vulnerable to the dogcatcher. Happily Edinburgh's lord provost, Sir William Chambers, was a lover of dogs and a director of the Scottish Society for the Prevention of Cruelty to Animals. Sir William not only arranged to pay for Bobby's dog license indefinitely, but also presented him with a collar engraved—on a brass plate—"Greyfriars Bobby, from the Lord Provost, 1867, licensed." (The collar, and Bobby's food dish, inscribed "Bobby's Dinner Dish," are preserved and on display in the nearby Huntly House museum.)

The statue of Greyfriars Bobby, a remarkable life-sized work of Victorian commemorative art in bronze, was commissioned by an English philanthropist, Baroness Angela Georgina Burdett-Coutts, and installed in 1873 atop a red granite drinking fountain "for dogs and passers-by." Latin and Greek inscriptions were duly affixed, and also one in English provided by the Town Council:

> A tribute to the affectionate fidelity of Greyfriars Bobby. In 1858 this faithful dog followed the remains of his master to Greyfriars Churchyard and lingered near the spot until his death in 1872. With permission erected by Baroness Burdett-Coutts.

Not by accident does this tale of a canine hero traverse social classes, from low to high, policeman to provost, barroom to baroness. Inevitably (we may think) American dog lovers also got into the act, collecting money for a gravestone for Bobby. But since the Skye terrier's actual resting place is not known, and since only persons, and not dogs, are permitted to be interred in Greyfriars (though a nearby Dogs' Cemetery holds the remains of soldiers' pets) they placed the marker over the grave of the master, thus commemorating the dog through the man, and the man as the owner—and beloved object—of the dog.

JOHN GRAY

DIED 1858

"AULD JOCK"

MASTER OF "GREYFRIARS BOBBY"

"AND EVEN IN HIS ASHES MOST BELOVED"

ERECTED BY
AMERICAN LOVERS OF "BOBBY"

The quotation marks tell their own story of the associative chain of love. The Americans come to "love" Bobby because he loved his "most beloved" master, a master whose nickname, "Auld Jock," makes him sound like the dog rather than the man. Meanwhile, supported by noble donors (Sir William Chambers, the Baroness Burdett-Coutts), reverenced by schoolchildren, given an affectionate sobriquet ("Greyfriars") that recalls St. Francis, Bobby the dog is translated into a kind of saint. The story of his preternatural faithfulness to the absent master and his quasi-miraculous survival through the kindness of strangers is told and retold. To his shrine and effigy flock pilgrims—four- and two-legged— who drink from his fountain, contemplate his relics (dog collar, food bowl), and meditate at the site of his (missing) grave. If there is an irony here it is only that saintliness seems to have become, indeed, a trait more "natural" to dogs than to humans—and that it is, nonetheless, human beings rather than Bobby's fellow canines who seek to derive an exemplary message from his story.

It is easy to dismiss this tale as a typical product of Victorian sentimentality and the period's love of kitsch (though I suppose the fountain might better be called an example of dogsch). But the dog faithful unto death is an old and cherished story. Montaigne tells the story of Hyrcanus, King Lysimachus's dog, who threw himself on his master's funeral pyre, as did the dog of a man called Pyrrhus. Or consider this example from Thomas Wilson's sixteenth-century *Arte of Rhetorique*, describing the "wonderfull" dog of the Roman Fulvius:

This *Fuluius* trauailing by the way was slaine with slaues, that laide in waite for him. His Dogge seeing his master dead, laie by him for the space of two daies. Whereupon when the man was missing, and search made for him: They found him dead with his Dog lying by him. Some maruelling to see the Dog lye there by his dead Master, stroke him and would haue driuen him from the dead corse, and could not; some seeing such kindnesse in the dog, and pitying him that he should ly there without meate two or three daies before: cast him a peece of flesh: wheeupon the Dog straight carried the meate to his masters mouth, and would not eate any whit himselfe, though he had forborne meate so long before. And last of all when the dead body should be cast into the

Riuer (according to the maner of the Romaines) the dog lept in after, and holding vp his master so long as he could, did chuse rather to dye with him, than to liue without him.

In our present century a dog named Shep, who belonged to Francis McMahon of Illinois, offered a modern American version of the Grey-friars Bobby saga. When McMahon fractured his skull and was taken to the hospital, the dog followed, taking up a vigil outside the door. At the moment of his master's death Shep reportedly began to howl. He kept up his vigil near the hospital for the next twelve years.

And then there is the story of Hachiko, an Akita who belonged to Professor Eisaburo Ueno of Tokyo University. Hachiko had the custom of meeting his master every day at the Shibuya subway station. When the professor died in 1925, Hachiko waited for him until midnight, and then went home alone. He repeated this act of fidelity every day for nine years, until his own death in 1934. A statue of Hachiko, paid for by his admirers, now stands at the subway exit where he waited so patiently for his master to return.

The Yuppie as Puppy

We might note that some of these animal behaviors, if faithfully followed by humans, would strike us as distinctly odd. It's one thing for Hachiko to meet his master's train for nine years; it's another for a bereaved human being to do the same. "Get on with your life," we say, and we mean it. But for that very reason, these icons of absolute and excessive fidelity offer us some sense of scale. The dog, by being "superhuman" in realms like fidelity and loyalty, gives us permission to temporize, vacillate, even fail.

Consider one contemporary film that contrasts human and canine fidelity. In *Fluke,* instead of dog waiting for a dead master to return, we have the story of a dead master who returns as a dog. *Fluke* was the dog movie of the year in 1995, its golden retriever hero, Comet—suitably disguised for the role as an endearing, dark-coated mutt—featured on the covers of glossy movie industry magazines. A remake of *Ghost* with a canine protagonist, *Fluke* had as its gimmick a dog who had once been a man—or, if you prefer, a man who was reborn as a dog. "I didn't know how to live as a man, and I didn't know how to live as a dog" was the line cited by reviewers summing up the film's "very poetic, beautiful" message. The man (Matthew Modine), dying in a road accident, reappears as an adorable puppy and revisits (through flashbacks) the scenario of his death. Convinced that his partner, who ran him off the road, was a murderer, he sets out to find his wife and child and protect them, only to learn that he himself was the bad guy—a bottom-line materialist, too busy to spend time with his family, who has, ironically, quarreled with his partner over the partner's desire to pioneer a better-engineered but more expensive automobile brake that would probably have saved his life.

In short, *Fluke* was *Ghost* with *Regarding Henry* thrown in (man becomes [1] dog or [2] mentally impaired in order to learn what family life is all about), a little bit of *Look Who's Talking* (Samuel L. Jackson as the voice of the streetwise and loyal stray Rumbo), a dash of Wegman (in a comical closet scene Fluke dons the hat and shoes he wore as a man to show his wife who he really is), a touch of *Tootsie* (like Dustin Hoffman's character, Fluke resolves in the closing moments to learn how to implement the life lessons he's learned, without the disguise), a bit of Greyfriars Bobby (boy and dog take refuge at the grave of the dead father—who in this version is now also the dog), and, of course, the requisite dollop of *Lassie Come Home* (dog struggles to travel many miles, finally arriving at local schoolhouse to await boy).

Why, a friend asked me, didn't Fluke just go back to his own house, since by this time he clearly remembered where he had lived when he was a man? Why did he have to seek out the wife and son in town after passing their home? My friend, usually very savvy in the ways of dog logic, had forgotten *Lassie* Rule Number One: if you want to go "home," you have to start with the boy at the schoolhouse door.

The real surprise of *Fluke*, though, was how painful it was to watch. Why do we worry about children being influenced by R-rated films when there are PG features like *Fluke*, *Black Beauty*, and *Babe* around to demonstrate vividly how cruel (some) humans can be? Fluke's life experience includes capture by animal control officers; separation from his mother and siblings; being caged in a shelter and slated to be "put to sleep" by an indifferent female bureaucrat and a sadistic male attendant; a catch-as-catch-can existence as a junkyard dog; kidnapping and incarceration in a laboratory where he is used as a test animal and almost blinded; grief over the death by shooting of his loyal companion, Rumbo; and —just when the audience may have thought his troubles were finally ended—his self-exile from the wife and son he has rediscovered, learned to love, and rescued. The penultimate scene shows the wife's fiancé (the erstwhile partner, now revealed as a modest and idealistic hero) presenting the son with: *a new puppy!* I could hardly believe it. Never mind the old dog—on with the new.

Meanwhile Fluke, having fled in the snow, finds what we are supposed to regard as self-knowledge and philosophical happiness in a sunny field miles away from any apparent source of food or habitation. That Rumbo reappears as a squirrel to chat him up about life did not comfort me a whit. I wanted him to go *home,* and right away. Perhaps this makes me insufficiently philosophical (a fact I have long suspected anyway) but I came away from *Fluke* full of fury, feeling manipulated but not instructed. *Fluke*'s writers and director would probably tell me I will respond more appropriately next time around, when I resurface as a born-again cocker spaniel. Oh, well—I've always wanted to be a blonde.

Do Dogs Have Souls?

> Dog that is born of bitch hath but a short time to live, and is full of misery. He cometh up, and is cut down like a flower; he fleeth as if it were a shadow, and never continueth in one stay.
>
> —Evelyn Waugh, *The Loved One*

Evelyn Waugh's brilliant little Hollywood satire, *The Loved One,* features an expatriate English writer contentedly employed in a pet cemetery called the Happier Hunting Ground. As he tells the bereaved owner of a dead Sealyham, "Every anniversary a card of remembrance is mailed without further charge. It reads: *Your little Arthur is thinking of you in heaven today and wagging his tail.*" But when Waugh's hero, Dennis Barlow, attends a funeral with full honors for an Alsatian, he is so moved by the prayer of a "non-sectarian clergyman" that he decides to set up in the pet funeral business for himself.

"Do dogs have souls?" I asked a dog-loving friend, who replied, without missing a beat, "They have pads." The old joke was pertinent enough: what we call in theological language a soul may have another less-fraught designation in canine terms. But does anyone doubt that, one way or another, the spirits of our pets live on?

Any child—or any adult, for that matter—who loses a pet to death wants to know what lies ahead for Bowser in the afterlife. "Harry," asks the kindly dog-lover Laura in *Beautiful Joe*, "do you think that dumb animals will go to heaven?" Harry, who reads the newspapers, is ready with "one writer's" opinion of the subject, which is that "among the best people of all ages have been some who believed in the future life of animals." Homer and some of the Romans and early Christians are among them, as are "Doctor Johnson, . . . Wordsworth, Shelley, Coleridge, Jeremy Taylor, Agassiz, Lamartine, and many Christian scholars."

Harry is not sure of the correct doctrinal position ("There's nothing definite about their immortality") but he knows what he thinks proper: "I wish with all my heart that we may find our dumb friends in paradise."

> "I think I would be happier in heaven if dear old Joe were there," said Miss Laura, looking wistfully at me. "He has been such a good dog. Just think how he has loved and protected me. I think I should be lonely without him."

Whereupon Harry promptly produces from his pocket "some poetry, or rather doggerel" that he cut out of the paper, beginning "Do doggies gang to heaven, Dad? / Will oor auld Donald gang?"

Laura herself believes that if any animal is destined for heaven, it should be the dog, "the friend to man," and tells a story about Adam and the dog: "When Adam was turned out of paradise, all the animals shunned him, and he sat weeping bitterly with his head between his hands, when he felt the soft tongue of some creature gently touching him. He took his hands from his face, and there was a dog who had separated himself from all the other animals, and was trying to comfort him."

When Edith Wharton compiled a list of her "ruling passions," the first item was "Justice and Order," and the second was "Dogs." ("Books," came third, followed by "Flowers" and "Architecture.") Her Pekinese, Miza and Mitou, were prime objects of her affections. Distressed by the Pope's refusal to support the Society for the Prevention of Cruelty to Animals in Italy (on the grounds that attributing souls to animals was a heresy), Wharton read a life of St. Francis, noting that the author distinguished between appropriate "sympathy" and excessive "sentimentality" toward animals. She herself "did not doubt for a moment," writes biographer R. W. B. Lewis, "that Mitou had a soul."

The question of whether animals have souls has fascinated philosophers from Aristotle to Thomas Aquinas, Thomas More, and René Descartes. Many religions around the world hold that souls are reborn in other bodies, so that the relationship between human and animal spirits is one of continuity rather than absolute distinction. Native American and Australian Aboriginal tribes celebrate the power of animal spirits. In Aboriginal "dream time" humans and animals are equal and can mate together, according to zoologist James Serpell. The director of communications for the Catholic Archdiocese of Boston told a reporter, with what the reporter regarded as "a little trepidation," that animals do not have immortal souls in the same way humans do. A rabbi at Hebrew College said that he thought animals did not have souls as human did, although they possess "a spark of divinity."

The congregation at a synagogue on Boston's South Shore spent an evening discussing the importance of knowing Jewish law; as a test case the discussant had chosen the question of whether or not it was permissible to say Kaddish for a dog.

Kaddish, the prayer recited by mourners in commemoration of their loved ones, is usually said for parents, siblings, or spouses. In the example provocatively and amusingly offered by the speaker, a member of a minyan (prayer group) names not a relative or friend but "Sam, my dog and my companion." As the narrative continues, "There are a few stifled laughs. There are some shocked looks. There is overt politeness. Kaddish is said. Later, there are lots of discussions."

The question of what the discussion leader called "Doggie Kaddish" was used as a way of exploring biblical texts, rabbinical commentaries, and responsa on both the uses of the Kaddish and the possibility that dogs have souls. Is it acceptable today to say Kaddish for a dog? How should the other members of the minyan have responded? "Mourners would be shocked and angered to see their father and mother listed alongside a dog or cat," wrote one Reform rabbi in an official responsum. "Whatever mourning for a pet which may occur should be conducted privately." A cantor suggested alternative good deeds instead, while another rabbi cited a text which seemed to authorize the saying of healing prayers for sick animals as well as sick people. The "answer" was left unresolved, open to further debate.

The word "pet" does not appear in the Bible or New Testament, where "animal" does multiple duty and humane care of all beasts is enjoined. "There is nothing in scripture that suggests any living thing other than man has a soul. To wonder about this is a projection of our anthopomorphic fantasy," notes pet-loss expert Wallace Sife. But on the other hand "there is nothing in the scriptures that *denies* the existence of a soul for any other creature of creation." When Sife, himself a professional bereavement counselor, consulted representatives of major religions on the question of pets and the afterlife, he got a series of fascinating, and perhaps symptomatic, responses. And nonresponses.

Buddhists, Episcopalians, Unitarians, and Jews all contributed some thoughts on this time-honored question. The senior rabbi emeritus of the Stephen Wise Free Synagogue in New York City explained that since animals are a part of God's creation, Sabbath laws apply to the animal kingdom. A subdean of the Episcopal Cathedral Church of St. John the Divine in New York (where an annual service is held for "the blessing of the animals") equivocates on the matter, shifting the emphasis to belief: "There are those who ask the question, 'Do animals have souls like ours, and will they be with us in an afterlife?' In a loss situation this question is best heard as an expression of the deep love of that which is lost in death. It is not so important to search for the answer." A representative of the Unitarian Universalist Association stresses that the human-animal bond is part of the "interdependent web of existence," and that since "it is a special strand of love and companionship that links pet and pet owner," it is fitting that we "find ways to mourn the loss and share the grief that the death of a pet brings." But Sife reports "Those faiths based upon a fundamentalist point of view felt that they had nothing to say about this personal pilgrimage." Presumably (despite the cautionary tale of *Fluke*) Rover cannot be born again, or at least cannot testify to the fact.

Most personal was the response of a spokesman from the Tibet Center, who urged mourners to "take positive actions," saying prayers for the pet, performing religious practices and dedicating them to the pet. "When my own cat 'Jack Benny' had kidney problems," he reported, "I bought a cassette recorder" and "played tapes of the teachings of His Holiness, the Dalai Lama, so the cat could hear them repeatedly. I am not the only one who does this," he added.

Indeed he is not. A list of suggestions by a bereavement counselor for dealing with the loss of a pet includes writing "a letter or will *from* your pet to yourself," making a list of all the loving memories of your deceased pet and writing *to* him or her, making an audio recording of yourself reading these memories, keeping a daily log or journal, holding a memorial service, and visiting an animal shelter "to look around, not adopt." (I find this last suggestion especially disturbing; the mourning pet owner is told "you have to be firm with yourself" about not adopting on this visit, however appealing you may find one of the animals you see.)

Dog Years

The pathos of the dog as faithful mourner, as lost beloved, and as symbol of the brevity but also of the value of life has given the dog an increasing role in the lives of people with AIDS and other illnesses. Paul Monette invokes the concept of "dog years" to describe the situation of persons with AIDS, where every single year must count for many. "What has it all got to do with the dog, exactly?" Monette wonders, when he and his partner begin to speculate whether Puck, a half Lab–half ridgeback cross, will survive them. "We were all living our lives in 'dog years' now, seven for every twelvemonth," he writes. "So don't tell me I had less time than a ten-year-old dog." Monette is a shrewd observer of both dogs and men, capable of looking pathos in the face without flinching. "Perhaps it is worse than sentimental, the direst form of denial, to still be weeping at dog stories," he said. "But I admit it." Puck, nicknamed Noble Beast by Monette's first partner, Roger Horwitz, who subsequently died, "came to represent the space left over from AIDS," the "human doggedness" not only to survive, but to live and love. Himself increasingly ill, with a new lover and a second male dog who sleeps curled up with the first, Monette seeks to find lessons in the companionship of the canine pair. "One of us is descended from wolves; one of us knows he's dying," he muses about himself and Puck. "We will not be returning from Troy, either of us."

"Who's going to take care of Puck?" was the question that woke Monette from sleep. His lover, Winston Wilde, promised to do so. And for many dogs orphaned by AIDS, a network of support and adoptive services has developed, both in the United States and elsewhere.

Rachel Tiven cherishes her mixed-breed, Sammy, two of whose previous owners died of AIDS. Rachel sublet a New York City apartment from Richard, a friend of a friend, who had developed full-blown AIDS. Because Richard's sister, with whom he went to live, already had three large dogs, Rachel got Sammy as well as the apartment. "At first," she recalls, "we said it was just temporary, till Richard got better." But

Richard got worse, and a few months later Rachel and Sammy went to his funeral. Only there, she said, did she realize "how large a role the dog had played in Richard's life. Sammy sat up front with the family, and everyone gushed over my fluffy mutt—almost as though he were Richard's alter ego."

Richard and Sammy were inseparable. "There are pictures of Sammy and Richard on Fire Island, Sammy and Richard in the city, Sammy and Richard hiking in the woods." But Richard was not Sammy's first owner. Sammy had been adopted from the ASPCA as a puppy by a man named Jim, who died of AIDS and left his dog to Richard. When Sammy went out to Long Island with the family for the private memorial service he jumped into a pile of Richard's clothes and started to howl.

"I don't think dogs have independent, nonsensory memory," says Rachel. "I don't think Sammy 'thinks' about Richard when he's padding around my dorm room, but it matters to me that I remember Richard as Sammy's daddy, and Jim before him. I'm glad I can give him a good home, and I suppose the story has a basically happy ending from the dog's point of view, but in sum total it makes me terribly sad. The simple fact that Sammy is my dog speaks to the way the plague devastated an entire community. I think of Jim, whom I never met, picking out a little black puppy from the pound. He couldn't possibly have known then that the puppy would outlive him and all of his friends."

Pets Are Wonderful Support (PAWS) is a San Francisco–based organization that helps improve the quality of life for people with AIDS by enabling them to keep their animal companions as long as possible. Pet food, veterinary-care vouchers, dog-walking services, grooming, foster care, and adoption placement are among the services PAWS provides to its over five hundred human clients and the almost 750 animals with whom they share their lives. Brochures on "safer pet guidelines" for persons with suppressed immune systems cautions against allowing pets to eat raw meat or drink from the toilet. Owners at risk for infection should avoid contact with the pet's bodily fluids, preferably by having someone else assist in cleaning up after accidents. The hardest guideline to obey may be the warning against pets licking your face. But, as an article on pets and PWAs in the journal *AIDS Patient Care* maintains, the dangers of pet-to-human disease transmission are slight, and the emotional benefits of pet-owning enormous. "If you're alone with this life-threatening disease, having the love of an animal who doesn't judge and would never leave you makes all the difference in the world," says one PAWS client. "My animals are my best friends."

PAWS was begun in 1987 after a San Francisco veterinarian noted that his HIV-positive clients were being urged by physicians to get rid of their companion animals for fear of infection. "The thing [the doctors] didn't realize," says Ken Gorczyca, D.V.M., "was the importance of the human/animal bond and how strong that was." Dr. Gorczyca investigated the scientific literature and found that there "really was nothing to support a position of giving up one's pets." From this beginning, PAWS evolved, and now serves clients with other immunosuppressing conditions (like cancer patients on chemotherapy) and at-risk populations (the elderly, pregnant women, diabetics) as well as people with AIDS.

The Pet Project, an organization developed in conjunction with the San Diego AIDS Project, works to assist people with AIDS in maintaining quality care for their pets. "Consider what it would be like to experience the fear of rejection by family and friends," says the Pet Project's Lorri Greene. "But animals don't reject us; they provide us with unconditional love." Greene notes that recent research suggests petting an animal can reduce stress levels. "Animals offer us a wonderful source of touch." Human-animal support services for people with AIDS/HIV include branches of PAWS, PALS (Pets Are Loving Support), and similar agencies in over twenty cities from Honolulu to Portland, Maine, and their numbers are growing. From PAWS of Southern Florida to PALS of Oklahoma City and POWARS (Pet Owners with AIDS Resource Service) of New York, volunteers are working to keep pet owners and their pets together for as long as possible.

Albin Swenson, sick with AIDS and out of money, hitchhiked with his pit-bull mixed-breed Hanna from Louisiana home to Rhode Island, declining any offers of travel that would separate him from his dog. "An animal has compassionate love," said Swenson. "They don't care what you do, they still love you. And that dog—he's my angel. When I get sick, he sticks by me." Picked up by an animal welfare volunteer—the only one to stop for him—Swenson was flown home with the financial assistance of an old friend and the SPCA of Northern Virginia, which gave $200 for Hanna's care.

In a tribute to his miniature poodle Willie, novelist Armistead Maupin touches briefly but finely on the depredations AIDS has made upon human and canine lovers. Willie, he says, was left for several months with a friend named Steve who had agreed to dog- and house-sit "in spite of serious concerns of his own." What those "concerns" are is never made explicit in this short piece; they do not need to be. When Willie wonders these days about whether Maupin's lover, Terry, will return from "his frequent daylong rounds of shops and doctors and drugstores," his master says:

> I wish we had a common language. I would tell Willie not to worry, that Terry will be home any minute now, no worse for wear, that the evening will still be ours to share. But I would also have to tell him, as best I could, about the dark constancy that has shaped our lives for the decade the three of us have been together. I would explain why Steve never comes to visit anymore and why, despite all the good things we both feel about Terry, we might not always have him with us in the bed.

Betty Carmack, a registered nurse who specializes in grief counseling related to pet loss or euthanasia, tells a moving story about pets and the community of AIDS patients. A man dying of AIDS was planning his memorial service when he realized that something was missing: "he wanted to make sure his dog could attend the service." But the dog, it turned out, died before his master. The man requested that his own ashes and his dog's be intermingled at his death.

Gay men with AIDS told Carmack that the physical closeness of their companion animals was a major comfort. When his cocker spaniel actually hugs him by putting her arms across his chest, one man said, "that is all I really need, when I'm able to be with her like that." Another reported that when he was not feeling well the dog seemed to sense it, "and stays right by me." Others found talking about illness easier with their dogs than with people. "My puppy helped me sort it out," said one man, recalling his initial diagnosis, "I just sat and talked with her." "I sat out on the porch with Sharpie, and I was able to talk with her and use her as a sounding board that helped me sort out my thoughts." And this: "By being able to confide in her and talk it out with her, that's real important to me." Often the dog acts as a mediator in conversations between a patient and his partner. "Our dog helps us communicate," said one man. "A lot of time she sort of begins the conversation in the sense that I'll be lying on the bed playing with her and [my partner] will come in and lie down too, and it's easier with both of us touching her to talk about things with her there." Buddy, another client's dog, is quite simply described as essential therapy, "the most important thing in my life."

Sometimes the dog's emotions, as voiced by the partner, can be used as a way of addressing difficult topics: "Sheba is concerned about your cough and she thinks you're getting weaker." The name "Sheba" here, one of the few given in these accounts, does double duty as a sign of loss (in William Inge's 1950 play it is the dog Sheba whose absence haunts the plot) and a signature of gay identity (as in Tony Kushner's *Angels in America,* where a pet named Sheba whose master develops AIDS is true to her name and doesn't "stick around"). In *Come Back Little Sheba,* to accept Sheba's death, rather than to fixate on her loss and hoped-for return, is an inkling of something like hope for the play's dramatic characters.

Come Back Little Sheba

With the advent of modern technologies, the manufacture of hope has moved into a new register. Sheba, it seems, might be coming back after all. Geneti-Pet, a Port Townsend, Washington, laboratory, stores blood samples from household pets in cryogenic suspension, looking forward to a time when technology can replicate the pet through DNA taken from its blood cells, in effect cloning the original and "enabling you to raise an animal that is identical in every way to your current or previous pet."

The consumer appeal of the brochure depends upon a familiar combination of loss and love. "Household pets bring us the gift of love every day of their lives," it begins. "The sad truth, however, is that our beloved dogs, cats, and other pets are with us for only a few years before death takes them away and we are left helpless and heartbroken. Until now."

For only $75 to process the blood sample, and $100 a year for storage, the laboratory holds out "strong hope" that Sheba can someday come back to life, though it does acknowledge that "science has not yet found the key to replication," so that "for obvious reasons, Geneti-Pet cannot guarantee success." Still, Geneti-Pet's brochure reminds the vacillating pet owner that there is no time to waste: "If you choose not to act now and your pet passes away or disappears, it will be impossible to obtain its DNA," and "once the animal is gone, it will be too late to change your mind."

Meanwhile, in Florida, an entrepreneur using already existing technology, freeze-dries dead pets so that they will always remain present to their owners. Jeff Weber of Jeff's Preservation Specialties, Inc., of Pinellas Park, Florida, charges fees from $400 (for small pets like birds and chipmunks) to around $1,800 (for Doberman pinschers). "When the pets are done," Weber explains, "they'll outlast the life of their owner. They retain natural characteristics no taxidermist could ever duplicate. That's why owners bring them to me." One satisfied customer "puts out water for her freeze-dried dog." Another "had his husky freeze-dried so he could put him beside the easy chair and pet his head while he watched television, just like he used to."

Somewhat to Weber's surprise, older pet owners seemed less interested in his services than younger ones, a response he attributed to elders' reluctance to be reminded of death and yuppies' desire to conquer it (or pay for it to go away). Most of his (human) clients are "younger, in their twenties, with no kids, from the Midwest." If business didn't pick up, he said he thought he might have to diversify, either by branching out into the world of dead humans (there is no Florida law against freeze-drying people) or—conversely—into the world of live dogs. One possible scheme he had in mind was "drug-sniffing dogs for the private sector," which parents could rent to check out their children's rooms.

Are these pet-preservation schemes in fact pilot projects for the preservation of human loved ones? For reasons that may be legal rather than technical, the Geneti-Pet folks say no. Jeff Weber, however, has had some conversations with a local funeral parlor about freeze-drying—and displaying—a human body in a posture and attitude "exactly as the deceased would like to be remembered by its living loved ones," perhaps with the addition of something he called "perpetual viewing chapels" in which the beloved could be permanently on display. But most of those who called to inquire about this extension of service to the human sector were really interested in their own preservation and "immortality" rather than that of a loved one. It's not yet clear that the same customer who likes to pet his freeze-dried pet husky in the living room while watching the tube would ante up $15,000 to $18,000 to have a spouse, partner, or friend preserved under glass, even in the most appealing posture and attitude.

As it turns out, in the nineteenth century stuffing a beloved pet was a common practice. "This mode of remembrance repulses me," wrote a

mid-century French pet-care specialist. "It's a sad thing to see one's little companion whose look was once so lively and bright forever immo-
bile and staring. Moreover, if one kept all his successors in this way,
one would end by having a somewhat cluttered and encumbering museum." Perhaps for that reason, he noted, it had become "the fashion
these days," to preserve only the head of the pet, or its coat. Even at the
beginning of the twentieth century some experts were still recommend-
ing stuffing and mounting: "You could have him stuffed in which case
you will have with you, always, something that will recall your favorite
to you." As Kathleen Kete notes, however, this began to change with
the founding of the Parisian pet cemetery at Asnières in 1899—in part
to halt the unsanitary disposal of dead dogs in the river Seine, but also
to recognize the emotional place of pets in modern life. "To secure a
patch of land to the animal who was a faithful companion, a consoler of
pain, who often has to his credit the rescue of human life and who in
recompense of his devotion is tossed on the garbage heap like the vilest
refuse."

The Pet Cemetery

The pet cemetery, so obvious a target for Waugh's satirical scorn, has
become a familiar American institution, with many advertising in the
pet directory of daily newspapers as well as in breed specialty journals.
And why not? The shorter life span of dogs and cats virtually ensures
that human survivors will be around to mourn.

Despite the historical primacy of the Parisian cemetery, most pet
cemeteries today are located, perhaps unsurprisingly, in the United
States. The International Association of Pet Cemeteries was founded in
1971 and has its headquarters in Land O'Lakes, Florida. The IAPC
lists a hundred pet cemeteries nationwide, from the Dearest Pet Memorial Cemetery of Manahawkin, New Jersey to the Paws Awhile Pet
Memorial Park in Richfield, Ohio and the Rolling Acres Cemetery,
Crematory, Funeral Home and Gift Shop in Lincoln, Nebraska. There
are three Pet Havens, three Pet Lawns, three Pet Rests and a Pets Rest,
a Noah's Ark, a Noah's Garden of Pets and a Noah's Gardens Pet Cemetery, and my favorite, the Rosa Bonheur Memorial Park of Baltimore,
Maryland (named for the trouser-wearing French painter of *The Horse
Fair*), which presumably inters horses as well as dogs and may, for all
I know, also cater to cross-dressed pets. The Bonheur Memorial Park is

one of the very few pet cemeteries—perhaps the only one—in the United States that permits pets and their owners to reside in adjacent plots. Most states outlaw the practice, though they do permit the ashes of owners and pets to be buried side by side. Meantime, for those who can't arrange to get one of these sites, the Virtual Pet Cemetery is one of several memorial parks for pets on the Internet. Eulogies for dogs (as well as cats, turtles, snakes, and budgies) from around the world are posted there.

There have been a few pet-cemetery scandals (in 1991 a Long Island pet cemetery dumped bodies into mass burial pits after assuring trusting mourners that their pets had been individually buried or cremated) but the vast majority of these businesses are pledged, as the IAPC declares, "to help other people and their family pet members, by providing sincere, realistic pet 'after care.'"

The paradox here is the same one we've been considering all along: why should it be so much easier to weep at the grave of "Heather: Queen of Scotties" or "Kettlewine Fritz: A dachshund of outstanding merit (1939–1952)"—both headstones in the Pine Ridge Cemetery for Animals—than at the headstone of a (doubtless worthy) human stranger? "The pet-human bond is sometimes greater than the human-human bond," the cemetery superintendent explained, and a social worker from the Massachusetts Society for the Prevention of Cruelty to Animals who conducts group discussions on coping with the loss of a pet suggested to a reporter that losing a pet can be more painful than losing a friend or relative because—in the reporter's words—"our love and then our grief are pure." Buried in Pine Ridge are the pets of Lizzie Borden (Donald Stuart, Royal Nelson, and Laddie Miller: "Sleeping awhile"), and Igloo, the short-coated fox terrier who went to Antarctica and back with Admiral Richard Byrd.

Igloo, Byrd's cherished companion (who would "wear his little union suit and fur cap" in Antarctica, as the *Times* indulgently reported), was "More Than a Friend," as his expensive tomb declared. When the explorer learned that his dog was near death he canceled two scheduled lectures (leaving a senator and assorted dignitaries in the lurch) and rushed back to Boston, arriving too late. He buried Igloo in a white casket with silver handles; a colleague from the expedition served as one of the pallbearers. A two-page obituary was published in the *Literary Digest*.

Igloo's white marble stone, described by a visitor as "iceberglike," is a monument not only to the Admiral's affection but also to what may seem to modern eyes to be his inconsistency. Honored upon his return from the Pole by the ASPCA and the American Humane Association for his devotion to his sled dogs, praised by *The New York Times* as an animal lover, Byrd had refused to fly food to his hardworking dogs despite their drivers' pleas. "You had better not depend on us at all. Left no dog food," he informed the waiting party of sledgers. With no recourse, the men built an execution snow wall and shot a number of dogs, reserving their carcasses to feed the remaining huskies. The sled dogs were workers; Igloo was a pet.

Many of the dogs from the Byrd expedition that did return died of distemper within the year. But when one of the survivors, Unalaska, a husky, was run over by a car in Monroe, Louisiana, three thousand schoolchildren participated in his funeral rites, and city officials announced that his portrait would be displayed on the walls of the new high school. Unalaska was buried in front of the American Legion Home, over the objections of legionnaires who complained that the site was reserved for war dead. "Sacred to the Memory of Unalaska," read the bronze plaque on his half-tone stone monument.

What does it cost to inter a dog today? It depends upon the degree of ceremony desired. A "country burial" (that is, a mass grave for pets) can cost under $50; cremation ceremonies cost $100 or $200; and an individual burial site, casket, and marker can run $300 to $500 and up. Obviously a mausoleum of the Igloo variety costs even more.

"STATUE OF YOUR OWN PET on handsome custom-made wooden urn," offered one listing in the "Pet Memorials" section of *Dog Fancy*. (A later version of this same advertisement declared reassuringly "mutts welcome.") Grieving owners could also avail themselves of the "St. Francis Personalized 'Mini' Marker," the "Pet Photo Urn" ("Porcelain china urns with 22 kt. gold trim. Your pet's photo permanently glazed on. An elegant and unique tribute to your devoted friend"), the "A Tribute to Dogs" wall hanging, bearing a "touching, sensitive poem [that] salutes the cherished dog who has unfortunately passed away. Free sample . . . specify blue or pink," a variety of granite, marble, and metal alloy pet markers and airtight caskets, a ceramic urn in the shape of a doghouse ("You choose colors and write epitaph"), and a "compassionate newsletter" called *It's Okay to Cry* that contains "stories of people who have lost a pet. Each touching story brings tears to your eyes and hope to your heart. . . . Satisfaction guaranteed." The purveyors of these products bear names like Serene Memorials, Faithful Friend, Reflections Pet Urns, and Pets Remembered ("Looking for a truly unique memorial for your beloved pet? We may have what you are looking for").

Pleasant Mountain Pet Rest of Plymouth, Massachusetts, offers rates "at a level that families from all walks of life can afford to return their pets' devotion." Presumably like the pets themselves in life, "the grounds are constantly maintained and groomed," and the cemetery thoughtfully includes in its information packet a brochure called "Ten Tips for Coping with the Loss of Your Pet." The "tips" are really questions, including "When is it time to euthanize my pet?"; "Should I stay during euthanasia?"; "What do I do now?" (This is the "tip" that deals with cemeteries, cremation, and home burial: "not a good option if you rent, or if you move frequently"); "What should I tell my children?"; "Will my other pets grieve?" ("Pets observe every change in the household. Certainly they're going to realize that someone is missing!"); and "Should I get a new pet right away?" ("You may find yourself making unfair comparisons"; "It's not a good idea to get a 'lookalike' pet"). This last suggestion is established lore in the realm of pet counseling, right up there with "Don't give puppies as Christmas presents," but—like all established lore, I guess—it is subject to individual exception. A woman I know lost her beloved Australian shepherd in a freak household accident (the dog, a clever forager, got into a hidden lode of baker's chocolate and was poisoned). Within days my grieving friend had been in touch with the breeder and had arranged to get a puppy from the same parents. The much-mourned Ingrid was not "replaceable," but her owner took comfort from knowing that Ilsa would be a family member who could carry on the connection.

Pleasant Mountain includes in its mortuary information a coupon offering "more help" in the form of a book called *Coping with Sorrow on the Loss of Your Pet*, described as a "complete, compassionate guide to every aspect of pet loss bereavement, including tested coping strategies that will help you and your family heal the pain of your loss." As is probably clear, I feel some ambivalence about these "tips" and, indeed, about the concept of pet cemeteries altogether. I'm not a fan of the language of "coping strategies" (especially "*tested* coping strategies") or of the collective notion of learning to "cope." The idea of "losing my pet," however, throws me into an emotional tailspin, if you'll pardon the pun. Losing my pet—okay, let's come down to painful cases; losing one of my golden retrievers, Wagner or Yofi—either to a dognapper or to the Great Dognapper in the Sky is an intolerable thought, and one that would probably not be rendered more tolerable by any number of tips on how to cope. So I find myself rejecting the "strategies" while acknowledging the emotions, and wishing that my temperament were more amenable to institutionalized "coping" than it seems to be. In the meantime I'll clearly have to cope with my unwillingness to countenance coping strategies. I think I regard them as a way of avoiding a pain that can't and shouldn't be avoided.

When the Time Comes

Even—or perhaps especially—when the death of a dog occurs by human decision, many people find themselves unprepared for the strength of their feelings. "I have always felt it was human arrogance that assumes that only people have souls," wrote columnist Anne Raver in a moving tribute to her fourteen-year-old shepherd-collie mix Molly, diagnosed by a veterinarian with a tumor of the spleen. Raver took Molly for a walk through farmland that she loved before taking her to the hospital for an injection that would end her life. "I wasn't prepared for how quick her death was," says Raver. "I'd expected, somehow, to have a minute or two left. To say one more goodbye, I guess. To apologize for taking her life."

Do dogs know when their time is coming? Can they tell when we start to agonize about making such a decision?

A friend of mine had a dog who had been with the family for years, and who had, in her fourteenth year, become incontinent and lethargic. Both human "parents" work outside of the home, and the children are grown and no longer live in the house; in addition, the adults' workplaces are seasonal; they must move from one house to another during the course of the year. The dog, beloved by everyone, including the local veterinarian, became a problem, a burden. It was hard to want to hug her, since she was frequently dirty, and she smelled. On the other hand, they all remembered her bounding youth—and middle age— with enormous love. Should they have her put to sleep because she seemed so miserable, and because they could not do anything to improve her situation? Family members gathered for a melancholy discussion, and it was decided that she would not move back with them from the summer to the winter quarters. The winter house was a city apartment; she would have to walk, or be carried, down several flights of stairs every time she needed to go out. The couple were distraught but reluctantly resolute. The grown sons wept, but were (almost) reconciled. And the dog? The day the family came to this decision, out of the dog's earshot, they encountered—to their amazement—a different animal, one who once again bounded with enthusiasm, kept herself clean, asked to go for walks and for rides in the car. She was a new dog—or rather, the old dog, the one they had cherished for fourteen years. The vet concurred: she had come back to (her former) life. There was no longer any question of putting her down, no question but that she would return with the couple to the city. How did this dog know that her fate had hung in the balance? No one had "told" her. And she had not been neglected before; quite the contrary. In the days of her deterioration they had tried to get her to go out, praised her when she did so, gave as much love as they could. So it was not that the family suddenly began paying attention to her where they had not. Her recovery was "just one of those things," subliminal, parapsychological, coincidental—who knows?

My friend Jonathan recalls that the old family dog of his childhood, Jeff, a black-and-white springer spaniel, came on the eve of his death (he died in his sleep) to bid ceremonious leave to each of the children. Of course Jonathan and his brothers had, he said, no sense of the impending event and dealt with Jeff unceremoniously, some shooing him away if they were busy with something else. It was only afterward that they realized what he had done. Jonathan was about eight at the time.

The owner of Max the Newfoundland wrote of his beloved dog's final months in 1875:

> The sweetness of his disposition and endearing qualities are sufficiently attested by the fact, that to the last, when sometimes his sickness entailed additional and disagreeable duties in regard to him, not a servant would hear to his days being shortened, and when he died there were those of the household who felt that though but a dog he had qualities which would have adorned a Christian.

Studies of how the loss of a companion animal affects human beings have been undertaken by a wide range of professionals, from psychologists, anthropologists, social workers, and philosophers to zoologists and veterinarians. One vet in Scotland did a fascinating comparative study of people's responses to human and animal death in a variety of circumstances: anticipation of impending death, activities following death, feelings following death, and thoughts on the "gap" left by the death. We are told, for example, that "replacement animals" can upon occasion be very successful, while "in the case of human bereavement, replacement as such does not occur." Other perceived differences were also striking: the guilt of the pet owner who may have had an animal euthanized to save it pain, the loneliness of the survivor whose grief for what friends regard as "just an animal" is not shared or even recognized, the comparative lack of ceremony in pet bereavement ("[pet] funerals are very unusual in the United Kingdom"), the need for a community of support.

Though some of the study's pronouncements seem like social science at its most owlish ("the 'boyness' of a son or the 'womanness' of a wife . . . can be compared with the 'dogness' of a dog; this is illustrated by statements such as 'It's good to have a boy [or woman] around the house'"), the issues it discussed were recognizable and oddly reassuring in their commonsensical way. Still, I found "replacement animal" an unsettling term: its very infelicity in a human context made the whole exciting and risky process of pet-getting seem coldly utilitarian. I do remember wondering whether Yofi's arrival as a puppy, right after Nietzschie's death, was "too soon," either for us or for our other dog Wagner. But it wasn't, though Wagner rather reluctantly gave up his new status as sole pet-in-chief. (I suppose this proves the study's point. It *is* definitely good to have a dog—or in my case, two—around the house.)

A social worker who leads group sessions at the Massachusetts Society for the Prevention of Cruelty to Animals today reports that people tend to feel guilty no matter what they decide about their pets' final days. Dogs near death, said Jane Nathanson, often look and behave as if they were perfectly well, eating full breakfasts and trotting into the vet's office on the day they are to be euthanized. Since the dog reposes full trust in the owner—and the owner, very often, reposes the same trust in the dog—making a decision about a dog's life and death can seem an intolerable responsibility.

Anne Raver found that Milan Kundera's *The Unbearable Lightness of Being*, with its scene of the dog Karenin dying of cancer, was a paradigm of her feelings about her own dog Molly. In Kundera's novel, when the dog becomes seriously and painfully ill and Tomas, a doctor, decides to give her a fatal injection, Karenin gives Tereza "a look of awful, unbearable trust. The look was an eager question. All his life Karenin had waited for answers from Tereza."

Karenin's death scene echoes, I assume consciously, that of King Lear's daughter Cordelia, in a play that we have already seen to present persistent and powerful analogies between dog and human love. Tereza "found a mirror in her bag and held it to his mouth. The mirror was so smudged she thought she saw drops on it, drops caused by his breath. 'Tomas! He's alive!' she cried," but Tomas shakes his head. "Lend me a looking-glass," cries the distraught Lear. "If that her breath will mist or stain the stone, / Why then she lives. "

> Why should a dog, a horse, a rat, have life,
> And thou no breath at all? . . .
>   Look on her, look, her lips,
> Look there, look there!—

The analogy is not farfetched, after all. Cordelia, too, is an emblem of unconditional—and silent—love.

The Literature of Grief

John Milton, following in the steps of the Roman Martial, was the quintessential poet of infant mortality. It was famously said of him that no dying child in the environs was safe from his ambitious and lamenting pen. A similar outpouring from poets, playwrights, and novelists has been occasioned by the death of dogs. From the English Byron to the Belgian Maeterlinck to modern American writers like Edward Albee and Maxine Kumin, the loss of a beloved dog has been the proximate cause of verse and prose in which grief and eloquence have contended together with ingenuity. But to call these works ingenious is not at all to call them disingenuous; it is rather, as was the case with Milton, that a combination of strong emotion and dramatic occasion in the context of a compelling minor genre has produced a series of quite remarkable small masterpieces.

Social as well as literary history plays an obvious role in this shift, since (happily) child mortality is not the common hazard that once it was, and, as no writer on dogs fails to mention, the dog's life is on average one-seventh of the human's. If you have a dog, you will most likely outlive it; to get a dog is to open yourself to profound joy and, prospectively, to equally profound sadness. Indeed it is not uncommon for people to say, as does one sympathetic character in Susan Conant's dog mysteries, that the loss of a dog was so painful that they will not get another, since they do not want to subject themselves to that kind of pain again. (As if to stress the point that anyone can have such feelings, Conant's vulnerable figure is a six-foot Irish cop.)

Columnist James Carroll, writing in *The Boston Globe*, tells of his reluctance to get a dog, despite his daughters' pleas—and of his pleasure once Sophie, a schnauzer, joined the family. Why had he resisted? Because the dog of his own childhood, Chris, a collie, had chased cars in the street and been run over by a milk truck. "I knew perfectly well that the fault was mine, because not only had I let Chris chase after cars, but I had thrilled—his speed, his deft courage—to watch him do it. So now my best friend—his eye never closed—was dead because of me. And why should I, after that, have ever wanted a dog again?" The adult Carroll, looking backward in time could admit to himself, "The truth is, I had never quite finished with Chris." And as he ran along the Charles River, with Sophie jogging companionably by his side, he "found himself imitating her uncomplicated exuberance," admiring her way of running, feeling that he, too, could achieve "an instant of pure flight," and saw that it was Sophie who had taught him. "Nice dog," a fellow jogger calls to him. And though his first instinct is to say she's his "kids' dog," he finds that he wants to say, instead, "She's mine" and "I'm hers."

As the authors of a book on aging dogs (and their owners) observe, "Poems and stories written to honor oldies that have passed on evoke a powerful response. People with minimal writing skills seem to become Brownings and Twains when it comes to penning a memorial to a beloved pet." Clearly, as we have seen, the Brownings and Twains also find solace in writing about their canine companions. And sometimes the dogs themselves get the last word.

Playing Dead

The governing conceit of the anthology *Unleashed* is that it contains a collection of "poems by writers' dogs." Thus what philosopher Jacques Derrida termed "the impossible sentence," Hamlet's "I am dead," comes to literary life in a series of poems supposedly written by dogs who have died. They are witty, and they can break your heart, or at least tweak it a little, if you are unwary and especially if you have, or have had, a dog.

"I left. I'd finished raising you," begins "Envoy" by Walter Kirn's Jolly Dog.

"*You* left," gently accuses Susan Minot's Jason in a poem called "Devotion," on the facing page—a litany of loving loss about the children of the household growing up, and growing away:

> *You* left. One by one there were less of you
> Less bicycles tipping off their stands. . . .
>
> You went, not I, with a suitcase shut.
> I loped after each car. . . .
>
> When the last who'd suck'd his bottle sleeping on my
>   fleecy side
> Left, I ambled off to where dogs bereft alone go,
>   and died.

Kate Clark Spencer's dog Bell contributes a poem called "When I Died on My Birthday," which begins, "My heart broke for you." And Ben Sonnenberg's Harry offers an epigram in the spirit of the Roman poet Martial, entitled "Stay," that reads in its entirety:

> I was a bad dog and didn't obey
> Any command, until today.

Perhaps closest to the "impossible sentence" spoken from the grave is "Buster's Visitation," a poem by Stephen Dunn's dog, who declares in the opening line "I'm a dead dog for real now." Playing dead, that most banal of dog tricks, has become a poignant final bow.

Loving Wills

We noted that one of the suggestions made by professional grief counselors is writing "a letter or will *from* your pet to yourself." This may sound excessively cute or anthropomorphic at first, something that one would never actually do. But in at least one case such a will was not only written but published, and did, so far as can be told, afford some comfort to the family.

When Eugene and Carlotta Monterey O'Neill's beloved dog Blemie
died of old age, O'Neill composed for his wife's consolation (and his
own) "The Last Will and Testament of Silverdene Emblem O'Neill,"
later printed as "For Carlotta." The voice of the "Will and Testament,"
is, of course, Blemie's:

> I have little in the way of material things to leave. Dogs are wiser
> than men. They do not set great store upon things. They do not
> waste their days hoarding property. They do not ruin their sleep
> worrying about how to keep the objects they have, and to obtain
> the objects they have not. There is nothing of value I have to be-
> queath except my love and my faith. . . .
>
> It is time I said good-bye, before I became too sick a burden
> on myself and on those who love me. It will be sorrow to leave
> them, but not sorrow to die. Dogs do not fear death as men do. We
> accept it as part of life, not as something alien and terrible which
> destroys life. What may come after death, who knows? I would
> like to believe with those of my fellow Dalmatians who are devout
> Mohammedans, that there is a Paradise where one is always
> young and full-bladdered. . . .
>
> I am afraid this is too much for even such a good dog as I am
> to expect. But peace, at least, is certain.

For months afterward O'Neill did not mention Blemie's name, but
frequently Carlotta saw him glance at the place on the hearth at their
California home, Tao House, where the old dog used to lie. Periodically
the playwright walked to the gravesite and paused where a marble
headstone reads "Blemie (Silverdene Emblem) / Born September 27,
1927, England / Died December 16, 1940, Tao House / Sleep in
Peace, Faithful Friend." At Christmas two years later O'Neill wrote to
his friend Sophus Keith Winther that "Blemie's ghost still benignly
haunts Tao House. Two days ago we waded through the mud out to his
grave beneath the pines at the foot of the hill to place a Christmas
wreath on it, hoping he would look down from the Paradise of Ten Bil-
lion Trees and Unrationable Dog Biscuits and pity us."

When writers' dogs die, the writers often write *about* them, if they don't
write *for* them. E. B. White's fond obituary for Daisy was published in
The New Yorker:

Daisy ("Black Watch Debatable") died December 22, 1931, when she was hit by a Yellow Cab in University Place. At the moment of her death she was smelling the front of a florist's shop. It was a wet day, and the cab skidded over the curb—just the sort of excitement that would have amused her, had she been at a safe distance. She is survived by her mother, Jeannie; a brother, Abner; her father, whom she never knew, and two sisters, whom she never liked. She was three years old. . . .

Her life was full of incident but not of accomplishment. Persons who knew her only slightly regarded her as an opinionated little bitch, and said so; but she had a small circle of friends who saw through her, cost what it did. . . . She died sniffing life, and enjoying it.

Sixty years later columnist Anna Quindlen commemorated the death of her dog in a mock obituary which, like Daisy's, was not really mock at all. "Jason Oliver C. Smith, a big dumb guy who was tan, died March 30 of lung cancer and old age," it began. "He was 13 years old and lived in New Jersey, Pennsylvania, and the back seat of the mini-van, behind the kids' seat."

He was born a golden retriever, although he never let it affect his behavior. He never appeared in a Ralph Lauren ad, never gamboled through a field of daisies and high grass by the side of a slim woman with a picture hat in a television commercial for feminine products. . . .

His career as a retriever coincided with a period of cataclysmic change. The New York City dog waste statute, commonly known as the pooper-scooper law, was enacted the year he was born. Late in life the animal rights movement swirled around him, and his master routinely threatened to make him into a coat.

His last illness came on the eve of the recent decision that stringent regulations governing pit bulls were discriminatory because breed specific. . . .

He lived in the city for most of his life, but he never wore a little plaid coat or a leather collar with fake gemstone, and he was never walked by a professional. . . .

At the time of his death, his license was current and he had had all his shots.

He is survived by two adults, three children, a cat named Daisy who drove him nuts, and his lifelong companion, Pudgy, whose spaying he always regretted, as well as a host of fleas who have gone elsewhere, probably to Pudgy.

At the combined family Easter Egg Hunt/Memorial Service held in his honor, he was remembered by one of the children as a "really smart dog."

Unfortunately, this was inaccurate. . . .

He will be missed by all, except Daisy.

He never bit anyone, which is more than you can say for most of us.

"More than you can say for most of us" is, in a way, the perfect canine epitaph.

The dogs in our lives, the dogs we come to love and who (we fervently believe) love us in return, offer more than fidelity, consolation, companionship. They offer comedy, irony, wit, a wealth of anecdotes, the "shaggy dog stories" and "stupid pet tricks" that are the commonplace pleasures of life. They offer, if we are wise enough or simple enough to take it, a model for what it means to give your heart with little thought of return. Both powerfully imaginary and comfortingly real, dogs act as mirrors for our own beliefs about what would constitute a truly humane society. Perhaps it is not too late for them to teach us some new tricks.

Coda

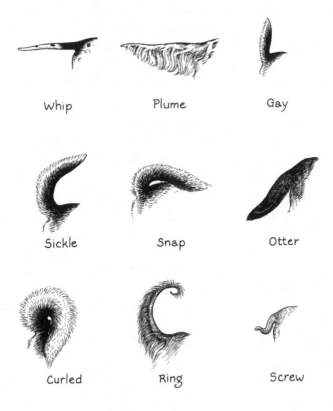

Whip

Plume

Gay

Sickle

Snap

Otter

Curled

Ring

Screw

What shall I do with this absurdity—
O heart, O troubled heart—this caricature,
Decrepit age that has been tied to me
As to a dog's tail?
    —William Butler Yeats, "The Tower"

One trick a dog doesn't need to learn is how to wag its tail. A wagging tail is the spontaneous sign of joyful recognition, and dog owners usually respond to it with a joyful recognition of their own. For the dog wears his heart on his tail.

Tell-tail. "What a wonderful indicator of happiness is the dog's tail," writes dog trainer Barbara Woodhouse, "the half-mast wag with the very tip of the tail, showing nervous expectation; the half-mast slow wag of the interested dog who wants to know what master is saying but doesn't quite pick it up; the full-mast wag of excitement and happiness when he is really happy."

Dogs' tails come in all shapes and sizes, from the long to the short to the virtually nonexistent, but whether curled, plume, gay (carried above the horizontal, as specified in several breed standards), sickle, otter, snap, ring, whip, or screw, the tail is among the most expressive of canine features, as well as the most elegant and graceful. "I have rarely found a dog with a gaily carried tail, which curled over its back or sideways, of any value," remarks the author of a book on British war dogs. "This method of carrying the tail seems to indicate a certain levity of character, quite at variance with the serious duties required." (No gays in the military?) The owners of some breeds, like the boxer, "dock" the tail—cut it short. In this case the whole dog may wag when the tail does. In puppies, no matter the breed, this tends to happen anyway; the tail of the dog tells the tale.

Dogs talk with their tails. They show happiness, recognition, love, greeting. When our golden retriever Nietzschie went (with a dog-sitting friend) to a lecture, he lay quietly on his side in the back of the room, disturbing no one (he was a very tactful dog)—except when latecomers entered. Then the quiet of the lecture hall was interrupted by a steady thump-thump-thump.

Trainer Jean Craighead George observes that "a tail wag, the equivalent of a human smile," is offered by dogs only to living things. "A dog won't wag its tail to its dinner or to a bed, car, stick, or even a bone," she says. I believe her. But there is an exception to every rule, and she hasn't met the well-named Wagner, who will enthusiastically greet just about anything, wagging his tail like a metronome. Whatever it is might *come* to life, he speculates. But then he's always been an optimist.

Another exception to the tail-wagging rule demonstrates its importance as a sign of spontaneous canine pleasure. This is an example from "art," not "life," but therein lies the point (or perhaps I should say, "Thereby hangs a tale"). As so often, the exemplary dog here is Lassie—or, in this case, Pal, who first played the role on screen.

The triumphant emotional climax of the first *Lassie* film comes when the exhausted collie, having swum rivers, climbed mountains, and endured storm, wind, and rain to reach the side of her beloved boy master, waits for him in the schoolyard where he has given up hope of her return. The boy descends the steps, dejected, and looks around: against all probability, Lassie is there! But Lassie, that consummate canine actor, here nonetheless misses a cue. For as the boy and dog greet one another, where is the wagging tail? Watch the film and you'll see what I mean. This is not a real reunion. This dog has seen this boy very recently. The tail, only faintly waving, is a dead (end) giveaway. Lassie is responding to an off-camera acting coach, not directly to the boy.

Tail-wagging is a sign of the sincere and the genuine—even if sincerity (as Sam Goldwyn once announced to an aspiring star) is the ultimate thing to learn how to fake.

Dogs may be good actors, but they are not good fakers. On the other hand, they *are* good manipulators and flatterers, able to make themselves look adoring, supplicating, or irresistibly cute when a biscuit or a piece of cheese is near. The hopeful tail wag by the door, the imperious high-tailed posture at dinnertime, are all perfectly sincere, even if the love being expressed is directed beyond the addressee—at, for example, that nice piece of chicken you don't seem to be wanting to finish. (Console yourself; it's *your* chicken he loves, after all.)

A "wag" is a joker, a mischievous person. Or dog. "Dogs," noted Max Eastman, "laugh with their tails." Wagner is a "wag" in this sense—a natural comic. Yofi, on the other hand, is more like Arnold Toynbee's vision of "America": "America," Toynbee is said to have said, "is a large, friendly dog in a very small room. Every time it wags its tail it knocks over a chair." (This was mid-century America; today's cultural historians might find other canine metaphors.)

A "slow tail wag, with tail at half-mast," explains Stanley Coren, can be interpreted as "I'm trying to understand you. I want to know what you mean, but I just can't quite figure it out." In my experience, it can also mean something like "I'm feeling guilty for what you're about to find out I've done"—Yofi used to do it whenever he'd chewed up a dishtowel. (My fault. Shouldn't have left them hanging at dog-level.)

A coda in music is a closing passage; it has come to mean, also, things like "addition," "end," "adjunct," "sequel." The word derives from the Latin for "tail." There are many proverbs and sayings about the relationship of the dog to the tail, all of which are intended to express, as proverbs and sayings do, home truths about human beings. "The tail is wagging the dog" is one of my favorites. Translation: something like "The unimportant has taken over the place of the important," or "Secondary conditions are replacing primary ones," or "You've got this backwards, you're doing this all wrong." But "the tail is wagging the dog" is, in a dog-centered universe (which we all might be better off for inhabiting) a *wonderful* sign, a sign of joy and exuberant pleasure. We should be so lucky.

"The tail wags the dog" is, in a sense, a capsule description of the argument of this book, if we understand by "tail" *dog* and by "dog" *human being*, or *human society*. Through the way we interact with dogs we can learn a great deal about how we interact with one another, about the present state of human living and human loving. The tail wags the dog. The dog wags us.

NOTES

Introduction

PAGE

13 "I love a dog": Bryan B. Sterling, *The Best of Will Rogers* (New York: Crown Publishers, 1979), p. 61.

13 "All knowledge": *Selected Short Stories of Franz Kafka*, Willa and Edwin Muir, trans. (New York: The Modern Library, 1952), p. 218.

13 When a three-week-old puppy: Jon Auerbach, "Hundreds Offer a Home for Puppy," *The Boston Globe*, March 8, 1995, p. 28.

14 A British Airways captain: "Pilot Who Diverted Plane for Dog Lauded," *The Boston Globe*, November 24, 1996, p. 17.

15 Sheba: "Dog's Best Mom": *The Boston Globe*, January 18, 1955, p. 3; "Man Who Buried Puppies Faces Jail," *The Boston Globe*, March 23, 1995, p. 10 (reprinted from *The Fort Lauderdale Sun-Sentinel*).

15 Fred was a stray beagle: Fred Kaplan, "Big Police Ally for a Dead Precinct Dog," *The Boston Globe*, November 9, 1995, p. 3. "Officers Ousted After Charges of Beating Dog," *The New York Times*, November 8, 1995, p. B2.

16 When nearly eighty: "N.H. Kennel Hoping for Hollywood Ending," *The Boston Globe*, September 7, 1995, p. 28.

16 Tetley, a Chihuahua: Chuck Sudetic, "Tetley's Saga: Friendly Finder Fools Subway Thief," *The New York Times*, May 9, 1995, p. B3.

17 Lyric, an Irish setter: James A. Duffy, "The Paws of Life," *The Boston Globe*, March 13, 1996, p. 1.

17 Lyric's exploits: Susan Bickelhaupt and Maureen Dezell, "Names and Faces, *The Boston Globe*, March 16, 1996, p. 22.

17 A study conducted: Karen Allen and Jim Blascovich, "The Value of Service Dogs for People with Severe Ambulatory Disabilities: A Randomized Controlled Trial," *The Journal of the American Medical Association*, April 3, 1996, vol. 275, No. 23, pp. 1001–1006.

17 Take the case of Bailey: "Tennessee Hog Dog," *The Boston Globe*, May 11, 1995, p. 3.

18   The stiff and stolid: Niall Kelly, *Presidential Pets* (New York: Abbeville Press, 1992), p. 65.
18   Franklin Delano Roosevelt's Scottie: ibid., pp. 70–71.
19   "You know, the kids": Earl Mazo and Stephen Hess, *Nixon: A Political Portrait* (New York: Harper and Row, 1967), p. 120.
20   Yuki once showed up: Kelly, *Presidential Pets*, p. 85.
20   Bill Clinton bid: Michael Blowen, "Names & Faces," *The Boston Globe*, May 12, 1993, p. 58.
20   "The Queen's corgis": Douglas Keay, *The Queen: A Revealing Look at the Private Life of Elizabeth II* (New York: St. Martin's Press, 1991), pp. 206–207.
20   "Who or what": "Social Study: Bill Blass" (*Vanity Fair*'s "Proust Questionnaire") *Vanity Fair*, August 1995, p. 164.
21   "The choice should be obvious": Carole Burns, "Pet Owners Are Claiming Their Own Piece of the Internet Turf," *The New York Times*, November 9, 1995, p. C6.
21   "click on a doghouse": *Anders CD-ROM Survey 1996* (Andiron Press, 1995), cited in "A CD-ROM Shoppers Guide," *Newsweek*, December 11, 1995, p. 14.
21   "A similar CD-ROM": Giles Foden, "Dogged Devotion," *The Guardian*, May 11, 1996, pp. 4–5.
21   "a British biologist": Rupert Sheldrake, "The Case of the Telepathic Pets," *New Age Journal*, October 1995, pp. 99–103.
22   "Dog lovers a plus": Eric Asimov, "Word for Word: The Personals," *The New York Times*, February 11, 1996, p. 7.
22   "Young men": Carla Koehl and Sarah Van Boven, "A Date with a Pedigree," *Newsweek*, January 22, 1996, p. 6.
22   A front-page article: *The New York Times*, "Arts and Leisure," August 7, 1994, section 2, p. 1.
22   "TV's Top Dog": *Entertainment Weekly*, December 3, 1993.
22   *How to Get:* Arthur J. Haggerty, *How to Get Your Pet into Show Business* (New York: Howell Book House, 1994).
22   Sandy, a multitalented mongrel: *Sandy: The Autobiography of a Star*, as told to William Berloni and Allison Thomas (New York: Simon and Schuster, 1978).
23   *Praise of the Dog:* Ethel E. Bicknell, *Praise of the Dog: An Anthology* (New York: Dutton, 1902); J. Earl Clauson, *The Dog's Book of Verse* (Boston: Small, Maynard & Co., 1916); Robert Maynard Leonard, *The Dog in British Poetry* (London: David Nutt, 1893), p. vii.
23   dog fiction: Jeanne Schinto's *The Literary Dog* notes, among her volume's predecessors, Edward Jesse's *Anecdotes of Dogs* (1846), J. St. L. Strachey's *Dog Stories from the 'Spectator'* (1895), Jerome K. Jerome's *Dog Stories by Zola and Others* (1904), J. Walker McSpadden's *Famous Dogs in Fiction* (1921, 1930), and Jack Goodman's

Fireside Book of Dogs (1943). Schinto, *The Literary Dog: Great Contemporary Dog Stories* (New York: Atlantic Monthly Press, 1990), p. 3.

23 Poncelet buys: Alessandra Stanley, "Great-Grandpa Is Now a Great Dane," *The New York Times,* January 12, 1994. Thierry Poncelet, *Sit! The Dog Portraits of Thierry Poncelet,* text by Bruce McCall (New York: Workman Publishing, 1993).

This art form, popular during the seventeenth and eighteenth centuries, is also being revived for the upscale mass market. The Plummer-McCutcheon mail-order catalog of the Hammacher-Schlemmer Company offers hand-painted, oil-on-canvas paintings of a military terrier, bulldog captain, military bull mastiff, or Lhasa apso—all with dog heads superimposed on human bodies. Julie Hatfield, "Shop Talk," *The Boston Globe,* May 9, 1996, p. 98.

23 "Fay is very versatile": Christine Burgin of the Wegman Studio, note to the author, May 21, 1995.

24 Is it the heat": "The Summer City," editorial, *The New York Times,* August 19, 1995, p. A18.

24 A company called Frosty Paws: "Hot Lines," *The Boston Globe Magazine,* October 2, 1994, p. 39.

24 Chicago's Comiskey Park: "Fido Says: Walk Me Out to the Ball Game": *Newsweek,* April 1, 1996, p. 8.

24 "Dog owners like": Emily Prager, "Fashion Unleashed," *The New York Times,* February 20, 1994, section 9, pp. 1, 8.

24 At a high-powered fund-raiser: "Every Dog Has His Day," *The New York Times,* September 10, 1995, p. 59.

24 "Dogs make": Julie V. Iovine, "Animal House," *The New York Times Magazine,* January 16, 1994.

25 "some dog owners": Will Judy, *The Dog Encyclopedia* (Chicago: Judy Publishing, 1936), p. 94.

25 "the ultimate nonfashion statement": John Budris, "Putting on the Dog," *The Boston Globe Magazine,* July 23, 1995, p. 17.

26 In Britain: Giles Foden, "Dogged Devotion," *The Guardian,* May 11, 1996, pp. 4–5. Lucia van der Post, "A Dog and Cat Fight Over Your Pennies," *Financial Times* Weekend, March 16–17, 1996, p. IV.

26 designer Betsy Speert: Cheryl and Jeffrey Katz, "Pet Project." Photographs by Eric Roth. *The Boston Globe Magazine,* November 6, 1995, p. 50.

26 "antique dog": Manhattan Art & Antiques Center, advertisement, *The New York Times,* December 8, 1995, p. C29.

26 the author of *The Blue Dog Book:* George Rodrigue, at The Time Is Always Now Gallery. Advertisement in *The New York Times,* December 8, 1995, p. C26.

26 Pogo's Light Biscuits: All from Rick and Martha Reynolds, *Dog Bites! Canine Cuisine* (New York: Berkley Books, 1992).

26 Southern California restaurant: Adam Pertman, "I'll have what Fido's Having," *The Boston Globe*, April 27, 1966, pp. 1, 12.

27 *Barron's:* Jay Palmer, "Pampered Pets: Well, Aren't You the Cat's Meow?" *Barron's*, April 1, 1996, pp. 29–34.

27 "Crispy Beef": "Giving a dog unhealthy water, even tap water, that you don't drink yourself could be considered a form of animal abuse—your children would drink pond water, too, if you let them," says Marc Duke, the founder of the Original Pet Drink company, manufacturers of Thirsty Dog Crispy Beef flavored carbonated water. Though he admits that "some dogs don't like Thirsty Dog, just like some people don't like Coca-Cola," he urges that the owner simply withhold other liquid until the dog decides to drink. Stephen P. Williams, "Unnecessary Objects: Drinks for Pets," *The New York Times Magazine*, August 20, 1995, p. 14.

27 the "bare-bones" costs: Leslie Eaton, "Hey, Big Spenders," *The New York Times*, "September 11, 1994, "Business" section, pp. 1, 6.

27 Health insurance: Elizabeth Lesly, "It's Health Insurance, for Pet's Sake," *Business Week*, February 1, 1993, p. 78.

27 "Our surveys show": Jay Palmer, *Barron's*, April 1, 1996, pp. 29–34.

28 "People treat their dogs": Katy Kelly, "Exclusive Summer Camps Are All in a Dog's Life," *USA Today*, June 19, 1995, p. 5D.

28 "It can be": Brooke Comer, "In Dogged Pursuit," *New York Magazine*, January 10, 1994, p. 14. The establishment in question is No Standing Anytime Ltd.

28 "One of the advantages": Bob Morris, "Laying Bare the Dog Days of Their Walking Lives," *The New York Times*, August 6, 1995, p. 44.

29 According to the Animal Veterinary: "Pills for Pet Peeves," *The Boston Globe*, August 15, 1994, p. 10.

29 Dog phobias: Janny Scott, "High-Rise Cat Syndrome: Summer Heat Brings an Increase in Urban Pet Afflictions," *The New York Times*, July 10, 1994, pp. 21, 27.

29 A speaker on holistic healing: *AKC Gazette*, December 1995, p. 100.

29 as critic Leonard Maltin noted: Leonard Maltin, *1996 Movie and Video Guide* (New York: Signet, 1995), p. 335.

30 "Sometimes just rotating": Lisa T. Wessan, letter to *New York* magazine, May 22, 1995, p. 12.

30 "How ironic": Linda J. Korb, letter to *New York* magazine, May 22, 1995, p. 12.

31 "The dread practice": Natalie Angier, *The Beauty of the Beastly: New Views on the Nature of Life* (Boston, New York: Houghton Mifflin, 1995), p. 169.

31 "Anthropomorphism is": Angier, C7.

31 "For many biologists": Dr. Harry Greene, University of California, Berkeley. Quoted in Angier, p. C7.

31 "It is necessary": Richard Klein, "The Power of Pets," *The New Republic*, July 10, 1995, p. 23.

32 "critical anthropomorphists": The term was coined by Gordon Burghardt, who teaches animal behavior at the University of Tennessee. Viva Hardigg, "All in the Family?" *U.S. News & World Report*, November 1, 1993, pp. 69–70.

32 "keeps getting pushed": Dr. Frans de Waal, Yerkes Primate Center in Atlanta. Angier, p. C7.

32 "We have a habit": Richard Powers, "A Game We Couldn't Lose," *The New York Times*, February 15, 1995, p. 13.

32 "This is a book": Elizabeth Marshall Thomas, *The Hidden Life of Dogs* (Boston: Houghton Mifflin, 1993), pp. vi–viii.

33 "Having something to say": Vicki Hearne, *Adam's Task* (New York: Alfred A. Knopf, 1987), 10.

33 "The family of tropes": Vicki Hearne, *Animal Happiness* (New York: HarperCollins, 1994), pp. 193–94. In another context, however, she cautions that "enthusiasm for the trope of anthropomorphism should not be allowed to obscure the blessed limits to a dog's understanding." Vicki Hearne, *Bandit: Dossier of a Dangerous Dog* (New York: HarperPerennial, 1991), p. 58.

33 "talking in highly anthropomorphic": Hearne, *Adam's Task*, p. 6.

33 "Many people think": Hearne, *Animal Happiness*, p. 82.

33 "an illustration": ibid., p. 71.

33 "by himself": ibid., p. 201.

33 "with his whining jealousies": Robert Louis Stevenson, "The Character of Dogs" (1883) in Robert Louis Stevenson, *Essays*, William Lyon Phelps, ed. (New York: Charles Scribner's Sons, 1918), pp. 237, 240–41.

34 "Two novels in which": Linda Gray Sexton, "Wise Dogs," *The New York Times Book Review*, May 21, 1995, p. 29.

35 "It's like a Normal Rockwell": See William S. Gray and May Hill Arbuthnot, *Fun with Dick and Jane* and other Elson-Gray Basic Readers (Chicago: Scott Foresman and Company, ca. 1930). Sam Shepard "Buried Child," in *Seven Plays* (New York: Bantam, 1986), p. 83.

35 Misha "had married": Thomas, *Hidden Life of Dogs*, p. 6.

35 "would wait": ibid., p. 57.

35 "evidently wishes to imply": Harriet Ritvo, "A Dog's Life," *The New York Review of Books*, January 13, 1994, pp. 3–4.

35 "Popular prejudice": Thomas, *Hidden Life of Dogs*, p. 57.

36 "that has been the basis": Fredson Thayer Bowers, *The Dog Owner's Handbook* (Boston: Houghton Mifflin, 1936), p. 13.

36 "We discovered": Konrad Lorenz, *King Solomon's Ring: New Light on Animal Ways*, Marjorie Kerr Wilson, trans. (New York: Mentor, 1991 [originally published in 1952]), p. 139. The Alsatian, "a son

of" his bitch Tito, "married the chow bitch Pygi. This happened quite against the will of my wife [Pygi's owner] who, naturally enough, wanted to breed pure chows. But here we discovered, as an unexpected hindrance, a new property of Lupus dogs [like the chow, descended from the wolf]: the monogamous fidelity of the bitch to a certain dog." The "true love of Pygi for her enormous and good-natured Booby" frustrated her mistress's desire to breed her with another chow: "She only wanted her Booby and she got him in the end." Here is the marital fidelity of Thomas's Misha and Maria (both, as huskies, also Lupus dogs), in this case dryly painted against the backdrop of (human) marital strife: Lorenz's claim for the superiority of Aureus dogs, like the Alsatian (German shepherd), and his wife's claim on behalf of the chow.

In *Never Cry Wolf* (New York: Bantam, 1979, p. 62) Canadian Farley Mowat described his relationship to a wolf named George and his "beautiful," "passionate," and "devilish" "wife," Angeline. "I became deeply fond of Angeline," writes Mowat, "and still live in hopes that I can somewhere find a human female who embodies all her virtues."

37   "And then it happens": Thomas Mann, *A Man and His Dog*, Herman George Scheffauer, trans. (New York: Alfred A. Knopf, 1930), p. 69. Originally published as *Herr und Hund* (Berlin: S. Fischer Verlag, 1918). Reflecting on this phenomenon in nineteenth-century France, historian Kathleen Kete has analyzed "the exaggerated place of canine affect as an idea within bourgeois culture." Kete, *The Beast in the Boudoir: Petkeeping in Nineteenth-Century Paris.* (Berkeley: University of California Press, 1994), p. 38.

38   "There, full of vermin": Homer, *The Odyssey*, Book 17, 11. 290–326. E. V. Rieu, trans.; C. H. Rieu, rev. trans. (London: Penguin, 1991), 263–64. The story of Argus is frequently evoked in subsequent stories of canine fidelity, as for example in the Author's Note to William Armstrong's *Sounder*. Armstrong recalls a gray-haired black man in the community who was a great storyteller and who taught the author to read. "He had come to our community from farther south, already old when he came. He talked little, or not at all, about his past. But one night at the great center table after he had told the story of Argus, the faithful dog of Odysseus, he told the story of Sounder, a coon dog."

38   "Nostalgia, in a dog?": Jeffrey Moussaieff Masson and Susan Mc-Carthy, *When Elephants Weep: The Emotional Life of Animals* (New York: Delacorte Press, 1995), p. xvii.

39   "The dog has": Barbara Woodhouse, *No Bad Dogs* (New York: Fireside, 1982), p. 57.

39 "Of the *memory*": William Youatt, *The Dog*. Edited, with additions, by E. J. Lewis (Philadelphia: Lea and Blanchard, 1848), p. 166.

39 "the place where": Robert Frost, "The Death of the Hired Man" (1914). In *The Poetry of Robert Frost*, Edward Connery Lathem, ed. (New York: Holt, Rinehart and Winston, 1979), p. 38.

41 Pet Share is: Good Age Fund, P.O. Box 338, Somerville, MA 02144.

A Dog's Life

43 "Whether dogs": Reinhold Bergler, *Man and Dog: The Psychology of a Relationship* (Oxford, England: Blackwell Scientific Publications, 1988), p. 14.

43 "Yesterday I was": Clark Gesner, *You're A Good Man, Charlie Brown* (New York: Random House, 1967), p. 22.

44 "I have known dogs": Robert Louis Stevenson, "The Character of Dogs" (1883) in Robert Louis Stevenson, *Essays*, William Lyon Phelps, ed. (New York: Charles Scribner's Sons, 1918), pp. 239–40.

44 The phrase . . . originally meant: *The Compact Edition of the Oxford English Dictionary* (Oxford: Oxford University Press, 1971). "dog," p. 578.

44 a nonfiction book: Amy Shojai, *A Dog's Life: The History, Culture, and Everyday Life of the Dog* (New York: Friedman/Fairfax, 1994).

45 "just like little dogs!": Dylan Thomas, *Portrait of the Artist as a Young Dog* (New York: New Directions, 1940), p. 84.

45 "I wanted to play": Virginia Woolf, *The Letters of Virginia Woolf*, Nigel Nicolson and Joanne Trautmann, eds. (New York and London: Harcourt Brace Jovanovich, 1979), vol. 5, pp. 161–62.

45 "a dog of birth": Virginia Woolf, *Flush: A Biography* (Harmondsworth, England: Penguin, 1983); originally published 1933), p. 24.

46 "For the first time": ibid., p. 20.

46 "She would make him stand": ibid., p. 32.

47 "can't bear me": Elizabeth Barrett Browning to H. S. Boyd, June 22, 1842, in *The Letters of Elizabeth Barrett Browning*, Frederick G. Kenyon, ed. (New York: Macmillan, 1908), vol. 1, p. 107.

47 "Before he was well out": Woolf, *Flush*, pp. 13–14.

48 "What was horrible": ibid., pp. 38–39.

48 "Things are not simple": ibid., p. 47.

49 "They entered": Woolf, *Flush*, p. 81.

49 "Did they not": ibid., p. 82.

50 "My poor Flush": Elizabeth Barrett Browning to Mary Russell Mitford, 3? March 1843, in *The Letters of Elizabeth Barrett Browning to Mary Russell Mitford, 1836–1854*, Meredith B. Raymond and Mary

Rose Sullivan, eds. (Winfield, Kan.: Armstrong Browning Library of Baylor University, The Browning Institute, Wedgstone Press and Wellesley College, 1983), vol. 2, p. 183.

50   "no hero": Elizabeth Barrett, letter to Mary Russell Mitford, September 4, 1843, in ibid., p. 295.

50   "He had refused": Woolf, *Flush*, p. 33.

50   "A throbbing rhythm": Gesner, *You're a Good Man, Charlie Brown*, p. 45.

51   So declares: "P.S.D.A. Dickin Medal: The Animals' V.C.," pamphlet (London: The Imperial War Museum).

51   "We have let": Jilly Cooper, *Animals in War* (London: Imperial War Museum, 1983), p. 56.

51   "My husband": ibid., p. 54.

52   "how seriously": ibid., p. 58.

52   "No animal": ibid., p. 54.

52   "The handler": Sergeant-Major Aylward of the R.A.V.C., quoted in ibid., p. 71.

53   "Great trouble is taken": ibid., p. 71.

53   "told me in his own way": ibid.

54   "a headline advertising": "Calling All Lassies," Michael Blowen, "Names and Faces," *The Boston Globe*, July 1, 1991, p. 35.

55   "The dog had met": Eric Knight, "Lassie Come Home," in *Dog Tales: Classic Stories about Smart Dogs*, photographs by Myron Beck, introduction by Richard A. Wolters (New York: Viking Penguin, 1990), p. 25.

55   "Stay here, Lassie": Knight, "Lassie Come Home," p. 32.

56   "a thousand miles": ibid., p. 37.

56   "Not a dog": ibid., p. 38.

56   "Mother!": ibid., p. 41.

57   "It ain't that": ibid., p. 42.

57   "Now, ma lad": ibid., p. 43.

57   "Does it look like": ibid., p. 44.

57   "I never owned": ibid., p. 46.

58   "In a day or so": ibid., p. 48.

58   "aristocrat": "A black-white-and-gold aristocrat" (Knight, pp. 25–26); "Lassie's skull was aristocratic and slim" (p. 46).

58   "collier": ibid., p. 33.

60   "I class myself": quoted in Robert Windeler, *Shirley Temple* (London: W. H. Allen, 1976), p. 98.

60   "rabbit-hearted": Albert Payson Terhune, "Hero," in *The Way of a Dog* (New York: Grosset and Dunlap, 1925), p. 12.

61   The editors of *Dog Fancy*: Kim Campbell Thornton, Betsy Sikora Siino, and Ellyce J. Kaluf, "The Dog Fancy Hall of Fame," *Dog Fancy*, March 1996, p. 45.

63 "antihero": *Benét's Reader's Encyclopedia,* third edition, ed. Katherine Baker Siepmann (New York: HarperCollins, 1987), p. 39.

64 "The whole horror": Mikhail Bulgakov, *The Heart of a Dog,* Michael Glenny, trans. (London: Collins Harvill, 1989), pp. 110–111.

64 "the great": ibid., p. 128.

64 "A peripatetic rogue": ibid., p. 761.

65 "picaroon forays": Mann, *A Man and His Dog,* Herman George Scheffauer, trans. (New York: Alfred A. Knopf, 1930), p. 80.

65 "Intimations of Immortality": "It is not now as it hath been of yore": Wordsworth, "Intimations of Immortality from Recollections of Early Childhood."

65 "get Skip to prop himself": Willie Morris, *My Dog Skip* (New York: Random House, 1995), pp. 11–12.

65 "There was something": ibid., p. 13.

65 "I never knew a dog": ibid., p. 38.

67 "The only rudiment": *Benét's Reader's Encyclopedia,* p. 898.

67 "Kindness to animals": Harriet Ritvo, *The Animal Estate* (Cambridge, Mass.: Harvard University Press, 1987), pp. 129–32.

67 "the *Uncle Tom's Cabin*": George T. Angell, "Our Dumb Animals," *Boston,* February 12, 1890, in George T. Angell, *Autobiographical Sketches and Personal Recollections* (Boston: American Humane Society, 1908), p. 94.

68 "My name is Beautiful Joe": Marshall Saunders, *Beautiful Joe* (Bedford, Mass.: Applewood Books, 1994; originally published 1894), p. 13.

68 "The wonderfully successful": Hezekiah Butterworth, introduction to ibid., p. 7.

69 "I am an old dog": ibid., p. 14.

69 "Boys and girls": ibid., p. 304.

70 "most farmers": ibid., p. 168.

70 "doggedly": ibid., p. 27.

70 "doggerel": ibid., p. 259.

70 "sheepish": ibid., p. 28.

70 "pawing the floor": ibid., p. 119.

70 "The story speaks": Hezekiah Butterworth, introduction to ibid., pp. 7–8.

70 "when at last": Charles F. Schimmain, *Our Max: A Memoir of a Four-footed Friend,* by "his chief mourner" (Boston: Loring, 1875), p. 38.

71 "first the dog": From Zbigniew Herbert, "First the Dog," in *Selected Poems,* Czeslaw Milosz and Peter Dale Scott, trans. (New York: The Ecco Press, 1968), p. 101.

71 "even-temperedness": Brian Harvey, *Race into Space: The Soviet Space Programme* (Chichester, Eng.: Ellis Horwood Ltd., 1988), p. 33. Joseph M. Rougeau, "Space: Into the Future," in *Space: National*

Programs and International Cooperation, Wayne C. Thompson and Steven W. Guerrier, eds. (Boulder, Col.: Westview Press, 1989), p. 159.

71 the Russian physiologist: James W. Humphreys, Jr., "Humans in Space: Medical Challenges," in Wayne C. Thompson and Steven Guerrier, eds., *Space: National Programs and International Cooperation* (Boulder, Col.: Westview Press, 1989), pp. 133–34.

72 "It was evidently": Ivan Pavlov, *Conditioned Reflexes: An Investigation of the Physiological Activity of the Cerebral Cortex,* G. V. Anrep, trans. (New York: Dover Publications, 1960), p. 11.

73 "one of the most important": ibid., p. 12.

73 "In all the cases": ibid., p. 410.

75 "Since there is": George Pitcher, *The Dogs Who Came to Stay* (New York: Dutton, 1995), pp. 48–49.

76 "Why . . . are owners": Barbara Woodhouse, *No Bad Dogs* (New York: Fireside, 1982), p. 65.

76 "With female dogs": ibid., pp. 66–68.

77 one puppy-training guide: Jill and D. Manus Pinkwater, *Superpuppy* (New York: Clarion Books, 1977), p. 26.

77 "Blemie," Carlotta once remembered: Louis Sheaffer, *O'Neill: Son and Artist* (New York: AMS Press, 1988), p. 518.

77 "The dog won't": Lawrence Kutner, "Parent & Child" column, "How Much Is That Relationship in the Window?" *The New York Times,* December 9, 1993, p. C11.

77 "Pavlov was not": Elisabeth Roudinesco, *Jacques Lacan & Co.: A History of Psychoanalysis in France, 1925–1985,* Jeffrey Mehlman, trans. (Chicago: University of Chicago Press, 1990), p. 36.

78 "Several fundamental questions arise": W. Horsley Gantt, introduction to Ivan Petrovitch Pavlov, *Lectures on Conditioned Reflexes.* Vol. 2: *Conditioned Reflexes and Psychiatry,* William Horsley Gantt, trans. and ed. (New York: International Publishers, 1941), p. 15.

78 According to Pavlov: ibid., pp. 180–81.

78 "Pavlov is the greatest fool": Personal conversations between Shaw and W. H. Gantt at Lady Astor's, July 1935. Ibid., p. 22.

78 "One can conceive": ibid., p. 84.

79 "chronic pathological inertness": ibid., p. 156.

"Talking Dogs"

82 "R is the dog's letter": Ben Jonson, *The Eighth Grammar* (1640), ed. Alice Vinton White (New York: Sturgis and Walton, 1909), pp. 50–51.

82 "I love you": A. R. Gurney, *Sylvia* (New York: Dramatists Play Service, 1996), p. 8.

82   "I think you're prejudiced": ibid., p. 14.

83   "as a present": William Shakespeare, *Two Gentlemen of Verona,* Act IV, scene iv, 1.6.

83   "Read the *Odyssey*": ibid., p. 68.

83   "I'll have to depend": ibid., p. 96.

83   "critic-proof": Vincent Canby, "Gurney's Notion of a Very Different Ménage à Trois," *The New York Times,* May 24, 1995, p. C15.

84   "Hey! Hey! Hey!": ibid., p. 18.

84   "Did I hear": ibid., p. 19.

84   "You seem to suggest": ibid., p. 58.

84   "A man and his dog": ibid., p. p. 22.

84   Sarah Jessica Parker's model: Jean Nathan, "A Shaggy Dog Story with a Cast That's Altogether Human," *The New York Times,* May 21, 1995, section 2, p. 5.

85   he hadn't brought his dog: Peter Filichia, "Stagestruck," *Theater-Week,* June 5–11, 1995, p. 12.

85   "That dog has taught": Peter Marks, "On Stage and Off," *The New York Times,* September 29, 1995, p. C2.

85   "The charming relations": Helen Keller, *A Tribute to a Dog.* Cited in Barbara Cohen and Louise Taylor, *Dogs and Their Women* (Boston: Little, Brown and Company, 1989), p. 52.

86   "Man himself": Charles Darwin, *The Expression of the Emotions in Man and Animals,* ed. Francis Darwin, Vol. 23 of *The Works of Charles Darwin,* ed. Paul H. Barrett and R. B. Freeman (New York: New York University Press, vol. 23, p. 8.

86   "Sir W. Scott's": ibid., pp. 89–91.

86   "I have been guilty": Jack London, "The Other Animals," in *Revolution and Other Essays* (New York: Macmillan, 1912), p. 238.

86   "Not that Buck": Jack London, *The Call of the Wild,* in *The Call of the Wild and White Fang* (New York: Bantam, 1963; originally published 1903), p. 37.

87   "I was unconscious": Joan London, *Jack London and His Times* (New York: Doubleday, 1939), p. 252.

87   understanding: London, *Call of the Wild,* p. 75.

87   "imagination": ibid., p. 51.

87   "surprise": ibid., p. 74.

87   "Buck felt vaguely": ibid., p. 66.

87   "sprang to his feet": ibid., p. 75.

87   "Often, such": ibid., p. 75.

87   "White Fang knew": Jack London, *White Fang,* in *The Call of the Wild and White Fang* (New York: Bantam, 1963; originally published 1903), pp. 284–85.

88   "began to 'talk'": Albert Payson Terhune, *Lad: A Dog* (New York: Puffin Books, 1993; originally published 1919), p. 268.

88 "to tell the Mistress": ibid., p. 282.

88 "the *human* side": ibid., p. 93.

88 *"Lassie* was my favorite": Andy Andrews, quoted in Ace Collins, *Lassie: A Dog's Life* (New York: Penguin Books, 1993), p. 188.

89 "O.K., Rinty": Benjamin Cheever, "Man's Best Friend and (Perhaps) Successor," *The New York Times,* January 4, 1994, section 2, p. 11.

89 a *New Yorker* cartoon: *The New Yorker Book of Dog Cartoons* (New York: Alfred A. Knopf, 1992), p. 4.

89 In ancient Greek mythology: Carl Kerenyi, *Asklepios: Archetypal Image of the Physician's Existence* (Princeton, N.J.: Princeton University Press, 1959), pp. 14–18. Barbara Hannah, Lectures 3–5 from C. G. Jung Institute (Küsnacht, Switzerland, 1953–54), p. 3. The suckling saga is reported by Freda Kretschmer.

90 Fools and court jesters: Eleanora M. Woloy, *The Symbol of the Dog in the Human Psyche* (Wilmette, Ill.: Chiron Publications, 1990), pp. 26–35.

90 "Again and again": C. G. Jung, *The Archetypes and the Collective Unconscious,* R. F. C. Hull, trans. (Princeton, N.J.: Princeton University Press, 1959), p. 231.

90 "The dog . . . appears": Woloy, *The Symbol of the Dog,* p. 29.

91 "of all the animals": Marie-Louise von Franz, cited in ibid., p. 23.

91 Assistance dogs: Peter J. Howe, "Furry Friends to the Disabled," *The Boston Globe,* April 3, 1996, p. 3.

92 A young girl: Cohen and Taylor, *Dogs and Their Women,* p. 24.

92 A ten-year-old boy: "Young Boy Saved from Death by Stray Dogs," Associated Press News Briefs, *The Harvard Crimson,* March 12, 1996, p. 4.

92 "there was criminal activity": "Mo. Prosecutor Discounts Story of Lost Boy, Dogs" (Reuters) *The Boston Globe,* May 2, 1996, p. 15.

92 "He is the only dog": John Steinbeck, *Travels with Charley: In Search of America* (Harmondsworth, England: Penguin Books, 1982; originally published 1962), p. 24.

93 "I tossed about": ibid., p. 267.

93 "Thought you had": ibid., pp. 249, 250, 267.

93 "Suppose your dog": ibid., p. 261.

93 "It is not done well": "Sir, a woman preaching is like a dog's walking on his hinder legs. It is not done well; but you are surprised to find it done at all." James Boswell, *Life of Johnson,* July 31, 1763.

93 doesn't even know": Steinbeck, *Travels with Charley,* p. 267.

94 "What's the matter": ibid., p. 220.

95 "A child has": Marshall Saunders, *Beautiful Joe* (Bedford, Mass.: Applewood Books, 1994; originally published 1894), pp. 27–28.

95 "I had never heard": ibid., p. 63.

95   "actively discouraged": Donald R. Griffin, *Animal Thinking* (Cambridge, Mass.: Harvard University Press, 1984), preface.

95   "Stand in front of your dog": John Ross and Barbara McKinney, *Dog Talk: Training Your Dog Through a Canine Point of View* (New York: St. Martin's Press, 1992), p. 253.

96   One of my favorite dog cartoons: Gary Larson, *The Far Side Gallery* (Kansas City, Kan.: Andrews, McMeel & Parker, 1984), unpaged.

97   "I am happy": Thomas Mann, *A Man and His Dog,* Herman/George Scheffauer, trans. (New York: Alfred A. Knopf, 1930), pp. 95–96.

97   "Probably you only hear": W. H. Auden, "Talking to Dogs," in *Complete Poems,* ed. Edward Mendelson (New York: Vintage, 1991), pp. 867–68.

97   Ross notes: Ross and McKinney, *Dog Talk,* p. 192.

97   overestimation of the object: see Sigmund Freud, "On Narcissism: An Introduction" (1914): *The Standard Edition of the Complete Psychological Works of Sigmund Freud,* ed. and trans. James Strachey (London: The Hogarth Press and the Institute for Psycho-Analysis, 1957), Vol. 14, p. 88.

97   "mutually satisfying": Nicholas Wade, "Method and Madness," *The New York Times Magazine,* July 3, 1994, p. 10.

97   "Do you chat": Patricia Gail Burnham, *Playtraining Your Dog* (New York: St. Martin's Press, 1980), p. 11.

98   "By now, I know": Warren Eckstein with Andrea Eckstein, *How To Get Your Dog to Do What You Want: A Loving Approach to Unleashing Your Dog's Astonishing Potential* (New York: Fawcett Columbine, 1994), pp. 14–15.

99   "as a family faculty": Elizabeth Barrett Browning to Mary Russell Mitford, 3? March 1843, in *The Letters of Elizabeth Barrett Browning to Mary Russell Mitford, 1836–1854,* Meredith B. Raymond and Mary Rose Sullivan, eds. (Winfield, Kan.: Armstrong Browning Library of Baylor University, the Browning Institute, Wedgstone Press and Wellesley College, 1983), vol. 2, p. 86.

99   "lying with his head": Elizabeth Barrett Browning to H. S. Boyd, March 2, 1842, in *The Letters of Elizabeth Barrett Browning,* Frederic G. Kenyon, ed. (New York: Macmillan, 1908), vol. 1, p. 100.

99   "Even her conversation": Norman MacCaig, "Praise of a Collie," in *The Rattle Bag,* Seamus Heaney and Ted Hughes, eds. (London and Boston: Faber and Faber, 1982), p. 351.

100   "Let's take": Carol Lea Benjamin, *Surviving Your Dog's Adolescence* (New York: Howell Book House, 1993), pp. 24–25.

100   "I've often had the feeling": Susan Conant, *A New Leash on Death* (New York: Berkley, 1994), 1.

100   "If malamutes": Susan Conant, *Dead and Doggone* (New York: Berkley, 1994), p. 49.

101	"The animals act naturally": René Descartes, *Treatise on Man*, cited in Stanley Coren, *The Intelligence of Dogs* (New York: The Free Press, 1994), p. 62. Descartes held that everything in animal behavior could be reproduced mechanically. Thus he was, for example, the predecessor of Ivan Pavlov, as of B. F. Skinner and other twentieth-century behaviorists. On the question of animal thoughts and souls, Descartes wrote to the Marchioness of Newcastle: "If they thought as we do, they would have an immortal soul like us. This is unlikely because there is no reason to believe it of some animals without believing it of all." As Coren points out, Descartes's dismissal of the idea that oysters and sponges might think, and therefore that a dog, which is also an animal, had thoughts, could as easily be extended to human beings: "Wouldn't a reasonable extension of this argument be, if a dog can't think, then neither can a human, for they, too, are both animals?"

101	"Machines which love": Ruthven Tremain, *The Animals' Who's Who* (New York: Charles Scribner's Sons, 1982), p. 173.

101	the Cartesian view prevailed: See, for example, Coren, *The Intelligence of Dogs*, p. 45. "When I first did my training in psychology, the belief was quite strong that dogs (and all other nonhuman animals) did not have consciousness. We were assured, for instance, that a beagle is not a conscious, thinking creature with self-awareness and emotional feelings but rather a beagle-shaped bag of reflexes, automatic responses, and genetic programming. We were encouraged to view dogs as simply biological machines."

102	"an extraordinary": Aljean Harmetz, "Jim Carrey's Lively Sidekick," *The New York Times*, August 7, 1994, Section 2, Arts and Leisure, p. 9.

103	It's striking: The original Disney feature film of *The Incredible Journey* was made in 1963—without the animal voice-overs.

103	"an indistinguishable tangle": Sheila Burnford, *The Incredible Journey* (New York: Bantam, 1987; originally published 1961), p. 147.

103	"The young dog": ibid., p. 101.

103	"A gaunt": ibid., p. 145.

104	"My father was a St. Bernard": Mark Twain, "A Dog's Tale" (1909) in *The Complete Short Stories of Mark Twain*, Charles Neider (Garden City, N.Y.: Hanover House, 1957), p. 489.

104	"I don't suppose": O. Henry, "Memoirs of a Yellow Dog," In *The Four Million* (New York: Doubleday, Page & Co., 1906), p. 110.

104	"I looked up": ibid., pp. 113–14.

105	"Ooow-ow-ooow-owow!": Mikhail Bulgakov, *The Heart of a Dog* (1925), Michael Glenny, trans. (London: Collins Harvill, 1989), p. 5.

105	"It takes a lot": ibid., p. 6.

105	"taxi": ibid., p. 62.

105   "talking dog": ibid., p. 82.

105   "That doesn't mean": ibid., p. 126.

105   "warm, comfortable": ibid., p. 128.

105   "woof-woof . . . Hathaway": Leon Rooke, *Shakespeare's Dog* (New York: Alfred A. Knopf, 1983), pp. 3–7.

105   "I remember once": ibid., p. 137.

106   "To err is human": Peter Mayle, *A Dog's Life* (New York: Alfred A. Knopf, 1995), p. 192.

106   "Don't you wish": ibid., pp. 82–84.

106   "Children who have dogs": Stephanie Loer, "Good Dog, Martha!" *The Boston Globe*, November 8, 1994, pp. 57, 64.

106   *The Quotable Dog:* Greg Snider (Chicago: Contemporary Books, 1994).

107   "An attempt": Amy Hempel and Jim Shepard, *Unleashed: Poems by Writers' Dogs* (New York: Crown, 1995), p. 14.

107   "At times": Karen Shepard, poem by Birch, "Glom: Labrador, 110 Pounds," in ibid., p. 79.

107   "*Huh*-huh": William Tester, poem by Skipper, "Complacencies of the Fenced Yard," in ibid., p. 24.

107   "He loves paw-long": Heather McHugh, "My Sheperd," in ibid., p. 143.

107   "You paused": R. S. Jones, poem by Scout, "Shelter," in Hempel and Shepard, *Unleashed*, p. 102.

107   "God I love": Lynda Barry, poem by her dog Bob Barker, "I love my master I love my master," in ibid., p. 94.

107   "Yoko": Thom Gunn, "Yoko," in *Collected Poems* (London, Boston: Faber and Faber, 1993), p. 299.

108   "Do you want": *The New Yorker Book of Dog Cartoons* (New York: Alfred A. Knopf, 1992), p. 20.

108   "Speaking personally": James Stevenson cartoon, in ibid., p. 99.

108   "It's always 'Sit'": ibid., p. 88.

108   "Woof woof woof": Jack Ziegler, in ibid., p. 55.

108   "From now on": Lee Lorenz, in ibid., p. 89.

108   "Once again": Michael Maslin, in ibid., p. 56.

109   "The quick brown *dog*": Robert Mankoff, in ibid., p. 95.

109   "'Beagle Press'": Charles M. Schulz, *The Snoopy Festival* (New York: Holt, Rinehart, and Winston, 1974), unpaged.

109   "My name is": "As dictated to Barbara Bush," *Millie's Book* (New York: William Morrow, 1990), p. 10.

109   "the Kerr part": ibid., p. 71.

109   "He Can Sit": Advertisement for Purina ONE Dog Formula (*Time*, January 15, 1996, p. 5).

110   "Flush was at a loss": *Flush: A Biography*, by Virginia Woolf (Harmondsworth: Penguin, 1983; originally published 1933), pp. 27–28.

110   Here the "dumb animals": It's perhaps of some minor interest to note
      that Lassie, too, was once a baked-bean salesdog. Sales zoomed up-
      ward when a picture of Lassie and Timmy appeared on the can of
      Campbell's Pork & Beans in the fifties. Ace Collins, *Lassie: A Dog's
      Life* (New York: Penguin, 1993), p. 114.

111   "From now on": Ross and McKinney, *Dog Talk*, p. 60.

111   "Randolph Gets Ruff": Patricia Nealon, "Randolph Gets Ruff," *The
      Boston Globe,* June 29, 1995, pp. 1, 10.

111   "Unpoopularity": Stuart M. Wise, "Unpoopularity," *The National
      Law Journal,* September 26, 1983, vol. 6, p. 43.

111   "No 'Flea Bargaining'": Martha Middleton, "No 'Flea Bargaining,'"
      The National Law Journal, October 14, 1985, vol. 8, p. 43.

111   "posing for *Vanity Fur*": *Millie's Book,* p. 22.

111   "Let's make no bones": Chris McConnell, "Reigning Cats and Dogs,"
      The Chicago Tribune, December 21, 1989, "Tempo" section, p. 1.

111   "To pun in succession": Richard Klein, "The Power of Pets," *The
      New Republic,* July 10, 1995, pp. 18–19.

112   "I don't believe": Saunders, *Beautiful Joe,* p. 166.

112   "Shunning": Emily Dickinson to Thomas Wentworth Higginson, Au-
      gust 1862. Letter 271 in Thomas H. Johnson, ed., *Emily Dickinson:
      Selected Letters* (Cambridge, Mass.: Harvard University Press, 1971),
      p. 178.

112   "a Dog—large": Emily Dickinson to Thomas Wentworth Higginson,
      25 April 1862. Letter 261 in ibid., pp. 172–73. Carlo's name seems
      to have come from the best-selling *Reveries of a Bachelor* by Ik Mar-
      vel (Donald G. Mitchell) (New York: Scribner's, 1850), a book Dick-
      inson admired. In *Reveries* Carlo—whose breed is not
      specified—belongs to the "bachelor" of the title, and sits by his side
      as he dreams. John Polidori, the author of *The Vampyre* (1819), also
      wrote a short story, "A Story of Miss Anne and Miss Emma with the
      Dog—Carlo," in which Carlo, a black-and-white Newfoundland,
      performs the breed's legendary feat of lifesaving to rescue a little girl
      who has been kind to him. See D. L. Macdonald and Kathleen
      Scherf, eds. *The Vampyre and Ernestus Berchtold; or, the Modern
      Oedipus: Collected Fiction of John William Polidori* (Toronto: Uni-
      versity of Toronto Press, 1994), Appendix C, pp. 187–90. Carlo is
      also the name of the slave George Harris's dog in Harriet Beecher
      Stowe's 1852 *Uncle Tom's Cabin.* George's master pelts Carlo with
      stones and drowns him, administering a flogging to George because
      he refuses to kill the dog himself. Stowe, *Uncle Tom's Cabin* (New
      York: Harper and Row, 1965), p. 19.

113   "my mute confederate": Emily Dickinson to Thomas Wentworth Hig-
      ginson, 9 June 1866. Letter 319 in Johnson, ed., *Emily Dickinson:
      Selected Letters,* p. 194.

113 "I think Carl[o]": Emily Dickinson to Thomas Wentworth Higginson, 25 April 1862, Letter 261 in ibid., pp. 172–73.

113 "He knew": Maurice Maeterlinck, *Our Friend the Dog*, Alexander Teixeira de Mattos, trans. (New York: Dodd, Mead, 1913), pp. 65–66.

113 "The little white dog": James Merrill, "The Victor Dog," in *Braving the Elements* (New York: Atheneum, 1972), pp. 70–71, lines 2–3.

113 Nipperie: Ruth Edge and Leonard Petts, *A Guide to Collecting His Master's Voice "Nipper" Souvenirs* (Harrow: The Kingswood Press, 1984).

114 "When I reflect": Franz Kafka, "Investigations of a Dog." *Selected Stories of Franz Kafka*, Willa and Edwin Muir, trans. (New York: Modern Library, 1952), p. 203.

114 "I began to enquire": ibid., p. 214.

114 "Anyone who has": ibid., p. 216.

114 "the mother weans": ibid., p. 215.

115 "All knowledge": ibid., p. 218.

115 "How long": ibid., p. 221.

115 "Was I really": ibid., p. 223.

115 "As Robert Browning": Woolf, *Flush*, p. 87.

116 "Perhaps they've made": Mary Morris, "Missing: A Dog's Doggerel," in Hempel and Shepard, *Unleashed*, p. 83.

116 Was Francis Bacon: "For take an Example of a Dog; And mark what a Generosity, and Courage, he will put on, when he finds himselfe maintained, by a Man; who to him is in stead of a *God*." Francis Bacon, "Of Atheisme," in *The Essayes or Counsels, Civill and Morall*, Michael Kiernan, ed. (Cambridge, Mass.: Harvard University Press, 1985), p. 53.

116 "Being quicker": W. H. Auden, "Talking to Dogs," in *Complete Poems* (New York: Vintage, 1970), p. 70–71.

117 "The fact was": Virginia Woolf, *Flush* (originally published 1933; London: Penguin, 1983), pp. 27–28.

Unconditional Lovers

119 "Millie, the young Springer": Larry Shook, *The Puppy Report: How to Select a Healthy, Happy Dog* (New York: Ballantine, 1992), p. 118.

119 "The eyes of a dog": Barbara Woodhouse, *No Bad Dogs* (New York: Fireside, 1992), p. 94.

120 "Love, genuine passionate love": Jack London, *The Call of the Wild* (New York: Bantam Books, 1963; originally published 1905), p. 74.

120 "had a way": ibid., p. 75.

120 "'As you love me'": ibid., p. 84.

120 "drew back": ibid., p. 86.

120　"But White Fang": Jack London, *White Fang*, p. 254.

121　"evolution": ibid., p. 253.

121　"I have a snapshot": George Pitcher, *The Dogs Who Came to Stay* (New York: Dutton, 1995), p. 7.

121　"The love that tied her": Milan Kundera, *The Unbearable Lightness of Being*, Michael Henry Heim, trans. (New York: HarperPerennial, 1991), pp. 297–98.

123　"Caesar once": W. R. Halliday, "Animal Pets in Ancient Greece," *Discovery* 3 (1922), pp. 151–54.

123　"This view of pet-keeping": James Serpell, *In the Company of Animals: A Study of Human-Animal Relationships* (Oxford, England: Basil Blackwell, 1986), p. 20.

123　"'gratuitous perversion'": Mary Midgley, *Animals and Why They Matter* (London: Penguin Books, 1983), p. 116.

123　"we are taught": Aaron H. Katcher, "Interactions Between People and Their Pets: Form and Function," in *Interactions Between People and Pets*, Bruce Fogle, ed. (Springfield, Ill.: Charles Thomas, 1981), p. 46.

123　"The human being": Konrad Lorenz, *Man Meets Dog*, Marjorie Kerr Wilson, trans. (Boston: Houghton Mifflin, 1955), p. 74.

123　"Anyone who": Midas Dekkers, *Dearest Pet: On Bestiality*, Paul Vincent, trans. (London and New York: Verso, 1992), p. 172.

123　"warm humanity": *The New Yorker*, review of Konrad Lorenz, *On Aggression*, quoted on the back cover of Konrad Lorenz, *On Life and Living*, Richard D. Bosley, trans. (New York: St. Martin's Press, 1990).

123　"deep sympathy": *The New York Times Book Review*, review of Konrad Lorenz, *On Aggression*, quoted on the back cover of ibid.

124　"like the Pekinese": Lorenz, "On the Humanization of Animals," in *On Life and Living*, p. 49.

124　"no longer an image": Alan Riding, "And God Created the Animal Lover," *The New York Times*, March 30, 1994, pp. C1, C8.

124　"No contest!": Jim Sullivan, "Names & Faces," *The Boston Globe*, February 26, 1994, p. 28.

124　"Of course it is harmless": Lorenz, *Man Meets Dog*, p. 74.

125　"The feelings that Ed": Pitcher, *The Dogs Who Came to Stay*, p. 66.

126　"all my defenses": ibid., pp. 21, 24, 25.

126　"A man and his dog": A. R. Gurney, *Sylvia*, p. 23.

126　"the combination": Barbara Cohen and Louise Taylor, *Women and Their Dogs* (Boston: Little, Brown, 1989), p. ix.

127　"fish without a bicycle": The phrase is a celebrated feminist slogan from the 1970s: "A woman without a man is like a fish without a bicycle."

127　"desperately unhappy": Paul Bennett, in Barbara Cohen and Louise Taylor, *Dogs and Their Women* (Boston: Little, Brown and Co., 1989), p. 8.

128   "replaced a six-foot Swedish husband": Jo Giese, in ibid., p. 100.

128   "maid of honor": Christie Fajkowski, in ibid., p. 18.

128   "People tell us": Jeri Wagner, in ibid., p. 26.

128   "I was going to have him fixed": Jane Kelley, in ibid., p. 78.

128   "the old dog, my love": John Cheever, *The Journals of John Cheever* (New York: Alfred A. Knopf, 1991), p. 193–94.

129   "altering the pronoun": Susan Cheever, *Home Before Dark* (New York: Bantam Books, 1991), p. 147.

129   Millie . . . seemed to think: "As dictated to Barbara Bush," *Millie's Book* (New York: William Morrow, 1990), p. 39.

129   "Pal and his male": Homer Dickens, *What a Drag: Men and Women and Women as Men in the Movies*. (New York: Quill, 1984).

130   "quite a trick": Ace Collins, *Lassie: A Dog's Life* (New York: Penguin, 1993), p. 94.

130   In another piece: ibid., p. 101.

130   "I discovered": *Millie's Book*, p. 19.

130   "Human beings fall": Dekkers, *Dearest Pet*, p. 31.

131   "Among the various dolls": D. W. Winnicott, *The Family and Individual Development* (London: Tavistock, 1965), p. 143.

131   "The best that can happen": ibid., p. 144.

131   Into this transitional arena: Psychologist Boris Levinson suggested some years ago that the dog could act as a transitional object, allowing children to respond to and accept issues like sexual feelings, sibling rivalry, aggression, and bowel habits. Levinson's initial suggestion that pets be allowed to be present during therapeutic sessions was greeted with skepticism, but by 1984 the American Psychiatric Association was sponsoring entire sections of its annual meeting on the topic of interactions between humans and their pets. See Boris Levinson, *Pet-Oriented Psychotherapy* (Springfield, Ill.: Charles C. Thomas, 1969), pp. 41–42, and Eleanora M. Woloy, *The Symbol of the Dog in the Human Psyche* (Wilmette, Ill.: Chiron Publications, 1990), pp. 16–17.

131   "These are the knickknacks": Roger A. Caras, *A Dog Is Listening* (New York: Summit Books, 1992), pp. 215–16.

132   "The toys": ibid., p. 218.

132   "I don't believe": J. R. Ackerley, *My Father and Myself*, p. 217.

133   "the One": Diary, 30 June 1950. Cited in Peter Parker, *Ackerley* (New York: Farrar, Straus and Giroux, 1989), p. 262.

133   More than one: Forster, quoted in ibid., p. 263.

133   One of my friends: Ackerley, *My Father and Myself* (London: Bodley Head, 1968), p. 218.

133   seeking a "husband": J. R. Ackerley, *My Dog Tulip* (New York: Poseidon, 1987), p. 57.

133   "never been married": ibid., p. 60.

134 "mightn't settle down": ibid., p. 69.

134 "frightfully keen": ibid., p. 96.

134 a physiological problem: Ackerley documents his own sexual problems, in this case with premature ejaculation, in the appendix to *My Father and Myself.*

134 "When she had me back": Ackerley, *Tulip,* p. 67.

134 "I felt, indeed": ibid., p. 88.

134 "Tulip's a good girl": ibid., p. 21.

134 "She seems to have been jealous": Ackerley diary, 9 January 1949. Cited in Parker, *Ackerley,* p. 292.

134 "the only 'dog book'": Lehmann, jacket blurb for *Tulip,* 2nd ed., cited in ibid., p. 264.

135 "the events I have related": Ackerley, *Tulip,* pp. 54–55.

135 "people love animals": Forster, 1934. *Time and Tide,* June 23, 1934.

135 "A lot of rubbish": Barbara Woodhouse, *No Bad Dogs,* p. 9.

136 "Lampl got his Jeanne": cited in Elisabeth Young-Breuhl, *Anna Freud,* p. 99.

136 "to confirm our judgment": Anna Freud, letter to Sigmund Freud, July 7, 1921, quoted in Elisabeth Young-Bruehl, *Anna Freud* (New York: Summit, 1988), p. 96.

136 "Wolf . . . has almost": Michael Molnar, *The Diary of Sigmund Freud, 1929–1939: A Record of the Final Decade* (London: The Hogarth Press, 1992), p. 214 (Thursday, 14 January 1937).

136 "For the doctor": Sigmund Freud, "Observations on Transference-Love" (1914). *The Standard Edition of the Complete Psychological Works of Sigmund Freud,* ed. and trans. James Strachey (London: The Hogarth Press and the Institute of Psychoanalysis, 1958), Vol. 12, p. 169.

137 "A number of independent": Ernest Jones, *The Life and Work of Sigmund Freud,* edited and abridged by Lionel Trilling and Steven Marcus (New York: Basic Books, 1961), p. 487.

137 "What Freud prized": Quoted in Molnar, *The Diary of Sigmund Freud,* p. 260.

137 This scenario is captured: ibid., p. 98. In 1930 the favored poem was from Jofi ("the nicest thing is a poem in Jofi's name, from Anna of course, in the company of a live little tortoise," he wrote), and a year later, on Freud's seventy-fifth birthday, the poem declared itself to be from "the union of quadrupeds—Wolf-Jofie-Tattoun." Tattoun was Jofi's "son." The tradition of the birthday poem presented by the dogs dates from 1926, when Wolf offered a greeting in rhyme, and continued through Freud's eightieth birthday, when the latest Yofi (the one to whom H.D. became attached) wandered "into my bedroom to show her affection in her own fashion, something she has never done before or after. How does a little animal know when a birthday comes

around?" Freud wondered to H.D. In H.D., *Tribute to Freud* (New York: New Directions, 1956), Appendix, p. 193.

137 "The dog would sit": Peter Gay, *Freud: A Life for Our Time* (New York: Norton, 1988), p. 540. Other analysts have also kept dogs in their consulting rooms while seeing patients, among them C. F. Baynes, Marie-Louise von Franz, Louis Kahn, and Eleanora M. Woloy. See Woloy, *The Symbol of the Dog,* p. 1.

137 "Yo-Fie . . . patiently": Anna Freud, "Foreword to *Topsy* by Marie Bonaparte," in *The Writings of Anna Freud,* vol. 8 (New York: International Universities Press, 1981), p. 360.

138 Martin suggested: Jennifer Stone, "A 'Psychoanalytic Bestiary: The Wolff Woman, the Leopard, and the Siren," *American Imago,* vol. 49, no. 1 (1992), p. 141.

138 "I was annoyed": H.D. *Tribute to Freud,* p. 162.

138 "the Professor" remarks: ibid., p. 166.

138 He had . . . promised: Barbara Guest, *Herself Defined: The Poet H.D. and Her World* (Garden City, N.Y.: Doubleday, 1944), p. 213.

138 "(1) According to": Sigmund Freud, "On Narcissism: An Introduction" (1914) *The Standard Edition,* Vol. 14, p. 90.

Sex and the Single Dog

141 "I am not a dog lover": see James Thurber, *Thurber's Dogs* (New York: Simon and Schuster, 1955), p. 208.

141 "What happened": A. R. Gurney, *Sylvia* (New York: Dramatists Play Service, Inc., 1996), p. 52. The speaker (needless to say?) is Sylvia, the dog.

142 "It would be incomprehensible": Sigmund Freud, *Civilization and Its Discontents* (1930), in *The Standard Edition of the Complete Psychological Works of Sigmund Freud,* James Strachey, ed. and trans. (London: The Hogarth Press and the Institute of Psycho-Analysis, 1961), vol. 21, p. 100n.

142 "One of the many": *Random House Historical Dictionary of American Slang,* J. E. Lighter, ed. (New York: Random House, 1994), vol. 1, A–G.

142 In the seventeenth century: Gordon Williams, *A Dictionary of Sexual Language and Imagery in Shakespearean and Stuart Literature* (London: Athlone Press, 1994), p. 400.

142 *How to Make:* Karen Salmansohn (New York: Workman Publishing Company, 1994).

142 Ancient literature: Aelian, VII. 19. Williams, *Dictionary of Sexual Language,* p. 401.

143 "A Damsel of *Tuscany*": Reported in Nicolas Venette, *Conjugal Love, or The Pleasures of the Marriage Bed* (1703) (New York: Garland Publishing, 1984), p. 159; Williams, *Dictionary of Sexual Language,* p. 402.

143 "abominable Mastive": *Last Words of Pride* (1658); cited in Williams, *Dictionary of Sexual Language,* p. 402.

143 still being retailed: John Dryden, 2 *Absalom and Achitophel,* 1. 437.

143 "just to kiss": *Bawd,* ca. 1782, p. 18. Cited in Williams, *Dictionary of Sexual Language,* p. 402.

143 "Panegyrick": *The Secret History of Clubs* (1709), p. 250.

143 Gould's 1682 satire: References cited in Williams, *Dictionary of Sexual Language,* pp. 402–403.

144 Police reports confirmed: Alain Corbin, *Women for Hire: Prostitution and Sexuality in France After 1850,* Alan Sheridan, trans. (Cambridge, Mass.: Harvard University Press, 1990), p. 124. Louis Fiaux, *Les Maisons de Tolérance: Leur Fermeture* (Paris: G. Carré, 1892), pp. 182–83, 393.

144 "The dog's penis": Laura Reese, *Topping from Below* (New York: St. Martin's Press, 1995), p. 364.

144 Golden Retriever: "Golden Retriever Faithfully Helps Students Do Senior Project Research." Advertisement for Apple Computer, *The Chronicle of Higher Education,* June 30, 1995, p. A18.

144 "It's lonely": "Man's Best Accessory," *People,* July 31, 1995, p. 86.

145 "We are not made": Midas Dekkers, *Dearest Pet: On Bestiality,* Paul Vincent, trans. (London, New York: Verso, 1994), p. 68.

145 "the greatest danger": ibid., p. 69.

145 "a very big mastiff": Marquis de Sade, *Juliette,* Austryn Wainhouse, trans. (New York: Grove Weidenfeld, 1968), p. 745.

145 "he started to nuzzle up": Nancy Friday, *My Secret Garden: Women's Sexual Fantasies* (New York: Pocket Books, 1974), p. 168.

145 "Nor is this woman": ibid., pp. 164–65.

146 "It is a pleasant duty": Dekkers, *Dearest Pet,* p. 64.

146 "In spite of the dangling penises": ibid., p. 1.

146 "respectable lady": ibid., p. 176.

147 "For pure erotic longevity": James Kincaid, *Child-Loving: The Erotic Child and Victorian Culture* (New York: Routledge, 1992), pp. 364, 392.

148 Joseph Pujol: Jean Rohain and F. Caradec, *Le Pétomane, 1857–1945: Sa Vie, Son Oeuvre* (Paris: Jean-Jacques Pauvert, 1967).

148 "Petting provides": Alfred Kinsey, Wardell B. Pomeroy, and Clyde E. Martin, *Sexual Behavior in the Human Male* (Philadelphia: W. B. Saunders, 1948), p. 539.

149 "Petting . . . is a word": Paul Robinson, *The Modernization of Sex* (1976). (Ithaca, N.Y.: Cornell University Press, 1989), p. 63.

149 "No biologist understands": Kinsey, et al., *Male*, p. 667.

149 A fascinating footnote: Alfred Kinsey, Wardell B. Pomeroy, Clyde E. Martin, and Paul H. Gebhard, *Sexual Behavior in the Human Female* (Philadelphia: W. B. Saunders, 1953), p. 503.

149 "In light of the above": Kinsey, et al., *Male*, p. 668.

150 "responsible for a good deal": Robinson, *Modernization of Sex*, p. 56.

150 "The elements": Kinsey, et al., *Male*, pp. 676–77.

150 "French kiss": ibid., p. 540.

150 "found it entirely credible": Robinson, *Modernization of Sex*, p. 56.

150 "A fair number": Kinsey, et al., *Male*, pp. 673–77.

151 "the majority of female contacts": Kinsey, et al., *Female*, p. 506.

151 "Type of Sexual Contact": Paul H. Gebhard and Alan B. Johnson, *The Kinsey Data: Marginal Tabulations of the 1938–1963 Interviews Conducted by the Institute for Sex Research* (Philadelphia: W. B. Saunders, 1979), p. 448.

151 "the psychiatrist Von Maschka": Dekkers, *Dearest Pet*, p. 137. Dekkers's source on legal prosecution is Roland Grassberger, *Die Unzucht mit Tieren* (Vienna and New York: Springer, 1968).

151 *Female Sex Perversion:* Maurice Chideckel, *Female Sex Perversion— The Sexually Aberrated Woman as She Is* (New York: Brown, 1963). Cited in Dekker, *Dearest Pet*, pp. 142–43.

152 "sneak dogs in the house": John Money, *Lovemaps: Clinical Concepts of Sexual/Erotic Health and Pathology, Paraphilia, and Gender Transposition in Childhood, Adolescence, and Maturity* (New York: Irvington, 1986), p. 254.

152 Hollander was visiting: Xaviera Hollander, with Robin Moore and Yvonne Dunleavy, *The Happy Hooker* (New York: Dell, 1972), p. 34.

153 "gave me an apologetic look": ibid., p. 35.

153 "Now, having written": Xaviera Hollander, with Robin Moore and Yvonne Dunleavy, *The Happy Hooker* (London: Grafton, 1987), pp. 299–300.

154 "sex addict": Michael Ryan, *Secret Life* (New York: Pantheon, 1995), p. 3. The episode with the dog, Topsy, is described on pp. 177–80.

154 "There's no rule": James Atlas, "The Age of the Literary Memoir Is Now." *The New York Times Magazine*, May 12, 1996, p. 26.

154 As his friend George Dennison recalls: Taylor Stoehr, *Here Now Next: Paul Goodman and the Origins of Gestalt Therapy* (San Francisco: Jossey-Bass, 1994), pp. 196–97.

154 "Paul took its head": George Dennison, memoir written for Goodman's *Collected Poems*. Quoted in Taylor Stoehr, *Here Now Next: Paul Goodman and the Origins of Gestalt Therapy* (San Francisco: Jossey-Bass, 1995), p. 194.

155　"The didactic burden": Dennison, in ibid., p. 195.

155　"When my younger brother" Dennison, in ibid., pp. 195–96.

155　"he had suppressed": Taylor Stoehr, Introduction to Paul Goodman, *A Ceremonial: Stories 1936–1940*, vol. 2 of *The Collected Stories of Paul Goodman* (Santa Barbara: Black Sparrow Press, 1978), p. 15.

156　"The Continuum of the Libido": written in 1938; in Goodman, *A Ceremonial*, p. 158. Brackets in the original.

156　"'Eia!'": ibid., p. 159.

157　as Taylor Stoehr remarks: Stoehr, *Here Now Next*, p. 192.

157　"Some in the audience . . . Pasiphaë": Paul Goodman, *Don Juan, or, The Continuum of the Libido*, Taylor Stoehr, ed. (Santa Barbara: Black Sparrow Press, 1979), pp. 55–56.

157　"These stories are not": Taylor Stoehr, letter to Marjorie Garber, September 18, 1994.

158　"Goodman's own campaign": biographical note in Goodman, *Don Juan*, p., 163.

Breeding

159　"Flush knew": Virginia Woolf, *Flush: A Biography* (Harmondsworth, England: Penguin, 1983), p. 24.

159　"There are two kinds of dogs": *Speculum Laicorum*, Cap. xxi. Quoted in G. R. Owst, *Literature and the Pulpit in Medieval England* (Cambridge: Cambridge University Press, 1933), p. 387.

160　"a bit of a mongrel": George Bernard Shaw, *Misalliance* (1914; New York: Samuel French, 1957), p. 135.

160　"We are glad": Eugene O'Neill, letter to Sophus Keith Winther, December 26, 1942, in *Selected Letters of Eugene O'Neill*, Travis Bogard and Jackson B. Breyer, eds. (New Haven: Yale University Press, 1988), p. 539.

161　"a duchess would almost": *The Complete Dog Book: Official Publication of the American Kennel Club*, 18th ed. (New York: Howell Book House, 1992), p. 403.

161　Gypsy Rose Lee: ibid., p. 433.

162　"Dogs reflect the culture": John Paul Scott and John L. Fuller, *Genetics and the Social Behavior of the Dog* (Chicago: University of Chicago Press, 1965), p. 432.

162　"Dogs have gone through": ibid., p. 397.

163　"true sportsmen": Cited in Harriet Ritvo, *The Animal Estate* (Cambridge, Mass.: Harvard University Press, 1987), p. 102.

163　"a dazzling amateur pugilist": Thierry Poncelet, *Sit! The Dog Portraits of Thierry Poncelet*, text by Bruce McCall (New York: Workman Publishing, 1993), p. 65.

163 the Dancing Clumbards: ibid., pp. 22–23.

164 here is a chart: information in this chart is derived from Ace Collins, *Lassie: A Dog's Life* (New York: Penguin, 1993), pp. 6–7.

165 "the true dog": Robert Louis Stevenson, "The Character of Dogs" (1883) in Robert Louis Stevenson, *Essays,* William Lyon Phelps, ed. (New York: Charles Scribner's Sons, 1918), pp. 243–44.

165 "Sometimes qualities": Ritvo, *The Animal Estate,* p. 106.

165 "an index": ibid., p. 115.

165 "The business of breeding": Kathleen Kete, *The Beast in the Boudoir* (Berkeley: University of California Press, 1994), p. 67.

165 "Most French dog shows": ibid., p. 68.

166 "the construction of French breeds": ibid., p. 70.

166 "The identification of owner with pet": Jean Robert, *Le Chien d'Appartement et d'Utilité: Education, Dressage, Hygiène, Maladies* (Paris, 1888), pp. 96, 97. Cited in Kete, *Beast in the Boudoir,* pp. 83–84.

166 "The clothed pet": Kete, *Beast in the Boudoir,* p. 85.

167 *Of English Dogges: Of English Dogges: Translation of the De Canibus Britannicis* (1570; translated 1576), Abraham Fleming, trans., published in *The Works of John Caius, M.D.,* E. S. Roberts, ed. (Cambridge: Cambridge University Press, 1912), pp. 1–42. Caius (1510–73) wrote his description of English dogs, *De Canibus Britannicis* (1570) for a sixteenth-century naturalist, Konrad von Gesner.

167 "snarr and snatch": Abraham Fleming, "To the Reader," Caius, unpaged.

167 "if I were your father's dog": *King Lear,* Act II, scene ii, ll. 131–32.

167 a "mongrel," a "cur," a "whoreson dog": *King Lear,* Act I, scene iv, ll. 48; 80–81.

167 "If we are led": *Flush,* p. 9.

168 "If there had been a Man Club": ibid., p. 11.

168 "Purity of race": H[erbert] A[lbert] L[aurens] Fisher, *A History of Europe.* Boston: Houghton Mifflin, 1939), p. 14. The author's Preface is dated December 4, 1934. The first edition was published in 1935.

168 "When we . . . estimate": Charles Darwin, *On the Origin of Species* (1859). Vol. 15 of *The Works of Charles Darwin,* ed. Paul H. Barrett and R. B. Freeman (New York: New York University Press, 1988), pp. 14–15.

169 "A dachshund dog": Midas Dekkers, *Dearest Pet: On Bestiality,* Paul Vincent, trans. (London, New York: Verso, 1994), p. 24.

169 "Max was of Newfoundland": Charles F. Schimmain, *Our Max* (Boston: Loring, 1875), p. 3.

169 "to the ladies": Stevenson, "The Character of Dogs," p. 240.

170 "He loves us": Maurice Maeterlinck, *Our Friend the Dog,* Alexander Teixeira de Mattos, trans. (New York: Dodd, Mead, 1913), p. 55.

170   "typical features": Cited in Sander L. Gilman, *Freud, Race and Gender* (Princeton, N.J.: Princeton University Press, 1993), pp. 73–74.

170   In ironic response: "How to Read Character at Sight," *Vanity Fair*, October 1919.

171   "Bashan cannot": Thomas Mann, *A Man and His Dog*, Herman Georg Scheffauer, trans. (Alfred A. Knopf, 1930), pp. 8–10.

171   "a Scotch collie": ibid., p. 27.

171   "manner of sitting": ibid., p. 22.

171   "his shoulder-blades": ibid., p. 36.

171   "the expression of his face": ibid., p. 11.

172   "proclaim a brave heart": ibid., pp. 11–12.

172   "Bashan enjoys": ibid., p. 72.

172   "simple" . . . "the enunciation": ibid., pp. 72–73.

172   "Bashan, you must know": ibid., p. 73.

172   "earthy": ibid., p. 94.

172   "for there is": ibid., p. 97.

172   "the aboriginal": ibid., p. 104.

172   "huge patriarchs": ibid., p. 108.

173   "Just as I am": Konrad Z. Lorenz, *Man Meets Dog*, Marjorie Kerr Wilson, trans. (Boston: Houghton Mifflin, 1955), p. 93.

173   "I was beginning": Susan Conant, *Black Ribbon* (New York: Bantam, 1995), p. 21.

173   "Chantal's Bouviers": *Dogs USA 1995 Annual Puppy Buyer's Guide and Owner's Manual* (October, 1994), p. 263.

174   "The American Polish Owczarek Nizinny Club": ibid., p. 349.

174   "Cottonkist Coton de Tulear": ibid., p. 292.

174   "Be Loved": ibid., p. 282.

174   "Right for you?": ibid., p. 323.

175   "The standard portrays": *The Complete Dog Book*, p. 27.

175   "Type . . . the characteristic": "Glossary," p. 714.

175   "the process of posing": *A Beginner's Guide to Dog Shows*. American Kennel Club publication, 1994, p. 11.

175   "very well built": Robert L. Chapman, ed., *New Dictionary of American Slang* (New York: Harper & Row, 1986), p. 412.

176   "merry and affectionate": *Complete Dog Book*, p. 103.

176   "friendly, reliable": ibid., p. 69.

176   "essentially scowling": ibid., p. 497.

176   "Sweetness of temperament": ibid., p. 290.

176   "The Alaskan Malamute": ibid., p. 238.

176   "As the sole purpose": ibid., p. 469.

176   "Properly clipped" . . . "stamped": ibid., pp. 583–84.

176   "the breed has a distinct personality": ibid., p. 586.

176   (Yet it may be well to note): Of Doberman pinschers, to be fair, we are told that "The judge shall dismiss from the ring any shy or vicious Doberman," ibid., p. 256.

176   "with family and friends": ibid., p. 248.

177   "a member of the family": ibid., p. 129.

177   "the Bull-and-Terrier Dog": p. 330.

177   "The Ladies' Dog Club": Susan Conant, *A Bite of Death* (New York: Berkley, 1991), p. 60.

177   "I grew up thinking": Susan Conant, *Dead and Doggone* (New York: Berkley, 1990), p. 100.

178   "There is an impression": *Complete Dog Book*, p. 497.

178   "Secondary sex characteristics": ibid., p. 584.

178   "The one great disadvantage": Fredson Thayer Bowers, *The Dog Owner's Handbook* (Boston: Houghton Mifflin, 1936), p. 5. The author, a celebrated literary bibliographer, was commemorated at his death by the reproduction of the title pages of two of his works in the memorial program; one was Bowers's landmark *Principles of Bibliographical Description* (1949), the other *The Dog Owner's Handbook*. Bowers was a breeder of Irish wolfhounds and a respected dog show judge who wrote, at one time, a column for the *American Kennel Gazette*. (So far as I know, no one has bothered to point out that "Bowers" is an easy anagram for "Bowser.") See David L. Vander Meulen, foreword to G. Thomas Tanselle, *The Life and Work of Fredson Bowers* (Charlottesville, Va.: The Bibliographical Society of the University of Virginia, 1993), p. viii, and Tanselle, pp. 126–27.

179   "bitches do *tend*": Roger Caras, *The Roger Caras Dog Book* (New York: Holt, Rinehart and Winston, 1980), p. 4.

179   "an intact female": Carol Lea Benjamin, *Surviving Your Dog's Adolescence* (New York: Howell Book House, 1993), p. 10.

179   "Females are often": The Monks of New Skete, *How to Be Your Dog's Best Friend: A Training Manual for Owners* (Boston: Little, Brown and Company, 1978), pp. 16–17.

180   "Everyone who has": Barbara Woodhouse, *No Bad Dogs* (New York: Fireside, 1982), pp. 65–66.

180   "Name choices": *Dogs: General Information* (The American Kennel Club, Inc., 1995), pp. 21–22.

181   from a recent dog show: catalog of the Eastern Dog Club Obedience Trial, December 1, 1995, Boston, Mass.

181   Entire books: Wayne Bryant Eldridge, *The Best Pet Name Book Ever* (New York: Barron's, 1990).

182   "Brain, fidelity": Albert Payson Terhune, *Lad: A Dog* (New York: Puffin-Penguin, 1993; originally published 1919), pp. 92–93.

183   "Much of the public's pity": Bowers, *Dog Owner's Handbook*, p. 234.

183 "He was magnificent": Terhune, *Lad,* p. 91.
183 "The up-to-date collie": ibid., p. 98.
185 "like that of an otter": *The Complete Dog Book,* p. 341.
186 Geraldine Rockefeller Dodge: William Secord, *Dog Painting 1840–1940: A Social History of the Dog in Art* (Woodbridge, England: Antique Collectors' Club, 1992), pp. 322–23.
187 A few years later: ibid., p. 162.
187 By the year of Cruft's: ibid., p. 276.
187 "In a curious way": Matthew Engel, "In the Lap of the Dogs," *The Guardian,* March 14, 1994, p. 2.
188 "A ribbon in Westminster": David Stout, "Self-importance Can Be Important, But Hold the Pendulous Dewlaps," *The New York Times,* February 12, 1995, p. 16.
188 "According to American": Conant, *Dead and Doggone,* p. 30.
188 the *New Yorker* published: Susan Orlean, "Show Dog," *The New Yorker,* February 20–27, 1995, pp. 161–69.
189 "Just like a diva": Frank Litsky, "Regal Afghan Hound Makes a Move to Front of the Pack," *The New York Times,* February 14, 1996, p. B17.
190 "glamour bitch": Vicki Croke, "Clumber Lumbers to the Top," *The Boston Globe,* February 27, 1996, p. 85.
190 "He stays in condition": Frank Litsky, "Brady, the Clumber Spaniel, Takes His Final Bow," *The New York Times,* February 14, 1996, p. B14.
190 "Clumber" . . . "Underdog": *The Boston Globe,* February 17, 1996, pp. 81, 85.
190 "Now our defining dog": Croke, "Clumber Lumbers," p. 85.
190 "the top dog": ibid., p. 81.
190 "long, low, and rather heavyset": Caras, *Roger Caras Dog Book,* pp. 40–41.
191 "a royal air": Croke, "Clumber Lumbers," p. 85.
191 Dachshund fancier: Bob Morris, "In Westminster Show Season, Dogs Are Party Animals." *The New York Times,* February 18, 1996, pp. 45, 48.
191 author of *Nop's Trials:* New York: Crown, 1984.
191 a stinging op-ed piece: Donald McCaig, "Gone to the Dogs," *The New York Times,* August 3, 1994, p. A21.
192 "Of the 11,000 events": Wayne R. Cavanaugh, "Kennel Club Doesn't Create Witless Canines," *The New York Times,* August 20, 1994, p. 22.
192 Other correspondents: Letters to the editor from: Kate Hutton, Sherlee Lantz, and Robert Lantz; and Randi Locke, *The New York Times,* August 20, 1994, p. 22.
193 "If close relatives": Dekkers, *Dearest Pet,* p. 87.

193 when Disney wanted: Sarah Von Boven and Lucy Howard, "Not Every Dog Has His Day." *Newsweek,* October 2, 1995, p. 10.

193 "If every breed": Vicki Croke, "Providing Golden Opportunities," *The Boston Globe,* November 11, 1995, p. 40.

194 When the Ohio legislature: "Man Bites Dog with Ohio's Vicious Dog Statue," *Cleveland State Law Review,* vol. 37, no. 1 (winter 1989), p. 120.

195 "actually generic": Deidre E. Gannon, *The Complete Guide to Dog Law* (New York: Howell Book House, 1994), pp. 89, 103.

195 A California insurance company: "Doberman Owners in California Feeling Pinch Over Household Insurance," *The Boston Globe,* March 26, 1995, p. 27.

195 "All the ladies": Vicki Hearne, *Bandit: Dossier of a Dangerous Dog* (New York: HarperPerennial, 1991), pp. 49–50.

195 "I have no wish": Bowers, *Dog Owner's Handbook,* p. 37.

196 The "wolf" legend is also described: Reginald Cleveland, *Cop: Chief of Police Dogs* (Springfield, Mass.: Milton Bradley, 1927), p. vi.

196 "very nearly": ibid., p. vii.

197 "Some of the nervous": Lorenz, *Man Meets Dog,* pp. 94, 96, 97.

197 "Alsatians . . . will hate": Woodhouse, *No Bad Dogs,* p. 121.

198 "Germany is a Dachshund": *Bandit,* p. 32.

198 "The Rottweiler is the guard-dog-of-the-moment": René Chun, "Have You Hugged Your Rottweiler Today?" *The New York Times,* August 14, 1994, p. 49.

198 a winning headline: "Man's Not-So-Best-Friends," *Time,* September 4, 1995, p. 20.

199 "If you pick up": Mark Twain, *Pudd'nhead Wilson* (1894). *Pudd'nhead Wilson's Calendar,* Chapter 16.

199 When Comet: *Variety,* June 5–11, 1995.

199 "No random-bred": Caras, *Roger Caras Dog Book,* p. 4.

200 An "alpha male": Stanley Coren, *The Intelligence of Dogs* (New York: The Free Press, 1994), p. 153.

200 "How large a pack": John Ross and Barbara McKinney, *Dog Talk* (New York: St. Martin's Press, 1992), p. 37.

200 "The biggest, toughest": ibid., p. 37.

201 "Two of my best friends": Dorothy Parker, Preface to James Thurber, *Men, Women and Dogs* (New York: Dodd, Mead, 1943), p. 17.

201 "lovable, vulnerable": Harrison Kinney, *James Thurber: His Life and Times* (New York: Henry Holt, 1995), p. 242.

201 "the saddened artist": ibid., p. 243.

Dog Law

203 "The dog and man at first were friends": Oliver Goldsmith, "Elegy on the Death of a Mad Dog," *The Works of Oliver Goldsmith,* ed. Peter Cunningham (Boston: Little, Brown and Co., 1854), vol. 1, pp. 105–106.

204 "When a dog bites a man": quoted in Frank M. O'Brien, *The Story of The (New York) Sun* (1918). Bogart was the city editor of *The Sun* from 1873 to 1890.

204 "canine jurisprudence": Roscoe Pound, "Dogs and the Law," *The Green Bag,* vol. 8 (1896), pp. 172–74.

205 Britain: See Deidre E. Gannon, *The Complete Guide to Dog Law* (New York: Howell Book House, 1994), pp. 153–64 for more on Britain's Dangerous Dog Act, passed July 25, 1991.

205 "spawning copy-cat legislation": Kim Thornton, "View Point," *Dog Fancy,* April 1992, p. 3.

205 "When you give": Douglas Martin, "Free-Range Canines," *The New York Times,* April 27, 1996, pp. 25, 28.

205 "canine liberation": Elizabeth Marshall Thomas, "Canine Liberation," *The New York Times,* May 1, 1996, p. A19.

205 "Park officers should": Rita Bradley, letter to the editor, *The New York Times,* May 4, 1996, p. 18.

205 "Parks and other public places": Lorna Hahn, ibid.

205 "have you ever seen": Deborah Galler, ibid.

205 "wild avifauna": Christopher Hayes, ibid.

205 "dog owners and non-dog owners": Jeffrey Zahn, ibid.

206 "they are considered": Tilly Mia Weitzner, ibid.

206 "emotion on their side": "Dog Days in the Parks," *The New York Times,* May 7, 1996, p. A22.

206 "One day": Jane DeLynn, *Real Estate* (New York: Poseidon Press, 1988), cited in ibid., p. A22.

206 "Dog Laws": Geeta Anand, *The Boston Globe,* November 27, 1995, pp. 13, 20.

207 "Used to be": Patricia Nealon, "Randolph Gets Ruff," *The Boston Globe,* June 29, 1995, p. 1.

207 A Little Rock . . . ordinance: Ordinance 6232, Little Rock, Arkansas. Mary Randolph, *Dog Law,* 2nd ed. (Berkeley: Nolo Press, 1994), p. 7/5.

207 "I had stopped": "Barking at Dog Draws a Citation," *The Boston Globe,* December 6, 1995, p. 90.

208 "Watch Your Steps": Jennifer McKim, "Watch Your Steps," *The Boston Globe,* April 2, 1995, p. 1.

208 "Dog droppings have become": *Town of Nutley v. Forney,* 283 A2d. 142, 116 N.J. Super. 567 (1971), quoted in Randolph, *Dog Law,* p. 2/21.

208 She sued for damages: *San Francisco Chronicle,* August 6, 1988, cited in ibid., 8/9.

208 A New York statute: *Schnapp v. Lefkowitz,* 101 Misc.2d 1075, 422 N.Y.S.2d 798 (1979), quoted in ibid., p. 2/22.

208 A French lawmaker's: "French Seek Dog Tax to Take Bite Out of Grime," (Associated Press) *The Boston Globe,* November 25, 1996, p. 9.

209 a debate in the House of Lords: Peter Alldridge, "Incontinent Dogs and the Law," *New Law Journal,* July 27, 1990, v.140.n.6466, p. 1067.

209 "radical departure": Randolph, *Dog Law,* p. 1/11.

209 In Atlantic Beach: "Dog Day After Court," Susan Bickelhaupt and Maureen Dezell, "Names & Faces," *The Boston Globe,* July 15, 1995, p. 26.

209 "I did one prenup": Jan Hoffman, "How They Keep It," *The New York Times Magazine,* November 19, 1995, p. 104.

210 "fear naething": Sir Walter Scott, *Guy Mannering* (1814) (Edinburgh: Adams and Charles Black, 1871), p. 152. The passage is cited in *The Complete Dog Book: Official Publication of the American Kennel Club* (New York: Howell Book House, 1992), p. 351.

210 "Like so many": Midas Dekkers, *Dearest Pet: On Bestiality,* Paul Vincent, trans. (London, New York: Verso, 1994), p. 171.

210 Ginger, a shepherd mix: Anne Ohle and Stuart M. Wise, *The National Law Journal,* March 15, 1982, p. 39.

210 "No Pets" provisions: Tina Cassidy, "Please, No Pets," *The Boston Globe,* July 23, 1995, pp. A1, A6.

211 "One of the common": Charles O. Gregory, Harry Kalven, Jr., and Richard A. Epstein, *Cases and Materials on Torts,* 3rd ed. (Boston: Little, Brown and Company, 1977), p. 491.

211 One self-help guide: Randolph, *Dog Law,* p. 11/15.

212 "unjustly penalize": Liz Palika, "Canine Laws," *Dog Fancy,* April 1992, p. 9.

212 In a Michigan case: Mary Patricia Cauley, *"People v. Kay:* Man's Best Friend?" *Detroit College of Law Review* Fall v. 1984.n.3, pp. 757–69.

212 Four hundred years ago: Dekkers, *Dearest Pet,* p. 116.

213 the continuing saga of Taro: Articles on Taro's case: Robert Hanley, "For New Jersey Dog, 1,000 Days on Death Row," *The New York Times,* October 14, 1993, p. B1. "Dog's Death Sentence Upheld by a Trenton Court," *The New York Times,* October 20, 1993, p. B5. Jerry Gray, "Trenton's Matter of State: Legislators and a Dog," *The New York Times,* December 3, 1993, p. B9; Robert Hanley, "Ruling Gives Reprieve to Dog on Death Row," *The New York Times,* January 27, 1994, p. B6; Jerry Gray, "Dog's Death Sentence Is Reduced to Exile," *The New York Times,* January 29, 1994, p. 1; Evelyn Nieves, "Owner of Pardoned Dog Narrows Choice of Exiles," *The New York Times,* February 3, 1994, p. B5; Robert Hanley; "Taro Leaves Death

Row, Jail, and New Jersey Soil, for Good," *The New York Times*, February 11, 1994; Kate Stone Lombardi, "Pardoned in New Jersey, Taro Incognito," *The New York Times*, March 20, 1994, Section 13WC, p. 1.

213 "Ready for a Milk-Bone": *People*, December 13, 1993, p. 88.

215 "large dogs": R. L. Suthard, "Law Enforcement's Best Friends," *The Police Chief*, January 1991, pp. 50–52.

215 "explosives detection": "Bomb Dog Teams," *FBI Law Enforcement Bulletin*, July 1990, pp. 12–13.

215 Within a period of three months: *FBI Law Enforcement Bulletin*, April 1990, pp. 6–7.

216 "a heart wrapped in fur": *The Complete Dog Book*, p. 572.

216 "All the dogs": neighbor Rick Christian, quoted in Nancy Gibbs, "Tracking Down the Unabomber," *Time*, April 15, 1996, p. 41.

216 "starring Jackie Walsh": Melissa Cleary, *Skull and Dog Bones* (New York: Jove, 1994), cover blurb.

216 "picked up a trail": *The Complete Dog Book*, pp. 161–62.

217 Consider the case: Joseph P. Fried, "A Sheepdog Flies into Kennedy with Drugs," *The New York Times*, December 6, 1994, p. B1, B3. Dennis Hevesi, "Man Who Used Dog to Smuggle Sentenced to 3 Years in Prison," *The New York Times*, April 27, 1995, p. B3.

217 "when the driver": Nadine Brozan, "Chronicle," *The New York Times*, October 7, 1995, p. 20.

217 a lively modern mystery: Robert Barnard, *Fête Fatale* (New York: Dell, 1985), pp. 180–81. Published in Great Britain as *Disposal of the Living*.

218 "There was also the evidence": Agatha Christie, *Elephants Can Remember* (New York: Dell, 1972), pp. 196, 225–26.

218 "Is there any point": Arthur Conan Doyle, "Silver Blaze" (1892), in *Sherlock Holmes: The Complete Novels and Stories*, vol. 1 (New York: Bantam, 1986), p. 472.

219 Lacking human eyewitnesses: "Simpson Prosecutors Use Dog to Fix Murder Time," *The New York Times*, February 9, 1995, p. B9. Adam Pertman, "Witnesses Testify to Dog's Yelps," *The Boston Globe*, February 9, 1995, p. 3.

219 "truly memorable": David Margolick, "Echoes of a Cry in the Night," *The New York Times*, March 22, 1995, p. C1.

220 "If he could": "News Hound," *People*, May 1, 1995, p. 55.

220 Yet another dog-walker: David Margolick, "Dog-Walking Neighbor of Simpson Contradicts His Account of When the Bronco Was Parked," *The New York Times*, April 1, 1995, p. 6.

220 "Barking . . . is one": Margolick, "Echoes of a Cry in the Night," p. C10.

221   Limousine driver: "Last Week in O.J. History," *The Boston Globe*, April 9, 1995, p. 77.

221   at least two persons: David Margolick, "Trying O. J. Simpson: $4,986,167 and Counting . . ." *The New York Times*, June 5, 1995, p. A10.

221   "Mr. Shapiro barks": David Margolick, "Jurors and Judge Ito: Their Private Lives," *The New York Times*, August 13, 1995, Section 4, "News of the Week in Review," p. 5.

221   at least five versions: *The Hound of the Baskervilles*, 1939 (directed by Sidney Lanfield; starring Basil Rathbone, Nigel Bruce, Richard Greene, Wendy Barrie, Lionel Atwill); *Hound of the Baskervilles*, 1959 (directed by Terence Fisher; starring Peter Cushing and Christopher Lee); *The Hound of the Baskervilles*, made for TV, 1972 (directed by Barry Crane; starring Stewart Granger, William Shatner, and Bernard Fox); *The Hound of the Baskervilles*, 1977 (directed by Paul Morrissey; starring Dudley Moore, Peter Cook, Denholm Elliott, Spike Mulligan, Joan Greenwood, Jessie Matthews, and Roy Kinnear); *The Hound of the Baskervilles*, made for TV 1983 (directed by Douglas Hickox; starring Ian Richardson, Donald Churchill, and Martin Shaw).

221   the first thing Holmes deduces: Arthur Conan Doyle, "The Hound of the Baskervilles" (1902), in *Sherlock Holmes: The Complete Novels and Stories*, vol. 2 (Toronto and New York: Bantam, 1986), p. 6.

222   "I have ample evidence": ibid., p. 39.

222   "A stranger then": ibid., p. 88.

222   "It was I": ibid., p. 105.

222   "the last who had seen": ibid., p. 56

222   "It is he who dogged us": ibid., p. 110.

222   "Evidently, many of these dogs": Jean Bethke Elshstain, "Why Worry About the Animals?" *The Progressive*, vol. 54, no. 3, p. 18.

223   "Ninety-seven dogs": Susan Conant, *Gone to the Dogs* (New York: Bantam, 1992), pp. 118–19.

223   "voicelessly trying": Susan Conant, *Dead and Doggone* (New York: Berkley, 1990), p. 139.

223   "You don't seem": ibid., p. 141.

224   In Arizona alone: Susan Netboy of Friends for Life, National Greyhound Adoption Network, "Greyhound Abuse and Rescue," letter to the editor, *Dog Fancy*, April 1992, p. 5.

225   "Sled dogs love": Mark Derr, "The Perilous Iditarod," *The Atlantic Monthly*, March, 1995, p. 123.

225   One of the several: *The Complete Dog Book*, p. 432.

225   "Yes, we are still eating dogs": James Piao, letter to the editor, *The New York Times*, September 13, 1994, p. A22.

226   "Dog meat": Andrew Lam, "It's a Man-Eat-Dog Culture," *The Los Angeles Daily Journal*, August 17, 1989, p. 6.

226   "dog farms": Kim Kyenan, "International Fund for Animal Welfare," *The Korea Times*, April 20, 1996, p. 6.

226   "Brigitte Bardot": Susan Bickelhaupt and Maureen Dezell, "Names & Faces," *The Boston Globe*, May 4, 1996, p. 26.

227   "The domestic dog": James A. Serpell, *In the Company of Animals* (Oxford and New York: Basil Blackwell, 1986), p. v.

227   "the pet emerged": Marc Shell, "The Family Pet," *Representations* 15 (summer 1986), p. 135. Shell cites Michael W. Fox, "Pet Animals and Human Well-Being," in William J. Kay et al., eds., *Pet Loss and Human Bereavement* (Ames, Iowa: 1984), p. 16: "For the British, eating dog is akin perhaps to cannibalism."

227   "frowned upon pet owning": Shell, "The Family Pet," p. 135.

227   "Hitler anthropomorphized": ibid., p. 138.

228   a 1983 novel: Dick King-Smith, *Babe: The Gallant Pig* (New York: Crown, 1985, first published in Great Britain in 1983 under the title *The Sheep Pig*).

228   "Since property": Anmarie Barrie, *Dogs and the Law* (Neptune, N.J.: T.F.H. Publications, 1990), p. 85.

228   In England in 1985: J. Leigh Mellor, "Hath a Dog Money?" *Taxation*, February 16, 1985, p. 357.

229   At one point: *Law Without Lawyers*, by Two Barristers-at-Law (London: John Murray, 1905). Cited in Mary Randolph, *Dog Law: A Legal Guide for Dog Owners and Their Neighbors* (Berkeley, California: Nolo Press, 1994), p. 1/10.

229   the animal was not protected: Randolph, *Dog Law*, p. 13/9.

229   As Constance Perin points out: in *Belonging in America* (Madison: University of Wisconsin Press, 1988), p. 136.

229   frantically struggling: Deborah Pines, "Court Rules Out Cause of Action for Death of Dog," *New York Law Journal*, February 16, 1994, p. 1.

229   "Hath a dog money?": *The Merchant of Venice*, Act I, scene iii, ll. 111–31. *The Riverside Shakespeare* (Boston: Houghton Mifflin, 1974).

230   Midas Dekkers, *Dearest Pet*, p. 118.

231   "The day *may come*": Jeremy Bentham, *The Principles of Morals and Legislation*, Chapter 17, section 1 (New York: Hafner, 1948), p. 311n.

232   "a veritable bible": Roswell C. McCrea, *The Humane Movement* (New York: Columbia University Press, 1910), p. 115.

232   "Don't you know": Harriet Beecher Stowe, *Uncle Tom's Cabin* (New York: Harper & Row, 1965; originally published 1852), pp. 19–21.

232   "Here, Topsy": ibid., p. 239.

232 "Stick out your hands": William H. Armstrong, *Sounder* (New York: Harper & Row, 1969), pp. 21, 24.

233 "It was more": Sydney H. Coleman, *Humane Society Leaders in America* (Albany, N.Y.: The American Humane Association, 1924), p. 33.

233 "which were then": ibid., p. 43.

233 in a notorious 1995 case: Michele R. McPhee, "Mutilated Pit Bull Found in Basement," *The Boston Globe*, November 29, 1995, p. 36; "Wounded Puppies Draw Calls of Concern," *The Boston Globe*, November 30, 1995, p. 35. "We've gotten hundreds of calls from people who were literally weeping over the dogs," said a hospital spokesman. The two puppies were nursed back to health at Angell Memorial Animal Hospital and adopted.

233 In 1907 in Britain: Jean Bethke Elshtain, "Why Worry About the Animals?" *The Progressive*, March 1990, p. 18.

234 "women were often located": ibid.

234 "a woman's preaching": James Boswell, *Life of Johnson* (1791), July 31, 1763.

234 "With the emergence": Elshtain, "Why Worry About the Animals?" p. 18.

234 "So far as animals are concerned": Immanuel Kant, *Lecture on Ethics*, 1. Infield, trans. (New York: Harper Torchbooks, 1963), pp. 239–40.

234 They seek to close the gap: Elshtain, "Why Worry About the Animals?" p. 18.

234 Animal Rights Law center: Neil MacFarquhar, "Mute Clients and Futile Cases Haven't Dulled Lawyer's Ardor," *The New York Times*, November 11, 1995, pp. 25, 28.

235 "If possessing": Peter Singer, *Animal Liberation: A New Ethics for Our Treatment of Animals* 2nd ed. (New York: Random House, 1990), p. 6.

235 "I am no more outraged": ibid., p. iii.

236 "There are barbarians": Voltaire, *Dictionnaire Philosophique*, "Bêtes."

236 Alexander Pope: in *The Guardian*, May 21, 1713. Singer, p. 203.

236 "To most people": Singer, *Animal Liberation*, p. 10.

237 "it is not helping": Gannon, *Complete Guide to Dog Law*, p. 6.

237 "there is a new school": Matthew Engel, "In the Lap of the Dogs," *The Guardian*, March 14, 1994, p. 3.

237 "a woman I'll call Lizzie": Susan Conant, *Black Ribbon* (New York: Bantam, 1995), p. 160.

237 "If you ground": Ingrid Newkirk, quoted in "Just Like Us?" *Harper's*, August 1988, p. 47.

237 Peter Singer takes: in *Animal Liberation*, p. 34.

237 "animal liberationists": Peter Singer, *The New York Review of Books*, February 2, 1989; reprinted in *The CQ [Congressional Quarterly] Researcher*, May 24, 1991, p. 317.

238 "Let me tell you": Jessica Szymczyk, "Animals, Vegetables and Minerals," *Newsweek*, August 14, 1995, p. 10.

239 In a famous court argument: George Graham Vest, *Charles Burden, Respondent v. Leonidas Hornsby, Appellant* (1870); cited in Mary Randolph, *Dog Law*, 9/26–27.

240 "O! Let me kiss" . . . "Filial ingratitude!" . . . "Mine enemy's dog": William Shakespeare, *King Lear*, Act III, Scene iv, ll. 14–16; Act IV, Scene vi, ll. 131–32; Act IV, Scene vii, ll. 36–37.

Dog Loss

241 "The old dog barks backward": Robert Frost, "The Span of Life," in *The Poetry of Robert Frost*, ed. Edward Connery Latham (New York: Holt, Rinehart and Winston, 1969), p. 308.

241 "He's not the finest character": Arthur Miller, *Death of a Salesman* (New York: Viking Press, 1958), p. 56.

243 "It is strange": J. C. Squire, "A Dog's Death," in *Collected Poems* (London: Macmillan, 1959), p. 33.

243 "Beneath this spot": George Gordon, Lord Byron, in *The Works of Lord Byron, Poetry*, vol. I, ed. Ernest Hartley Coleridge (New York: Octagon Books, 1966), pp. 280–81.

244 "Frederick the Great of Prussia requested": Nancy Mitford, *Frederick the Great* (Harper & Row, 1970), p. 291.

244 In the 1930s: Beth Daley, "Flag Lowering on the Rise," *The Boston Globe*, August 16, 1995, p. 33.

244 "Max is dead": Charles F. Schimmain, *Our Max: A Memoir of a Four-Footed Friend* (Boston: Loring, 1875), p. 3.

244 "Until the last": ibid., p. 36.

244 "I have lost": Maurice Maeterlinck, *Our Friend the Dog*, Alexander Teixeira de Mattos, trans. (New York: Dodd, Mead, 1913), p. 3.

244 "succeeds in piercing": ibid., p. 41.

244 "The dog is really": ibid., pp. 62–63.

245 "the Dog is the noblest": Emily Dickinson to George H. Gould (?), February 1850. Letter 34 in Johnson, *Selected Letters*, p. 37.

245 "Hills—Sir": Emily Dickinson to Thomas Wentworth Higginson, 25 April 1862. Letter 261 in ibid., p. 172.

245 "thoughts of such": Thomas Wentworth Higginson to Emily Dickinson, May 11, 1869. Letter 330a in ibid., p. 198.

245 "Whom my Dog understood": Emily Dickinson to Thomas Wentworth Higginson, early 1866. Letter 316 in ibid., p. 192.

245 "I wish for Carlo": Emily Dickinson to Thomas Wentworth Higginson, 9 June 1866. Letter 329 in ibid., p. 193.

245 "I came across a photograph": Willie Morris, *My Dog Skip* (New York: Random House, 1995), p. 3.

246 "'Skip died'": ibid., p. 121.

246 "Willie Morris takes": Winston Groom, the dust jacket blurb for ibid.

247 "The dog of your boyhood": Morris, *My Dog Skip*, p. 122.

247 "One of my patients": Wallace Sife, *The Loss of a Pet* (New York: Howell Book House, 1993), pp. 25–27.

248 "strive[s] laboriously": *Topsy*, 151. Compare this to Virginia Woolf, *Flush* (originally published 1933; Penguin edition London, 1983), pp. 27–28: "Flush was equally at a loss to account for Miss Barrett's emotions. There she would lie hour after hour passing her hand over a white page with a black stick; and her eyes would suddenly fill with tears; but why? . . . Then again Miss Barrett, still agitating her stick, burst out laughing. . . . What was there to laugh at in the black smudge that she held out for Flush to look at? . . . when he watched the same finger for ever crossing a white page with a straight stick, he longed for the time when he too should blacken paper as she did."

248 "The growth under Topsy's lip": ibid., p. 105. When Bonaparte is about to depart on a vacation in the south of France, she writes elegiacally, "In a few weeks, Topsy, I shall come back from over there with a tanned skin and a book you cannot read . . . when I return . . . you will, doubtless, either be healed or doomed" (p. 109).

248 "Topsy, Topsy": ibid., p. 123.

248 The "sentence" of oral cancer: Lynn Whisnant Reiser thinks Topsy's victory over cancer "must have expressed" for both the Freuds and Bonaparte "the wish that Freud would yet recover," while allowing all the human participants to "keep some distance" from their suffering. "Topsy—Living and Dying: A Footnote to History," *Psychoanalytic Quarterly*, vol. 56, no 4 (1987), p. 687.

249 "Does Topsy realize": Michael Molnar, *The Diary of Sigmund Freud, 1929–1939: A Record of the Final Decade* (New York: Charles Scribner's Sons, 1992), p. 233.

249 Freud visited: Gary Genosko, introduction to *Topsy*, p. 25.

249 "a distressing symptom": Ernest Jones, *The Life and Works of Sigmund Freud,* edited and abridged by Lionel Trilling and Steven Marcus (New York: Basic Books, 1961), p. 529.

249 "You promised me": ibid., p. 530.

250 "Although none of us": Susan Cheever, *Home Before Dark* (New York: Bantam, 1991), p. 149.

250 "For weeks": Willie Morris, *My Dog Skip*, p. 53.

250 "Music has no heart": William Wordsworth, "Incident: Characteristic of a Favourite Dog," in *Wordsworth, Poetical Works,* Thomas

Hutchinson, ed., Ernest de Selincourt, rev. (New York: Oxford University Press, 1969), pp. 384–85.

251   "Not free from boding thoughts": William Wordsworth, "Fidelity" (composed 1805, published 1807) in *Wordsworth, Poetical Works*, p. 385.

252   "The Dog or Horse": William Wordsworth, "Essay Upon Epitaphs." Originally published in *The Friend*, 22 February 1810, then printed as a note to *The Excursion*, Book V (1814). In W. W. Merchant, *Wordsworth: Poetry and Prose* (Cambridge, Mass.: Harvard University Press, 1967), p. 605.

252   When Emily Brontë died: Elizabeth Gaskell, *The Life of Charlotte Brontë* (London: Penguin, 1985; originally published 1857), p. 358. Rebecca Fraser, *The Brontës: Charlotte Brontë and Her Family* (New York: Fawcett Columbine, 1988), p. 319.

252   "during Miss Branwell's reign": quoted in Winifred Gérin, *Anne Brontë* (London: Allen Lane, 1959, 1976), p. 67.

253   Emily Brontë soon had: Gaskell, *Charlotte Brontë*, pp. 268–69.

254   "Poor old Keeper!": quoted in Fraser, *The Brontës*, p. 297.

254   "The dogs seemed": Charlotte Brontë, letter to Ellen Nussey, 23 June 1849. Quoted in Fraser, *The Brontës*, p. 327.

255   "or some caress": Charlotte Brontë to William Smith Williams, 25 June 1849. Quoted in ibid., p. 328.

255   "Poor old Keeper died": quoted in Gaskell, *Charlotte Brontë*, p. 465.

255   "He had come": ibid.

255   Greyfriars Bobby: Forbes Macgregor, *The Story of Greyfriars Bobby* (Edinburgh: Ampersand, 1981).

257   Montaigne tells: Michel de Montaigne, "Apology for Raymond Sebond," in *The Complete Essays of Montaigne*, Donald M. Frame, trans. (Stanford: Stanford University Press, 1965), p. 346.

257   "This *Fuluius*": Wilson's Arte of Rhetorique, G. H. Mair, ed. (Oxford, England: Clarendon Press, 1909), p. 193.

258   a modern American version: Betsy Sikora Siino, "Psychic Phenomena," *Dog Fancy*, October 1995, p. 39.

258   A statue of Hachiko: Robert Rosenblum, *The Dog in Art from Rococo to Post-Modernism* (New York: Harry N. Abrams, 1988), p. 10.

258   "very poetic": Gene Siskel, *Siskel & Ebert* (television review).

260   "Dog that is born": Evelyn Waugh, *The Loved One: An Anglo-American Tragedy* (Boston: Little, Brown, 1948), p. 122.

260   "Every anniversary": ibid., p. 21.

260   "Harry . . . do you think": Marshall Saunders, *Beautiful Joe* (orig. pub. 1894; reprinted Bedford, Mass: Applewood Books, 1994), p. 258.

261   "I wish": ibid., p. 258.

261   "I think": ibid., p. 259.

261   "When Adam": ibid., p. 260.

261 "ruling passions": R. W. B. Lewis, *Edith Wharton: A Biography* (New York: Harper & Row, 1975), p. 160.

262 The director of communications: Vicki Croke, "Do All Dogs Go to Heaven?" *The Boston Globe*, April 15, 1995, p. 55.

262 "Doggie Kaddish": Joel Lurie Grishaver presented this example as what he called "Halakhic Action Adventure 3: 'Kaddish for Sam, My Dog and Companion.'"

262 "Mourners would be shocked": Walter Jacobs, *Contemporary American Reform Responsa* (New York: Central Conference of American Rabbis, 1987).

262 "There is nothing": Wallace Sife, *The Loss of a Pet* (New York: Howell Book House, 1993), p. 141.

263 The senior rabbi emeritus: Rabbi Balfour Brickner, in ibid., pp. 138–39.

263 A subdean: Reverend Canon Joel A. Gibson, in ibid., p. 143.

263 A representative of the Unitarian: Reverend Dr. Tracy Robinson-Harris, in ibid., p. 144.

263 "Those faiths": ibid., p. 137.

263 a spokesman from the Tibet Center: the Venerable Khyongla Rato Rinpoche, in ibid., p. 146.

263 A list of suggestions: Sife, pp. 149–53.

264 "What has it all": Paul Monette, "Puck," in *Last Watch of the Night: Essays Too Personal and Otherwise* (New York: Harcourt Brace & Company, 1994), pp. 1–28.

265 Brochures on "safer pet guidelines": See "Safe Pet Guidelines for Patients with HIV Disease," by Ken Gorczyca, D.V.M., © 1991 Pets Are Wonderful Support, San Francisco, CA.

265 "If you're alone": brochure from PAWS, 539 Castro Street, San Francisco, California 94114. An up-to-date listing of other regional human-animal support services resource centers can be obtained by writing to PAWS.

266 "The thing": interview with Ken Gorczyca by Firewind, in *Footsteps*, October 1992, p. 8.

266 "Consider what it would be like": quoted in Barbara J. Burton, "Pets and PWAs: Claims of Health Risk Exaggerated," *AIDS Patient Care*, February 1989, p. 35.

266 Albin Swenson: "A Dying Man and His Dog Go Home," *The Boston Globe*, September 10, 1995, p. 38.

266 a tribute to his miniature poodle: Armistead Maupin, "The Kiss Patrol," in Michael J. Rosen, ed., *Dog People: Writers and Artists on Canine Companionship* (New York: Artisan, 1995), p. 132.

267 Betty Carmack . . . tells: Burton, "Pets and PWAs," p. 34.

267 When his cocker spaniel: Betty J. Carmack, "The Role of Compan-

ion Animals for Persons with AIDS/HIV," *Holistic News Practice*, vol. 5, no. 2 (1991), pp. 24–31.

268 "enabling you to raise": brochure from Geneti-Pet, Port Townsend, Washington. "Jurassic Bark," *Harper's*, September 1994, p. 28. Henry Alford, "Unnatural Selection," *The New York Times Magazine*, November 13, 1994.

269 "When the pets": Pat Jordan, "Freeze-Dried Memories," *Time*, February 13, 1989, pp. 16–20.

269 "This mode of remembrance": Alfred Bonnardot, *Des petits chiens de dames, spécialement de l'épagneul Nain* (Paris, 1856). Quoted in Kathleen Kete, *The Beast in the Boudoir* (Berkeley: University of California Press, 1994), pp. 89–90.

270 "You could have him": Mme. Charles Boeswillwald, *Le Chien de luxe: Comment élever, dresser, et soigner nos chiens* (Paris, 1907). Quoted in ibid., p. 90.

270 the unsanitary disposal: a problem publicly under discussion at least since 1830, notes Kete, ibid., p. 90.

270 "To secure": Bibliothèque Marguerite Durand, dossier Durand— Cimetière des Chiens. Cited in Kete, ibid., pp. 90–91.

270 International Association of Pet Cemeteries: cited in Sife, *The Loss of a Pet*, p. 155.

271 Virtual Pet Cemetery: "Requiems for Pets: Guilt Rides the Internet." *The New York Times Magazine*, March 17, 1996, p. 21.

271 "The pet-human bond": Vicki Croke, "A Place to Say Goodbye," *The Boston Globe*, September 26, 1995, p. 25.

271 "wear his little union suit": *Beyond the Barrier: The Story of Byrd's First Expedition to Antarctica* (Annapolis, Md.: Naval Institute Press, 1990), p. 41.

271 A two-page obituary: *Literary Digest*, May 9, 1931, p. 9. Rodgers, *Beyond the Barrier*, p. 267.

272 "You had better": Rodgers, *Beyond the Barrier*, pp. 202–204, 256.

272 "Sacred to the Memory": *The New York Times*, July 10, 1931. Rodgers, *Beyond the Barrier*, p. 268.

272 "STATUE OF YOUR OWN": *Dog Fancy*, January 1996, p. 116.

272 "St. Francis": *Dog Fancy*, February 1996, p. 102.

273 "the grounds": brochure for Pleasant Mountain Pet Rest, 76 Liberty Street, Plymouth, Mass.

273 "Ten Tips": Moira Anderson-Allen, "Ten Tips for Coping with the Loss of Your Pet," excerpted from Anderson-Allen, *Coping with Sorrow on the Loss of Your Pet* (Olympia, Washington: Peregrine Press, 1994).

274 "I have always felt": Anne Raver, "A Loyal Friend, a Link to Paradise," *The New York Times*, April 28, 1994, p. C8.

275 "The sweetness": Charles F. Shimmain, *Our Max: A Memoir of a Four-Footed Friend* (Boston: Loring, 1875), p. 36.

276   "replacement animals": Mary Stewart, "Loss of a Pet—Loss of a Per-
       son: A Comparative Study of Bereavement," in *New Perspectives on
       Our Lives with Companion Animals,* ed. Aaron Honori Katcher and
       Alan M. Beck (Philadelphia: University of Pennsylvania Press,
       1983), p. 404.
276   "funerals are very unusual": ibid., p. 399.
276   "the 'boyness' of a son": ibid., p. 401.
277   "a look of awful": Milan Kundera, *The Unbearable Lightness of Be-
       ing,* Michael Henry Heim, trans. (originally published 1984; New
       York: Harper Perennial, 1991), p. 300.
277   "found a mirror": ibid., p. 302.
277   "Lend me a looking-glass": William Shakespeare, *King Lear,* Act V,
       Scene iii, ll. 262–64, 307–12.
278   "I knew perfectly well": James Carroll, "The Family Dog Taught Me
       Something I Needed to Know." *The Boston Globe,* March 15, 1996, p.
       15.
278   "Poems and stories": Bonnie Wilcox and Chris Walkowicz, *Old
       Dogs, Old Friends: Enjoying Your Older Dog* (New York: Howell
       Book House, 1991), pp. 201–02.
279   "I left": Walter Kirn, "Envoy," in *Unleashed: Poems by Writers' Dogs,*
       Amy Hempel and Jim Shepard, eds. (New York: Crown Publishers,
       1995), p. 154.
279   "*You* left": Susan Minot, "Devotion," ibid., p. 155.
279   "My heart": Kate Clark Spencer, "When I Died on My Birthday,"
       ibid., p. 164.
279   "I was a bad dog": Ben Sonnenberg, "Stay," ibid., p. 172.
279   "I'm a dead dog": Stephen Dunn, "Buster's Visitation," ibid., p. 170.
280   "The Last Will": "For Carlotta" (New Haven: Yale University Press,
       1956).
280   "I have little": Quoted in Sheaffer, *O'Neill: Son and Artist,* p. 519.
280   "Blemie's ghost": Eugene O'Neill, letter to Sophus Keith Winther,
       December 26, 1942, in *Selected Letters of Eugene O'Neill,* Travis
       Bogard and Jackson B. Breyer, eds. (New Haven: Yale University
       Press, 1988), p. 539.
281   "Daisy ('Black Watch Debatable')": E. B. White, "Obituary," *The
       New Yorker,* March 12, 1932, p. 16.
281   "Jason Oliver C. Smith": Anna Quindlen, "Mr. Smith Goes to
       Heaven," *The New York Times,* April 7, 1991, p. E19.

Coda

283   What shall I do: William Butler Yeats, "The Tower" (1926). *The Col-
       lected Poems of W. B. Yeats* (New York: Macmillan, 1956), p. 192.

INDEX

Abandoned dogs, 40
Abuse of animals, 23, 223–24
Accessories, dogs as, 24–25, 144
Accomplices, dogs as, 217
Ackerley, J. R., 132–35
Actaeon, 44
Addams, Charles, *241*
Adopting dogs, 40–42
Advertising, 21, 53–54, 108, 109–10,
    112, 147, 148, 173–75
Agassiz, Jean Louis, 261
AIDS, 264–68
Airedales, 52, 171
Albee, Edward, 277
"All-American" dogs, 185–86, 198–200
Alpha males, 200
Alsatians, 52, 196–97
Alston-Myers, Lisa Jane, 191
Alter, Eleanor, 209–10
Altering dogs, 75–76, 179
Ameche, Don, 102
American Dog Owners Association, 212
American Humane Education Society, 68
American Humane Society, 42, 67, 224,
    225, 236, 272
American Kennel Club
    and breeding dogs, 163, 175, 177,
        178, 185, 188, 191–92, 194
    criticisms of, 191–92
    and favorite dogs, 198
    and legislation, 212
    and naming dogs, 180–81
    and showing dogs, 185, 188
American Society for the Prevention of
    Cruelty to Animals, 15–16, 233,
    236, 272

Amory (Cleveland) Fund for Animals,
    236
L'Amour est une Fête (Bourdon), 144
Anaclitic personality, 138–39
Andrews, Andy, 88–89
Angell, George Thorndike, 68, 232
Angier, Natalie, 31
Animal Happiness (Hearne), 21
Animal Hero Award (Massachusetts), 54
*Animal Liberation: A New Ethics for Our
    Treatment of Animals* (Singer), 235,
    236
Animal Liberation Front, 236
Animal rights, 231–33, 234–39
Animal Veterinary Medical Association,
    29
Annie (Broadway show), 22, 45, 60
Anthropomorphism, new, 30–35, 103,
    227
Antiheros, dogs as, 61–64
Antis (war dog), 51
Aquinas, Thomas, 262
Arcadia (Sidney), 167–68
Arete (show dog), 191
Argus (*The Odyssey*), 38, 44, 54, 56,
    241–42
Aristotle, 105, 262
Arnold, Matthew, 33, 34
Arte of Rhetorique (Wilson), 257–58
Asclepius (mythical god), 89–90
Asta (*The Thin Man*), 216
Astrophel and Stella (Sidney), 143
Atlas, James, 154
Auden, W. H., 97, 116
Authors, dogs as, 22–23, 64–67, 109,
    278–79

Babe (film), 102, 192, 228, 259
Bacon, Francis, 116, 244
"Bad Dog" (computer program), 21
Bad dogs, 194–97. *See also* Vicious dogs
Bailey (Sundquist's dog), 17–18
Balto (film), 61
Bambi: A Forest Life (Salten), 68
Bandit (Vicki Hearne's dog), 195, 197
Barbera, Michelle M., *141*
Bardot, Brigitte, 124, 213, 226–27
Bark Up (procanine group), 206
Barking, laws against, 207
Barnard, Robert, 217–18
Barraud, Francis, 113
Barrie, J. M., 83
Bashan (Thomas Mann's dog), 65, 97, 171–73
Batchelder, Ann, 41
Battina (William Wegman's dog), 23
Baxter, Percival, 244
Bear (search dog), 127
Beautiful Joe (Saunders), 67–70, 94–95, 112, 224, 232, 260–61
Beauty (war dog), 51
Beckman, Robert, 228
Beethoven's Second (film), 36, 66
Bell (Kate Clark Spencer's dog), 279
Benjamin, Carol Lea, 100, 179
Benji (film dog), 130, 199
Bennett, Paula, 127
Bentham, Jeremy, 231
Bergh, Henry, 233
Bergler, Reinhold, 43
Bernese mountain dogs, 161
Bestiality. *See* Sexual fantasies
Bible, 262–63
Bichon frise, 161
Biff (Champion Hi-Tech's Arbitrage) (show dog), 188–89
Biography, of dogs, 64–67
Bird dogs, 167
Bisexuality, 129
Biting, legislation about, 211–13
Black Beauty (film), 259
Black Beauty (Sewell), 67, 68, 69, 232
Black Dog (catalog company), 25–26
Blass, Bill, 20
Bleak House (Dickens), 116
Blemie (aka Silverdene Emblem) (Eugene O'Neill's dog), 77, 160, 280
Blood (*A Boy and His Dog*), 60
Bloodlines (Conant), 223

Bloom, Harold, 182
Boatswain (Lord Byron's dog), 176, 243–44
Bodger (*The Incredible Journey*), 103
Bogart, John B., 204
Bomb-sniffing dogs, 215
Bonaparte, Marie, 248–49
Bones Dog and Catalogue, 26
Boodgie (David Hockney's dog), 26
Boomer (Henry J. Stern's dog), 205
Borden, Lizzie, 271
Borzois, 198
Boston, Massachusetts, legislation in, 206–7, 208
Bourdon, Sylvia, 144
Boxers, 176–77
Boy (Peter Mayle's dog), 44, 70, 106
A Boy and His Dog (film), 60
Boyd, Hugh Stuart, 47, 99
Brady (aka Clussexx Country Sunrise) (show dog), 190–91
Bratton, William J., 16
Breeding
    and advertising, 173–75
    and best of opposite sex, 177–80
    "fancy," 173–77
    and inbreeding, 191–93
    legislation about, 205
    and mixed breeds, 166–68
    and studs, 162–65
    and Victorian era, 165–68
Brian (companion dog), 188
Brian (war dog), 51
Britain
    dog breeding in, 165–66
    dog shows in, 187–88
    dogs in wills in, 228
    humane societies in, 233
    legislation in, 205, 209, 233
    national breeds of, 198
    stealing dogs in, 228–29
    vivisection in, 233
    war-dog school in, 51–52
British Dalmatian Club, 193
Broderick, Matthew, 84–85
Brontë, Anne, 253, 254
Brontë, Charlotte, 253, 254–55
Brontë, Emily, 252–55
Brown, Buster, 44
Brown, Charlie, 43, 109
Browning, Elizabeth Barrett. See *Flush: A Biography* (Woolf)

Bruno (war dog), 52
Buck, 86–87, 120. See also *The Call of the Wild* (London)
Buddy (guide dog), 91
Bulgakov, Mikhail, 64, 105
Bulldogs, 160–61, 171, 198
Bullseye, 217
Burlingham, Dorothy, 136
Bush, George, 19. *See also* Millie
"Buster's Visitation" (Stephen Dunn's dog), 279
Butcher, Susan, 224, 225
Butterworth, Hezekiah, 68, 70
Buz (hero dog), 61
Byrd, Richard, 223, 271–72
Byron, George Gordon, Lord, 176, 243–44, 277

Caius, John, 161, 167
Calendars, dogs on, 23
California, legislation in, 226
California Federation of Dog Clubs, 195
Call names, 181
The Call of the Wild (London), 66, 86–87, 120
Cambridge, Massachusetts, legislation in, 207–8
Camp Gone to the Dogs, 28
Camp Wingford, 28
Camps, for dogs, 28
Can You See Me Yet? (play), 85
Canby, Vincent, 83
Caras, Roger, 113, 131–32, 179, 180, 190–91, 199–200
Cargill, John, 220
Carlo (Emily Dickinson's dog), 112–13, 245
Carmack, Betty, 267
Carrey, Jim, 147–48
Carroll, James, 278
Cartoons, 108–9. *See also specific cartoonist*
Cashew, 92
Cassiopeia (John Cheever's dog), 128–29
Catalogs, dog-theme, 25
Cavalier King Charles Club, 192
Celebrity dogs, 22–23. *See also specific dog*
Cemeteries, 270–74
Cerberus (mythical dog), 90
Challenge to Lassie (film), 56
Champion (war dog), 52

Chance (*Homeward Bound*), 103
Charley (William Bratton's dog), 16
Charley (John Steinbeck's dog), 64, 92–94
Charlotte's Web (White), 227–28
Charlton, Anna E., 235
"The Chase" (Somerville), 86
Checkers (Richard Nixon's dog), 19, 20
Cheever, Benjamin, 89
Cheever, John, 128–29, 249–50
Chiens de Brie, 52
Chihuahuas, 144
Child-Loving (Kincaid), 147
Children, and love of dogs, 92, 124
The Children of Men (James), 123
China, dog meat in, 225–26, 227
Chinese crested, 161, 225
Chow chows, 178, 197, 225
Chris (James Carroll's dog), 278
Christianity, 227
Christie, Agatha, 218
Clark, Marcia, 219, 221
Cleary, Melissa, 216
Cleveland, Reginald, 61
Cliché (Dorothy Parker's dog), 160
Cliff (police dog), 215
Clift, Anthea, 228
Clinton (Bill) family, 20
Close, Glenn, 193
Clothing, 24–26, 146–47
Clumber spaniels, 190–91
Cock, Samuel, 143–44
Cokey, 217
Coleridge, Samuel Taylor, 261
Collectibles, 26
Collies, 215
Come Back, Little Sheba (Inge), 268
Comet (celebrity dog). See *Fluke*
The Company of Dogs (catalog company), 25
The Complete Dog Book (American Kennel Club), 175, 176–77, 178
Conant, Susan, 100, 111, 177, 188, 216, 223–24, 237, 278
Cone, Ed, 125–26
"Continuum" (Goodman), 157
Cookbooks, 26
Cooper, Jilly, 52
Cop: Chief of Police Dogs (Cleveland), 61, 196
Coren, Stanley, 21, 30, 99, 216, 285
Corgis, 20, 197
Coriolanus (Shakespeare), 230

Courage of Lassie (film), 54, 56
Crime
  accomplices in, 217
  detectives of, 215–17
  motives for, 217–18
  victims in, 222–25
  weapons in, 221–22
  witnesses to, 218–21
Crimson Tide (film), 62–63
Croke, Vicki, 190
Cross-species mating, 148–52
Crowninshield, Frank, 170–71
Cruft, Charles, 187
Crufts Dog Show (Britain), 187
Custody of dogs, 209–10
Cyberspace, dogs in, 21, 24

Dachshunds, 20, 191, 198
Daisy Dog (Paul Goodman's dog), 158
Daisy (E. B. White's dog), 280–81
Dalmatians, 160
Damhoudere, Joost de, 230
Dancing Clumbards, portrait of, 163
Dancing dogs, 163
Dangerous dogs, 212
Daphne (*Look Who's Talking Now*), 102, 103
Dart (Wordsworth), 250
Darwin, Charles, 38–39, 86, 168–69, 237
Darwinism, 121
Davis, Geena, 56, 82
Day-care centers, 28
De Ville, Edward "Coupe," 163
Dead and Doggone (Conant), 223–24
Dekkers, Midas, 130, 145, 146, 151, 169, 193, 210, 230
DeLynn, Jane, 206
Dennison, George, 154–55, 158
Derrida, Jacques, 278
Descartes, René, 73, 74, 100–101, 114, 234, 235–36, 262
Detectives, dogs as, 215–17
Deucie (therapy dog), 41
Developmental narratives, of dogs, 74–77
DeVito, Danny, 102
Dickens, Charles, 66–67, 116
Dickens, Homer, 129
Dickin Medal, 51, 53, 222
Dickinson, Emily, 112–13, 176, 245
Diderot, Denis, 144
Disabled people, 88–94, 211
Divorce, 209–10

Dixon, Jeanne, 214
DNA, of dogs, 268–70
Doberman pinschers, 195, 212, 215
Dodge, Geraldine Rockefeller, 26, 186
Dodo (war dog), 53
Dog, definitions of, 142
Dog Fancy magazine, 61, 112, 173, 204, 205, 212, 272
A Dog Is Listening (Caras), 113
A Dog Loop (film), 144
Dog meat, 225–28
Dog Talk (Ross), 95–96, 110–11
Dog World magazine, 220
"Dog years," 264–68
Dog-care handbooks, 166
Dog-O-Rama (New York City), 24
Dognapping, 16–17, 228–29
Dogo Argentino, 205
"A Dog's Death" (Squire), 243
A Dog's Life (Mayle), 21, 44, 106
Dogs and Their Women (Cohen and Taylor), 126–27
Dogs Today magazine, 26
Dogs USA magazine, 173
The Dogs Who Came to Stay (Pitcher), 75, 125–26
"Dogz: Your Computer Pet" (CD-ROM), 21
Dole, Bob, 20, 111
Don Juan (Goodman), 157
Down and Out in Beverly Hills (film), 29
Doyle, Conan. *See* Holmes, Sherlock
Drs. Foster & Smith (catalog company), 25
Drug smuggling, 217
Dryden, John, 143
"Dulux dog" (advertisement), 21
Dumb dogs, 94–101, 110
Dunn, Stephen, 279
Dying dogs, 274–78
Dylan (dog loss), 243

Eastern Dog Club Show, 186–87
Eastern Dog Club, 198–99
Eastman, Max, 285
Eating dogs, 225–28
Eckstein, Warren, 98–99
Eddie (*Frasier*), 22
Edgar (John Cheever's dog), 129, 249–50
Edward VII (king of England), 190
Edwards, Glenn, 16–17
Eighner, Lars, 64

Eisenhower, Mamie, 19
"Elegy on the Death of a Mad Dog" (Goldsmith), 203–4
Elgar, Edward, 114
Eliot, T. S., 180
Elizabeth II (queen of England), 20
Ellis, Havelock, 151
Elshtain, Jean Bethke, 222, 233–34
England. *See* Britain
English Kennel club, 162–63
"Essay upon Epitaphs" (Wordsworth), 252
Estés, Clarissa Pinkola, 30–31
Eustis, Dorothy, 91
Evie (*We Think the World of You*), 133, 134
Experimental animals, 233–34, 235–36, 237

Fairytales, dogs in, 90
Faithfulness of dogs, 249–58
Fajkowski, Christie, 128
Fala (Franklin Delano Roosevelt's dog), 18–19
Family values, 15, 35, 59, 123
Far from Home: The Adventures of Yellow Dog (film), 38, 60
Farfel (puppet dog), 93
Fashion, 24–26
Fay Ray (William Wegman's dog), 23
Feminism, 126–28
Feminization of dogs, 234
Fenjves, Pablo, 219–20
Ferenczi, Sandor, 137
Fernville Lord Digby (advertising dog), 21
"Fetch" (computer program), 21
Fiction. *See* Literature; *specific author or book*
"Fidelity" (Wordsworth), 250–51
A Fig for Momus (Lodge), 143
Fila Brasileiro, 205
Finley, Timothy, 85
"First the Dog" (Herbert), 71
Fisher, H.A.L., 168
Floral (Friends and Lovers of Riverside Area Life), 205
Florio, James, 213
Flossy (The Brontës' dog), 253, 254, 255
Fluke (film), 60, 102, 199, 216, 239, 258–60

Flush: A Biography (Woolf), 45–50, 66, 99, 110, 115–16, 117, 159, 168
Fly (*Babe*), 102
Ford, Gerald, 20
Forster, E. M., 133, 135
Foster, Susan, 193
France, 165–66, 198, 208–9
Francione, Gary L., 234–35
Frank (Jan Hooks' dog), 85
Frank, Morris, 91
Franz, Marie-Louise von, 91
Fred (stray dog), 15–16
Frederick the Great (emperor of Prussia), 244
Freud, Anna, 136, 137–38, 248–49
Freud, Sigmund, 49, 73, 74, 97, 135–39, 142, 182, 248–49
Friday, Nancy, 145–46
Friends, dogs as best, 37, 126–27, 239–40
Frost, Robert, 241
Frosty Paws, 24
Fulvius (Roman emperor), 257–58
Funerals, 272–73

Galton, Francis, 170
Gaskell, Elizabeth, 253–55
Gay, Peter, 137
Gender issues, 129–30, 178–80, 197, 198
Geneti-Pet (laboratory), 268
Genetics, 162, 191–92
George, Jean Craighead, 284
George V (king of England), 190
Gerberg, Mort, *119*
German shepherds, 176, 178, 192, 195–97, 212, 215. *See also* Alsatians
Germany, legislation in, 209
Giese, Jo, 127–28
Ginger (Gary Larson), 96–97
Ginger (two-family dog), 210
"Golden Retriever" (computer program), 21, 144
Golden retrievers, 176, 193, 215
Goldsmith, Oliver, 203–4
Good Age Fund, 41
Good Dog! magazine, 198
Goodman, Paul, 154–58
Gorczyca, Ken, D.V.M., 266
Gould, Robert, 143
Graham, Barbara, 31

Grasper (The Brontës' dog), 252–53
Grassberger, Ronald, 151
Gravely, Rex, 14
Gray, Harold, 60
Gray, John. *See* Greyfriars Bobby
Great Danes, 144
Greene, Lorri, 266
Greyfriars Bobby, 56, 240, 255–57, 259
Greyhounds, 167–68, 224
Grief, literature of, 277–78
Guide dogs, 91
Guiterrez, Gerald, 85
Gunn, Thom, 107–8
Gunther, Hans F., 170
Gurney, A. R., 82–85, 108, 126, 141
Guy Mannering (Scott), 161

Hachiko, 258
Hackman, Gene, 62–63
Haggerty, Arthur J., 22–23
Halfond, Brie, 213
Handsome Dan (Yale mascot), 160–61
Hanna (Albin Swenson's dog), 266
The Happy Hooker (Hollander), 152–54
Happy Trails Pet Resort, 28
Harry (Ben Sonnenberg's dog), 279
H.C. (sled dog), 225
Health care, for dogs, 27–28
Hearne, Vicki, 21, 30, 33, 34, 195, 197,
    216, 237
The Heart of a Dog (Bulgakov), 64, 105
Heimel, Cynthia, 124
"Heinz dogs," 201
Helpfulness, of dogs, 88–94
Hempel, Amy, 106–7
Henry IV (Shakespeare), 230
Henry, O., 104–5, 199
Her (Lyndon Johnson's beagle), 19
Herbert, Zbigniew, 71
Herding dogs, 162, 215
Hero (fictional dog), 60–61
Heroes
    and "a dog's life," 44, 60–61
    commercialism of dogs as, 53–54
    and dogs as antiheroes, 61–64
    Lassie as prototype of dog, 54, 55–60
    police dogs as, 215–16
    war dogs as, 50–53, 54
Herriot, James, 34
The Hidden Life of Dogs (Thomas), 20–21
Higginson, Thomas Wentworth, 113, 245

The Hills of Home (film), 56
Him (Lyndon Johnson's beagle), 19
Hinnant, Bill, 43, 85
Hirschfeld, Magnus, 151
Hockney, David, 26
Hollander, Xaviera, 152–54
Holloway, Roy, 190
Holmes, Sherlock, 218–19, 221–22
Homecoming, 37–39
Homer, 261
Homeward Bound: The Incredible Journey
    (film), 38, 60, 102, 103
Hooker (*Shakespeare's Dog*), 105
Hooks, Jan, 85
Hoover, Herbert, 18
Horwitz, Roger, 264
"The Hound of the Baskervilles" (Doyle),
    221–22
Hounds, 167–68
How to Be Your Dog's Best Friend (Monks
    of New Skete), 179–80
How to Get Your Pet into Show Business
    (Haggerty), 22
"How to Read Character at Sight" (*Vanity
    Fair*), 170–71
"How to Say Fetch" (Hearn), 216
*How to Make Your Man Behave in 21
    Days or Less, Using the Secrets of
    Professional Dog Trainers*, 142
Human Hero Award (Massachusetts), 54
Human interest stories, about dogs, 14,
    16, 111, 242
Humane education, 67–70
Humane societies, 231–32, 233–34. *See
    also* American Humane Society
Hyrcanus, 257

Iditarod Trail International Sled Dog
    Race, 224–25
Igloo (Admiral Byrd's dog), 271–72
Indigo Girls, 236
Inge, William, 268
Insurance, for dogs, 27–28
The Intelligence of Dogs (Coren), 21, 99,
    216
International Association of Pet Cemeter-
    ies, 270
Internet, 271
"Investigations of a Dog" (Kafka),
    114–15
Irish Wolfhound, 160

Jackson, Samuel L., 102
James, P. D., 123
James, William, 73
James Spratt Company, 187
Jason (Susan Minot's dog), 279
Jason (Anna Quindlen's dog), 281–82
Jeff (Jonathan Aaron's dog), 275
Jeff's Preservation Specialties, Inc., 269
Jingle Dog (singing group), 101
Jo Fi (Sigmund Freud's dog), 136
Jock (war dog), 52
Johnson, Don, 60
Johnson, Lyndon B., 19–20
Johnson, Samuel, 93, 125, 234, 261
Jolly Dog (Walter Kirn's dog), 279
Jones, Ernest, 137, 249
Jones, R. S., 107
Jonson, Ben, 82
Judy (boxer war dog), 51
Judy (English pointer war dog), 50–51
Juliette (Sade), 145
Julius Caesar (Shakespeare), 230
Jungian psychology, 90–91

Kaczynski, Ted, 216
Kaddish, 262
Kafka, Franz, 13, 64, 114–15
Kant, Immanuel, 234
Karenin (*The Unbearable Lightness of Being*), 121–22, 129, 276–77
Katcher, Aaron, 123
Kato (Nicole Brown Simpson's dog), 219–21
Keaton, Diane, 102
Keaton, Michael, 56, 82
Keeper (Brontë's dog), 252, 253–54
Keller, Helen, 85–86
Kelley, Jane, 128
Ken-L Ration, 54
Kete, Kathleen, 165–66, 234, 270
Kimi (Holly Winter's dog), 224. *See also* Conant
Kincaid, James, 147
King Lear (Shakespeare), 167, 230, 240, 277
King Solomon's Ring (Lorenz), 36
King Timahoe (Nixon's dog), 19
King Tut (Herbert Hoover's dog), 18
Kinsey, Alfred, 132, 148–49, 150–51
Kirn, Walter, 279

Klein, Richard, 31, 111–12
Knight, Eric, 54, 55–60
Knitting with Dog Hair, 25
Koenig, Marcia, 127
Korea, eating dogs in, 226–27
Korea Animal Protection Society, 226
Krypto (*Superman*), 44
Kumin, Maxine, 277
Kundera, Milan, 121–22, 129, 276–77

Laboratory animals, 235, 236, 237–38, 239
Labradors, 198, 215
Lacan, Jacques, 47
Lad: A Dog (Terhune), 61, 83, 88, 102, 183
Lady and the Tramp (film), 102, 199
Laika (Russian space dog), 71–72, 222
Lam, Andrew, 226
Lamartine, Alphonse Marie Louis de, 261
Lampl, Hans, 136
Landseer, Edwin, 42, 161
lang, k.d., 236
Lapdogs, 144
Larson, Gary, 96–97
Lassie (fictional/film dog)
  biography of, 45
  and canonization of dogs, 34
  cartoon about, *13*
  casting of, 129–30
  commercialization of, 21
  and helpfulness, 91, 94
  as hero, 54, 55–60
  and homecoming, 38
  love of, 129–30
  mentioned, 196, 215
  tail of, 284–85
  as talking dog, 83, 89
Lassie (film), 21, 90
Lassie (Knight), 34, 54
Lassie Come Home (film), 38, 59–60, 259, 284–85
"Lassie Come-Home" (Knight), 55–59, 66
Lassie (television program), 59, 88–89, 130
Leader (Bob Dole's dog), 20, 111
Lee, Gypsy Rose, 161
Lehmann, Rosamond, 134
Lehrer, Lonnie, 214
Levin, Harry, 182
Lewis, R.W.B., 261

Liberty (Gerald Ford's dog), 20
Life expectancy, 243
Lineage, 164
Lodge, Thomas, 143
Lollipop (rescue dog), 40–41
Lombroso, Cesare, 170
London, Jack, 65, 74–75, 86–88,
    120–21, 233
Look Who's Talking Now (film), 102–3
Lopez, Rosa, 220
Lorenz, Konrad, 36–37, 38–39, 123–24,
    135, 169, 173, 197
The Loss of a Pet (Sife), 247–48
Lost dogs, 242–43
Love, Iris, 191
Love of dogs
    evolution of, 121
    and love of humans, 14–15, 123–24,
        125, 135
    passionate, 132–34
    and transference, 136–37
    and transitional objects, 130–32
    women's, 121–22, 124, 126–30
Love Given O're (Gould), 143
The Loved One (Waugh), 242, 260
Lovelace, Linda, 144
Luath (*The Incredible Journey*), 103
Lucifer (*Juliette*), 145
Lun Yug (Sigmund Freud's dog), 136
Lupa (George Pitcher's dog), 75, 125–26
Lyric (heroic dog), 17, 91

Macbeth (Shakespeare), 166–67
McCaig, Donald, 191–92
McCaig, Norman, 99
McCall, Bruce, 163
McCarthy, Susan, 31, 38
McClellan, A., 53
McHugh, Heather, 107
McMahon, Francis, 258
Madonna, 144, 145
Maeterlinck, Maurice, 113, 169–70, 244,
    277
Maida (Walter Scott's dog), 86
Malamute, Alaskan, 176
Malteses, 144
Maltin, Leonard, 29
A Man and His Dog (Mann), 65, 171–73
Man Meets Dog (Lorenz), 123, 173
Man Ray (William Wegman's dog), 23
Mankoff, Robert, 109
Mann, Thomas, 37, 65, 97, 171–73

Maria (*The Hidden Life of Dogs*), 35
Mark, Marky, 147
Marriage, between dogs, 35–37, 133–34
Martha Calling (Meddaugh), 106
Martha Speaks (Meddaugh), 106
Martin, Richard, 233
The Mask (film), 21, 101–2
Maslin, Michael, 108
Massachusetts Society for the Prevention
    of Cruelty to Animals, 54, 68, 95,
    210–11, 271, 276
Masson, Jeffrey Moussaieff, 31, 38
Mastiffs, 167
Mating
    cross-species, 148–52
    See also Breeding
Maupin, Armistead, 266–67
Max (film dog), 22, 101–2
Max the Newfoundland, memoir of, 244,
    275
Mayle, Peter, 21, 44, 70, 106
Mazur, Debi, 144
Meddaugh, Susan, 106
"Memoirs of a Yellow Dog" (O. Henry),
    104–5
Memory, of dogs, 38–39
The Merchant of Venice (Shakespeare),
    230
Merrill, James, 113
A Midsummer Night's Dream (Shake-
    speare), 81, 143, 150, 230
Mike the Dog, 29
Milk-Bone dog biscuits, 53–54
Miller, Arthur, 241
Miller, Ben, 210
Millie (Bush springer spaniel), 19, 20,
    45, 64, 109, 111, 129, 130
Millie's Book (Millie), 19, 64, 109
Milton, John, 277
Minot, Susan, 279
Misha (*The Hidden Life of Dogs*), 35
"Missing: A Dog's Doggerel" (*Unleashed*
    collection), 116
Missing persons, 215
Missy (*Beethoven II*), 36
Mitou (Edith Wharton's dog), 261
Miza (Edith Wharton's dog), 261
Modine, Matthew, 102
Molly (Anne Raver's dog), 274
Monette, Paul, 264
Money, John, 152
Money, dogs as owners of, 228, 229–30

Mongrels. *See* Mutts/mongrels
Monks of New Skete, 179–80
Monsieur Grat (René Descartes' dog), 101
Montague, Allison, 154–55
Montaigne, Michel Eyquem de, 257
Monterey, Carlotta. *See* Blemie
More, Thomas, 262
Morris, Willie, 21, 65, 199, 245–47, 250
Mountain dogs, 166
Mugford, Roger, 26
Music (Wordsworth), 250
Mutts/mongrels, 162, 168, 201
My Dog Skip (Morris), 21, 65, 199, 245–47
My Dog Tulip (Ackerley), 132–35
My Life as a Dog (film), 70–71
My Secret Garden (Friday), 145–46
"My Shepherd" (McHugh), 107
Mystery stories, dogs in, 21, 100, 111, 163, 215–17, 218–19, 223
Mythology, dogs in, 89–90, 157. *See also* *specific character*

Names for dogs, 180–82
Nana (*Peter Pan*), 83
Narcissistic personality, 138–39
Narcotics dogs, 215
Nathanson, Jane, 276
National Center for Family Literacy, 109
Nationalism, 197–98
Neutering, 75–76, 179
"New abolitionists," 234–39
New Jersey, vicious dog law in, 213–14
New York City, legislation in, 205–6
The New Yorker magazine
    Biff profile in, 188–89
    cartoons in, *13, 43, 81, 119,* 201, *203, 241*
    White's obituary for Daisy in, 280–81
Newfoundlands, 144, 160, 176
Newkirk, Ingrid, 237
Newspapers, about dogs, 26
Nick Carter (detective dog), 216
Niehaus, Honey, 27–28
Nietzschie (author's dog), 29, 39, 181–82, 276, 284
Nipper (RCA Victor dog), 113–14
Nixon, Richard, 19
Nixon (film), 19
No Bad Dogs (Woodhouse), 135
Nurock, Kurt, 101
Nussey, Ellen, 252–53, 254

Odysseus. *See* Ulysses
Of English Dogges (Caius), 161, 167
Old Possum's Book of Practical Cats (Eliot), 180
Old Yeller (film), 34, 199
Oliver Twist (Dickens), 66–67
"One-bite law," 211–13
O'Neill, Eugene, 77, 160, 196–97, 280
101 Dalmatians (film), 34, 66, 193
Ordeal (Lovelace), 144
Orlean, Susan, 188–89
Oscar (advertising dog), 26
Our Dogs newspaper, 26
Our Friend, the Dog (Maeterlinck), 169–70, 244
Our Gang (films), 197
The Overthrow of Stage-Players (Rainolds), 141–42

Paintings, of dogs, 26, 163–64
PALS (Pets Are Loving Support), 266
"Panegyrick upon my Lady *Fizzleton's* Lap-Dog" (Ward), 143
Parin, Vasel, 71–72
Parisian dogs, 166
Park, Allan, 221
Park Bench Cafe (Huntington Beach, CA), 26
Parker, Dorothy, 160, 201
Parker, Sarah Jessica, 82–85
Parks, 205–7
Patton (film), 61–62, 63
Pavlov, Ivan, 71–74, 77–79
Pedigree Mealtime, 188
Pedigrees, 164
Pedigrees (catalog company), 25
Pelléas (Maurice Maeterlinck's dog), 113, 244
People for the Ethical Treatment of Animals (PETA), 236, 237, 238
People's Dispensary for Sick Animals (Britain), 51, 53
Percy (Thomas Mann's dog), 171, 173
Perin, Constance, 229
"Personal Automated Wagging System" (P.A.W.S.) (CD-ROM), 21
Perversions, 148–52
Pet cemeteries, 242
Pet Nosh (superstore), 27
Pet Project, 266
Pet Share, 41–42
The Pet Show (radio program), 29–30

Petco Animal Supplies (superstore),
    27
Pete (in O. Henry), 104–6
Pete the Pup (*Our Gang*), 197
Petimony, 209–10
Pets & People Foundation, 40–41
Pets Are Wonderful Support (PAWS),
    265–66
Petsmart (superstore), 27
Petstuff (superstore), 27
Petting, 148–52
Philosophers, dogs as, 114–17
Physiognomy, 170–71
Piao, James, 225–26
Picano, Felice, 133
Pit bulls, 177, 194–95, 197–98, 205,
    212, 233
Pitcher, George, 75, 121, 125–26
Pleasant Mountain Pet Rest, 272
Plutarch, 122–23
Police dogs, 184, 196, 215
Politicians, 17–20
Poncelet, Thierry, 23, 163
Poodles, 160, 176, 198
Poop, picking up, 207–9
Popcorn, Faith, 144
Pope, Alexander, 104, 236
Pornography, 144, 149
Portrait of the Artist as a Young Dog
    (Thomas), 45, 201
Pound, Roscoe, 204–7
POWARS (Pet Owners with AIDS Re-
    source Service), 24, 266
"The Power of Pets" (Klein), 111–12
Powers, Cindy, 17
"Praise of a Collie" (McCaig), 99
Preservation of pets, 268–70
PRIDE (Providing Responsible Informa-
    tion on a Dog's Environment), 225
Property, animals as, 228–29, 234–35
Puck (Paul Monette's dog), 264
Pujol, Joseph, 148
Punch (war dog), 51

Queenie (J.R. Ackerley's dog), 132–35
Quindlen, Anna, 281–82
The Quotable Dog, 106–7

Race, 168–71, 172
Racism, 195, 232–33, 235
Rahv, Philip, 157
Rainolds, John, 141–42

Rameau (*Topping from Below*), 144
Raver, Anne, 274, 276
RCA Victor, 113–14
Real Estate (DeLynn), 206
Recordings, novelty, 101–2
Reese, Laura, 144
Reitman, Ivan, 36
Remus (Pitcher's dog), 75, 125–26
Reno (film dog), 215–16
Rentals
    dog, 22
    house, 210–11
Replacement animals, 276
Rescue groups, 193
Rescuers, dogs as, 40–42, 215
Richardson, E. H., 51
Rifleman Khan (war dog), 51
Rights, animal, 231–33
Rin Tin Tin, 24, 60, 89, 91, 94, 102, 196,
    215
Ritts, Herb, 148
Ritvo, Harriet, 35, 67, 162–63, 165, 201
Rivers, Joan, 144
Rob ("para dog"), 50
Robinson, Paul, 149, 150
Rocks (*Look Who's Talking Now*), 102–3,
    199
Rodrigue, George, 26
Rogers, Will, 13
Rolling Stones, 142
Romance, dogs for, 22
Romances, medieval, dogs in, 90
Rooke, Leon, 105
Roosevelt, Franklin Delano, 18–19
Roosevelt, Theodore, 197
Ross, John, 95–96, 97, 110–11
Rottweilers, 198, 215
Roudinesco, Elisabeth, 77
Rowdy (Holly Winter's dog), 223, 224.
    See also Conant
Royal Society for the Prevention of
    Cruelty to Animals, 233
Rumbo (film dog), 102
Russell, Chuck, 102
Rutgers University Animal Rights Law,
    234–35
Ryan, Michael, 154

Sade, Donatien Alphonse François,
    Comte de, 145
St. Bernards, 171
St. Christopher, 90

Sally (Broderick's dog), 84–85
Salten, Felix, 68
Salukis, 162
Sam (dog phobia), 29
Sammy (Richard's dog), 264–65
Samson (best man dog), 23
San Mateo County, California, legislation in, 205
Sandy, The Autobiography of a Star, 22–23, 45, 64
Sasha (singing dog), 101
Saunders, Margaret Marshall, 67–70, 94–95, 232
Sayers, Dorothy, 163, 221
Schulz, Charles M., 43, 85, 109
Schur, Max, 249
Scooby-Doo (cartoon dog), 216
Scott, George C., 61–62
Scott, Walter, 86, 161, 210
Scout (R.S. Jones' dog), 107
Secret Life (Ryan), 154
Seeing Eye, 90
Self-help books, 30–31
Senior dogs, 40
Senior people, 40–42
Serpell, James, 123, 227, 262
Sévigné, Madame de, 101
Sewell, Anna, 67, 232
Sex
    and breeding, 178–80
    and cross-species mating, 148–52
    and fantasies about dogs, 141–52, 154–58
Sexton, Linda Gray, 34
Sexual fantasies, 141–52, 154–58
Shadow (*Homeward Bound*), 102, 103
Shady Spring Kennels, 28
Shaffer, Charlotte Katz, 28
Shakespeare, William, 36, 81, 83, 105, 143, 150, 166–67, 230, 240
Shakespeare's Dog (Rooke), 105
Shanahan, Danny, *13,* 89
Shapiro, Robert, 221
Shaw, George Bernard, 78, 160
Sheba (*Come Back, Little Sheba*), 268
Sheepdogs, 166, 217
Shell, Marc, 227
Shelley, Percy Bysshe, 261
Shep (faithful dog), 258
Shepard, Jim, 106–7
Shepard, Sam, 35

Shepherds, 162, 167, 196. *See also* Alsatians; German shepherds
Shields, Brooke, 25
Shih Tzu, 176
Shook, Larry, 119
Showing dogs, 182–91
Sidney, Philip, 143, 167–68
Sife, Wallace, 247–48, 263
Silverdene Emblem. *See* Blemie (Eugene O'Neill's dog)
Simpson (O. J.) trial, 219–21
Singer, Peter, 235, 236, 237
Singing dogs, 101–2
Sirius (star), 144
Skip (Willie Morris' dog), 65, 199, 245–47, 250
Sled dogs, 223, 224–25, 272
Smith, Liz, 191
Snoopy, 43, 50, 85, 109
Society for the Prevention of Cruelty to Animals (Italy), 261
Socks (Clintons' cat), 20
Somerville, William, 86
Son of Lassie (film), 54
Sonnenberg, Ben, 279
Sophie (James Carroll's dog), 278
Sorel, Edward, *203*
Souls of dogs, 260–64
Sounder (film), 232–33
Space animals, 71–72. *See also* Laika
Spaniels, 143, 167–68, 176, 190–91, 192, 198
Spaying, 75–76, 179
Speculum Laicorum (anon.), 159
Speechless (film), 56, 82
Speert, Betsy, 26
Spencer, Kate Clark, 279
Spooner, Paul, 92
Sporting dogs, 162, 224–25
Squire, J. C., 243
Stacking, 175
"Standard" dogs, 175–76
Stanley (David Hockney's dog), 26
Stealing dogs, 228–29
Steinbeck, John, 64, 92–94
Steiner, Peter, *81,* 108
Stevenson, J. (cartoonist), *43*
Stevenson, Robert Louis, 33–34, 44, 112, 165, 169, 180
Stipe, Michael, 236
Stock dogs, 162
Stoehr, Taylor, 155–56, 157–58

Stowe, Harriet Beecher, 68, 232
Strachey, Lytton, 45, 49
Stud Book (American Kennel Club), 163
Stud Book (English Kennel Club),
    162–63
Studs, 162–65
Stuffing pets, 269–70
Sundquist, Don, 17–18
Superman/Superboy (fictional character),
    44, 61
Superpup (television program), 61
Superstores, pet, 27
Swenson, Albin, 266
Sylvia (Gurney), 82–85, 108, 126, 141
Symbols, dogs as, 19
Szymczyk, Jessica, 238

Tails of dogs, 283–86
"Talking to Dogs" (Auden), 97, 116
The Taming of the Shrew (Shakespeare),
    143, 230
Tao (fictional cat), 103
Taro ("death row dog"), 213–14, 235
Taxes, 228
Taylor, Elizabeth, 60
Taylor, Jeremy, 261
Television. *See specific dog or program*
Temple, Shirley, 60
"Ten Tips for Coping with the Loss of
    Your Pet" (Pleasant Mountain Pet
    Rest), 272
Terhune, Albert Payson, 60–61, 65, 83,
    88, 183
Terriers
    American Staffordshire, 177, 194
    Cairn, 198
    Dandie Dinmont, 161, 209–10
    as main variety of dog, 167
    Scottish, 160, 197
    Skye, 161
    Yorkshire, 144
    See also Pit bulls
Therapy, pet, 29–30, 40–42
Thomas, Dylan, 45
Thomas, Elizabeth Marshall, 20–21, 30,
    32–33, 35–36, 38–39, 205
Thomas, Rufus, 142
Thurber, James, 70, 97, 141, *159*, 201
Tige (Buster Brown's dog), 44
"Tintern Abbey" (Wordsworth), 65
Tippy (Paul Goodman's dog), 156, 157
Tiven, Rachel, 264–65

Togo (dog hero), 61
Tomiko, 24
"Top dog," definition of, 200
Top Dog (film), 215–16
Top Dog (singing group), 101
Topper (Paula Bennett's dog), 127
Topping from Below (Reese), 144, 158
Topsy (Marie Bonaparte's dog), 248–49
Tosa Inu, 205
Toto (*The Wizard of Oz*), 60, 90, 198
Toynbee, Arnold, 285
Trademarks, dogs as, 113–14
Tramp (*Lady and the Tramp*), 102,
    199
Trans-Species Unlimited, 236
Travels with Charley (Steinbeck), 64,
    92–94
Travels with Lizbeth (Eighner), 64
Truesdale, Tina, 188
Truesdale, William, 188, 189
Tryst of Grandeur (show dog), 189–90
Tulip (Ackerley), 132–35
Twain, Mark, 104, 199
Two Gentlemen of Verona (Shakespeare),
    83, 230
"Typey" dogs, 175

Ulysses (Odysseus), 38, 44, 54, 56, 241–
    42
Unalaska (sled dog), 272
The Unbearable Lightness of Being (Kun-
    dera), 129, 276–77
Uncle Tom's Cabin (Stowe), 68, 232
Underdogs, 200–201
United Kennel Club, 194, 212
United States, dogs representative of,
    197–99
United States Border Collie Club, 191,
    192
Unleashed (Hempel and Shepard), 107,
    116, 278
Urban Canine Conservancy, 205
Urich, Robert, 109–10
Ursa (dog hero), 127

Vest, George Graham, 239–40
Vicious dogs, 212, 213–14
"The Victor Dog" (Merrill), 113
Victoria (queen of England), 161, 187
Victorian era, 165–68, 201, 240
Vietnam, 226
Vivisection, 233–34, 235–36, 237

Voltaire, François Marie Arouet de, 235–36

Voyage to Lethe (Cock), 143–44

Wagner, Jeri, 128
Wagner (author's dog), 39, 40, 182, 273, 276, 284, 285
Wald, Stanley, 41
Walker, Alice, 236
"Walking the Dog" (song), 142
War dogs, 50–55, 222
Ward, Edward, 143
Washington, Denzel, 62–63
Waugh, Evelyn, 242, 260, 270
We Think the World of You (Ackerley), 133, 134
Weber, Jeff, 269
Weddings, dogs at, 128
Wegman, William, 23
Weimaraners, 160, 177
Westminster Kennel Club, 183, 186, 188–91
Wetherbee, Roland, 16
Wharton, Edith, 261
White, E. B., 280–81
White Fang (London), 60, 74–75, 87–88, 120–21, 233
Whitman, Christine Todd, 214, 235
Wilberforce, William, 231
Wilde, Winston, 264
William (tax dog), 228, 229
Willie (Maupin's dog), 266–67
Wills, from pets, 279–82
Willy (*Patton*), 61–62
Wilson, Thomas, 257–58
Wimsey, Lord Peter (fictional character), 163
Winnicott, D. W., 131, 135

Winter, Holly (fictional character). *See* Conant, Susan
The Wizard of Oz (film), 60, 90, 198
Woggs (R.L. Stevenson's dog), 33–34
Wolf (Terhune), 61
Wolf (Anna Freud's dog), 136–37
Wolfhounds, Irish, 160
Women
    and love of dogs, 121–22, 124, 126–30, 151
    See also Feminism; Gender
Women's suffrage, 233–34
Woodhouse, Barbara, 39, 76, 119, 135, 180, 197, 284
Woolf, Virginia, 45–50, 110, 115–16, 117, 159, 167–68
Wordsworth, William, 65, 250–52, 261
World War I, 51, 52, 91, 114, 197–98
World War II, 50–51, 52, 53
Wray, Fay, 23

Yale University, mascot of, 160–61
Yankee Golden Retriever Rescue, 193
Yeats, William Butler, 283
Yofi (author's dog), 40, 98, 182, 273, 276, 285
Yofie (Sigmund Freud's dog), 136, 137–38
Yoko (Thom Gunn's dog), 107–8
You Gotta Have Bark , 205
You're a Good Man, Charlie Brown (Broadway show), 43, 85
Youth, loss of, 245–47
Yuki (Lyndon Johnson's dog), 19–20

Zanuck, Darryl, 19

PERMISSIONS

PHOTO CREDITS

First Page: *Alice and Louis* by March Avery; *Double Portrait*, Lucian Freud: Collection PaineWebber Group Inc.

Family Values: Lassie images: Archive Photos.

Home Is Where the Dog Is: *Couple on a Mattress*, 1984; *Hoboken Lady and Her Dogs*, 1983; *Strays on Car*, 1987: © Robin Schwartz.

Talking Dogs: *His Master's Voice*, Francis Barraud: used by permission of EMI Records Limited in certain countries, permission in the Americas, Japan, and Hong Kong courtesy of General Electric Company; RCA Victor logo: The Bettmann Archive; Jimmy Nelson's "Farfel"®, Jimmy Nelson Collection; *Sylvia:* Joan Marcus; *You're a Good Man, Charlie Brown*: Billy Rose Theatre Collection, The New York Library for the Performing Arts, Astor, Lenox and Tiden Foundations.

Dog Stars: *101 Dalmatians, Lady and the Tramp, Homeward Bound: The Incredible Journey:* © Disney Enterprises, Inc.; *Beethoven II:* Copyright © 1993 by Universal City Studios, Inc. Courtesy of MCA Publishing Rights, a Division of MCA Inc. All rights reserved. Dorothy and Toto from *The Wizard of Oz:* Corbis-Bettmann.

A Dog and His Boy: Rin Tin Tin: Corbis-Bettmann; Dickie Moore and Pete: The Bettmann Archive; *Paul and His Dog*, Nadar: Collection of the J. Paul Getty Museum, Malibu, California; Tintin: © Hergé/Moulinsart-1996; Superboy and Krypto are trademarks of DC Comics copyright ©1970. All rights reserved. Used with permission.

Eminent Canines: *Lord Gristle*, Thierry Poncelet: Stephanie Hoppen Picture Archive Limited; Sir Edwin Landseer's *The Connoisseurs* published by Henry Graves & Co., 1867: Collection of The Dog Museum; *Keeper—from Life*: Courtesy of the Brontë Society; Boatswain: City of Nottingham Museums–Newstead Abbey; Greyfriars Bobby: Harvey Wood/Still Moving Picture Company.

Doggy Style: *Back East:* © William Wegman, 1988, Courtesy PaceWildenstein MacGill Gallery, New York; *Jonah and Lypsinka at POWARS Benefit*, 1995: © Robin Schwartz; Walk for the Animals: Evan Richman/*The Boston Globe*.

Hot Dogs: Marky Mark: Annie Leibovitz / Contact Press Images; *Untitled (Storyville Portrait)*, E. J. Bellocq: Courtesy Fraenkel Gallery, San Francisco; *Nude with Dog*, Gustave Courbet: Musée d'Orsay.

Dogs of War: Laika: Archive Photos; Admiral Byrd and dog: The Bettmann Archive; World War I recruiting poster: Bowman Gray Collection, Wilson Library,